# The
# Concise Oxford
# Dictionary of
# Geography

Susan Mayhew
*and*
Anne Penny

Oxford   New York
OXFORD UNIVERSITY PRESS
1992

*Oxford University Press, Walton Street, Oxford* ox2 6dp

*Oxford New York Toronto*
*Delhi Bombay Calcutta Madras Karachi*
*Petaling Jaya Singapore Hong Kong Tokyo*
*Nairobi Dar es Salaam Cape Town*
*Melbourne Auckland*
*and associated companies in*
*Berlin Ibadan*

*Oxford is a trade mark of Oxford University Press*

*First published 1992 as an Oxford University*
*Press paperback and simultaneously in a*
*hardback edition*

*British Library Cataloguing in Publication Data*
*Data available*

*Library of Congress Cataloging in Publication Data*
*Mayhew, Susan.*
*The concise Oxford dictionary of geography /*
*Susan Mayhew and Anne Penny.*
*p. cm—(Oxford reference)*
*1. Geography—Dictionaries. I. Penny, Anne. II. Title. III. Series.*
*910.3—dc20 G63.M39 1992 91–30530*
*ISBN 0–19–866157–6*
*ISBN 0–19–282565–8 pbk*

*Printed in England by Clays Ltd, St Ives plc*

100971490

# How to use this book

This dictionary provides coverage in one volume of the terms used in both human and physical geography. There are over 5,000 definitions across the following fields: cartography, surveying, remote sensing, statistics, meteorology, climatology, biogeography, ecology, simple geology, soils, geomorphology, population, migration, settlement, agriculture, industry, transport, development, and diffusion.

Headwords are printed in bold type and appear in alphabetical order. However, some entries contain further definitions. These have been included under the headword to avoid unnecessary repetition and to indicate some of the wider applications of the headword. Many entries have an asterisk. This points the reader to cross-references. In a very few cases the cross-reference as indicated does not have the exact wording as in the entry, but is close enough to make further reference possible.

# A

**aa** See *block lava.

**abiotic** Non-living, usually describing certain factors in an *ecosystem.

**ablation** Loss of ice from a glacier by, for example, melting and evaporation.

Ablation also results from *sublimation, the *calving of icebergs, and *avalanches. In temperate and subpolar regions, melting is the most important process in ablation, whereas in the Antarctic, the most important ablation process is calving.

At the edges of the glaciers, where ablation has occurred, large quantities of *debris accumulate to form **ablation moraines**. The zone of net ice loss from a glacier is the **ablation zone**.

**Abney level** A surveying instrument which can measure angles to within 10 seconds of an arc.

**aborigine** An indigenous type existing in a land before the invasion or colonization by another type. This term is especially used for the original inhabitants of Australia.

**abrasion** The grinding away of bedrock by fragments of rock incorporated in ice, water, or wind. Abrasion is an alternative term for *corrasion. The mass of solid removed varies with the size, density, and velocity of the particles and the density of the *vector bearing these particles. Ice ceases to be an effective agent for abrasion when the weight of the ice is thick enough to promote *plastic flow. An **abrasion platform** is a rock platform extending from the foot of a sea cliff.

**abscissa** The horizontal, or *x*-axis, of a graph. Where a *causal factor or an *independent variable can be clearly defined, it is recorded along the abscissa.

**absenteeism** A failure to show up for work. In Britain in 1971 there was a clear increase in absenteeism from the South-

East to the North. This may be due to a higher level of less attractive jobs away from the South-East. Absenteeism may be caused by ill health or by a voluntary decision not to work.

**absolute drought** In Britain, this is a period of 15 days, on none of which more than 0.25 mm of rain falls.

**absolute humidity** The amount of water vapour in a given volume of air, generally expressed in terms of grams per cubic metre.

**absolute stability** If a parcel of rising air cools more rapidly than the air around it, it will cease to rise. This is the condition of absolute stability. Correspondingly, if it cools less rapidly, it will continue to rise. This is **absolute instability**.

**absolute zero** The lowest temperature theoretically obtainable: $-273.15\,°C$.

**absorption** The process by which a material or system takes in another material or system.

**abyssal** At great depths; over 3000 m below sea level—thus, **abyssal plain** and **abyssal deposits**. The word abyssal for a rock has now been replaced by *plutonic. The term **abyssal zone** is variously used to indicate the deepest region of the sea or that part of a lake not penetrated by sunlight.

**accelerated erosion** See *soil erosion.

**accelerated soil erosion** See *soil erosion.

**accelerator** A factor which increases the momentum of a boom or slump in an economy so that small changes in demand, for example, lead to a greater industrial advance or decline.

**acceptable dose limit** The highest safe level of an introduced substance; the maximum level at which the substance poses no health hazards to the environment in which it is used.

**accessibility** The ease of approach to one location from other locations. This may be measured in terms of the distance travelled, the cost of travel, or the time taken. In *network analysis, accessibility may be expressed by measures of *connectivity, but there are also non-mathematical aspects. Accessibility may also be seen in social and economic terms; for example, it is argued that class structures limit people's access to services. An **accessibility index** is a simple measure of accessibility for any selected *node.

**accordant drainage** Surface drainage which follows the *dip of the strata it flows over.

**accordant junctions, law of** This states that tributaries join a stream or river at the same elevation as that of the larger watercourse; thus there is no sudden 'drop' in the level of the tributary. This means that tributaries are *graded to the level of the junction.

**accordant summits** Hill or mountain tops at the same level. This has been seen as evidence of uplift and later *dissection.

**accreting margin** See *constructive margin.

**accretion** 1. The growth of land by the offshore deposition of sediment. Accretion is most active in *estuaries, particularly within the tropics. *Spits and *tombolos are features of accretion.

2. The growth of a landform by the addition of deposits; *seif dunes grow by accretion.

3. The increase in size of particles by additions to the exterior, as in the formation of hailstones.

**acculturation** The adaptation to, and adoption of, a new culture. This may occur simultaneously as two cultures meet but more often occurs as an immigrant group takes to the behaviour patterns and standards of the receiving group.

**accumulated temperature** From a specified date, the length of time for which mean daily temperatures have fluctuated about a given temperature. For arable farming, 5.5 °C is the minimum temperature for growing crops. It is therefore possible to calculate the accumulated temperature for a given area to assess the suitability of that area for arable farming.

**accumulation** The employment of *surplus value as capital or its reconversion into capital.

**acid** A substance containing hydrogen ions which can be neutralized by an *alkali. The *pH of acid is below 7.

The term 'acid' as applied to rocks or lava has an entirely different meaning. See *acid rock.

**acid rain** When *fossil fuels are burned, dioxides of sulphur and nitrogen are released into the air. These dissolve in atmospheric water particles to form acid rain.

Any form of atmospheric water with a *pH of less than 5.6 is properly termed **acid precipitation**. When the concentration of sulphur dioxide reaches 0.2 ppm, acid precipitation is toxic to vegetation; humans are at risk when the concentration rises above 1 ppm.

**acid rock** In geology, an igneous rock composed predominantly of silica or silicate minerals such as mica.

**acid soil** A soil with a *pH of less than 7.

Acidity in a soil may be due to the *leaching out of *cations when *precipitation exceeds *evapotranspiration. The cations are replaced by hydrogen ions. Other factors include the nature of the vegetation, and thus the *humus, and the acidity of the parent rock. Examples of acid soils are *podzols and *brown earths.

**acre** A unit of area, defined in British law as 4840 square yards (0.4 ha).

**actinometer** An instrument which measures the intensity of electromagnetic radiation, usually that of the sun.

**action space** The area in which an individual moves and makes decisions about his or her life, including, for example, shopping, studying, or working; the set of places of which an individual is aware.

Localities which are well known by an individual are more often chosen as the site for activity. See also *activity space.

**active glacier** A glacier which is receiving new ice above the snow line, but losing ice by *ablation below the snow line.

**active layer** The layer of soil subject to periodic thawing located above the *permafrost in *tundra. This thawing may occur daily or only in summer. Many *periglacial processes occur in the active layer, such as *frost heaving, *frost thrusting, *ice wedging, *gelifluction, and the formation of *patterned ground.

**active permafrost** That layer of *permafrost which thaws because of human activity but then refreezes.

**active system** A *remote sensing system that transmits its own electromagnetic radiation.

**activity allocation model** A form of planning which lays down the location of activity within an area. An accurate forecast is made of future population, industry, trade, housing, and so on. Future needs in these fields are indicated and the planner then allocates new developments to the most suitable points in the area. From this it is possible to model the flows of people within the area which result from this planning.

**activity index** A measure of the extent to which a local authority develops policies to attract industry. Such policies may range from the provision of sites to the construction of factories.

**activity rate** The percentage of people of working age who are actually employed. This may be calculated for a region or a nation. A low activity rate can indicate high unemployment. In many cases it includes those seeking work. A low rate, for example for women, may indicate a desire not to work.

**activity space** That part of *action space with which an individual interacts on a daily basis.

**actual isotherm** An *isotherm derived from actual temperatures. Usually, a temperature reading is adjusted to show the value it would have if its meteorological station were at sea level. Thus, for every 150 metres of altitude, 1 °C is added to the temperature.

**actuarial data** *Demographic statistics, having a bearing on births and deaths.

**adaptation** Any change in the structure or functioning of an organism that makes it better suited to the environment. **Adaptive radiation** is the 'fanning out' of new groups of organisms into new niches over time as the result of the stimulus of changed conditions.

**adaptive behaviour** Reasoned behaviour that makes deliberate choices in an attempt to bring about an optimal result. By contrast, **adoptive behaviour** shows a lack of conscious choice.

**additional worker hypothesis** The view that a rise in unemployment leads to a rise in the working population. As the major wage earner becomes unemployed, other members of the family who were not part of the system now seek employment in order to sustain the household.

**adiabatic** A temperature change involving no transfer of heat to or from another material or system.

Any **adiabatic temperature change** results from a change in pressure. As air rises, pressure decreases, volume increases, and temperature falls. The speed at which the temperature of rising air falls with altitude is the **adiabatic lapse rate**. Dry, rising air expands with height. The energy needed for this expansion comes from the air itself in the form of heat. The result is a fall in temperature of approximately 10 °C per 1000 m. This is the **dry adiabatic lapse rate (DALR)**. If the rising air becomes saturated to *dew point, condensation of vapour into water droplets will occur. This condensation is accompanied by the release of *latent heat. This heat partly offsets the cooling of the air with height, so that the **saturated adiabatic lapse rate (SALR)** is some 6 °C per 1000 m.

**adiabatic chart** See *aerological diagram.

**adit** A tunnel driven horizontally into a hillside for the purpose of mining.

**administrative principle** The principle advanced by Christaller which proposes that, in a region with a highly developed system of central administration, settlement is arranged such that one larger centre administers six smaller centres. The number of settlements at progressively lower levels follows the sequence 1, 7, 49, 343 . . . This hierarchy is known as k=7.

**adobe** Bricks of sun-dried earth or clay. **Adobe houses** are made from such bricks. The term has been extended to include alluvial clay and *playa clay.

**adret** The sunny slope of a hill or valley side. In the Northern Hemisphere adret slopes face south; in the Southern Hemisphere they face north. Adret slopes are warmer because they receive more *insolation. See *ubac.

**adsorption** The bonding of gases or liquids to solid particles by physical or chemical means.

**advanced gas-cooled reactor, AGR** A nuclear reactor where the heat of the reaction is transmitted to carbon dioxide under pressure. The hot gas is then used to heat water to make the steam which turns turbines.

**advection** The horizontal transfer of heat. Advective transfers occur in air streams, in ocean currents, and in surface *runoff. These horizontal transfers redress, in part, the imbalance of *insolation between the tropics and the poles. **Advection fog** forms when a warm, moist stream of air moves horizontally over a cooler surface and is chilled below *dew point.

**adventitious population** Population living in the countryside by choice and not because they are employed in rural occupations.

**aeolian, eolian** Wind-borne. The term is applied to landforms that have been shaped to some extent by the wind.

**aeration** The spread of air into a material. The **aeration zone** is that layer of rock or soil lying above the water table where the pore spaces are at least partly filled with air.

**aerial photography** The recording, from height, of the characteristics of an area by the use of photographic film.

**aerobic** Referring to any living organism or process which depends on atmospheric oxygen for the release of energy from foodstuffs during the process of respiration. **Aerobic respiration** uses gaseous or dissolved oxygen. See *anaerobic.

**aerological diagram** A chart plotting the factors which determine the movement of air. Variations of temperature, pressure, dry and saturated *adiabatic lapse rates, and *saturated mixing ratio lines are plotted against height in a *tephigram. An **adiabatic chart** may be used to predict the *convective condensation level.

**aerology** The study of the air.

**aeroplankton** Microscopic organisms floating in the atmosphere.

**aerosols** In meteorology, minute particles of sea-salt, dust (particularly silicates), organic matter, and smoke. Aerosols enter the atmosphere by natural processes— such as volcanoes—and by man's activities— such as the burning of *fossil fuels. Aerosols absorb heat and may act as *condensation nuclei.

**aesthetic landscape** The landscape in terms of taste and beauty. Similar economic systems, like wheat farming on the Prairies of Canada and the Great Plains of the USA, give rise to different aesthetic landscapes. Some landscapes are actually created according to contemporary taste as exemplified in the parklands of English country houses.

**afforestation** The planting of trees.

**aftershock** A relatively minor tremor or a series of tremors occurring after an earthquake.

**age** 1. In geology, a subdivision of an *epoch.

2. Historically, a period of time characterised by a particular technology or culture, as in the *Stone Age.

**age dependency** The dependency of those members of the population too young or too old to be employed full-time on the contributions of those in full employment. As population growth slackens in developed societies and as health care improves, there are large numbers of retired people whose accumulated savings have been eroded by inflation and who cannot, therefore, support themselves. The aging of the population means that fewer workers are obliged to support increasing numbers of old people. The **dependency ratio** is the ratio between those between 15 and 65 years of age and the rest of the population.

**age of towns scheme** A scheme of town classification advanced by Taylor who saw towns developing and changing through time. Infantile towns have a haphazard distribution of shops and houses with no factories. In juvenile towns differentiation of zones begins and shops are separated. The adolescent town has scattered factories but no clear zone of high-quality housing, which develops in early mature towns. Lastly, the mature town has separate commercial and industrial area and clear zoning of housing types from the poorest to the most expensive.

**age/sex pyramid** A set of two *histograms set on a vertical axis and back to back which depicts the numbers of the two sexes in different age groups. Males are usually on the left with females on the right. The youngest group is at the base, the oldest group at the apex. Actual figures or percentages of the age-groups may be used.

The importance of such diagrams is that they can show, in pictorial form, the varying population structures and past histories of different types of society. For example, in many less developed countries, the pyramid will have a very wide base. Western nations, on the other hand, have fewer children and more old people so that the pyramid is more cylindrical.

**age structure** The composition of a population by age-groups. Three types of structure have been identified: the West European with fewer than 30% of children and more than 15% of old people; the North American type with 35–40% of children and 10% of old people; and the Brazilian type with 45–55% of children and 4–8% of old people. The type of age structure has a profound effect on the future of the population with dependent elderly at one extreme and explosive population growth at the other.

**agglomerate** A rock composed of sharp fragments set in a fine matrix especially when formed of volcanic material.

**agglomeration** The concentration of activities, usually industries, in the same location. It may also apply to concentrations of urban settlement.

**agglomeration economies** For an industry, the benefits of locating in a densely peopled and highly industrialized area. The market is large, but concentrated in a relatively small area. Transport costs are therefore low, so that many specialized industries can evolve since local demand is sufficiently high. *Functional linkages are common.

**aggradation** The deposition of wind- and water-borne deposits which builds up the land surface.

**aggregate** 1. A group of soil particles held together by electrostatic forces, *polysaccharide gums, and *cementation by carbonates and iron oxides.

2. In statistics, the collection of individuals under consideration, used for studies on a general scale.

**AGR** See *advanced gas-cooled reactor.

**agribusiness** Large agricultural operations which are run like an industry. A single business can be concerned with the whole of agricultural output: the ownership of land, the agricultural process, the manufacture of agricultural machinery, the processing of the product, and its shipment. This is typical of agribusinesses in the USA. European equivalents are not generally as all-embracing. An agribusiness is characterized by very large production units, and management by administrators and accountants rather than farmers. The farm is but one feature of the business and may be only a minor part of it.

**agricultural density** The density of the agricultural population per unit area of farmed land. It is, however, rather difficult to define and isolate the 'agricultural' population.

**agricultural geography** The geography of the cultivation of the land including the spatial expression of cultivation.

**agricultural location theory** An attempt to explain the pattern of agricultural land use in terms of costs, distance, and prices. One explanation is concerned with the effect of the city on rural land use. It is predicted that circular zones of different agricultural production will surround the city. Zones may also occur beside a coastal strip, or along both sides of a transport artery. A pattern of agricultural land use zoning may occur from a unit as small as a single farm to one as large as a subcontinent. The classic theory of agricultural location is that of *von Thünen.

**agricultural revolution** The discovery of new agricultural techniques which increase output. In Britain, the agricultural revolution occurred in the late eighteenth century and was based on new machinery and the use of rotations. See *green revolution.

**agricultural system** Any method of farming may be seen as part of an agricultural system. 'Inputs' include seeds, water, pesticides, herbicides, fertilizer, and livestock which are introduced to the 'plant'—the buildings, machinery, and land. The 'output' is the produce of the farm.

**agroforestry** The use of the land for forestry as well as agriculture. The interplanting of *Leucaena* trees with maize brought about a threefold increase in maize yields in Nigeria, since *Leucaena* 'fixes' atmospheric nitrogen in the soil which is then, with the addition of leaf litter, much more fertile.

**agro-town** A town of up to 20 000 people with agriculture as the main economic activity. As such they are not truly *urban settlements, although they may be the only significant settlements in the region. Agro-towns occur in parts of Mediterranean Europe and may find their counterparts in the Yoruba regions of West Africa.

**Agulhas current** A warm *ocean current off the coast of south-eastern Africa.

**aid** The provision of resources from developed to less developed countries. This is usually from the Western democracies to the Third World, but oil-exporting nations usually give the most in terms of total GNP. Aid may take the form of finance or credit or other forms such as expertise, education and training, and advanced or *intermediate technology. Food aid may be supplied in emergencies. There is a trend by Western European nations to give most to their ex-colonies.

Ostensibly, the provision of aid is to encourage development but its donors may well be rewarded by interest payments from the receiving nation or by political allegiance. Furthermore, agencies such as the International Monetary Fund or the World Bank may impose a restructuring of the economy as a condition of receiving aid. The 'charities', or *Non-Governmental Organizations, also provide aid but with fewer conditions and more emphasis on development. See *neo-colonialism.

**aiguille** French for pyramidal peak or *horn.

**air frost** See *frost.

**air mass** An area of the *atmosphere that, horizontally, has more or less uniform properties, especially of temperature and *humidity, and extends for hundreds of kilometres.

Air masses obtain these attributes from their areas of origin, known as **source regions**, where conditions are sufficiently similar to confer uniform properties to the overlying air. They become less uniform with movement into different areas and with time.

The classification of air masses is twofold: firstly by the nature of the source region—land, **continental air mass, c**, or sea, **maritime air mass, m**—and secondly by the latitude of the source area—arctic, A, polar, P, or tropical, T. These two methods combine to distinguish most air masses, such as cA—continental arctic, mP—maritime polar, mT—maritime tropical, and so on. See also *secondary air masses.

**air parcel** A theoretical volume of air. A simple analysis of the likely behaviour of air can be made by assigning the relevant qualities to an air parcel and predicting its movements according to the laws of physics.

**air pressure** See *atmospheric pressure.

**air–sea interaction** The transfer of heat, momentum, solids, liquids, and gases between the atmosphere and the oceans. These transfers occur because the latter two constitute a single system in terms of matter, forces, heat, and other forms of energy. Thus, small processes like wind stress and *evaporation are of essential importance in the *general circulation of the atmosphere and oceanic circulations. Similarly, larger processes, such as *planetary winds, will affect oceanic circulation. Ocean temperatures are critical in determining *depression tracks.

**airstream** A current of air, a wind, coming from an identifiable source.

**alas** In a *periglacial landscape, a large, steep-sided, flat-bottomed depression which can be several kilometres across. Lakes often occur in alases which may form the basis of *pingo development.

**Alaska current** A cold *ocean current.

**albedo** The proportion of the sun's radiation that is reflected from any surface, such as clouds or bare rock. The total albedo of the earth is about 35%.

**Aleutian low** An atmospheric *low above the north Pacific. Here, a series of depressions is interrupted by occasional *highs.

**alfisol** A soil order of the *US soil classification. See *brown earth.

**algae** A large and diverse group of simple plants that contain chlorophyll and can therefore photosynthesize. Algae live in aquatic habitats or in moist regions inland.

**algal bloom** The dense spread of algae which results from changes in the chemistry and/or temperature of lake water. The addition of phosphorus as a result of pollution from fertilizers is an important factor in the growth of algal blooms. The bloom will disappear if the input of fresh phosphorus ceases.

**algorithm** A process of calculations, supported by mathematical proof, used to bring about a solution to a problem.

**alidade** A surveying instrument used with a *plane table to establish the angles between the survey line and a particular feature. It comprises two separate sights, one at each end of a rule.

**alienation** The separation of the individual from the products of his labour and the means of production such that he becomes an adjunct of the machine he uses rather than a whole person. The idea of alienation has been used as a powerful concept to explain the rise of urban ills such as violent football fans, street gangs, and alcohol and drug addiction.

**alimentation** The input of snow and ice to a glacier by the formation of *firn, the refreezing of meltwater, or the action of an avalanche.

**alkali** A substance which neutralizes, or is neutralized by, *acid. Alkalis are generally oxides, hydroxides, or compounds such as ammonia which dissolve in water to form hydroxide ions. Alkalis have a *pH of more than 7. Hence **alkaline soil**. An **alkali flat** is a level area in an arid region overlain by alkali salts.

**alkaline** In lava and rocks, containing less than 50% silica.

**alkaline soil** Any soil which has a *pH above 7. This alkalinity usually reflects a high concentration of carbonates, notably those of sodium and calcium.

**Allen's rule** This states that in many species, extremities such as ears and tails are larger in varieties living in a hot climate than in related types found in cold climates. This enables animals living in hot climates to dissipate excess heat through these extremities while animals in cold climates minimize heat loss. Some writers contest the validity of this 'rule'.

**Allerød** A warmer phase of less intense glaciation during the last *glacial of the *Pleistocene.

**allogenic** Existing locally, but originating in a different area. Thus, an allogenic stream is one fed from outside the local area.

**alluvial fan** A fan-shaped landform composed of *alluvium dropped by a river after it loses momentum as it enters a broad valley from a narrow, upland course. An **alluvial cone** is similar in origin, but tends to have a steeper slope. Cones tend to grow from seasonal streams in semi-arid or arid areas. **Alluvial flats** are level tracks of land beside rivers. The river may cut into the flats to form an **alluvial terrace**.

**alluvium** A general term for all deposits laid down by present-day rivers, especially at times of flood.

There is a marked tendency to restrict the term alluvium to fine-grained deposits such as *silt or silty clays.

**Alonso model** An explanation of urban land use and land values. It is grounded on the concept of *bid rents whereby the urban land user seeks central locations but is willing to accept a location further from the city centre if rents are lower in compensation. The use that can extract the greatest return from a site will be the succesful bidder. To this basis, Alonso, in a study of housing, added the quantity of land required, variations in the amount of disposable income used on land, and transport costs on one hand and on all goods and services on the other. If the amount of goods and services is held constant, the price of land should decrease with increasing distance from the centre. The well-off will choose to live at lower densities at the edge of the city; the poor remain in high-density occupance near the city centre. Each household represents a balance between land, goods, and accessibility to the workplace.

The assumptions on which this theory rests range from all land being of equal quality to lack of planning constraints. This means that the theory is a long way from reality although it does reflect some aspects of urban morphology.

**alp** The shoulder of land above a *glacial trough. The alp runs from the break of slope above the trough to the summer snowline. An **alpine glacier** is synonymous with a valley glacier and **alpine topography** denotes those features of glaciation found in upland areas.

**alpha index,** $\alpha$ In *network analysis, the ratio of the actual number of circuits in a network to the maximum possible number of circuits in that network. It is given as:

$$\alpha = \frac{e - v + p}{2v - 5} \times 100$$

where $e$ = edges, $v$ = vertices, $p$ = number of graphs or subgraphs.

Values range from 0%—no circuits—to 100%—a completely interconnected network.

**Alpine orogeny** The building of 'young' fold mountains from the Verkhoyansk of the USSR through Europe to the Sierra Nevada of the USA dated at approximately 65 million years BP.

**Altaid orogeny** A period of mountain building in central Europe and Asia dating from the late *Carboniferous to the *Permian.

**alternative technology** Technology based on renewable, rather than non-renewable, resources.

**altimeter** An instrument used to plot altitude. The **pressure altimeter** is based on the change of pressure with height and the **radio-altimeter** on the time that radio waves take to 'bounce' back to a recording device on an aeroplane. An **altimetric frequency curve** shows the frequency with which various heights of land occur within a given area.

**altiplano** The high plateau, specifically in Bolivia, lying between the east and west of the Andes.

**alto-** Prefix referring to clouds between 3000 and 6000 m high, as in **alto-*stratus**, a grey sheet of medium cloud, or **alto-*cumulus**, a tall cloud formation of middle altitude.

**ambient** Surroundings, of the surroundings. **Ambient temperature** is the temperature all round a given point.

**amelioration** An improvement; in climatology, the term is usually applied to a change to a warmer climate. However, the term is misleading as such a change may be an improvement for one species but a deterioration for another.

**amenity** Pleasantness; those aspects of an area such as housing, space, and recreational and leisure activities which make it an attractive place to live in.

**amphidromic point** The point around which *tides oscillate. Thus, while there are tides along the coasts of East Anglia and the Netherlands, there is a point in the sea between the two where there is no change in the height of the water.

**ana-** From the Greek *ana*, 'upwards'. Rising air, as at an *ana-front or in an *anabatic wind.

**anabatic wind** When the sides of a mountain valley are heated further, and more

rapidly, than the valley floor, the warmer air will rise upslope, creating an anabatic wind.

**anaerobic** Describing any organism or process which can or must exist without free oxygen from the air. Thus, an **anaerobe** can live without air and **anaerobic decomposition** and **anaerobic respiration** can occur in the same circumstances.

**ana-front** A cold front where warm air rides over the cold segment.

**anastomosis** The division of a river into two or more channels with large, stable islands between the channels.

**anastomotic drainage** See *drainage patterns.

**anchor tenant** In a new shopping centre, a shop, such as a nationally known chain store, which will attract many customers is encouraged and may even be granted a lower rent. This is an anchor tenant which provides customers for smaller shops.

**ancillary linkage** A link, which may benefit both, between two different forms of land use. Thus, building societies are increasingly located in high streets. The presence of the shops attracts clients to the building societies, while the provision of cash points encourages shoppers.

**andesite line** Essentially, the boundary between the *basic rocks of the oceanic *crust and islands and the *acid rocks of the continental crust in a belt surrounding the Pacific. It is the boundary between oceanic *sima and continental *sial. **Andesite** is an intermediate *igneous rock.

**anemometer** An instrument for recording wind speed. A simple **vane anemometer** consists of three semi-conical cups mounted on a vertical spindle and attached to a generator. The cups are driven by the wind; the faster they move, the greater the generator output. This output may be calibrated directly onto a continuous paper trace.

The use of a wind-vane keeps a **pressure-tube anemometer** facing the wind. The wind pressure is transmitted down a tube and is then converted into a print-out.

**angle of repose** The maximum slope of a scree. Angles of repose vary with rock type.

**annual growth rings** For each year of a tree's growth, two concentric zones are added to the trunk, one formed in the spring and the other during late summer. It is possible to count the rings and thereby to estimate the age of the tree. Variations in the width of the rings are used as evidence for past changes in the climate.

**annular drainage** See *drainage patterns.

**anomie** The lack of traditional social patterns within a group. It is said that this may be engendered by *urbanization where life can be led under conditions of anonymity and where social relations are transitory. The individual becomes alienated from his folk or rural background, he no longer feels part of a group and his status is more bound to his efforts than to his birth. The consequence is a feeling of being lost. The rise of anomie in the city has been contested by those who feel that for every loss caused by urban living there is a gain.

**Antarctic** Denoting regions south of the **Antarctic circle**, 66.6 °S. The major landmass within this latitudinal zone is **Antarctica**. Within the Antarctic circle, the sun does not rise on 21 June (winter *solstice in the Southern Hemisphere) or set on 22 December (summer solstice in the Southern Hemisphere).

**Antarctic air mass** These *air masses originate within the *Antarctic and have similar properties to *Arctic air masses.

**Antarctic convergence** The zone in the seas around Antarctica where cold, heavy seas sink below the warmer waters to the north.

**Antarctic meteorology** Winters are severe, with characteristic double temperature minima (two separate periods of very low temperatures), due to the absence of *insolation for several winter months, and to the frequent exchange of air with that of lower latitudes. *Blizzards are common. Temperatures rise in late summer as the long waves of the *westerlies bring incursions of warmer air. Nevertheless, precipitation is still almost always in the form of snow, since maximum temperatures, occurring at the summer (December) *solstice, rarely exceed 0 °C.

**antecedent** Prior to, before, as in *antecedent drainage patterns. **Antecedent moisture** is the amount of moisture already present in the soil before a specified rainstorm.

**antecedent drainage** A river, or rivers, which persists in the same course in spite of the formation of a ridge across its path. It can do so because as the land rises, the river keeps pace by cutting downwards.

**anthracite** A hard, compact type of coal containing over 85% of carbon, burning smokelessly and slowly, generating much heat.

**anthropogeomorphology** The study of man as he affects the physical landscape. This effect may be direct, as in building a dam to make a reservoir, or indirect, as in subsidence caused by mining.

**anticline** See *fold.

**anticlinorium** See *fold.

**anticyclone** A region of relatively high *atmospheric pressure commonly some thousands of kilometres in diameter, also known as a high. Anticyclones appear on weather charts as a series of concentric, widely spaced *isobars of 1000 *millibars and above. The weather associated with mid-latitude anticyclones is warm, sunny, and dry in summer, and either cold and frosty or foggy in winter.

The interiors of continental land masses lose heat in winter through *terrestrial radiation. The air above is cooled by contact to form a shallow layer of cold, heavy air, known as a **cold anticyclone**. Such systems are semi-permanent over Siberia and north-west Canada in winter.

When the warm air of a *Hadley cell subsides, **warm anticyclones** occur. These are semi-constant features of *subtropical latitudes. When the warm Azores high moves north-east to Britain in summer, the weather is unusually fine. This is due to the compression of the air as it descends, causing *adiabatic warming.

In *mid-latitudes, at intervals of several years, the *jet stream divides into northerly and southerly branches. This causes a series of low- and high-pressure cells to form. The latter are known as **blocking anticyclones** and prevent the normal flow of *depressions into north-west Europe. Unusually long periods of fine, dry weather result in summer. Winters are very cold, but rather dry.

**anti-dip stream** A stream flowing in a direction roughly opposite to the *dip of the rocks over which it runs.

**antidune** An impermanent ripple in the bed of a stream. The antidune migrates towards the head of the river as the steeper, upstream slope is added to by sediments moving downstream, while the gentler, downstream slope is eroded.

**antipodes** Points on the earth's surface which are diametrically opposite to each other.

**antitrades** Westerly winds in the upper atmosphere above, and in contrast to, the easterly *trade winds at ground level.

**anvil shape** In meteorology, a broad and massive cloud shape with a flattened crown that is much wider than the base.

**anyport** A model of port development suggested by Bird. Initially, a primitive port grows around a natural, sheltered harbour. As the port grows, marginal quay expansion occurs and the port's quays are of greater size in relation to the town. The next step—marginal quay elaboration—sees the extension of jetties and the cutting of docks. After this, as the port continues to grow, there is dock elaboration as new docks are excavated downstream. The next stage—simple linear quayage—sees the rationalization of existing quays and docks to provide better facilities. Finally, specialized quayage develops with facilities for *containers and for *Ro-Ro traffic. As these seven stages occur, the activity of the port moves seawards.

**AONB** See *Area of Outstanding Natural Beauty.

**apartheid** The system of racial segregation first promulgated by the National Party of South Africa in 1948. **Petty apartheid** operated in small but not insignificant ways: facilities such as lavatories, transport, parks, and theatres have been divided into two groups—White and non-White. Although apartheid has been officially dropped, its effects are still to be seen in the human geography of South Africa. Apartheid within a city was applied to every urban South African area. Housing was zoned for racial groups so that areas for Bantu, Coloureds, Asians, and Whites were allocated. On a national scale 'independent republics' (homelands) were planned so that every non-White was allocated to a different major tribal group. These homelands were expected to operate independently, providing their non-White inhabitants with a right to vote within their confines. In fact, many non-Whites still live in the townships near the cities.

**aphelion** The point on a planet's orbit when it is furthest away from the sun it circles. On 4 July, the earth is at aphelion, 152 000 000 km from the sun.

**apogee** The point on a moon's orbit when it is furthest away from the planet it circles. When our moon is furthest from earth, its effect on the tides is at its least. **Apogean tides** are thus at their least extreme, with a small tidal range.

**Appalachian orogeny** A period of mountain building in North America during the *Permian and the *Triassic. It corresponds with, but is slightly later than, the *Armorican and *Hercynian orogenies of Europe.

**apparent time** Local time, established from the time when the sun is at its highest, at noon.

**Appleton layer** The upper layer of the *ionosphere, roughly 300 km above the earth's surface. Radio waves can be bounced off the Appleton layer.

**applied geography** The use of geographical facts and techniques in order to solve problems. Thus, the local government re-organisation in Britain in 1974 was based on the concept of the *city-region, *threshold populations can indicate the viable location of a shop or a service, and *bid-rent curves can throw light on urban development.

**applied geomorphology** The study of the interactions between geomorphology and human activity. Thus, applied geomorphology covers the following:
1. The specialized mapping of land-forms, such as slope elements, which affect or may be affected by human activities, and which are not mapped by other disciplines.
2. The interpretation of features shown on aerial photographs or by *remote sensing methods.
3. The monitoring of changes in the environment, especially when those changes bring risks to society.
4. The assessment of the causes of these changes, notably of those which develop as hazards to man.
5. The remedies to such hazards.
6. The recognition of the consequences of human activity in geomorphology.

**appraisive image** The meaning invoked by a particular place, usually with regard to its attractions. Individuals may see images in an affective manner, mirroring their emotions, or in an evaluative sense, judging objectively between places.

**appropriate technology** Equipment and processes most suited to the prevailing technology of a region. Thus, the introduction of ox-ploughing may be more suitable than the provision of tractors.

**apsis,** pl. **apsides** On an orbit around a planet or sun, the higher apsis is the most distant point on the orbit from the centre and the lower apsis is the nearest point. The **line of apsides** is the imaginary line that links the two.

**aquaculture** The use of waters, other than the sea, for agricultural production, usually the production of fish. See also *fish farming.

**aquiclude** A rock which does not allow the passage of water through it.

**aquifer** A rock which will hold water and permit its passage. A **confined aquifer** is one sandwiched between two *impermeable rocks. Water runs into this aquifer where the rock is exposed to the surface or lies below the *water table.

**aquifuge** A rock which cannot absorb water and through which water cannot pass.

**arable farming** The cultivation of crops.

**arable land** Originally meaning fit for cultivation, as opposed to pasture or woodland, it is now applied to agricultural land used for growing crops.

**arch** In coastal geomorphology, an arch is made when two caves occurring on either side of a headland are cut until they meet. Arches are relatively temporary features of the landscape, as roof fall isolates the seaward end which then becomes a *stack.

**Archimedes' screw** An instrument, resembling a large corkscrew within a tube, used for lifting irrigation water from a channel. It is now rarely seen.

**archipelago** Originally an island-studded sea, such as the Aegean Sea, now a group of islands.

**Arctic** Denoting regions within the **Arctic Circle**, i.e. north of 66.6 °N. Within these regions the sun does not set on 21 June (the summer *solstice in the Northern Hemisphere) nor rise on 22 December (the winter solstice in the Northern Hemisphere).

**Arctic air masses** These are exceedingly cold, with the Arctic Ocean as their source region. Such air masses should not be confused with polar *air masses.

In climatology the Arctic is defined in terms of the treeless zone of *tundra and of the regions of *permafrost in the Northern Hemisphere.

**Arctic front** A quiet front, located between latitudes 50 °N. and 60 °N., where cold Arctic air meets slightly warmer Polar air. It is not very active because the temperature difference be- tween the two air masses is slight.

**Arctic meteorology** The Arctic regions experience an annual cycle of winter 'night' and summer 'day'. In winter, highs and lows traverse the area, but most have little effect on surface weather except for *cold lows which cause medium- and high-level clouds. These partially offset radiational cooling. Most weather results from the intensely cold ground air which is chilled by contact with land losing heat from strong *terrestrial radiation, since winter clouds are otherwise scarce. Only infrequently do depressions penetrate the *inversions so formed. Winter temperatures are close to – 40 °C. Although snowfall is slight, winds cause frequent blizzards and drifting. In spring, days are longer and sunny but temperatures remain low because incoming *solar radiation is reflected back into the atmosphere from the snow surface. In summer, some depressions bring thicker cloud and light rain. The snow- and ice-melt in June and July keep air temperatures over the pack ice close to 0 °C. Skies are usually overcast over coastal areas, but by late afternoon temperatures in inland areas may rise to 15–20 °C.

**Arctic sea smoke** A form of *steam fog.

**arcuate delta** A fan-shaped *delta, like that of the Nile.

**areal differentiation** A recognition of the different regions of the earth's surface which is aimed at interpreting the variations in the character of the settled world; a traditional regional geography. With the development of *systematic geography through the *quantitative approach, many geographers abandoned regional geography. Now, the systematic themes are generally recognized, while it is accepted that every process will be modified according to the unique nature of each separate environment.

**Area of Outstanding Natural Beauty, AONB** An area, supervised by the relevant local authority, in which development is very carefully considered so that the beauty of the landscape is not diminished. 6% of England and Wales is covered by AONBs.

**arena** A shallow, roughly circular depression which has been eroded in soft rock and which is rimmed by more resistant rocks.

**arenaceous** Sandy in texture, or applied to rocks composed of cemented, usually quartz, sand.

**arête** A steep knife-edge ridge between *cirques in a mountainous region.

**aretic** Without flowing streams, as in hot deserts where any precipitation infiltrates the arid ground or evaporates.

**argillaceous** Clay-like in composition and texture or applied to rocks containing *clay minerals and clay-sized particles. An **argillic horizon** contains an accumulation of clay formed by *illuviation.

**arid** Lacking moisture, hence **aridity**, which occurs when *evapotranspiration exceeds *precipitation.

**aridisol, aridosol** In the *US Soil Classification, the equivalent of a *desert soil.

**arithmetic mean** A numerical value representing the average worth of a set of data. It is calculated by adding together all the values of a set and dividing the total by the number of values. It is quick and easy to calculate but the presence of an unusually high or low value distorts the mean from a truly central value. Furthermore, it is unreliable when the data set contains only a few values. The mean of *grouped data may be established by multiplying the mid-point of each class by the number of observations in each class, summing these figures and dividing the sum by the total number of values in the data set.

**arithmetic progression** A series of numbers with the same interval between each, as in 1, 2, 3 . . . or 2, 4, 6 . . . . Malthus believed that food production followed an arithmetic progression (see *Malthusianism).

**arkose** A coarse-grained sandstone formed of broken and eroded particles of *granite or *gneiss.

**Armorican orogeny** A mountain-building movement, beginning in Europe in the *Carboniferous and lasting into the *Permian. Some use the term as a synonym for the *Hercynian.

**array** In statistics, a set of observations.

**arroyo** A straight-sided, flat-floored periodic watercourse, cut in alluvium and found especially in the south-eastern USA.

**artesian basin** A *syncline of permeable rocks with outcrops at the crest of the syncline. Water from rain or streams seeps into this *aquifer. Eventually the rock becomes saturated and the water is under pressure. If a borehole is sunk at depth to tap the water, an **artesian well** forms from which the water will flow upwards without pumping.

**artificial recharge** The filling, or partial filling, with water of an *aquifer by means of *recharge wells.

**ash** See *pyroclast. An **ash cone** may be the result of a volcanic eruption.

**ash flow** Synonymous with *nuée ardente.

**aspect** The direction in which a valley side or slope faces. In deeply cut east–west orientated valleys, the slopes facing the equator receive more sun and are more attractive to settlement than the shaded sides of the valley.

**asphalt** A naturally occurring tar.

**assart** The taking in by individual farmers of previously waste, often forest, land in medieval Britain.

**assimilation** The absorption of an immigrant group into a receiving community. Initially the migrant group is segregated from the host culture but then there is often a blurring of cultural lines. The rate of assimilation, which resembles *acculturation, depends on the race, religion, customs, occupations, and culture of the migrants. **Behavioural assimilation** is the absorption of the incoming group into the host community while **structural assimilation** is concerned with the distribution of incomers within society. See *integration.

**assisted area** A part of Britain where government intervention is thought to be necessary to boost economic development or at least to halt its decline.

**associated number** Also known as the König number, the associated number of a *node is the number of *edges from that node to the furthest node from it. This is a *topological measure of distance, in edges rather than in kilometres. A low associated number indicates a high degree of *connectivity.

**association, plant association** A plant *community unit. The term has been variously defined, but one widely used definition of an association is a floral assemblage with a characteristic dominant and persistent species.

**asthenosphere** That zone of the earth's *mantle which lies beneath the relatively rigid *lithosphere. The asthenosphere is composed of hot, semi-molten, and therefore deformable, rock.

**asymmetric, asymmetrical** Lacking symmetry. An **asymmetrical fold** has one limb dipping more steeply away from the axis than the other. An **asymmetrical valley** has one side sloping more steeply than the other.

**Atlantic climatic stage** After the dry, cold, *boreal stage of climate, associated with the maximum extent of the *Ice Age, there was a milder, moister phase known as the Atlantic. In Britain this stage began c.7000 BP.

**Atlantic polar front** The *front over the North Atlantic between a tropical maritime *air mass to the south and a polar maritime air mass to the north.

**Atlantic Suite** A *petrographic province marked by *Atlantic-type coasts, block faulting, and *alkaline rocks.

**Atlantic-type coast** A coastline where the trend of ridges and valleys runs transverse to the coast. If the coastal lowlands are inundated by the sea, a *ria or *fiord coastline may result.

**atmosphere** 1. The layer of air surrounding the earth. This layer has an average composition, by volume, of 79% nitrogen, 20% oxygen, 0.03% carbon dioxide, and traces of *rare gases. Also present are atmospheric moisture, ammonia, *ozone, and salts and solid particles.
 2. A unit of air pressure; one atmosphere is equal to the pressure exerted by the weight of a column of 760 mm of mercury at 0 °C, under standard gravity, at sea level.

**atmospheric cells** Air may move, with a vertical circular motion, northwards or southwards in a vertical cell, such as the *Hadley cell which extends roughly from the equator to 30 °N. This cell was thought to be the result of *convection, and is hence known as a **thermally direct cell**, but its origin is now considered to be more complex.
 Atmospheric cells are major components in the transfer of heat and momentum in the atmosphere from the equator to the poles. In the 1950s, the existence of **horizontal cells**, also fulfilling this role, was established.

**atmospheric heat engine** The system of energy which drives and controls the nature of the pressure, winds, and climatic belts of the earth's surface. It is powered by incoming *solar radiation and variations in *insolation over the earth's surface.

**atmospheric instability** The state in the atmosphere of a body of air which is likely to rise. The initial rise may be prompted by the relative warmth of the body. If it cools less rapidly than the *environmental air, it will continue to rise.

**atmospheric moisture** Water, in liquid or gaseous form, present in the atmosphere.

**atmospheric pressure** The pressure exerted by the weight of the *atmosphere.
 Atmospheric pressure, measured in *millibars, decreases logarithmically with height.

**atoll** A *coral reef, ring or horseshoe-shaped, enclosing a *lagoon. An **atollon** is a small atoll on the margin of a larger one.

**atomic power** See *nuclear power.

**atomistic economy** See *segmented economy.

**attrition** In geomorphology, the wearing away of particles of debris by contact with other such particles, as with river pebbles.

**aureole** See *metamorphic aureole.

**Aurora Borealis** Coloured and white flashing lights in the atmosphere north of the Arctic Circle. The lights are the result of the ionization of atmospheric molecules, at low temperatures, by solar and cosmic radiation. This phenomenon also occurs in the *Antarctic, where it is termed **Aurora Australis.**

**authority constraint** In *time–space geography, a limit to an individual's actions, such as the use of a day nursery or a library, because some activities are available only at certain authorized times.

**autochthonous** Referring to events occurring within, rather than outside, an environment.

**autotrophe** An organism which uses light energy to synthesize sugars and proteins from inorganic substances. Green plants are by far the most common autotrophes. Hence **autotrophic.**

**avalanche** A rapidly descending mass, usually of snow, down a mountainside. **Powder avalanches** consist of a moving amorphous mass of snow. **Slab avalanches** occur when a large block of snow moves down a slope and can cut a swathe through the soil and sometimes erode the bedrock if the snow is wet. A rush of air—an **avalanche wind**—may be produced by an avalanche.

Avalanches of other substances occur and are distinguished by the type of material involved, e.g. **debris avalanche**, **rock avalanche**.

An avalanche may be triggered off by its own weight, by undercutting at the foot of the slope, by the pressure exerted by water in the pores of snow or debris, or by earthquakes. An avalanche may form an **avalanche cone**.

**aven** A vertical opening or shaft into a limestone cave.

**average** A measure of *central tendency; the most representative value for a group of numbers. The term is usually synonymous with the *arithmetic mean.

**awareness space** Any locations known of by an individual before a decision about such places is made. For example, an in-dustrialist will choose to locate in a site of which he has previously been aware rather than in somewhere of which he has no knowledge.

**axial plane** An imaginary surface dividing, as symmetrically as possible, the two limbs of a *fold.

**axis of the earth** A line joining the North and South Poles and around which the earth rotates every 24 hours.

**azimuthal map projection** A *map projection constructed so that all the points on the map are at the correct *bearing and distance from the centre.

**azonal** Referring to a soil without soil *horizons, such as a young soil developing on a bare rock surface. *Alluvium and *sand dunes are examples of azonal soils.

**Azores high** An *anticyclone usually found in the northern Atlantic over the Azores islands. In summer, it can extend over Britain, where it brings fine, hot weather.

# B

**back-arc region** The region beyond the *volcanic arc, away from the mid-*oceanic ridge. It may show signs of convergence, such as faulting or folding, or of divergence, such as crustal thinning and subsidence.

**background level** The naturally occurring level of pollution or radiation.

**backhaul rate** A cheap transport rate offered to a customer using a service which would otherwise be unused. For example, empty iron-ore wagons returning to the point of supply may be used to haul other goods like coal at a discount rate since otherwise they would return empty or containing only ballast.

**backing** Of winds in the Northern Hemisphere, a change in direction in an anticlockwise movement, e.g. from westerly to southerly. The converse applies in the Southern Hemisphere.

**backshore** That part of a beach lying above the ordinary limit of high tides but below the cliff foot.

**back slope** That slope of a *cuesta which is more gentle.

**back wall** The steep slope at the back of a *cirque.

**backwash** The return flow of water downslope to the sea after the *swash has moved upshore.

**backwash effect** Myrdal argued that economic growth in one area adversely affects the prosperity of another. Wealth and labour moves from poorer, peripheral areas to more central regions of economic growth and the industrial production of wealthy regions may well undercut the industrial output of the poorer regions. This draining of wealth and labour together with industrial decline is the backwash effect.

**backwearing** The erosion of a slope whereby the slope maintains a constant angle as it retreats. See *parallel slope retreat.

**bacteria** Single-cell organisms. Their importance in geography lies in their role in the formation and development of soils. See *gley soils and *polysaccharide gums.

**badlands** Arid lands, generally bare of vegetation, which have been cut into a maze of ravines and sharp-crested hills. The term comes from the badlands of South Dakota, USA, but is now applied generally.

**bajada** The American name for a series of *alluvial fans which have coalesced along the foot of the mountains.

**balanced growth** A strategy of growth with an equal emphasis on agriculture and industry. Agricultural development provides the food required and releases labour from the land to engage in industry. Industrial wealth stimulates markets for agricultural growth—or such is the theory. Unbalanced growth denotes a strategy which focuses on agriculture or industry alone.

**balanced neighbourhood** A neighbourhood which contains groups from all levels of society. Such a neighbourhood does not usually occur spontaneously and has to be planned. It is hoped that a balanced neighbourhood will benefit all the 'lower' groups when they come into contact with 'higher' groups who will develop powers of leadership. One criticism of this concept is that there will be no sense of community when the members come from disparate backgrounds. A more fundamental criticism would be that it is based on an outmoded view of society.

**balance of payments** Commonly, the difference in a nation's economy between the income from exports and the cost of imports.

**Baltic shield** The rigid, relatively stable, and usually flat area of pre-Cambrian rock found in Finland and eastern Scandinavia.

**band** In *remote sensing, a part of the electromagnetic spectrum. Each sensor has its own band specification and each sensor's bands have specific uses in the way they highlight or subdue information. Band colour combinations are frequently used in making images.

**bankfull discharge** The *discharge of a river which is just contained within the banks. It is difficult to measure bankfull discharge in the field since not all rivers have clearly defined, crested banks.

**bankfull stage** The condition of a river which is only just contained by its banks.

**banner cloud** A long, flat cloud forming on the lee of a mountain peak. Air flows down the lee side and is warmed *adiabatically. The air then rises and cools. A sequence of descent and ascent continues with distance from the peak until all the water droplets in the cloud evaporate and cloud formation ends.

**bar** 1. An accumulation of marine sediment which may be exposed at low tide. The crest of the bar generally runs parallel to the coast, but may extend across an *estuary or a bay.

2. Within a river, a deposit of *alluvium which may form temporary islands. **Alternating bars** develop as patches of alluvium form along alternate sides of a straight channel. **Braid bars** form within a channel and cause the river to split up. Braid bars are roughly diamond-shaped and are generally aligned along the course of the channel. **Point bars** form on the inner curves of a meandering river where the *discharge is low.

**barbed drainage** One effect of river *capture is that the direction of flow of a stream may be reversed. When this occurs, tributaries may meet the main river at an obtuse angle; this is barbed drainage.

**barchan** See *sand dune.

**bar graph** A diagram consisting of a number of narrow rectangular bars each of a length proportional to the data represented. In a **compound bar graph**, one large bar is split up into different portions which illustrate the breakdown of the data. Not to be confused with *histogram.

**baroclinic** With a literal meaning of 'sloping air', this term is applied to regions where different air masses meet and there is a pressure gradient. In such areas, known as **baroclinic zones**, the *isotherms at height show a sudden fall, i.e. there is a sudden increase in the *meridional temperature gradient. In the baroclinic zones of the mid-latitudes spontaneous generation of weather systems such as depressions and thunderstorms is common.

When the temperature gradient along the *meridians is very steep, *atmospheric cells break down into cyclonic and anticyclonic *eddies. This failure is known as **baroclinic instability**, and is characterized by the ascent of warmer, and the descent of colder, air.

**barometer** An instrument for measuring *atmospheric pressure. The **mercury barometer** measures the height of a column of mercury, in a glass tube, which the atmosphere can support. The **aneroid barometer** consists of a metal box from which most of the air has been removed. The flexible sides expand and contract as atmospheric pressure varies. The same system is used in an *altimeter. A **barogram** records changes in *atmospheric pressure as a pen marks a revolving cylinder.

**barometric gradient** See *pressure gradient.

**barotropic** In meteorology, describing a part of the atmosphere where pressure and temperature are uniform at any given height, as in an ideal *air mass.

**barrage** A structure built across a river or estuary in order to restrain water.

**barrier** A ridge in the sea of sand or shingle, running parallel to the coast or across an *estuary and above water at normal tides. Barriers are thought to have originated during the *Flandrian transgression when the sea engulfed coastal plains. The clay and silt was carried offshore and the coarser sand and shingle were thought to have been pushed landward. A **barrier island** is long and narrow, usually having beaches on the seaward side. **Barrier beaches** are long, sandy ridges lying above high tide level; **barrier chains** are barrier beaches and islands strung along a coastline. For barrier in human geography, see *diffusion barrier.

**barrier lake** Any lake formed by a naturally occurring barrier made, for example, of rock, *moraine, or *lava.

**barrier reef** A *coral reef stretching along a line parallel with the coastline but separated from it by a wide, deep *lagoon.

**barrio** A *shanty town.

**barrow** A communal burial mound built from the *Stone Age until Saxon times. **Long barrows**, up to 100 m long and 20 m wide, were the earlier form, while **round barrows** were introduced during the *Bronze Age.

**barysphere** This term may refer to the *core and *mantle of the earth, but is often used inexactly.

**basal complex, basement complex** The ancient *igneous rock base of continents which lies beneath Precambrian rocks.

**basal slipping, basal sliding** The advance of a glacier by slow movement close to its bed. This form of ice movement occurs in *warm glaciers where the ice at the base is at its *pressure melting point.

**basalt** A very fine-grained *igneous rock derived from volcanic upwellings. Molten basalt spreads very rapidly to form lava sheets often hundreds of kilometres across. Basalt may crack into hexagonal columns. It is the principle rock of the sea bed and accounts for 90% of all volcanic eruptions. It is composed primarily of plagioclase feldspar and pyroxene. Hence **basaltic** and **basaltic lava**.

**base flow** The usual level of a river. The river can maintain the base flow during dry periods when it is fed by a flow of *ground water.

**base level** The lowest level to which the course of a river is cut down. This level may be sea level or the level of a waterfall or lake, but streams rarely erode as far as base level.

**base line** An accurately surveyed line over land which is to be mapped. It is the basis from which other readings can be taken.

**basic** In lava and rocks, dark, dense material containing 50% or less of silica.

**basic workers** Also termed city-forming workers, these are workers who bring wealth into the city by providing goods and services for the *umland, thereby earning the exchange necessary to finance the city's needs.

**basic/non-basic ratio** In and around a city, the ratio of *basic (city-forming) to *non-basic (city-serving) workers. This ratio is difficult to calculate. One method is to collect data from firms about the percentage of sales within the city and outside it. A firm of 100 workers may sell 60% of its product in city markets. 60 of its workers are therefore classified as non-basic while 40 are classified as basic. It is also possible to establish the basic/non-basic ratio by the use of questionnaires for a sample population.

This ratio expresses the power of the city as it influences its region. The ratio seems to be linked with city size; the larger the city the higher the proportion of non-basic workers. This is because the amount of trade within the city increases as the city grows.

Difficulties occur in the calculation of the ratio because of problems arising from the definitions of urban and rural regions and because many workers are involved in output which is both basic and non-basic. See *economic base theory.

**basin and range** A landscape where ridges made of asymmetric *fault blocks alternate with lowland basins. In the USA, the basin and range country lies between the Sierra Nevada and the Wasatch Mountains.

**basin cultivation** A form of tropical cultivation where low earth ridges enclose small fields—basins. The ridges are to check *runoff from heavy tropical rains, conserving soil moisture and limiting soil erosion.

**basin irrigation** A form of *irrigation where flood water is led into man-made, shallow, and wide depressions.

**basket of eggs topography** A series of *drumlins irregularly grouped about the landscape.

**bastide** A planned, fortified strongpoint and centre of economic development created in the Middle Ages, mostly in France. The rectilinear street pattern contrasts strongly with the irregular, cramped layout of most medieval towns.

**batholith, bathylith** A massive *intrusion, at least 100 km$^2$ in area and extending 20–30 km down into the layer of *magma. Erosion may expose all or part of the upper surface of the batholith.

**bathymetry** The measuring of water depth, mainly of seas and oceans but sometimes of deep lakes.

**bathyorographical** Of a map, showing submarine as well as land contours.

**battery farming** An *intensive form of poultry farming where birds are kept in small cages stacked one on top of another. Provision of food and water is automatic. See *factory farming.

**bauxite** The major ore of aluminium, usually occurring as a form of clay which results from the weathering of tropical rocks. Its main constituents are aluminous *laterite and hydrous aluminium oxides.

**bay** A wide-mouthed recess in the line of the coast, filled with sea water and with open access to the sea.

**bay bar, baymouth bar** A ridge of mud, sand, or shingle extending across a bay. It may be formed when *spits stretch out from each side of the bay and meet. Alternatively, it may be the result of landward movement of an *offshore bar.

**baydzharakh** A dome-shaped polygon, some 3–4 m high and up to 20 m wide found in a *periglacial landscape. It is brought about as the *active layer deepens and the *ice wedges begin to thaw.

**bay-head** At the head of a bay. Hence, **bay-head beach** and **bay-head delta**.

**baymouth bar** *Bay bar.

**beach** An accumulation of *sediment deposited by waves and *longshore drift along the coast. Beach material is very well sorted and the size range tends to be very limited at any particular beach; pebble beaches usually have very little sand, and sand beaches have little shingle. The size of the sediment determines the slope of a beach. Shingle and pebble beaches are steeper than sandy beaches. Beach ridges are formed in sand, resulting from the production of successive *berms.

**beach budget** Most beaches are in equilibrium—the material removed by erosion is compensated for by deposition. If this budget is upset by the building of substantial breakwaters or sea walls, sand beaches may disappear as their source of supply is cut off. Since beaches contribute to the protection of the coastline, the disappearance of a beach can lead to the problem of increased marine erosion.

**beach cusp** A series of small bays—a matter of metres—demarcated by cones of shingle with the pointed ends facing seawards.

**bearing** The horizontal angle between a *base line and any point viewed by a surveyor. A **true bearing** is taken from *true north; a **magnetic bearing** from *magnetic north.

**Beaufort scale** A scale of wind strengths, devised in 1805 by Admiral Sir Francis Beaufort, and modified in 1926. The scale ranges from light winds (1–3) to breezes (4–6) and to gales and hurricanes (7–12). Winds are now generally expressed in metres per second or miles per hour.

**bed** 1. The floor of a body of water.

2. In geology, a layer of sedimentary rock which stands out because of structure, composition or texture. **Bedding** is the arrangement of beds in a rock, while a **bedding plane** separates the distinctive layers of rock.

**bed-floor roughness** The *frictional force of a river bed. A rough bed of boulders, pebbles, and potholes exerts more friction than a smooth, silky channel. It is difficult to quantify bed roughness; usually a somewhat subjective, comparative assessment is made as in 'moderately smooth'.

**bedforms, sedimentary bedforms** In hydrology, forms developed by a flow of water over a mouldable river bed. Bedforms range in size from ripples in the sand, a few centimetres apart, to 'dunes' tens of metres in length.

Bedforms appear to develop further as stream power increases. Initially, the bed is flat; the **plane bed**. With an increasing discharge, small ripples form and develop into dunes. There follows a transitional zone with a plane bed again. With further increases in discharge, standing waves are set up in the water, creating dunes and antidunes.

**bedload** The material which is moved along a river bed by pushing and *saltation. Bedload is usually composed of sands and pebbles but when the water level is high and the current strong, boulders may be moved.

**bedrock** The unweathered rock which underlies the soil and *regolith or which may be exposed at the land surface.

**bedrock fracture** Bedrock is broken up by the impact of large blocks of rock which are incorporated into glacier ice and are moving with the glacier.

**behavioural geography** This suggests that, far from being an *economic man, an individual is a complex being whose perception of the environment may not correspond with objective reality. A distinction is made between the objectively observed environment—things as they are—and of the perceived environment—things as they are seen by the individual. Thus, it is not the fact that a being is living on an island that is significant, it is how he or she perceives that island. An island could be seen as a prison or as a base from which to explore. Behavioural geography is concerned with understanding the flow of events which produce, reproduce, or transform a system; an analysis of processes rather than outcomes. It is concerned with the selectively abstracted structures (mental maps) which are used as part of the decision-making process, whether by individuals or by corporations. The worth of such decisions depends upon the perceptions of the decision-maker and his or her ability to respond to that perception.

**behavioural matrix** An array of information set out in columns and rows concerned with decision-making by an individual or corporation. The rows, rising in value from left to right, indicate the ability of the decision-maker to use incoming information. The columns indicate the quality of information, rising from top to bottom. As firms grow, they should receive more information and be more able to use that information. This results in a diagonal movement towards the lower right of the matrix which symbolizes perfect decision-making. A firm with high ability and a high level of information would tend to seek the *optimum location, while a *satisficer, located near the top left of the matrix, will have a more random location pattern.

Criticisms of the matrix include the point that information and the ability to use it are not independent of each other, and that only crude and arbitrary measures can be used to quantify the levels of the two *vectors.

**behavioural model** A *model which takes into account the vagaries of human nature rather than depending on the concept of *economic man.

**behaviourism** The view that the actions of an individual occur as responses to stimuli. Through constant repetition, the individual learns to make the same, 'correct' response to a given stimulus. Thus it becomes possible to predict behaviour for each stimulus. Behaviourism is thought by many to oversimplify human behaviour and take no account of the mental processes involved in the perception of, and response to, a stimulus.

**bench** A narrow, naturally occurring *terrace backed by a steep slope.

**bench mark** A notch cut in a resistant material, such as a rock outcrop or a stone-built building. In Britain, it shows, to one place of decimals, the height of the mark OD (above the *datum level).

**beneficiation** Concentrating the mineral content of an ore by *ore-dressing, smelting, and pelletizing. Beneficiation usually takes place close to the site of an ore body prior to its transportation to a manufacturing region.

**Benguela current** A cold *ocean current off the south-western coast of Africa.

**Benioff zone** The zone of earthquakes usually caused as an oceanic *plate plunges below a continental plate. The intense friction as the plates rub against each other generates earthquakes of increasing depth.

**benthic** Occurring at the base of bodies of water—lakes, oceans, and seas irrespective of water depth. Hence **benthic zone**, **benthic division**. **Benthos** refers to life attached to the bottom or moving in the bottom mud.

**Bergeron–Findeisen** theory states that minute droplets of water within a cloud will only coalesce around ice crystals. Without the presence of ice crystals, water droplets can remain unfrozen at temperatures of −20 °C. Such droplets are supercooled. At these low temperatures, ice crystals act as *condensation nuclei and larger crystals

may be formed. When the fall-speed of these ice masses is greater than the upward movement of air currents, they will fall. As they descend they may melt to form rain. This theory does not account for the development of all precipitation from clouds, since tropical *cumulus clouds can give rain when the cloud-top temperature is 5 °C or more. See also *coalescence theory.

**Bergman's rule** states that, in warm-blooded animals, species living in cold climates tend to be larger than related species living in hot climates. Some writers question the validity of this 'rule'.

**bergschrund** A deep tensional *crevasse formed around the head of a *cirque glacier. The crevasse forms as ice falls away downslope.

**berm** A narrow, horizontal ridge of beach deposits running parallel to the shore, above the *foreshore.

**beta index, β** A simple measure of *connectivity relating the number of *edges to the number of *nodes. It is given as:

$$\beta = \frac{\Sigma e}{\Sigma v}$$

where $e$ = edges, $v$ = vertices (nodes).
  The greater the value of β, the greater the connectivity.

**betterment** The unplanned increase in the value of land as a result of actions taken not by the owner but by others. The granting of *planning permission usually brings about betterment.

**B horizon** See *horizon.

**bid-rent curve, bid-price curve** The decrease in cost paid for land rents with distance from the market, usually a city centre. Since transport costs rise with distance from the market, rents tend to fall in compensation. Different forms of land use—agricultural, industrial, retail, service, or housing—generate different bid rents. See *Alonso model.

**bifurcation ratio** In a drainage basin, the ratio of the number of streams of a given order to the number of streams of the next, higher, order. The ratio varies with the different classifications of stream orders.

**binary distribution** A *city-size distribution in which a number of settlements of similar size dominate the upper end of the hierarchy.

**bioclastic** Of a rock, made up of broken organic remains.

**bioclimatology** The study of climate as it affects living organisms.

**biodegradable** Describing matter that can be broken down by the natural action of living organisms, usually *aerobic bacteria.

**bioengineering** The use of the chemical processes arising from living organisms in an industrial or agricultural context. An example is the production of methane gas from animal dung.

**biogeochemical cycle** The cyclical movement of energy and materials within *ecosystems. This cycle is applied to specific materials, such as copper or carbon.

**biogeography** The study of the distribution of life forms, past and present, and the causes of such distributions. Biologists usually omit man from these studies while geographers may stress human intervention.

**biogeosphere** The upper crust of the earth ending at the maximum depth of organic life.

**bioherm** An ancient mass of rock formed from sedentary organisms, such as corals. It is often surrounded by rocks of a different origin.

**biological control** The attempt to reduce numbers of pests by the use of predators, either from within the community, or by introduction from outside. Although there have been some successes, notably the control of prickly pear in Australia by the moth *Cactoblastis*, most efforts have had at most partial success and have had to be backed up by the use of pesticides. It

should be noted that effective predators are not usually indigenous.

**biological indicator** An organism used to detect the degree of chemical activity. Lichen, for example, can be used to determine levels of atmospheric sulphur dioxide.

**biological magnification** The buildup of toxins from pesticides, herbicides, and domestic and industrial waste such that these toxins are more and more concentrated in living organisms with movement up the *trophic levels of *food webs. The toxins are not easily broken down and hence they accumulate in the organisms at the top of food webs.

**biological oxygen demand, BOD** The requirement of oxygen for respiration by aquatic organisms. Deeper levels of water may have insufficient oxygen since the water is too deep for the solution of atmospheric oxygen.

**biomass** The total mass of all the organisms inhabiting a given area or of a particular population or *trophic level.

**biome** A naturally occurring community characterized by distinctive life forms which are adapted to the broad climatic type. Major biomes are *tundra, *coniferous (boreal) forest, temperate forest, *tropical rain forest, *savanna, temperate grassland, and *hot deserts. A biome is an idealized type; local variations within a biome are sometimes more significant than variations between biomes. The present-day biomes have evolved in the last 10 000 years.

Smaller biomes are recognized, such as rocky coast biomes or coral reef biomes. In this way, the term is not synonymous with *formation.

**biosphere** The zone where life is found. This is recognizable where the land surface meets the atmosphere, and extends from 3 m below the ground and for some 30 m above it. The biosphere also comprises that region of waters, some 200 m deep, where most marine and freshwater life is found.

**biota** The collective term for all the organic part of a given *ecosystem.

**biotechnology** The application of biological knowledge and techniques to technology.

**biotic** Living; sustaining or having sustained life. **Biotic factors** are exerted by those organisms which affect the existence of a species.

**biotic potential** The maximum population that an area can reach.

**biotic pyramid** A graph showing the *biomass at each *trophic level. Bars are drawn each side of an imaginary axis with the lowest trophic level at the bottom. The overall shape reflects the decreasing amount of biomass with movement up the trophic levels.

**biotite** *Mica.

**bird's foot delta** See *delta.

**birth control** Techniques to limit family size including contraception, sterilization, and abortion. Birth control is seen as a solution to problems of *overpopulation and has been encouraged by many Third World countries. The results have not been as successful as might have been hoped, partly because reaching all sections of society in a nation requires more resources than are generally available and takes an enormously long time. Furthermore, introducing birth control involves complex social factors—children are seen, in many societies as 'wealth', and childbearing is seen as a major function of a married woman. Some governments, like Cuba, do not support birth control, thinking that population is a resource, and it is banned by many religious groups.

**birth rate** The number of births in a year per 1000 of total population taken at the mid-year mark. This is the **crude birth rate** since it is not adjusted to take account, for example, of the proportion of the population which is of childbearing age. The crude birth rate may be expressed as

$$B/P \times 1000$$

where $B$ = the number of births, $P$ = total population.

The **standardized birth rate** indicates what the crude birth rate would have been for a population if the age and sex composition of that population were the same as in a population selected as standard.

**biscuit-board topography** A flat or rolling upland cut into *cirques along its length.

**black box** The view, used in *behavioural geography, that the workings of the human mind cannot be analysed; all that can be observed is the input and output. The input is a stimulus and the output is behaviour but the process in between is as inaccessible as the contents of a sealed black box. This concept of an inaccessible process is also used in physical systems.

**black earth** See *chernozem.

**black frost, black ice** A coating of transparent ice, not readily visible; hence its danger to road users.

**black smoker** Dark particles of sulphides can be dissolved out of the *oceanic crust. Near the mid-*oceanic ridge, sea water penetrates the cracks in the newly formed crust. This water picks up sulphides, is heated, and is propelled upward through the vents to form a black smoker.

**blanket bog** A continuous covering of bog, mostly comprising peat. Only steep slopes and rocky outcrops are dry. Bog formation depends on high humidity and rainfall.

**blind valley** A steep-sided valley in an area of *karst scenery which ends in an abrupt cliff facing up the valley. This is usually the point at which any overland drainage disappears down a *streamsink.

**blizzard** A strong wind which whips up particles of ice and dry, powdery snow. The snow in a blizzard is not falling, but is carried up from snow on the ground.

**block** Of volcanoes, see *pyroclast.

**blockbusting** A technique, used by estate agents in the USA, of inclining residents of a white neighbourhood to move out because they fear that the district is to be taken over by black families.

**block diagram** A drawing, usually of a landform or landforms designed to give a three-dimensional impression by the use of perspective.

**block disintegration** The break-up by *mechanical weathering of jointed and *bedded rock along the lines of weakness. *Frost shattering is the most common agent.

**block faulting** The division of parts of the earth's crust into roughly rectangular blocks bounded by *faults.

**block field, block stream** A sheet of angular rock fragments in spreads or lines in a *periglacial landscape. Some writers maintain that this debris is formed *in situ* by *frost shattering. Others suggest that the blocks have ridden down on the top of saturated debris during *gelifluction.

**blocking anticyclone** See *anticyclone.

**block lava** Sometimes termed *aa, this lava has a thick skin broken into jagged blocks. Its chemical composition is identical to that of *pahoehoe. These two lava formations often occur in the same lava flow.

**block mountain** A mass of upland, bounded by *faults. The surrounding rocks may have sunk, the mountain block may have risen, or both may have occurred.

**blowhole** A crack in the top of a cliff through which air and sea water blow. The blowhole is fed from the seaward end via joints and tunnels.

**blow-out** A *deflation hollow.

**bluff** A steep, almost vertical, cliffed section of a river bank.

**bocage** A landscape of small fields surrounded by low hedges. The term was first applied to the fields of Brittany and Normandy although field enlargement has destroyed much bocage in Normandy.

**BOD** See *biological oxygen demand.

**bog** An area of wet, spongy ground thick with partially decomposed vegetation.

**bogaz** Narrow, deep fissures found in *karst lands and formed as solution deepens and widens the natural joints in the rock.

**bog peat** Acid, brown, only partially decomposed organic matter.

**Bølling** A glacial *interstadial of some 200 years' duration, beginning at about 12 350 years BP.

**Bora (fall-wind)** A cold winter wind blowing down from the mountains on to the eastern Adriatic coast.

The wind develops when a cold continental *air mass crosses a mountain range and is forced to descend because of the *pressure gradient. Despite *adiabatic warming, this cold air displaces warmer air. The term is now applied to winds of similar origin in any other region.

**bore** The current of the incoming tide up a river producing a wall of water which moves upstream.

**boreal** The term means northern and is used, with a capital, to designate a time of cold, dry weather beginning in Britain between 7500 and 5500 years BC.

**boreal forest** See *coniferous (boreal) forest.

**bornhardt** A dome-shaped rock outcrop more than 30 m high, and sometimes several hundred metres in width. The origin of these features is problematical. They may have been exposed by the stripping of the *regolith, either by *parallel slope retreat or by the *downwearing and removal of soil.

**borral** A soil order of the *US soil classification. See *chernozem.

**Boserup model** The view that increases in population size stimulate agricultural change. At the earliest stage, small families subsist through forest *fallow where land is used for two years or so and is then left for 20 to 25 years. As population rises, *bush fallowing and short periods of fallow are used with increasingly intense cropping and shortening fallows. Further population growth is followed by annual cropping which consists of harvesting one crop a year with a fallow of a few months only. Multi-cropping is stimulated by further population increase and is the most intensive system of agriculture.

**boss** A roughly circular *igneous intrusion, a few square kilometres in area and lying at a steep angle to the ground surface.

**boulder clay** A now outmoded term for *till. It is an inexact term as till does not always contain boulders.

**boulder field** As distinct from a *block field, this is an area of boulders which is the result of *spheroidal weathering. When the weathered layers are removed by water, the corestones are left as rounded boulders.

**boundary** A line marking the limits of a unit of land, often a geographical region, but also of economies or societies, such as a ghetto. Different cultural groups are divided by **ethnic boundaries**. **Physical boundaries** follow natural features such as rivers, and **geometric boundaries** follow lines of latitude and longitude. A distinction is made between **antecedent boundaries** which demarcate territories before they are settled, like the 49th parallel between Canada and the USA, and **subsequent** boundaries which evolve together with the society they encompass. See *frontier.

**bounded rationality** A decision-maker has neither the time and space nor the ability to arrive at an optimal solution and many individuals may not seek to optimize at all. The idea of bounded rationality is that individuals strive to be rational having first greatly simplified the choices available. Thus, instead of choosing from every location, the decision-maker chooses between a small number.

**bourne** A temporary stream occupying a *dry valley.

**box canyon** In the USA, a canyon with steep, almost vertical walls.

**B.P.** Before the present day.

**brackish** Of water, slightly saline.

**braided channel** A river channel which has deposited *bars and islands around which the river flows. It has been shown that, for a given *discharge, braided channels slope more steeply than meandering channels. Braiding occurs when the discharge fluctuates frequently, when the river cannot carry its full load, where the river is wide and shallow, where banks are easily eroded, and where there is a large *bedload. The position of the bars is changeable. Braiding differs from *anastomosis in that the islands are longer lasting in the latter case.

**Brandt Report** A publication (1980) concerned with the problems of the Third World—the South—and its relationships with the more developed world—the North.

**braunerde** See *brown earth.

**Brazil current** A warm *ocean current off the east coast of Brazil.

**break, breaking point** The point at which the field of influence of one settlement ends and that of another begins. This can be calculated according to the *gravity model equation:

$$d_{jk} = \frac{d_{ij}}{1 + \sqrt{\frac{P_i}{P_j}}}$$

where $d_{jk}$ is the distance of the breaking point from town $j$, $d_{ij}$ is the distance between towns $i$ and $j$, $P_i$ is the population of town $i$, and $P_j$ is the population of town $j$. The number of shops in each settlement may be used rather than population.

**break of bulk point** The point at which a cargo is unloaded and broken up into smaller units prior to delivery. This minimizes transport costs. This frequently happens at waterfront sites and imports are often processed to cut costs. At break of bulk points costs are incurred through goods being transferred from one mode of transport to another. Processing before the transfer leads to lower costs.

**break of slope** A sudden change of gradient as in a river after *rejuvenation or when a band of resistant rock stands out.

**breccia** Any rock which consists of sharp fragments of different rocks cemented together.

**brickfielder** A hot, dry, and dusty northerly wind affecting south-east Australia in the summer.

**bridle path** A path suitable for walkers and horse riders but banned to vehicles.

**bright lights district** An area of the *CBD given over to entertainment and hotels.

**brightness** In *remote sensing, the degree of light emitted from an area.

**brine** A strong solution of common salt in water. Shallow pits known as **brine pans** are used to make salt by evaporation.

**Broad, Broads** A series of shallow, freshwater lakes linked by water courses found in East Anglia. They result from extensive peat digging in the Middle Ages.

**broadleaved** A tree leaf that is wide in relation to its length. Most broadleaved trees are *deciduous.

**Bronze Age** A time after the *Neolithic when **bronze**—an alloy of copper and tin—was used to make implements. This age also saw the development of the wheel, the domestication of draught animals, and the use of writing and arithmetic.

**brown earth, brown forest soil** A *zonal soil associated with areas where the natural vegetation is, or was, deciduous woodland. Brown earths may have a thick litter layer and generally have an A *horizon rich in *humus and containing iron and aluminium *sesquioxides in small, crumb-like *peds. This horizon merges into a lighter B horizon which has blocky peds and is weakly developed. There is little *leaching although the soils are free-draining.

**brown podzolic soil** See *podzol.

**brush** Small trees and shrubs.

**buffer state** A generally neutral state which lies between two powerful and potentially belligerent neighbours. Invasion by its more powerful neighbours is often the lot of a buffer state.

**buran** An icy, snow-laden wind of central Asia.

**bush** An area of low, woody plants and grasses, usually uncleared, as in the **bush veld** of South Africa.

**bush fallowing** A type of subsistence agriculture where land is cultivated for a period of time and then left for some years to recover its fertility. This was a feature of *infield–outfield cultivation in Britain, of areas of upland farming, and of the tropics.

**business climate** The environment of an area in relation to industrial output. This is difficult to quantify but factors affecting the business climate include local legislation, the attitude of public officials, and the availability of finance.

**butte** A small, flat-topped, steep-sided hill of layered strata, probably the residue of a larger feature and cited by some to be evidence of *parallel slope retreat.

**Buys Ballot's law** This states that if an observer faces the direction *to* which the wind is blowing, the lower pressure will be to the left in the Northern Hemisphere. The reverse is the case in the Southern Hemisphere. This law can be used to predict wind direction once the location of the lower pressure is known.

# C

**C 14 dating** Carbon 14 dating is used on organic remains and is based on the existence of this isotope of carbon in living matter. After death, no more carbon 14 is added to the remains. The dating is based on the rate of decay of the radioactive isotope and the proportions of C 14 to the more abundant C 12.

**caatinga** Thorny woodland composed of drought-resistant species found in north-eastern Brazil.

**cadastre** A record of the area, boundaries, location, value, and ownership of land, achieved by a **cadastral survey**.

**Cainozoic, Caenozoic, Cenozoic** The most recent *era of earth's history stretching approximately from 65 million years BP to the present day.

**cairn** A rough mound of stones piled up as a route marker, as a boundary indicator, or as a memorial.

**calcareous** Containing calcium carbonate or limestone and/or chalk. **Calcification** is the replacement of any matter by calcium minerals. Calcification of soil occurs when calcium carbonate is deposited in the B *horizon.

**calcrete** A *duricrust made up mostly of calcium carbonate.

**caldera** A sunken crater at the centre of a volcano, formed as a result of subsidence. As the *magma founders, so the centre of the volcano collapses.

**Caledonian orogeny** A mountain-building movement in north-west Europe between about 430 and 360 million years BP.

**calibration** The adjustment of a model so that it will fit special circumstances. The values used within a particular model, such as the *gravity model, need to be modified to local circumstances before it can make predictions.

**caliche** In the American south-west, an encrustation of calcium.

**California current** A cold *ocean current.

**calm** An atmosphere without movement. Calms are associated with *anticyclones and with certain latitudes such as the *horse latitudes and those of the *doldrums.

**calving** The breaking away of a mass of ice from an iceberg, an *ice front, or a glacier.

**cambering** The rounding at the edge of a cap rock occurring in *periglacial landscapes where there are underlying clays. As clays thaw, they are squeezed out and the cap rock cracks and sags at the edges.

**Cambrian** The oldest *period of *Paleozoic time stretching approximately from 570 to 500 million years BP.

**Campbell-Stokes recorder** An instrument for measuring and recording hours of sunshine. The sunlight is focused through a lens and then burns a line, which extends with movements of the sun, onto a card.

**campo** A Brazilian *savanna probably formed by burning and tree felling.

**canal** An artificial watercourse cut for inland navigation. Canals came into prominence in England in the late eighteenth century because of the poor state of the roads and the cheapness of water transport. As all-weather roads and railways developed, the canal became outmoded. Canals are still used for short hauls of bulky and non-perishable goods and canalized rivers are an important mode of transport in larger countries.

**Canaries current** A cold *ocean current.

**canopy** The upper layer of a woodland or forest where the crowns of the trees are at approximately the same height.

**canyon, cañon** In South-West USA, any valley. Otherwise, a steep-sided, deep valley in arid and semi-arid regions, formed by *dissection.

**CAP** See *Common Agricultural Policy.

**capability constraint** In *time–space geography, a limit to an individual's actions because of biological needs, like food and sleep, and because of restricted facilities, like access to public transport.

**capacity** In hydrology, the maximum amount of debris that the stream can move as *bedload. The capacity is dependent on the *discharge and on the nature of the load; a stream may be able to carry more weight if the particles are small than if the load were of large boulders.

**cape** A headland jutting out into the sea.

**capillary** In a soil, the fine spaces between soil particles. The particles attract soil moisture and surface tension is strong enough to cause moisture to rise up through the soil, above the water table. This is **capillary action**.

**capital** One of the *factors of production, capital includes all the items designed by society to further the creation of wealth. Plant, machinery, and buildings are **fixed capital** while **floating capital** includes raw materials, fuels, and components. **Finance capital** is the money needed for production.

**capital goods** Goods which are used to create other goods.

**capital-intensive** An economic system needing high levels of investment, frequently in the form of finance *capital. See *labour-intensive.

**capitalism** An economic system based on the private ownership of *capital and the workings of a free market. In *Marxist terms, an arrangement whereby one class—the capitalists, or bourgeoisie—owns the *factors of production while the workers possess only their labour. According to Marxism, capitalism exploits the workers.

A more general usage defines capitalism as a system where the factors of production are privately owned. Sales occur for profits in markets which are free in the sense that, subject to the constraints of the law, *entrepreneurs are able to engage in business. The implicit assumption is that individuals are rewarded in relation to their economic contribution.

**cap rock** A *stratum of resistant rock overlying less resistant rock. The more resistant rock is often undercut by erosion of the lower rock. The term is also applied to an *impermeable rock overlying an *aquifer.

**capture, river capture** When a river is extending its channel upstream by *headward erosion, it may come into contact with the headwaters of a river which is less vigorous. The headwater from the minor river may be diverted into the more rapidly eroding channel. There is often a sudden change of stream direction at the point of capture; this is the **elbow of capture**. See also *misfit stream and *wind gap.

**carbonaceous** Containing carbon; as, for example, in coal or *peat.

**carbonation, carbonation-solution** A form of weathering whereby **carbonic acid**—water with dissolved carbon dioxide—dissolves limestone.

**carbon cycle** Carbon is supplied to the *biosphere as carbon dioxide during volcanic eruptions. Most of this is dissolved in the sea or incorporated into calcareous sediments which then harden to form limestones and dolomites. As these rocks are folded and raised above sea level, they are subjected to solution by weak carbonic acid and form sediments once more. This is the largest and slowest of the carbon cycles. The shortest cycle involves respiration by plants and animals whereby carbon dioxide is expired and *photosynthesis by plants which change carbon dioxide and water into organic compounds. It has been suggested that a third carbon cycle exists in the burning of fossil fuels. Carbon dioxide is emitted and can be once again incorporated by living organisms. These may then be a source of fuel. It is this third cycle that seems to be out of balance; carbon dioxide is being emitted far more rapidly than it can be absorbed during photosynthesis. This increase in atmospheric carbon dioxide may lead to an increase in the warming of the atmosphere. See *greenhouse effect.

**Carboniferous** A *period of *Paleozoic time stretching approximately from 345 to 280 million years BP. This period can be subdivided into the Mississippian and the Pennsylvanian periods.

**cardinal points** The major points of the compass—North, South, East, and West.

**carnivore** Any animal which eats the flesh of other animals. Within a *pyramid of numbers, **top carnivores** are usually the least numerous, largest, and most complex animals and are at the top of the pyramid.

**carrying capacity** The maximum potential number of inhabitants which can be supported in a given area. The concept was first advanced in *ecology, where the 'inhabitants' are plants, was extended to livestock, but now is increasingly used in terms of the optimum numbers of users of recreational facilities where the upper limit is set at the point where the environment deteriorates.

**cartel** A system whereby producers divide up the market between themselves, avoiding direct competition and not encroaching on each other's share of the market.

**Cartesian coordinate system** A reference grid used to locate a point. Two reference lines—the *ordinate ($x$-axis) and the *abscissa ($y$-axis)—are drawn at right angles to each other, intersecting at the point of origin of the system. The location of a point is given in terms of distance from the origin along each axis.

**cartogram** Broadly defined as a map using statistical symbols, a more specialist usage defines a cartogram as a type of map transformation based on other than a true scale.

For example, a voting map of Britain may show the size of counties in relation to the numbers of voters in each electoral unit. Some attempt is made to show the shapes of countries and regions involved and these are positioned in the correct geographical context.

**cartography** The production of maps and charts and the study of the same.

**cascading systems** See *systems.

**case-hardening** The production of a resistant *weathering rind consisting mainly of iron and magnesium hydroxides, and sometimes of amorphous silica. The origin of these materials is under dispute; some writers claim they come from the interior of the rock, others that the rind is composed of wind-borne minerals.

**cash cropping** The growing of a crop to produce goods for sale or for barter rather than for the subsistence of the farmer and family.

**caste** A position in society inherited from parents at birth and from which there is no transfer throughout life. The system is at its strongest in India where people of high caste are respected but those of the lowest caste—the untouchables—work in the most menial occupations.

**cataract** A step-like succession of waterfalls.

**catastrophism** The belief that geological strata and other landscape elements were formed by sudden, isolated, and forceful events.

**catch crop** A fast growing plant which is intercropped between the rows of the main crop. It is often used as *green manure.

**catchment area** 1. In human geography, the region which is served by a city.

2. In hydrology, the region drained by a river and its tributaries; the *drainage basin.

**categorical data** Data which can be placed into categories which are mutually exclusive, such as age-groups. **Categorical data analysis** is a statistical technique which uses methods similar to those of a *regression analysis.

**catena** A sequence of soil types arising from the same parent rock, but distinct from each other because of the variations arising from differences in topography such as drainage, slope position, *leaching, and *mass movement.

**cation** An atom, or group of atoms with a positive charge. **Cation exchange** is the process whereby a cation in solution is absorbed by a solid, replacing a different cation. Thus, in soil science, if a potassium salt is dissolved in water and applied to a soil, potassium cations are absorbed by soil particles, and sodium and calcium cations are released.

**causal analysis** The search for the cause or causes of particular events and objects.

**causal factor** One variable which causes change in another. Statistical techniques which test the strength of the postulated link include the *Student's *t*-test and the *chi-squared test.

**cave** A large, natural, underground hollow, usually with a horizontal opening. The largest and best-developed caves and **caverns** (large caves) are found in areas of *karst scenery.

Karst caves result from solution but *corrasion by water-borne sediments and pebbles is also important. The collapse of cave roofs causes much of the hummocky appearance of karst.

**caving** The collapse of an undercut river bank.

**cavitation** The process by which bubbles in a liquid collapse close to a solid surface. Cavitation causes shock waves by this collapse. It is an erosional *hydraulic force, usually occurring downstream of local obstructions on the river bed.

**cay** See *key.

**CBD, Central Business District** The heart of an urban area, usually located at the meeting point of the city's transport systems, which contains the highest percentage of shops and offices. Land values are high, land use is at its most intense, and, in many countries, development is upwards rather than sideways. Within the CBD, specialist areas, such as a jewellery or garment-making, may arise in order to benefit from *external economies.

**celerity** In a river, the square root of the product of the acceleration due to gravity and the mean depth of the river flow. See also *Froude number.

**cell** See *atmospheric cell.

**cellular clouds** Honeycomb-like clouds, seen only from satellite photographs, with a diameter of around 30 km. Their origin is not fully understood, but is connected with the movement of cold air over a warmer sea surface.

**Celsius scale** A scale of temperature with 99 divisions between 0°—the freezing point of pure water—and 100°—the boiling point of pure water. These temperatures are established at sea level and under a standard pressure of 760 mm. The scale was formerly called Centigrade.

**cementation** The binding together of particles by adhesive materials. Sedimentary rocks are often bound together and hardened by cementation.

**Cenozoic** See *Cainozoic.

**census** A survey, usually into the size and nature of a population. A census is taken for a particular point in time, and while some nations require their people to note where they were at the time of a census,— **de facto census** others ask for the respondents' place of residence—**de jure census.** As well as a head count, a census, in the developed world, would inquire into, for example, birthplace, age, sex, marital status, qualifications, occupation, family structure, and fertility.

**Central American Common Market** An economic community of Central American states designed to promote trade and development by the easing of tariff barriers and establishing intergovernmental links.

**Central Business District** See *CBD.

**central business height index** A measure of the intensity of land use within the *CBD. The total floor area of all stories of a building is compared with the ground floor area of the building under consideration. The higher the index, the more intensive the urban land use.

**central good, central function, central service** Any good, function, or service at a *central place.

**centrality** The degree to which a town serves its surrounding area. This depends on the ease of access to the town and the range of goods and services offered. The centrality of a town is not necessarily commensurate with its population.

Christaller used the occurrence of telephones to indicate centrality at a time when the ownership of telephones was not as universal as it is today. The equation he used was

$$Z_z = \frac{T_z - E_z \cdot T_g}{E_g}$$

where $T_z$ is the number of telephones in the central place, $E_z$ is the population of the central place, $T_g$ is the number of telephones in the region served, and $E_g$ is the population of the region. $Z_z$ is the index of centrality. The higher the index, the greater the centrality.

**centrality of population** A central point in the distribution of a population within a country which has the same population numbers on every side. The **mean centre of a population distribution** is the point at which the squares of the distances of all the population from the centre is at a minimum. This is very complicated and lengthy to calculate.

The **median centre** is the point at which travel distances for all the population to converge is lowest and the **modal centre** is the area with the maximum population density.

**centralization** A concentration of administration or production at a central point, possibly to the detriment of the *periphery.

**centrally planned economy** Generally speaking, this term has been used as a synonym for communist economies. The *factors of production are owned by the state. Their deployment is planned from the administrative capital which leads to the creation of an enormous bureaucratic superstructure. From there, the generalized plans will be broken into different sectors or regions. True central planning requires an enormous quantity of information which may be difficult to gather at the centre. Some charge central planning with inefficiency.

**central place** A settlement or nodal point which, by its functions, serves an area round about it for goods and services.

**central place system** The distribution of a hierarchy of *central places, appearing as a network.

**central place theory** A theory, advanced by Christaller and, later, Lösch, concerned with the way that settlements evolve and are spaced out. Christaller envisaged an *isotropic plain with an even distribution of purchasing power. Travel costs were the same in any direction and all parts of the plain were served by a central place so that the spheres of influence of the central places completely filled the plain. Central goods and services were to be purchased from the nearest central place and no excess profit was to be made by any central place. Christaller contended that each central place should have a hexagonal market area since this polygon represents the most effective packing of the plain and is most nearly circular.

To ensure that goods and services are freely available, central places emerge in the middle of a hexagon containing six lower order places. One higher order place will serve a total of two lower order neighbours. This may mean that two distinct lower order places are served or that the central place will serve one-third of each of the six lower order places surrounding it. This will bring to two the total of lower order places served, and with the addition of the central place itself, three places are served. This method of serving the market is known as the k = 3 system. A different system of hexagons would evolve if transport costs are to be minimized. The hexagon is rotated so that the settlements are located evenly at the mid-point of the hexagon's sides. Now the central place serves a half share in the surrounding six settlements; a total of three places plus the central area. Therefore k = 3+1 = 4; the k = 4 system. The most efficient pattern for the administration of settlements sees all six lower order centres inside the hexagonal area of the central place, k = 7.

All these places fit into a hierarchy. Higher order places stand out from the hexagonal pattern of lower order centres, but are themselves packed in hexagons around an even higher order central place. Christaller envisaged this hierarchy as going all the way up to major regional centres. It should be said that hexagonal patterns are very rarely found in real life.

Lösch, who had worked independently of Christaller, extended these ideas. He plotted the ten smallest market areas, each with a different k value. Each network surrounded a common central place. Tracings of each network were laid over each other and the tracings were located so as to produce the largest number of places occurring for each k value. The result was a central place with city-rich and city-poor areas spread out in wedges around the major central place. Such a pattern is found around Indianapolis.

Common sense tells us that the basic postulates of these models do not exist but they still give insight into the nature of town development and distribution.

**central tendency** A synonym for average, most often expressed as an *arithmetic mean, a *median, or a *mode.

**central vent eruption** Also known as a pipe eruption, this is a volcanic eruption from a single vent or a cluster of centrally placed vents. Eruptions of this type form conical volcanoes.

**centrifugal** Moving away from a centre.

**centrifugal forces** Those forces which encourage a movement of people, business, and industry away from central urban areas. Such forces include congestion, restricted sites, high local taxes and rents, obsolete technology, and lack of *amenity.

**centripetal** Moving towards a centre.

**centripetal acceleration** In meteorology, the force acting into the centre of a high- or low-pressure system which causes winds to blow along a curved path, parallel to the *isobars. It is of greatest significance in *hurricanes and *tornadoes.

**centripetal drainage** See *drainage patterns.

**centripetal forces** Those forces which move people, business, and industry towards a centre. These forces include *accessibility, *functional linkages, *agglomeration economies, and *external economies.

**chaco** The almost level *savanna and *scrub woodland between the Andes and the river Paraguay.

**chain** A series of connected features, such as islands. A **mountain chain** is a series of roughly parallel mountain ranges.

**chain migration** A movement of population whereby one person migrates, to be followed by others of the same family. Later, friends or more distant relatives may follow.

**chalk** A pure form of *limestone composed of the shells of minute marine organisms together with spherical or egg-shaped particles of calcium carbonate.

**channel** Any natural or man-made watercourse. The **channel capacity** of a river is its cross-sectional area in square metres, but the limits of the channel at each bank are not easy to assess.

Water in the channel will experience **channel resistance** which slows or impedes the flow; friction with the bed is the major cause. See *bed-floor roughness.

Various classifications of **channel types** have been suggested. The typology may be based on the shape of the channel and its network, the nature of the bank and bed and the way in which these affect the channel, or the capacity of the river to carry sediment.

**channel order** See *stream order.

**chapparal** A *biome characterized by short, woody, and dense bushes having permanent, thick, hairy, or leathery leaves to restrict loss of water through transpiration in summer. Seed-eating rodents and birds abound together with small mammals. All may be preyed upon by wolves and big cats.

Chapparal is found on the west coasts of continents between 30 and 40 °N. and S. of the equator. Summers are dry with average temperatures above 20 °C and winters are mild and moist.

**charter group** A group representing the most typical culture of a host community as a model for immigrants. This is often established by the first settlers. Thus, English-speaking, White, Protestant, culture to some extent dominates the USA in spite of the influx of many different groups.

**chase** In medieval England, an unfenced but private hunting ground held by a commoner and therefore subject to common, rather than forest, law.

**chatter mark** In glaciology, a mark made upon a surface by a rock embedded in ice. Chatter marks are crescentic in shape and have been attributed to tension in a rock as ice pulls across it. The 'horns' of the crescent point in the direction of the ice flow.

**chelate** A chemical substance formed from the bonding of organic compounds to metallic *ions, especially ions of aluminium, iron, and magnesium. The *leaching out of chelates is **cheluviation**.

**chelation** The formation of *chelates. By this process, some relatively insoluble materials may become soluble so that they are released into the soil.

**chemical weathering** The breakdown of rocks by chemical means such as *corrosion, *hydrolysis, *oxidation, and some forms of *organic weathering.

**chemotrophic** Of a *primary producer which can obtain energy from chemical reactions rather than from the sun.

**chernozem** A *zonal soil with a deep A *horizon, rich in *humus from decomposed grass, and dark in colour.

Also known as **black earths**, chernozems develop on mid-latitude continental interiors where grassland is, or was, the natural vegetation.

Chernozem development is associated with temperate climates which have marked wet and dry seasons. There is sufficient moisture to permit the decay of the grass litter into humus, but not enough for *leaching to be significant. The B horizon is lighter brown, but is often absent. The lower horizons are often rich in calcium compounds. In *US soil classification chernozems fall into the category of *mollisoils, sub-order boroll.

**chestnut soil** A *zonal soil found in grasslands more arid than those under which *chernozems develop. These grasslands are sparser, so that there is less *humus.

The *xerophytic nature of much of the grassland under which chestnut soils develop also retards the development of humus. In the B *horizon, there is an accumulation of calcium carbonate. In *US soil classification, chestnut soils fall into the category of *mollisoils, sub-order xeroll.

**child–woman ratio** The ratio of the number of children below five to the number of women of childbearing years, which may be expressed as:

$$\frac{P_{0-4}}{Pf_{15-49}} \times 100$$

where $P$ refers to a population, the numbers refer to their ages, and $f$ denotes women.

In the absence of universal registration of births, the child–woman ratio is a relatively good indicator of fertility.

**chinook** A warm, dry wind descending from the Rocky Mountains of North

America. The *adiabatic temperature change brought about as the wind descends resembles the warming of the European *foehn. The chinook occurs sporadically between December and February, bringing dramatic rises in temperature. It develops if air streams from the Pacific replace the normal high-pressure cells existing over the Great Plains.

**chi-squared test** A statistical technique used to find the significance of the difference between one or more frequency distributions and a hypothetical, expected distribution. An assertion is made—e.g. the pebbles in a river bed become progressively smaller from source to mouth. This assertion is then restated as a *null hypothesis—there is no difference in pebble size along the course of a river. It is this null hypothesis which must be rejected if the assertion is to be proved true. The formula is given as:

$$\chi^2 = \frac{\Sigma (O - E)^2}{E}$$

where $O$ = observed (actual) frequencies, $E$ = expected frequencies.

The significance of the value of chi-squared is read from a graph, using the appropriate degrees of freedom. If the point derived from the coordinates falls above the 0.1% line, for example, there is less than a 0.1% probability that the null hypothesis is true and therefore that there is a greater than 99.9% probability that the assertion is true.

**chlorophyll** A green pigment found in the cells of most plants and vital for the absorption of light energy during *photosynthesis.

**chorography** The establishment and description of geographical regions. As such, it is the study of *areal differentiation.

**choropleth** A map showing the distribution of a phenomenon by shades to indicate the density per unit area of that phenomenon. The greater the density of shading, the greater the density in reality. Choropleths give a clear but generalized picture of distribution and this may mask finer details. The choice of values for the classes may affect the visual picture given.

**c.i.f. (cost, insurance, freight) pricing** A form of *uniform delivered pricing in an import or export context where prices are quoted with reference to a port.

**cinder cone** A cone formed by fragments of solidified lava thrown out during a volcanic explosion. Some volcanoes are made of alternate layers of **cinder** and *volcanic ash.

**circuit of capital** In order to pay for the other *factors of production the capitalist must forward finance capital. Upon their purchase, this money is transformed into commodities. These are processed and transformed into saleable goods which will realize finance capital. This may then be reinvested.

**circular and cumulative growth** See *cumulative causation.

**circulation** The movement of capital, labour, goods, and services throughout the economy. More specifically, in population geography, the word applies to short-term repetitive movements of individuals where there is no intention to effect a change of residence. For example, many West African men move to cities after harvesting their crops. Employment opportunities are greater there, but the workers return to the land before the rains to plough, plant, and weed their crops.

**cirque** Also known as a **corrie** or **cwm**, this is a circular hollow cut into bedrock during glaciation. The side and back walls are steep but the front opens out downslope. Cirques may be up to 2 km across. During glaciation, ice is thickest in the centre of the cirque and is thought to undergo rotational slipping, thus overdeepening the cirque floor but merely riding over the low bar at the mouth.

The formation of cirques remains unclear. The sides and back are subject to intense physical weathering and it is suggested that *frost shattering occurs at the base of the *bergschrund, but such a crevasse cannot be deep because ice becomes plastic when it is more than 40–60 m thick (according to the elevation). A cirque may contain a **cirque glacier**.

In the temperate zones of the Northern Hemisphere, cirques face outward in directions between north-east and south-west. This is due in part to decreased insolation on north-east facing slopes and in part to the buildup of drifted snow in the lee of westerly winds.

**cirro-, cirrus** Like a lock of hair; referring to high, slender clouds with a feathery appearance. When these coalesce to form a thin layer of high cloud, they are termed **cirro-stratus**. Patchy, mottled high cirrus is **cirro-cumulus**, often called a **mackerel sky**. This forms above very active warm fronts. See also *cloud.

**city** A large urban centre functioning as a central place which can provide very specialized goods and services. No limiting figures of population size or areal extent have been agreed on. In the UK, a city has a cathedral.

**city-filling activity** Activity which provides goods and services for use within the city. A synonym for non-basic activity (see *non-basic worker).

**city-forming activity** An activity, such as the provision of goods and services, which contributes to the economic well-being of the city by attracting income from beyond the city. A synonym for basic activity (see *basic worker).

**city-region** The city and its *hinterland.

**city-size distribution** The ranking of cities within a nation according to size and place in the hierarchy. Several patterns may be recognized: see *settlement hierarchy.

**city state** A city having independent sovereignty and so powerful that it can command its surrounding territory. One example is the city state of Kano in early Nigerian history.

**clachan** A *hamlet in the Scottish Highlands; usually a formless collection of houses with a church.

**class** A concept which recognizes different strata in society. Pre-industrial societies saw class in terms of rank, resting on tradition and an intricate system of rights and duties. Capitalist societies see class as defined by socio-economic status, as in the *Registrar General's classification.

**classification** In *remote sensing, the process of assigning individual *pixels of a multi-spectral image to different categories. Each category is derived from observations made on the ground (*ground truth).

**class interval** The set of limits by which data are classified, as in 0–4, 5–9, 10–14, and so on. Fixing of class limits for use in *histograms or *choropleths can change the impact of the data thus sorted. Class intervals may be set by equal groupings, at 'natural breaks' in the data or as part of a logarithmic sequence.

**clast** A rock fragment or a pebble, over 5 mm in diameter and forming part of a *sedimentary rock. A rock composed of such fragments and pebbles is **clastic**.

**clay** In a soil, mineral particles less than 0.002 mm in size. When dry, clay is hard; when wet it swells and becomes pliable and sticky. **Clay colloids** are finely divided clays dispersed in water. These particles have a negative surface charge which attracts positively charged ions. These minute particles are among the most reactive constituents of a soil.

**clay micelles** Individual clay particles, platey in form, with a diameter of less than $2\mu$, having a negative charge and therefore being able to attract cations within a soil.

**clay mineral** Not clay-sized particles, but a group of minerals created by the intense weathering of rock. Clay minerals affect the physical properties of soils because they expand when wet.

**clay pan** A more or less *impermeable clay below the soil surface which causes waterlogging.

**clay-with-flints** A deposit of clay containing flint, often in *pipes or potholes, which overlies chalk. It has been suggested that this deposit comes from the weathering of chalk.

**clear felling** The practice of cutting down all the trees on a site. This leaves the ground unprotected against erosion and is unattractive.

**cleavage** The fine splitting of a *metamorphic rock along lines of mica flakes, and usually at right angles to the original *bedding planes.

**cliff** A steep rock face, usually facing the sea.

**climate** The average weather conditions of a region. The recorded average is the result of many years of observations of weather.

**climatic change** Evidence of climatic change ranges from differing geological strata to the study of pollen grains and tree rings.

The early climatic history of the world is not well understood but it is known that during the last 55 million years the earth has been cooling, and that during the last million years there have been alternating periods of glacial and *interglacial episodes. The causes of climatic change include changes in the earth's orbit and axis, volcanic activity, variations between the distribution of land and sea, and, possibly, changes in the composition of the earth's atmosphere. Recent research suggests that the actions of man are altering the climate. See *greenhouse effect.

**climatic formation** A group of vegetation categorized according to the climate which controls it. Unlike an *edaphic formation, this vegetation group occurs in very large units.

**climatic geomorphology** Also known as **climatomorphology**, this is the association of types of landform with different climates. Some geomorphologists believe that the processes operating in climatic zones give rise to specific landforms e.g. *periglacial landforms in *tundra climates.

**climatology** The study of the climates of the earth, their origin and their role as elements of the natural environment.

**climax** The last possible stage in the development of natural vegetation. After this point the vegetation is in equilibrium with physical conditions and only minor changes should occur.

**climax community** An *ecosystem which undergoes no change and perpetuates the existence of the species concerned. This can be seen as the final stage of a *succession.

**climograph** A graph of monthly average temperature plotted against average humidity. The monthly points are joined by a line. The shape and location of line thus drawn indicates the nature of climate in terms of heat and humidity.

**clinometer** An instrument used to establish angles, usually on a hillslope and more rarely along bedding planes.

**clint** The raised portion of a *limestone pavement lying between the *grikes.

**closed system** A system marked by clear boundaries which admit of no movement of energy across them. The *entropy of any closed system never decreases.

**cloud** A visible dense mass of water droplets and/or ice crystals suspended in the air. Clouds generally form when air is forced to rise: at a *front, over mountains, or because of *convection.

Clouds mirror the atmospheric processes which cause them. *Cirrus often indicates the presence of the *jet stream or the approach of a warm front. As the front gets nearer, these clouds coalesce to form cirro-*stratus. With the advent of the front, the cloud becomes lower and thicker, forming *alto-stratus. Where the front nears ground level, *nimbo-stratus may form. At active ana-fronts all these clouds may take on a more *cumulus form.

Atmospheric *convection currents are generally indicated by the presence of cumulus or even cumulo-nimbus clouds. A cumulus cloud will often form over a heated surface and then shift with the wind, so that a further cumulus is formed over the same 'hot spot'. If this process continues a line of cloud—a **cloud-street**—is formed.

*Turbulence, generated by moderate winds, is a common cause of stratus cloud, which is often trapped beneath an *inversion. Turbulence also gives rise to a nearly continuous sheet of strato-cumulus cloud.

As air rises over mountain barriers, condensation occurs, and lens-shaped or **lenticular clouds** form above the peaks. Where the mountain is not substantial enough to cause air to rise entirely above it, a **banner cloud** may form. This is a cloud which develops to one side of the peak, stretched out by the prevailing wind. A **castellanus cloud** looks like a series of turrets.

**cloud cover** The proportion of the sky that is overcast, assessed visually, and expressed most commonly in eighths (*oktas).

**cloud seeding** *Seeding of clouds.

**Club of Rome** A society of one hundred members ranging from academics such as scientists, social scientists, economists, and teachers, to managers and civil servants. Its publication *Limits to Growth* in the early 1960s argued the necessity of slowing down population growth in order to ward off *Malthusian checks.

**clustered** The layout of a feature, especially settlements, closely together in a group.

**CMEA** See *Council for Mutual Economic Assistance.

**coalescence theory** The *Bergeron–Findeisen theory cannot explain the formation of all tropical rainfall since ice crystals are often absent in tropical clouds. The coalescence theory, advanced by Langmuir, suggests that the small droplets in clouds become larger by coalescence until they are sufficiently heavy to fall. As they fall, they collide with other droplets, becoming still larger. The deeper the cloud, the bigger the drops grow and the faster they fall. The biggest raindrops thus formed are around 5 mm in diameter.

**coastal dune** A ridge or hill which forms when marine deposits of sand are blown to the back of the beach. The rate of formation and the extent of these dunes is dependent upon the supply of sand to the beach.

**coastal plain** A fairly level low-lying area bordering the coast, and perhaps formed by *fluvial deposition. Coastal plains often occur along *emergent coasts.

**cockpit karst** The arrangement of star-shaped hollows surrounded by steep, rounded hills found in tropical karst country. Cockpits—the hollows—can be 100 m deep and usually contain a *streamsink.

**coefficient of dispersion** A statistical measurement which indicates the nucleation or dispersion of settlement. For a rural unit,

$$C = \frac{p \times n}{P}$$

where C is the coefficient of dispersion, $p$ equals total population of the rural unit, $P$ is the population outside the main village, and $n$ is the number of settlements. The higher the coefficient, the less the settlement is dispersed.

**coefficient of localization** Also known as the index of concentration, this measures the degree of concentration of a given phenomenon, such as industry, over a set of regions. The coefficient, L, is the sum either of the positive or of the negative deviations of the regional percentage of workers in the given industry from the corresponding regional percentage of workers in all industry. A value of 0 would indicate that employment in the given industry is distributed very evenly over the regions. A value of 1 indicates extreme concentration of industry in only one region. This statistic alone is not very helpful but it may be used to compare two different regions or two different industries.

**coefficient of variation** The *standard deviation of a data set expressed as a percentage of the *arithmetic mean. It is used in comparing two apparently similar data sets.

**cognition** Those processes involved in the gathering, organization, and use of knowledge, hence **cognitive**. Much of *behavioural geography is concerned with cognition, the way in which people see and respond to outside stimuli.

**cognitive dissonance** A mismatch between what is perceived and what is—between cognition and reality—so that an individual may seem to act irrationally.

**cognitive mapping** The acquisition, coding, storage, manipulation, and recall of spatial information within the mind. Cognitive mapping simplifies the complexity of the landscape and the *mental map derived thereby is held to influence behaviour.

**cohesion** Adhesion; the force by which materials are held together. Cohesion is the result of chemical and electrostatic forces.

**cohort** A group of people who experience a significant event, such as birth or marriage, during the same period of time, usually a year but also in five-year groups. Thus, all children born in the UK in 1980 would form the birth cohort of 1980. **Cohort analysis** traces the subsequent vital history of cohorts. **Cohort fertility** is the total of live births to a particular birth or marriage group.

**col** 1. In the landscape, a pass between two peaks or ridges.
2. In meteorology, a narrow belt of low pressure between two *anticyclones. Here, *isobars are few and therefore winds are slack.

**cold desert** A tract of arid, sparsely vegetated land experiencing low temperatures; also a synonym for *tundra.

**cold front** See *front.

**cold glacier** A glacier with its base well below 0 °C, frozen to the bedrock. Cold glaciers move very little and therefore effect very little erosion.

**cold low** Also known as a **cold pool**, or a **polar low**, these terms refer to areas of low pressure and temperature in the middle *troposphere. Such lows do not appear on surface *synoptic charts, but are important in *Arctic and *Antarctic meteorology.

A second type of cold low is the **cut-off low**, formed in mid-latitudes by the cutting off of polar air from the main body of cold air, nearer the poles. This occurs during periods of low index circulation (see *Rossby waves). Such lows are associated with unsettled weather and, in summer, thunderstorms.

**cold occlusion** An *occlusion in which the cold air to the rear is colder than the cold air it undercuts.

**cold water desert** An arid, but often foggy, desert affected by an offshore coastal current. Precipitation is slight because incoming airstreams cool as they pass over the current and rain falls out to sea.

**collective farm** A farm owned by the state, made by the merging of farms which used to be owned by individuals. In the USSR, the kolkhoz collective farm differed from the sovkhoz, or state farm, in which the peasants were the employees of the state. The kolkhoz was owned jointly by its members, who were paid in accordance with the profits of the farm. Each worker in the kolkhoz could also farm a small plot on his own. Collective farms predominated in Eastern Europe. They are generally marked by low productivity; peasant farmers achieve a much higher level of productivity on their own plots.

**collectivism** A school of thought which maintains that the *factors of production and the means of distribution should be owned by all and not by individuals who might pursue their self-interest at a cost to the state. It advocates public control, which is not necessarily brought about by state ownership.

**collision margin** In *plate tectonics, the boundary of two continental plates. Such margins are a hybrid type because two slabs of continental crust that eventually collide were initially separated by oceanic crust with passive or destructive margins. The oceanic crust is consumed, leaving the two continental crusts. At such a margin the lower plate is not consumed but, together with the upper plate, forms a double layer of crust, as in the Himalayas.

**collision theory** This states that raindrops grow by colliding and coalescing with each other, especially in tropical maritime *air masses. See also *Bergeron–Findeisen theory and *coalescence theory.

**colloid** Any substance so finely divided that it consists of molecules or groups of molecules dispersed in a gas or liquid. Colloids rarely settle. See *clay colloids.

**colluvium** The mixture of soil and unconsolidated rock fragments deposited on, or at the foot of, a slope.

**colonial animal** An animal, like the individuals making up a coral, which is not fully separate from others of its species.

**colonialism** The acquisition and colonization by a nation of other territories. In this respect, colonialism is as old as society. The term took on a more specific meaning in the late nineteenth century when colonists saw it as the extension of 'civilization' from Europe to the 'inferior' peoples of 'backward' societies. It may also be seen as a search for raw materials, new markets, and new fields of investment. Although independence from former colonisation has been achieved almost everywhere, some claim that it has been replaced by *neocolonialism.

**colony** In ecology:
1. A collection of plants and animals living in one place.
2. A group of species newly arrived in a habitat.
In human geography:
1. A settlement formed in a foreign country which is ruled by the home country. Properly speaking, colonies are those settlements which become home to citizens of the controlling power. (See *colonialism.)
2. Those American settlements which shook off British rule in 1776. Hence, **colonial** is applied in the USA to the artefacts of that time and place.

**combe, coombe** In South-East England, a short, deep, steep-sided hollow or valley, usually found in chalk country.

**COMECON** The Council for Mutual Economic Assistance, a trading bloc formed to encourage the trade and economy of the East European nations and the USSR. The members were the USSR, Poland, Czechoslovakia, Hungary, Romania, Bulgaria, East Germany, Mongolia, and Cuba, with Yugoslavia as an associate.

**command economy** An economy typified by state control of the *factors of production and by centralized, state planning.

**commercial agriculture** Any agricultural system which is geared to the sale of its produce.

**commercial geography** A form of geography, now superseded, concerned with the production and supply of raw materials, including agricultural output and finished goods.

**commercial ribbon** A form of *ribbon development where service and retail outlets develop along the major routes radiating outward from the city. Such development is confined to the lots adjoining the main roads.

**commodity** A *good which has an exchange value. It may also mean raw material.

**Common Agricultural Policy, CAP** A policy of *EC intervention in agriculture aimed at making production more efficient while farmers are paid reasonable prices. The most commonly used strategy is the subsidy on certain types of farming or certain crops. *Set-aside grants are also available to reduce the farmed acreage.

**common field** In medieval times, an open field with common rights of cultivation and grazing.

**common land** Land which is privately owned, perhaps by an individual or a local authority, but over which others have legal rights.

**common market** An economic association of states into a single trading market having little or no restriction of movement of individuals, capital, goods, and services within it and with a united trading policy towards non-member states. See *EC.

**communism** Historically, the principle of communal ownership of all property; basic economic resources are held in common. Modern communism is grounded in the ideas of Karl Marx. He hoped to see a society with no socio-economic difference between, for example, manual and intellectual labour, or urban and rural life. Social relations would be regulated by the maxim, 'from each according to his ability and to each according to his needs'. Centrally planned economies have been developed in accordance with this ideology and there have been many forms of communism, all supposedly seeking the classless society.

**community** 1. In ecology, a naturally occurring, non-random, collection of plant and animal life within a specified environment. The community is named after the physical environment, such as a freshwater lake community, or after the dominant species, such as an oak woodland community.

2. In human geography, a group of people living in the same town, village, or suburb in sympathetic association. This is not always the case; communities can be strongly divided.

**community charge** In the UK, a shortlived form of local taxation (also known as the poll tax) whereby a fixed charge is paid per adult.

**commuting** The movement from suburban or rural locations to the place of work and back. Hence **commuter village** and **commuter zone**. Commuting is usually on a daily basis but can occur weekly. Most commuting is **in-commuting** involving movement into the city to work but **reverse commuting** also occurs where residents in the inner city travel daily to workplaces in the suburbs. **Lateral commuting** involves the journey from one residential location to another as the suburbanization of industry develops.

**compaction** The compression of silt, clay, or soil. Compaction of soil eliminates soil pores so that the resulting soil is poorer.

**comparative advantage** The advantage of some nations or regions to produce goods better and more cheaply than less favoured nations or regions. This comparative advantage leads to trade as nations exchange those goods which they can produce more easily for goods not readily produced at home. The advantage is usually seen in resources of raw materials and labour, but very often the competitive performance of producers is based on better marketing, delivery, reliability, and quality control.

**comparative cost analysis** An analysis of industrial costs in order to establish a *least-cost location. However, it is not always easy to calculate total costs when a large number of inputs are involved, and *agglomeration economies and *external economies are difficult to express in financial terms.

**compatibility** In land use, being able to accommodate more than one form of activity. In **complete compatibility**, two uses may exist side by side at the same time, like walking and hill farming. **Partial compatibility** means that different activities, like water skiing and fishing, can only take place at different times in the same place. The concept is usually applied to recreational land use.

**competence** In hydrology, the largest size of particle that a river can carry. Just as the *discharge of a river varies with climate, *bed-floor roughness, and so on, so the competence of the river will vary.

**competition** Competition occurs when a necessary resource is sought by a number of organisms. **Intraspecific competition** occurs within a single species; **interspecific competition** occurs between different species.

**complementarity** An expression of mutual dependency based on an ability to produce goods in one area which are needed in another. Initially, complementarity was seen as operating in two very different regions, but is now held to occur between similar environments with different regional specialities.

**complementary region** An area served by a *central place. Central places with *high order goods and services have a larger complementary region than places offering low order goods and services.

**components of change** An accounting procedure for studying changes in economic activity, most often in manufacturing. Changes may occur *in situ* as employment grows or declines by births or deaths, as new plants open and old ones close, and through migration of plants into and out of an area.

**compression** In geology, a force pushing into a part of the earth's crust, causing it to buckle.

**compressive flow** In glaciology, valley floors exhibit ridges and hollows, probably because the glacier was moving in different ways along its length. Where a glacier is slowing up, the flow is compressive. The planes of weakness curve upwards and outwards. In zones of compression, the ice may bring up material from the valley floor, thus eroding the valley; compressive flow accentuates pre-existing hollows.

**compressive stress** See *stress.

**compulsory purchase order** A directive to enforce the purchase of land by government or local authorities from a private land owner. Orders may be issued for redevelopment or for building new roads.

**concealed unemployment** A situation whereby individuals—primarily housewives—know that there are no jobs available and do not register as unemployed.

**concentration and centralization** The propensity of economic activity to congregate in a restricted number of central places. Such concentration is aided by *functional linkages and *external and *agglomeration economies. The centralized core tends to develop at the expense of the periphery. Industry is in the control of fewer and fewer capitalists and the growth of *multinational corporations has seen the direction of economic activity all over the world vested in a few headquarters.

**concentration theory** The concept of a hierarchy of industrial developments whereby each level is linked to the next. Any two units, at whatever level, are linked to one unit above. Thus, two industrial plants merge into one industrial district while two industrial districts form one manufacturing town.

**concentric zone theory** The theory, proposed by Burgess, that urban land use may be classified as a series of concentric zones. Zone I, the *CBD, lies at the centre of the city. Zone II is in transition. It is the first zone of invasion by migrants to the crowded, multi-occupied part of the city. Within this Zone are the *ghetto areas; these are not necessarily slums. In Zone III are the working men's houses, the area of second-generation immigrants, one step up from Zone II. Zones IV and V are residential: Zone IV for the better-off and Zone V for the commuters. All these Zones are held to have evolved separately and without planning. They result from the competition of different socio-economic groups for land. This competition results in variations in the cost of land and, therefore, causes segregation within a city.

**concordance of summit levels** Synonymous with *accordance of summit levels.

**concordant** Complying with. In geomorphology, relief and drainage may be concordant with geological structure.

**concordant coast** Synonymous with *Pacific coast.

**condensation** The change of a vapour or gas into liquid form.

This change of state is accompanied by the release of *latent heat, which alters the *adiabatic temperature change in rising air. Condensation in meteorology can be caused by the following:

the cooling of a constant volume of air to *dew point,

the expansion of a parcel of air without heat input,

the evaporation of extra moisture into the air,

the fall in the moisture-holding capacity of the air due to joint changes in volume and temperature,

contact with a colder material or *air mass.

Note that water vapour can be cooled to well below 0 °C before condensation occurs. See *Bergeron–Findeisen theory.

**condensation level** The point at which rising air will cool to *dew point, condense, and form clouds.

**condensation nuclei** Microscopic particles, found in clouds, which attract water droplets. These droplets coalesce to form a raindrop. This will descend when its fall-speed is greater than the velocity of upward air currents in the cloud.

Condensation nuclei may be particles of dust, soot, salt, or, in the *Bergeron–Findeisen theory, ice crystals. Silver nitrate crystals have been used to attract water droplets in a cloud and thus initiate rain. This is known as **seeding clouds**.

**conditional instability** The *instability of a parcel of air. It is brought about by the presence of water vapour, cooling at the *SALR. It will continue to cool less rapidly than the *environmental air as long as the air is moist. Air may become unstable when it reaches *dew point.

**conduit** A channel or pipe, possibly natural in formation, which conveys liquids.

**cone** In geomorphology, a relief feature, circular or semicircular in plan and rising to a point in the centre.

**cone volcano** A volcanic peak with a roughly circular base tapering to a point.

Cones may be built solely of *lava or of *scoria, or of an interbedded combination of the two. Lava flows and layers of *pyroclasts form **composite cones**. **Parasitic cones** form through smaller vents on the flanks of the volcano.

**conflict theory** The view that more is achieved by conflicting interests than by co-operation.

**confluence** The junction of one stream with another.

**conformable** In geology, of strata deposited one above the other in geological sequence with no breaks.

**congelifluction, congelifluxion** A form of *mass movement which occurs in *periglacial environments. Water builds up near the surface because the ground below is frozen. This water acts as a lubricant for matter sliding downslope.

**congelifraction** Freeze-thaw. The process of *frost shattering.

**congeliturbation** In a *periglacial landscape, the heaving, thrusting, and cracking of the ground by frost action.

**congestion** The restriction of the use of a facility by overuse. The term is generally used to indicate the slowing of urban traffic because too many vehicles are competing for too little space, but it can be applied to any excessive demand for any one facility. Congestion on a routeway depends on the carrying capacity of the route, the volume of traffic, and the varying proportions of the total freight and passenger traffic carried by competing means of transport. The effects of congestion involve long and often costly delays, road accidents, air pollution, and noise. These are difficult to quantify in terms of cost and the individual may have little control over them.

**conglomerate** 1. A *sedimentary rock composed of rounded, water-borne pebbles which have been naturally cemented together.

2. A grouping of industries producing a number of unrelated products.

**coniferous (boreal) forest** This occurs naturally between 55 and 66 °N. where winters are very cold, short summers are warm, and precipitation, around 600 mm per annum, falls mainly as snow. Pure *stands are common and species are relatively few. Trees are evergreen and leaves are needle-shaped, restricting surface area and preventing loss of water by transpiration. Undergrowth is sparse. Animal species are dominated by insects, and seed-eating rodents such as mice and squirrels abound. Larger animals include deer, bear, wolves, foxes, and medium-sized cats.

**conjunction** The condition of two planets which, when seen from the earth, lie one in front of the other. When the earth, moon, and sun are in conjunction, the forces affecting *tides are at a maximum and *spring tides occur.

**connate water** Also known as **fossil water**, this is water laid down in sedimentary rocks and sealed off by overlying beds.

**connectivity** In *network analysis, the degree to which the *nodes of a network are directly connected with each other. The higher the ratio of the *edges to the nodes in a network, the greater the connectivity.

**consequent drainage** A water course flowing in the same direction as the *dip of the underlying strata.

**consequent stream** A river that develops on a newly formed surface, such as a recently uplifted coastal plain, and follows its slope.

**conservation** Conservation had its origin in the USA where attention was drawn in the 1950s to the damage done by mining in the Appalachians. It may be defined as the protection of natural or man-made resources and landscapes for later use. A distinction is made between conservation and preservation; a conserver recognizes that man will use some of the fish in a lake but a preserver would ban fishing in the lake entirely. Species, habitats, and man-made landscapes may be conserved. **Land use conservation** considers the conflicts between human land use and the protection of the natural environment.

Conservation protects resources for future use by banning reckless exploitation. It promotes more efficient extraction methods, recycling, and an end to wasteful use of non-renewable resources. A major theme is the conservation of soil, perhaps the most abused of the natural resources. Conservation is both rational, since it extends resources for the use of future generations, and morally sound. It is argued that man has no right to bring about the extinction of species and environments which have value on aesthetic, scientific, and recreational grounds.

**conservative margin** In *plate tectonics, a plate margin where the movement of the plates is parallel to the margin. The San Andreas Fault in California is a conservative boundary with the Pacific side of the fault moving northwards in relation to a south-moving block on the continental side.

**conspicuous consumption** Consumption marked by a disregard for waste and a desire to be seen as wealthy. For example, new goods may be bought to replace serviceable but dated goods.

**constant slope** The straight, sloping element of a hillslope, thought by some to undergo *parallel slope retreat.

**constructive margin** In *plate tectonics, a boundary where two plates are moving apart from each other, as at an *oceanic ridge, and where *magma flows upwards and outwards, as the plates move apart. These are also known as **accreting margins** or **diverging margins**.

**constructive wave** A **spilling wave**, with a long wavelength and a low crest, which runs gently up the slope of the beach. Such waves are thought to deposit material. Spilling waves usually occur on gently sloping beaches.

**consumer** 1. Those organisms in all the *trophic levels, with the exception of the producers (see *production). These include *herbivores, *carnivores, *omnivores, and *parasites. **Primary consumers** subsist on plant material alone. **Secondary consumers** feed on primary consumers, and so on.

2. One who uses goods and services. Certain assumptions are made in economics about the consumer. He will use goods commensurate with their price such that a fall in the price of a commodity will lead to increased consumption. So will a rise in income, and the reverse is held to be true.

**consumer goods** Goods and services produced for the individual. **Consumer durables,** like cars, are consumer goods which can be used many times.

**contact field** The pattern of contacts existing between an individual and those who surround him for the *diffusion of innovations which may range from information to epidemics. Near the 'sender' the probability of contact will be strong but this will weaken progressively with distance.

**contact metamorphism** See *metamorphism.

**container** A metal box of standard size, used for the transport of cargo by road, rail, or water. Containers may be moved easily and quickly from one mode of transport to another and are packed by the dispatcher so that a minimum of handling is required. **Containerization** has revolutionized transport systems in the developed world.

**contextual effect** In *electoral geography, a response in their voting by groups within society rather than by individuals. Voters may be influenced by the views of others in the community and may be more moved by local than national issues.

**contiguous zone** A zone of the sea beyond the *territorial seas of a nation over which it claims exclusive rights. In law, the contiguous zone extends between 12 and 24 nautical miles from the coastline. From **contiguous,** meaning neighbouring.

**continent** One of the main continuous bodies of land on the earth's surface. Commonly, seven continents are recognized: Africa, Antarctica, Asia, Australia, Europe, North America, and South America. Geologically, the boundaries of a continent lie offshore at the gentle slope of the *continental shelf. In this sense, the continents include their neighbouring islands; thus Britain is part of Europe, and may be termed a **continental island**.

A **subcontinent** is a large land mass forming part of a continent, e.g. the Indian subcontinent. Large islands such as Greenland are also classed as subcontinents.

**continental air mass** See *air mass.

**continental climate** A type of climate associated with the interior of large land masses in mid-latitudes. Without the moderating influence of the sea, temperatures are extreme in summer and winter. Precipitation is low.

**continental crust** That part of the outer, rigid surface of the earth which forms the continents. Continental crust is thicker than *oceanic crust, but is less dense.

**continental divide** The major *watershed of a continent.

**continental drift** The theory that continents which are now separate were united in a supercontinent. The idea originated from the apparent jigsaw fit between the Americas and Africa.

In 1915, Wegener suggested that an original supercontinent, which he called Pangaea, split into two large continents, Laurasia to the north and Gondwana to the south. These two split again to form the continents as we know them. Wegener's evidence for this theory included the presence of the same geological structures and deposits on each side of the Atlantic. Further evidence is provided by fossils of a small reptile found both in Africa and Latin America. Yet more evidence comes from a reconstruction of an ice cap radiating from South Africa which has left its mark across the southern continents. The intervening basins between the continents are occupied by oceans.

**continental platform** A continent together with its *continental shelf.

**continental shelf** The gently sloping submarine fringe of a continent. This is ended by a steep **continental slope** which occurs at around 150 m below sea level. The two make up a **continental margin**.

**continental shield** A *shield of the magnitude of a continent.

**continuous media** Fixed pipelines and transmission cables used for the transport of energy over permanent routes. Such networks are only profitable when they are used to the full since they are very expensive to construct.

**continuous variable** A variable, such as the distance between two towns, where any value may be recorded, including fractions. There are no clear-cut or sharp breaks between possible values.

**contour** A line on a map joining places of equal heights, and sometimes equal depths, above and below sea level. The **contour interval** is the vertical change between consecutive contours.

**contour ploughing** A method of ploughing parallel to the contours rather than up or down a slope. It is used to check soil erosion and the formation of gullies.

**contraception** Any form of *birth control which prevents fertilization of the ovum.

**contrast stretching** In *remote sensing, the expansion of the range of *digital numbers from the area under survey to a larger range to improve the contrast in the resulting image.

**control variable** An attribute used for sorting data into categories, usually for subsequent analysis or for sampling.

**conurbation** A group of towns forming a continuous built-up area.

**convection** The process by which heat is transferred from one part of a liquid or gas to another, by movement of the liquid or gas itself. In the atmosphere, warmer, lighter air moves upward and is replaced by colder, heavier air. This is the **free convection** of a **convection current.**

The upward movement of an air parcel over mountains, at fronts, or because of *turbulence is known as **forced convection**.

**convection rain** When *convection occurs in a parcel of moist air, the rising air will cool. Further cooling will cause condensation of the water vapour in the air, and rain may result.

If the air is very moist, the cooling results in condensation, and hence the release of *latent heat. This causes the rising air to accelerate, and very tall *cumulonimbus clouds form.

**convective condensation level** The point of saturation for an air mass. It can be located on a *tephigram at the intersection of the *environmental lapse rate curve and the *saturated mixing ratio line. The saturated mixing ratio line corresponds to the average mixing ratio in the layer between 1000 and 5000 m.

**convenience distance** The ease, or otherwise, of travel. A town 50 km away may be well served by transport and thus 'nearer' than one 20 km away which is badly served.

**convenience goods** *Low-order goods like milk, bread, and occasional groceries which are bought locally with little consideration of the price charged since purchases are usually on a small scale and convenience is rated more highly than economy.

**conventional name** The name given by foreigners to a place. For example, München becomes Munich in English.

**conventional sign** A symbol used on a map and explained by a key.

**convergence** 1. In *plate tectonics, the coming together of plates.

2. In meteorology, air flowing together from two different air masses. Convergence is usually associated with a vertical

increase in the height of the atmosphere, associated with the ascent of air, and frequently causes weather events. See also *Inter-Tropical Convergence Zone.

**converging margin** See *destructive margin.

**co-operative** In *agricultural geography, an association of farmers developed in order to reduce costs and increase efficiency. Purchases of equipment, seeds, fertilizers, and fodder can be made in bulk, thus lowering costs. Conversion of crops into marketable goods can be made on a wider scale.

**coppice** As a verb, to cut off the trunk of a young tree close to the ground to encourage the growth of side shoots. From this, the noun, coppice—a small woodland managed in this way.

**copse** A small wood.

**copyhold** A right to farm land given if the tenant was able to produce a copy of the relevant entry on the *court roll.

**coral reef** An offshore ridge, mainly of calcium carbonate, formed by the secretions of small marine animals. Corals flourish in shallow waters over 21 °C and need abundant sunlight, so the water must be mud-free. **Fringing reefs** lie close to the shore, while **barrier reefs** are found further from the shore, in deeper water. A **coral atoll** is a horseshoe-shaped ring of coral which almost encircles a calm lagoon. Many coral reefs are hundreds of metres deep and yet corals will not grow at depths of more than 30–40 m. It has been suggested that deep reefs have formed during a long period of subsidence. Thus, coral forms in shallow waters and then sinks. New coral will then form on the top. **Coral sand** results from the breaking up of coral.

**cordillera** An extensive mountain *chain. The term usually refers to the Andes or to the series of mountain chains of western North America.

**core** 1. The central part of the earth. The inner core has the properties of a solid and the outer core those of a liquid. The core is dense, very hot, and probably composed largely of iron.

2. The centre of the *core–periphery model.

**core area** The heartland of a nation, usually more advanced than the rest of the nation, with an intense feeling of native culture and nationality.

**core region** In a nation, a centre of power where innovation, technology, and employment are at a high level. Core regions may often flourish at the expense of peripheral regions. (See *core-periphery model.) To solve problems of underdevelopment, some nations have concentrated resources at planned cores like Brazilia or Tema.

**core–frame concept** A model of the *CBD which recognizes a core of intensive land use indicated by high-rise buildings. Shops and offices abound and the core is the central point of the transport systems. Beyond the core lies the frame where land use is less intensive. Here are found warehousing, wholesaling, garaging and servicing of cars, and medical facilities.

**core–periphery model** Friedmann maintained that the world can be divided into four types of region. *Core regions are centres, usually metropolitan, with a high potential for innovation and growth, such as São Paulo in Brazil. Beyond the cores are the upward transition regions—areas of growth spread over small centres rather than at a core. Development corridors are upward transition zones which link two core cities such as Belo Horizonte and Rio de Janeiro.

The resource-frontier regions are peripheral zones of new settlement, as in the Amazon Basin. The downward transition regions are now declining because of exhaustion of resources or because of industrial change. Many 'problem' regions of Europe are of this type.

This concept may be extended to continents. The capital-rich countries of Germany and France attract labour from peripheral countries like Spain, Greece, Turkey, and Algeria. Higher wages and prices are found at the core while the lack of employment in the periphery keeps wages low there. The result may well be a balance of payments crisis at the periphery or the necessity of increased exports from the periphery to pay for imports. In either case, development of the periphery is retarded.

**corestone** See *boulder field.

**Coriolis force** The deflection of moving objects, especially of airstreams, produced by the rotation of the earth on its axis. This is not a real force, but the curving pattern of an airstream, produced as the earth beneath it moves, appears to be the result of a force. This apparent force has its greatest deflective effect at the poles, and its least effect at the equator. This deflection reduces the efficiency of an *atmospheric cell to transport heat polewards.

**corrasion** The erosive action of particles carried by ice, water, or wind. Corrasion is another term for *abrasion.

**correlation** The link or relationship existing between two or more variables. Where there is a **positive correlation** between two variables, an increase or decrease in one is matched by a similar change in the other. Conversely, a **negative correlation** sees one variable increase while the other declines. Several statistical methods are used to determine the strength of the correlation, that is, the *correlation coefficient.

**correlation coefficient** A measurement of the strength of a correlation between two variables, derived from statistical techniques such as *Spearman's rank method and the *product moment method. The values of the coefficient run from +1 (very strong positive correlation) through 0 (no correlation) to −1 (very strong negative correlation). Correlation coefficients may also be calculated for multiple *regressions.

**corridor** A limb of one state's territory through that of another, usually to gain access. The most famous is the Polish corridor, an extension of Poland to give it access to the Baltic coast ports of Danzig (Gdańsk) and Gdynia.

**corrie** See *cirque.

**corrosion** The erosion of rock by *solution or by chemical action: *carbonation, *hydration, *hydrolysis, and *oxidation.

**co-seismal line** A line connecting those points on the earth which experience the waves from an earthquake simultaneously.

**cost–benefit analysis** A technique whereby projected public schemes are evaluated in terms of social outcomes as well as the usual profit and loss accounting. The technique begins by assessing the costs, benefits, and drawbacks of the scheme, including side-effects such as the generation of noise. Financial values are assigned to these, including qualities, like aesthetic appearance, which are not usually associated with cost. As most major projects are developed over a long period of time, costs must reflect future conditions. The decision whether to implement the project is made in the light of this analysis.

This method is far from trouble-free. It is difficult to determine which items should be included, and difficult to put a price on intangibles, such as aesthetic experience. The discounting of future costs is problematic, reflecting, as it must, some arbitrary interest rate.

**cost curve** The line depicting the relationship between the cost of an item and the volume of output. Unit costs are high at low levels of production, falling as *economies of scale cause unit costs to fall. Having fallen to a minimum, unit costs rise again as *diseconomies of scale come into play.

**cost–space convergence** The increasing similarity in accessibility and costs of any location and of its products so that hitherto distant and expensive products are now in competition with local industries. Of increasing importance in this convergence are changes in transport—motorways and airways—since the 1950s and the transfer of information via the telephone system, computer, and facsimile machine.

**cost structure** The breakdown of production costs into the expenditure for individual inputs. These include materials, marketing, capital, land, and labour. The cost structure determines the way in which a firm reacts to changes in the industrial environment.

**cost surface** A three-dimensional diagram with the horizontal axes delineating the area under consideration and the vertical axes showing in relief spatial variation in costs. These may be the cost of a single item or of total production.

**cottage industry** The production of finished goods by a worker, sometimes together with his family, at home. The products may be sold directly to the public by the worker, or to an entrepreneur who pays according to the number of goods produced. Cottage industry now exists in Britain only in the textile trade and is found in some less developed countries.

**coulee** See *meltwater channel.

**Council for Mutual Economic Assistance, CMEA** See *COMECON.

**counter-radiation** The long-wave radiation emitted from the earth after it has absorbed the shorter-wave radiation of the sun.

**countertrade** A trading system under which a country will accept exports from another country if that country accepts its own goods in return. Countertrade makes trading easier for those countries lacking in foreign exchange. It allows a nation to export goods for which world demand is low and is a way of buying in high technology.

**counter-urbanization** The movement of people and industry away from the city. This may occur spontaneously as cities become expensive, polluted, and congested or may be encouraged by governments.

**country park** An area of the country which has facilities for recreation such as picnicking, walking, riding, fishing, and so on; an opportunity for the public to enjoy the countryside at little distance from the city.

**country rock** A pre-existing rock which has suffered later igneous *intrusion.

**county** A basic unit of local government in Britain based on the medieval feudal earldoms, but much altered in the nineteenth and twentieth centuries.

**coupling constraint** In *time–space geography a limit to an individual's actions because of the necessity of being in the same space and time as other individuals.

**court roll** In Britain, the record of the activities of a medieval court.

**cove** A small bay on a rocky coast.

**cover crop** A fast growing crop planted in the rows between the main crop to protect the soil from erosion caused by heavy rainfall.

**crag and tail** A mass of rock—the crag—lying in the path of a glacier which protects the softer rock in the lee beyond it—the tail. The rock of the tail is a lee-effect depositional landform. A small scale example of this effect is the formation of morainic ridges in the shelter of individual boulders.

**crater** A circular depression around the vent of a volcano. Craters form the summit of most volcanoes. They occur where lava overflows and hardens or where the walls collapse as the *magma sinks down the vent after an eruption. Water may accumulate here to form a **crater lake**.

**craton** A core of stable continental crust within a continent and composed wholly or largely of Precambrian rocks with complex structures. Two types of craton are recognized: **platforms**, which are parts of cratons on which largely undeformed sedimentary rocks lie, and *shields.

**creep** The slow, gradual movement downslope of soil, *scree, or glacier ice. Most creep involves a deformation of the material, i.e. *plastic flow.

**crescentic dune** See *sand dune.

**Cretaceous** The youngest *period of *Mesozoic time stretching approximately from 136 to 65 million years BP.

**crevasse** A vertical or wedge-shaped crack in a glacier. It can vary greatly in width, from centimetres to tens of metres. The maximum depth of a crevasse is about 40 m because at that depth ice becomes plastic and any cracks merge within the ice. **Transverse crevasses** occur when the ice extends down a steep slope. **Longitudinal crevasses** form parallel with the direction of flow as the ice extends laterally. **Marginal crevasses** occur across the sides of a glacier as friction occurs between the ice and the valley walls. **Radial crevasses** fan out when the ice spreads out into a lobe.

**critical group** The group most susceptible to damage by a particular form of pollution. If emissions are low enough to avoid damage to the critical group, then the rest of the population will be deemed to be unharmed. Identification of the critical group is not always easy, however.

**critical isodapane** According to *Weber's theory, the costs of a good increases with transport costs from the point of production. The critical isodapane is the *isopleth where this increase is exactly offset by the savings made by the decreased costs brought about by cheaper labour.

**critical temperature** In agriculture, a temperature of vital significance to a plant, such as the temperature below which growth will not occur.

**critical theory** A view of Marxism which is open-ended and continuously self-critical; in this way, Marxist theory will not be paralysed. This view takes into account some of the less familiar parts of Marx's work such as the aesthetics of a mass society, but the central interest is the relationship between social structure and social changes in a capitalist society.

**crofting** A form of *subsistence farming mostly characteristic of north-west Scotland. Farms and fields are small and usually inherited. One or two cows may be kept and sheep roam over common uplands. Crofting was traditionally supported by fishing and cottage industry—spinning and weaving—and is now linked to the tourist trade.

**crop combination analysis** A technique evolved by Weaver to delimit agricultural regions which, he argued, are not regions of simple monoculture as suggested by the names Corn Belt, Cotton Belt, or Spring Wheat Belt, but are areas of combinations of crops.

Theoretical areal values of crop combinations are established so that two crop combinations take 50% each of the available land, three crop combinations take 33% of land each, and so on. The real life figures for each crop in the combination are compared with the theoretical figures and the crop combination with the best 'fit' to the theoretical figures is used to classify the area.

**crop marks** Areas within a field of some plants which are differently coloured, or shorter, and which stand out in aerial photographs. The plants respond to the different soil moisture conditions above ruined buildings, or to the extra soil nutrients in refuse pits. Aerial photographs of crop marks may indicate lines of old buildings, field patterns, original hedgerows, and roads.

**crop rotation** *Rotation of crops.

**cross-bedding** In a sedimentary rock, the arrangement of beds at an angle to the main bedding plane. The term *current bedding is also used.

**cross-cutting relationships, law of** This states that an *igneous rock is younger than any rock it cuts across.

**cross-section** In human geography, a 'snapshot' of society and its landscape at one moment in time to reconstruct a past geography. In physical geography, a transverse section of relief.

**cross-valley profile** A section of a valley drawn at right angles to the course of a river at a given point.

**cruciform village** A village which has developed around an intersection of two different routes.

**crude rate** A *vital rate which is not adjusted for the age and sex structure of a population.

**crumb** In soil science, a spheroidal cluster of soil particles, i.e. a type of *ped. Soils of a **crumb structure** permit the percolation through them of air and water.

**crust** The outer shell of the earth including the continents and the ocean floor. This is the *lithosphere, formed of *sial and *sima. Sial overlies sima in the continental crust but sima forms most of the ocean floor, i.e. the oceanic crust.

**cryophilous crop** A crop which will not fully flower and seed unless it has experienced low temperatures earlier in its growth. Examples include some varieties of wheat, peas, potatoes, and apples.

**cryostatic pressure** The pressure exerted on rocks and soil when freezing occurs. As the *freezing front advances, the pressure of the soil moisture increases since it is trapped. Such pressure can separate individual grains of soil, forming a mass of fluid mud. This may be driven near to the surface where it domes up the ground or where it forms mud blisters.

**cryotic** Having temperatures below 0 °C. **Non-cryotic** areas have temperatures above freezing point. The boundary of two such areas is the **cryofront** or *freezing front.

**cryoturbation** This term is variously used. It can represent all the weathering processes that prevail in a *periglacial landscape or be extended to include the churning up of rocks and soil. Some writers reserve the term for irregular displacements of soil horizons, while using the term periglacial *involutions for more regular disturbances.

**crystal fractionation** The separation of pooling magma into different rocks such as *gabbro or *basalt.

**crystal growth** The growth and expansion of crystals of salt or ice along cracks and fissures in a rock. This expansion causes pressure and splits up the rock.

**crystalline** Consisting partly or wholly of crystals. Thus, **crystalline rocks**, which are *igneous or metamorphic (see *metamorphism). The slower the rate of cooling of the rock, the larger the crystals.

**cuesta** A ridge with a *dip slope and a *scarp slope. Cuestas occur in gently dipping strata which have been subjected to erosion.

**cultural distance** A gap between the culture of two different groups, such as that between the culture of rural societies and that of the cities.

**cultural ecology** The study of the interactions of societies with one another and with the natural environment. It seeks to understand and explain the adaptations of human behaviour and social institutions to the environment.

**cultural geography** The study of the impact of human culture on the landscape. Themes which have been explored include the effects of plant and animal domestication, fire, hydrological techniques, farming methods, and settlements.

**cultural hearth** The location in which a particular culture has evolved. Sauer controversially chose South Asia and the northern Andes as the cultural hearths for the development of agriculture based on vegetative propagation. Central Mexico and Asia Minor are seen as hearths for the much later seed planting. Urban hearths are relatively easy to date, but the developmental sequence is disputed.

**cultural landscape** The landscape which results from many generations of human occupance. Many features of present landscapes were fashioned by past societies who effected more or less permanent changes. The cultural landscape is evolved from the natural landscape by a cultural group.

**cultural region, cultural area** A region characterized by a common culture. A distinction can be made between the ethos of London and that of the Western Isles.

**culture** Learned behaviour which is socially transmitted such as customs, belief, technology, and art. The word has many connotations and a geographer might define it differently from, say, an archaeologist. Culture is the primary factor affecting the way in which man responds to the environment. The **cultural landscape** is a man-made landscape as it expresses the response of a culture to its natural surroundings.

**culture contact** The meeting of different *cultures. Movement from one culture to another may cause the disorientation known as **culture shock**.

**cumec** A measurement of *discharge. One cumec is one cubic metre of water per second.

**cumulative causation** The progressive unfolding of events connected with a change in the economy. These changes apply to a whole set of variables as a consequence of the *multiplier effect. Thus, the location of a new factory may be the basis of more investment, more jobs both in that factory and in ancillary and service industries in the area, and have a better *infrastucture which would, in turn, attract more industry. The momentum of change is self-perpetuating, and investment should continue to be attracted to the area. A further part of Myrdal's ideas is that this process of improvement is made at a cost to some other part of the economy; that regions prosper as others feel the loss of investment and the outmigration of the fittest of their populations.

Three stages of regional economies occur: the pre-industrial phase with few regional inequalities; a time when cumulative causation is working, where regional inequalities are greatest because of the *backwash effect; and a third stage where the *spread effect stimulates growth in the periphery.

Cumulative causation, like the multiplier, also works 'backwards'—as a major factory closes, the effects are felt throughout the local economy.

**cumulative frequency curve** Also known as an *ogive, this is a curve drawn by plotting the value of the first class on a graph. The next plot is the sum of the first and second values, the third plot is the sum of the first second and third values, and so on. Cumulative frequency graphs are useful in indicating class groupings for a *choropleth.

**cumulo-nimbus** A low-based, rain-bearing *cumulus cloud, dark grey at the base and white at the crown, which spreads into an *anvil shape. The shape of the crown is due to the levelling effect of strong upper air winds.

**cumulus** An immense, heaped cloud with a rounded, white crown and a low horizontal base, stretching up to as much as 5000 m in altitude.

**current bedding** Fine layers which run at an angle to the main bedding planes in a sedimentary rock. Current bedding, also known as *cross or *false bedding, occurs when the currents depositing sediment change the direction of flow.

**currents** The rate of flow of a **river current** varies with depth because friction operates along the bed and sides. The *thalweg is located in the deepest part but all currents change as discharge increases. **Tidal currents** are associated with the rise and fall of the sea. The velocities of ebb and flow vary with the morphology of the coast and any outflow of fresh water. *Rip currents form in the nearshore zone and balance the inflow of sea shore currents. They may form a loosely circular pattern of flow as they pass through the surf zone.

*Ocean currents are driven by the planetary winds.

**curvilinear relationship** In a graphed plot of two variables, the relationship between the two which shows up as a curved line.

**cusec** A unit of measurement of flow; it means cubic feet per second.

**cusp** A hollow in a beach, U-shaped in plan with the arms of the U pointing seawards. Beaches tend to have a series of cusps which are formed when outgoing *rip currents and incoming waves combine to set up nearly circular water movements along the beach.

**customs union** A common market encompassing two or more states within whose boundaries there is free trade, with no tariffs or barriers to the movement of goods.

**cut-off low** See *cold low.

**cwm** See *cirque.

**cycle** A series of features and/or events recurring in much the same sequence.

**cycle of erosion** The notion, first introduced by the American geographer W. M. Davis, that a high-level land surface would be eroded until the whole surface was lowered. Interim stages would show the successive widening and lowering of valleys as rivers and *mass movement shaped the landscape. Davis's theory was based on fluvial landscapes; other cycles have been suggested, for example, in arid lands. The concept of a cycle of erosion is not now generally accepted.

**cycle of industry** The cycle of industry recognizes times of industrial development and, perhaps, decline. Initially, in its infancy, a region is concerned with *cottage and primary industry. Few industrial towns exist, and urban centres are market towns. The stage of youth sees the emergence of a factory system based on localized resources and/or innovations, accompanied by the development of an *infrastructure. The mature region has experienced large-scale development of manufacturing industry and economic development. The system of industries and services is highly complex, and centres are interconnected by public transport. The mature region may well, however, have derelict buildings and slums. Some regions experience continued maturity while others decline into senility as problem regions where growth is slow, there is overdependence on one or a few industries, the infrastructure is declining, and unemployment is high. Attempts may be made to rejuvenate these areas, usually primarily by government action.

**cycle of occupation** The growth in numbers and density of population which then declines, to be followed by a second cycle of population growth.

**cycle of poverty** A vicious spiral of poverty and deprivation passing from one generation to the next. Poverty leads very often to inadequate schooling and then to poorly paid employment. As a result, the affordable housing is substandard and it may be that crime will increase in these areas of deprivation. Stress is increased and health levels are poor. The children growing up in such areas start off at a disadvantage, and so the cycle continues.

**cyclogenesis** The formation of *cyclones, especially for mid-latitude depressions (also known as frontal wave depressions). Cyclogenesis occurs in specific areas, such as the western North Atlantic, western North Pacific, and the Mediterranean Sea.

Cyclogenesis is primarily the result of *convergence of air masses. But cyclones are areas of low pressure. How does this fit with the occurrence of air masses piling up together? Quite simply, because cyclogenesis occurs when *divergence in the upper *troposphere removes air more quickly than it can be replaced by convergence at ground level. The net result is low pressure.

The significance of upper air movements in cyclogenesis is also indicated by the link with *Rossby waves. Surface depressions develop below the downstream, or eastern, limbs of Rossby waves, where the airflow is divergent. Furthermore, the routes of mid-latitude cyclones, known as *depression tracks, closely parallel the movements of the upper air *jet stream.

**cyclomatic number** In *network analysis, the number of circuits in the network. It is given by:

$$\mu = e - v + p$$

where $e$ = number of edges, $v$ = number of vertices (nodes), $p$ = number of graphs or subgraphs, $\mu$ = cyclomatic number.

A high value of the cyclomatic number indicates a highly connected network. There exists a significant relationship between the level of economic development of a region and the cyclomatic number of its major transport networks.

**cyclone** An area of low atmospheric pressure with winds moving in a spiral about the central low. This spiral movement is anticlockwise in the Northern Hemisphere and clockwise in the Southern Hemisphere. Synonymous with *depression.

# D

**daily urban system** The area around a city within which commuting to the city centre takes place.

**dairying** The production of milk, almost entirely from cows, but also from goats and sheep. It is an agricultural system with very high labour and plant costs but using relatively little land. Income is earned throughout the year but there are some difficulties of overproduction. Dairying is only possible at any distance from the city by means of specialist transport.

**dale** In northern England, a river valley.

**Dalmatian coast** A drowned seashore with the main relief trends running more or less parallel with the coastline. The old mountain peaks appear as islands above the flooded valleys. Compare with *Atlantic type coast.

**DALR** Dry adiabatic lapse rate. See *adiabatic.

**dambo** A shallow, low-lying area with no distinctive drainage channels but located at the head of a drainage system.

**Danelaw** The areas of northern and northeast England settled by Scandinavians in the ninth and tenth centuries and over which Danish law prevailed.

**Darcy's law** This states that the flow of *ground water from one site to another through a rock is proportional to the difference in water pressure at the two sites. Darcy's law does not hold good for well-jointed limestone which has numerous channels and fissures.

**dating** The establishment of the age of features, events, or products. See *C 14 dating, *dendrochronology, *lichenometry, *geomagnetism, and *varve.

**datum level, datum line, datum plane** The zero altitude base from which all other altitudes are measured to produce contours on a map. This base level for a British map is the *ordnance datum.

**daylight saving** A system whereby time is advanced by one hour (or more) from the *standard time of an area in order to extend the period of daylight at the end of the working day.

**dead** In geomorphology, a landform no longer active. **Dead caves** are no longer subject to marine erosion since they are now well above sea level. **Dead cliffs**, also above sea level, are similarly free from marine erosion although *subaereal denudation still occurs.

**deadweight tonnage** The total weight of all the effects of a ship—cargo, passengers, crew, fuel, stores, fresh water, and baggage—when loaded to her safe load line.

**death rate** The number of deaths in a year per 1000 of the population as measured at mid-year. This **crude death rate** may be expressed as:

$$\frac{D \times 1000}{P}$$

where $D$ = the number of deaths, $P$ = the mid-year population.

This is a crude rate because no allowance is made for different distributions of age and sex. For example, Sri Lanka had a crude death rate of 5 per 1000 during the 1970s compared with 9–12 per 1000 in North-West Europe. The low rate for Sri Lanka is a reflection of the youth of its population and does not imply lower mortality in the higher age groups. A **standardized death rate** compares the rate to a real or assumed population which is held to be standard. Thus the standardized death rate for an age and sex category which is labelled sa is

$$\frac{\sigma(P_{sa} D_{sa})}{P} \times 1000$$

where $P$ = standard population, $P_{sa}$ = number of population of sex and age category sa, $D_{sa}$ = specific annual death rate of sex and age category sa. See *mortality.

**debris** Material such as scree, gravel, sand, or clay formed by the breaking up of minerals and rocks. Through the air, debris is transported by *saltation and *deflation, in water, debris moves in solution, in suspension, by rolling and by saltation. In ice, debris can be carried on the glacier—supraglacially, within the glacier (englacially), or beneath the glacier (subglacially). Debris movement downslope is *mass movement.

**debris fall** See *fall.

**decalcification** The *leaching out of calcium carbonate from a soil *horizon by the downward movement of soil water.

**decentralization** A process of counteracting the growth of favoured metropolitan areas. Even while the city is still growing, it has many negative aspects such as congestion, noise, pollution, crime, and high land values. Such problems are a spur to spontaneous movement away from the cities. From a wider point of view, governments may favour decentralization to restore the fortunes of declining regions which suffer from an outflow of population and where the services and *infrastructure are underused.

Governments may attempt to decentralize by discouraging new investment at the centre and encouraging growth in the *depressed areas. Incentives for such relocation include grants, loans, tax concessions, and the provision of industrial premises.

**deciduous forest** In the cold season of temperate latitudes, a tree's water supply is restricted when the temperature falls below 0 °C. In order to lessen losses of water, deciduous trees shed their leaves until the spring brings more available moisture.

**decision-making** The choice of one particular strategy in the attainment of a goal.

In earlier models, *economic man was seen as the decision-maker, but he has generally been replaced by the *satisficer who is not blessed with perfect knowledge, who works with *bounded rationality, and who seeks only a satisfactory solution. Decision-making is viewed in the light of *behavioural geography, and the variety of incoming information and the range of the individual's abilities to use that information may be expressed in a *behavioural matrix. A theoretical basis to decision-making has been attempted through considerations of *risk, *uncertainty, and *game theory. More successful generalizations, however, have been based on case studies. These may show a stimulus such as higher demand for a product. The response of the industrialist may be to expand. From this decision comes the need for an extended site or a new plant. This location decision then demands a host of smaller decisions. Experiencing the results of the decision will then lead to feedback which may affect future decisions.

**declining region** A region suffering the economic decline associated with closure of factories, outmoded industry, and high unemployment. Services also decline as incomes fall and governments may be concerned with halting such uneven development.

**declining slope retreat** See *downwearing.

**décollement** The movement of underlying strata which is moved during folding as it adheres to the upper layers. This layer, together with the overlying beds, rides easily over an assemblage of older rocks.

**decomposers** Simple organisms which obtain their nutrients from dead plant or animal material by breaking it down into basic chemical compounds. A **decomposer chain** can run from a relatively large organism, such as a fungus, to smaller organisms such as bacteria.

**deduction** Deducing or inferring the general from the particular; using particular statements as premises from which future developments are shown to proceed logically. Deduction provides laws from which outcomes may be predicted but such prediction plays little part in human geography because of the extreme complexity of the systems involved.

**deep** Beneath the ocean, a long and relatively narrow depression over 5500 m in depth. Deeps, also known as ocean *trenches, occur at *destructive margins.

**deepening** A fail in atmospheric pressure at the centre of a *low.

**deep weathering** In the warm, moist tropics, chemical weathering is very strong and can affect rocks to a depth of more than 50 m. One school of thought suggests that *tors are an exhumed form of deep weathering.

**deer forest** A stretch of moorland, usually without trees, managed for deer stalking.

**defensible space** The environment used by its inhabitants to build their lives in and to feel secure.

**deferred junction** Of a tributary when it cannot join a river because of the raised banks of the *levée. The tributary flows parallel to the river before it finally joins it. See *yazoo.

**deficiency disease** A disease brought about because some vital element is missing in the diet. The food lack is generally of protein, vitamins, or minerals. It is claimed that over half the human population of the world suffers or has suffered from malnutrition, leaving the victims debilitated.

**deflation** The action of the wind in removing material from a surface and lowering that surface. Deflation is most effective where extensive areas of non-cohesive deposits are exposed, as in *loess or in dry lake beds. It may scoop out a shallow depression known as a **deflation hollow**.

**deflocculation** See *flocculation.

**deforestation** The clearance of forests by cutting and/or burning.

**deformation** In geology, the change in the shape, size, or structure of a landform, rock stratum, or region, caused by *tectonic activity.

**deglaciation** The retreat and removal of a glacier or ice sheet from an area.

**deglacierization** Synonymous with *deglaciation.

**deglomeration** The movement of activity, usually industry, away from areas of concentration. Deglomeration occurs when the advantages of *agglomeration are outweighed by its disadvantages—high land costs and rents, constricted sites, congestion, and pollution.

**deglomeration economies** Forces such as congestion and high land values which lead to *decentralization.

**degradation** 1. The lowering of a surface by weathering and subsequent erosion.
2. A deterioration in a soil as a result of *leaching.

**de-industrialization** The decreasing significance of industrial employment in developed capitalist economies. The term is often reserved for manufacturing industry and the decreasing significance usually applies to employment. This may not be a good yardstick since an industry with a decreased labour force might well contribute to the national economy in terms of output and exports.

**delta** A low-lying area found at the mouth of a river and formed of deposits of *alluvium. Deposition occurs as the river's speed, and hence its silt-carrying capacity, is checked when it enters the more tranquil waters of a lake or sea. Furthermore, clay particles *flocculate in salt water, become heavier, and sink. Post-glacial rises in sea level have increased the slowing effect of the sea and some deltas grow by as much as 200 m a year. Other, older, deltas may be eroded. The morphology of a delta is the result of the interplay of the following factors: the input of sediment from the river, the density and depth of the sea water, waves, currents, and any *tectonic activity in the region. **Cuspate deltas** have a pointed seaward end. **Lobate deltas** have a curved seaward end and **digitate** or **bird's foot deltas** have long 'fingers' of alluvium extending into the sea. **Inland deltas** form in hot, arid areas of inland drainage where water is gradually lost through evaporation.

**demand** In economics, the volume of goods which purchasers are willing to buy. This depends on their incomes and preferences, the price of other products, and the price of the product concerned. When preferences alone are isolated, demand can be seen on a **demand curve** which shows demand falling as prices rise. Together with supply, demand determines prices in competitive markets.

**demand cone** A depiction of the falling away of demand for a good with distance from the market which is due in principle to the increasing cost of transport.

**demersal** Of marine life, living near the sea bed.

**demographic regulation** The notion that a population will restrict its fertility when a reduction of mortality causes population to grow beyond the ability of the environment to sustain it. This is not a simple response and is accompanied by changes in society in an attempt to maintain an equilibrium.

**demographic relaxation theory** The view that overpopulation leads to war. A major example is the professed desire for *Lebensraum*—space in which to expand—shown by the German government in the late 1930s and which led to the invasion of Czechoslovakia and Poland. The resulting wars destroy populations. In this way, war is seen as relieving overpopulation.

**demographic transition** An account, but not a complete explanation, of changing rates of fertility, mortality, and *natural increase. These changes are held to occur as a nation progresses from a rural, agrarian, and illiterate state to a predominantly urban, industrial, literate one. Four stages may be recognized.

The reasons for falling death rates are improved nutrition and living conditions and health care. The reasons for falling fertility are less clear. Certainly, fertility rates have fallen in countries such as France before reliable contraceptives were developed. Various reasons for falling fertility have been suggested.

1. The breakdown of the *extended family, which means more stress for parents.

2. In a 'modern' industrial society the labour value of children is low whereas in peasant society children contribute to the labour force from an early age.

3. With the provision of pensions, it is no longer necessary to have children as a support in old age.

4. More women are in work.

5. As standards of living rise, more wealth is needed to bring up children.

6. Where infant mortality is low, fewer babies are needed to ensure the survival of the family unit.

**demography** The statistical and mathematical study of human populations, concerned with the size, distribution, and composition of such populations. The main components of this study are *fertility, *mortality, and *migration. See also *population studies.

**demoiselle** An earth pillar with a protective cap of rock.

**dendritic drainage** See *drainage patterns.

**dendrochronology** The technique of dating living wood by counting the annual growth rings. Recently, the study of *isotopes within the rings has yielded information about past temperatures and the width of the rings gives information about times of drought.

**denitrification** The breaking down of nitrates by bacteria, releasing free nitrogen. See *nitrogen cycle.

**density** See *population density.

**density anomaly** An unexpected variation in the density of part of the earth's crust.

*Gravity anomalies can be linked to density anomalies in the lower mantle.

**density-dependent factors** The checks to population growth which are the result of overcrowding, such as *competition. **Density-independent factors**, like fire and drought, will occur whatever the state of the population.

**density gradient** The rate at which an intensity of land use or population density falls with distance from a central point. Clark noted that population density declines exponentially with increasing distance from the city centre.

**denudation** The laying bare of underlying rocks by the processes of weathering and erosion.

**dependence** The condition in which a society is able to develop, in part or in full, only by reliance on another nation for income, aid, political protection, or control. A degree of dependence can be fostered only when one society comes into contact with another. Nearly all today's 'underdeveloped' societies were once viable and could satisfy their own economic needs but they were often torn apart after contact with a colonial power. It is therefore maintained that Europe did not 'discover' the dependent, underdeveloped countries; on the contrary, it created them.

**dependency ratio** See *age dependency.

**dependent variable** A variable which depends on one or more variables which may control it or relate to it.

**depopulation** The decline, in absolute terms, of the total population of an area. See *rural depopulation.

**deposition** The dropping of material which has been picked up and transported by wind, water, or ice.

**depressed area** An area, usually within a developed nation, where capital is scarce and labour, plant, and *infrastructure are underemployed. Depressed areas develop because their economic activity has been outmoded, often because of competition from cheap labour in the Third World, and because of world recessions. Competition also comes from newly industrialized areas. Victorian cities decline as the better-off move to rural and suburban areas. Currently, unemployment in the inner cities of Britain runs at four times the national average. See *development areas.

**depression** 1. An area of low pressure (roughly, below 1000 *millibars). The term is usually applied to *mid-latitude depressions. Depressions also occur as *cold lows, *lee depressions, *monsoon depressions, polar lows (see *mesometeorology), and *thermal lows. See also *cyclogenesis.
2. A time of low economic activity and high unemployment.

**depression tracks** The usual paths taken by *mid-latitude depressions. These paths are influenced by the courses of the *jet streams, by sources of energy, such as warm sea surfaces, and by mountain barriers.

**deprivation** Loss; lacking in provision of desired objects or aims. Within the Third World deprivation may be acute; the neccesities of life such as water, housing, or food may be lacking. Within the developed world basic provisions may be supplied but, in comparison with the better-off, the poor and the old may well feel a sense of deprivation.

**deranged drainage** A medley of islands, lakes, marshes, and streams developed on irregular *till.

**derelict land** Abandoned land, often covered with deserted and ruined buildings or old railway sidings.

**desalination** The conversion of salt water into fresh by the partial or complete extraction of dissolved solids. The methods used include distillation, electrodialysis, freezing, and reverse osmosis. The processes are relatively simple but costly.

**descriptive statistics** Statistics which are used to describe a state which exists at the present or existed in the past.

**desert** An arid area of sparse vegetation, such that much of the ground surface is exposed. Scanty vegetation can be due to very high, or very low temperatures (as in *cold deserts), or to an excess of potential *evapotranspiration over precipitation. See *hot desert.

**deserted village** A village site once inhabited but now abandoned. Most English deserted villages were abandoned in the late Middle Ages and traces may be seen in the landscape in the form of old building lines, lumps of masonry, clumps of stinging nettles, and isolated churches.

**desertification** The spread of desert-like conditions in semi-arid environments. The causes of desertification are by no means clear, and some writers suggest that pastoral *nomadism, once thought to degrade the environment, may represent the best use of desert areas.

**desert pavement** A surface consisting of large angular or rounded rock fragments lying over mixed material. These rocky fragments are thought to have been left behind after wind or water has removed the lighter material. Desert pavements can protect surfaces from *deflation.

**desert soil** Most desert soils show little development of soil *horizons because the climate is too dry for chemical *weathering or the formation of humus. *Leaching occurs only occasionally after sporadic rain, and this downward movement of soil water is soon reversed by evaporation.

**desert varnish** A film of iron oxide or quartz on desert rocks. The precise cause is disputed; some recognize desert or **rock varnish** as being *weathering rind, but the polishing of rock by fine wind *abrasion is also significant.

**desilication, desilification** The process by which silica is removed from a *soil profile by intense weathering and *leaching. Desilication is common in wet, tropical regions and leads to the formation of a firm but porous soil with a reduced capacity to store water.

**desire line** A straight line constructed on a map to symbolize a trip between two locations.

**deskilling** The breaking down of jobs into smaller units, each to be tackled separately, so that low levels of skill are required for restricted tasks. It is associated with the development of the assembly line, standardized production techniques, and automation.

**destructive margin** In *plate tectonics, the zone where two plates meet and one plate is forced below the other. As it descends into hotter regions, the lower plate is consumed in the *subduction zone.

**destructive wave** A **plunging wave**, with a short wavelength and a high crest, which breaks so that the water crashes downwards from the wave crest and erodes the beach. Plunging waves generally occur on steeply sloping beaches.

**determinism** The view that man's actions are stimulated and governed by some outside agency like the environment or the economy. Man has no choice in regulating his actions, which may be predicted from the external stimuli which triggered them.

**detritivore** An animal which feeds on fragments of dead and decaying plant and animal material.

**detritus** 1. In geomorphology, fragments of weathered rock which have been transported from the place of origin.
2. In ecology, dead plants and the corpses and shed parts of animals.

**developed** Applied to a country or region with an advanced economy, fully using all required resources, and enjoying a high standard of living. See *development indicators.

**developing** This term is now used in preference to *underdeveloped as a more neutral world.

**development** The use of resources to improve the standard of living of a nation. This definition is based on the more obvious distinctions in living standards between developed and less developed countries, but it may be that a change to 'western' conditions is not in the best interests of a Third World nation.

**Development indicators** as used by the World Bank include details of birth and death rates, fertility, life expectancy, health, urbanization, industrialization, production, consumption, investment, capital, income, education, energy consumption, and trade. These indices of development are simply concerned with statistics and do not indicate social structures and patterns of behaviour; it is possible to get only a narrow view of a society and its wealth.

**development area** A depressed area in need of investment in industry and *infrastructure. In Britain from 1947 to 1981, investment was deflected from prosperous areas by the failure to grant development certificates. Other methods of inducing investment in development areas include grants, tax concessions, loans, and the provision of industrial premises.

**development control** A measure by central government to regulate the location of new industry in Britain. An Industrial Development Certificate (IDC) must be granted by the Department of Trade and Industry, which regulates the availability of the IDC according to the size of the plant and the location selected. IDCs are not required in *assisted areas. Local authorities also control industrial development but may be overruled by central government.

**development stages growth theory** A theory of growth which suggests that all economic development passes through the same sequence. Initially, there is a subsistence economy, but with better transport, regional specialization develops and village industries emerge. Agriculture becomes more intensive and industrialization takes place. Over time, processing gives way to service industries.

**Devensian** In Britain, the last stage of the *Pleistocene where icy periods alternated with warmer ones.

**devolution** The means by which a state allows a degree of independence to a political unit within its boundaries. With the rise of nationalism, devolution may be seen as one way to avoid ethnic unrest.

**Devonian** A *period of *Paleozoic time stretching approximately from 395 to 345 million years BP.

**dew** A type of precipitation where water droplets form on the ground, or on objects near the ground.

Dew forms when strong night-time *terrestrial radiation causes the ground to cool. At the end of a clear night, air in contact with the ground may be chilled to *dew point. If this cooling brings about temperatures below 0 °C, frost rather than dew will form.

**dew point** The temperature at which condensation begins to occur as moist air is cooled. The dew point of an *air mass varies with its initial temperature and humidity.

Dew point is determined by the use of a **dew point hygrometer** in which a polished surface is reduced in temperature until water vapour from the atmosphere condenses on to it.

**dew pond** A pool made to provide a water supply in a dry region such as a chalk or limestone upland. The sides and bottom are lined with impermeable clay to retain the water which generally comes from rainfall rather than from dew.

**dialectic** A theory of the nature of logic. Dialectic is the logic of reasoning. The determination of truth is arrived at by the assertion of the theory—thesis—and its denial—antithesis, and then the synthesis of the two to form a new theory.

**diatom** A type of alga with silica in the cell walls and occurring singly or in colonies. Diatoms are one type of *plankton, and their skeletons, deposited on the sea floor, form **diatom ooze**, particularly in oceanic regions between latitudes 50 °S. and 60 °S.

**diatreme** A passage, generally sloping upwards, which has been forced through sedimentary country rock by volcanic activity.

**differential erosion** This occurs when some rock strata are more resistant to erosion than others, so that the former stand out as ridges between depressions in the softer rocks.

**differential share** See *shift share analysis.

**diffluent col** In glaciology, a low pass at a valley side which has been cut by ice spreading out over the *col from its own valley to an adjoining one.

**diffluent glacier** A glacier breaking away from a larger valley glacier and crossing over a low pass.

**diffusion** The widespread dispersal of an innovation from a centre or centres. This innovation may be anything from an epidemic disease to a political belief. The innovation spreads through in a **diffusion wave**, a ripple of the new factor spreading from one location to another.

   **Expansion diffusion** is the spread of a factor from a centre with the concentration of the things being diffused also remaining, and possibly intensifying, at the point of origin. An example of this is the introduction of high-yielding crops. **Relocation diffusion** similarly spreads from a centre but the innovation moves outwards, leaving the centre. An example of this is the movement of a bush fire. **Hierarchic diffusion** passes through a regular sequence of orders as when an innovation in a metropolis spreads out to cities, then towns, and finally to villages. The order may also be based on class and the innovation may spread up or down the hierarchy. **Cascade diffusion** concerns only movement down an order or hierarchy.

**diffusion barrier** Any obstacle which checks the *diffusion of an innovation. Four types of barrier may be encountered. A **superabsorbing barrier** stops the message and destroys the transmitter—the point of origin. An **absorbing barrier** stops the message but does not affect the transmitter. A **reflecting barrier** stops the message but allows the transmitter to transmit a new message in the same time period. A **direct reflecting barrier** deflects the message to the nearest available location to the transmitter.

**diffusion curve** The graphical representation of the spread of a new development from its inception to its general use. The curve has a typical S-shape. Initially only a few innovators and early adopters are prepared to experiment with new techniques—about 16% of the population. As the idea gains ground, the majority—the next 68%—accept the innovation. Finally, the laggards take notice.

**digital data** In *remote sensing, data shown or stored in binary. The **digital number (DN)** is the value recorded for the quality of each *pixel, usually from a range of 0–255.

**dike, dyke** A vertical or semi-vertical wall-like igneous *intrusion which cuts across the *bedding planes of a rock. Dikes often form in swarms. **Ring dikes** are vertical circular sheets around a central intrusion. **Dike-springs** of water may emerge along the line of a dike.

**dilatation** *Pressure release.

**diminishing returns, law of** The principle that further inputs into a system produce ever lower increases in outputs. Any extra input may not produce an equal or worthwhile return.

**dip** The angle of inclination of a rock down its steepest slope. Dip is the angle between the maximum slope and the horizontal. A **dipslope** occurs where the slope of land mirrors the slope of the underlying *strata. A **dip stream** follows the dip of the rocks over which it flows.

**discharge** The quantity of water flowing through any cross-section of a stream or river in unit time. Discharge is usually measured in cubic metres per second—cumecs—and can be calculated as $A \times V$ where $A$ is the cross-sectional area of a stream and $V$ is the velocity.

**discontinuous media** Forms of the transport of energy which can be used flexibly along different routes and to different locations, as with oil tankers and lorries. The journey may have a number of different links by water, rail, and road.

**discordant** At odds with, not complying with. **Discordant coastlines** cut across folds and faults, **discordant drainage** is not related to the *dip of the underlying rocks, and in a **discordant junction** a tributary suddenly falls steeply just before it reaches the river.

**discovery depletion cycle** The progression which unwinds as a non-renewable resource is exploited. The sequence begins with the discovery and early development of the resource, followed by rapid expansion leading to peak production. As reserves are depleted, output falls until the resource is exhausted.

**discrete variable** A variable which is broken down into separate size categories where no fractions are possible. For example, the number of cars travelling to a town can only be expressed in whole numbers—fractions cannot exist.

**discrimination** The treatment of ethnic or social minorities in a different way from the majority. **Positive discrimination** favours the minority group; more often negative discrimination occurs, with opportunities limited for the minority group.

**diseconomies** Financial drawbacks. **Diseconomies of scale** occur when an enterprise becomes too large, where sites become constricted, where the flow of goods is congested, and, perhaps, where the workforce is alienated. **Diseconomies of urbanization** are associated with the high cost of labour, land, and transport in cities.

**dispersal** In biology and *biogeography, the scattering of seed as a plant species colonizes.

**dispersed city** A plan of city structure as envisaged by Frank Lloyd Wright with one-family houses surrounded by open space. Shops and factories lie between housing areas and population densities are low enough to give a rural effect. The whole city is to be served by a network of super-highways.

**dispersed settlement** In comparison with *nucleated settlement, a settlement pattern characterized by scattered, isolated dwellings. Highlands, poor soils, and ubiquitous water supply help to create dispersed settlement as do cultural factors; lowland Wales has dispersed settlement whereas lowland England inclines to nuclear villages.

**dispersion diagram** A plot of the spread of values in a distribution. A vertical axis is used and each value is shown as a dot.

**dissection** The cutting down of valleys by river erosion. Thus, a **dissected plateau** is a level surface which has been deeply cut into by rivers, leaving a close network of valleys with hills in between.

**dissolved load** Material carried in solution by a river.

**dissolved oxygen** Oxygen from the atmosphere and from photosynthesis is dissolved in the upper levels of all bodies of water and is vital for the maintenance of most aquatic life. The amount of oxygen present decreases with depth, rising temperatures, and with the oxidation of organic matter and pollutants. The amount of oxygen used by organisms depends on their *biological oxygen demand.

**distance Absolute distance** is expressed in physical units such as kilometres and is unchangeable. **Relative distance** includes any other kind of distance such as **time distance**, which is measured in hours and minutes and changes with varying technology. Thus, a location 6 hours away by train is only 90 minutes away by air. **Cost distance** is expressed in terms of currency and varies with the transport mode, the volume and type of traffic and goods, and their destination. **Convenience distance** expresses the ease of travel.

**distance decay** The lessening in force of a phenomenon or interaction with increasing distance from the location of maximum intensity.

**distributary** A branch of a river or glacier which flows away from the main stream and does not return to it.

**distribution** 1. The physical layout of a feature over an area, such as forest land.

2. The dispersal of payments to the *factors of production for the output achieved.

3. The function of *tertiary industry in delivering goods, that is wholesaling, warehousing, and retailing.

4. The spread of varying observations within a population.

**district** In behavioural urban geography, a clearly identifiable section of a city, having a distinct *image and geographical extent.

**districting algorithm** A system, usually using computers, of drawing up electoral boundaries so that the constituencies conform to more or less equal size limits of population. Boundaries may not be manipulated to favour one party. Such a system can be produced but the altered constituencies thus derived have not been taken up by politicians.

**diurnal** Over the course of one day. Hence, **diurnal range**, the difference between the maximum and minimum temperatures in one day, and **diurnal rhythm**, the regular physiological changes taking place within an organism over each day.

**divergence** In meteorology, the spreading out of an air mass into paths of different directions. Divergence is associated with the vertical shrinking of the atmosphere and the descent of air.

**diverging margin** See *constructive margin.

**diversification** A measure taken to spread industrial commitment over a large range of activities so that there is no overdependence on one. The term can also refer to the extent to which this takes place. Diversification can take place within a single firm by taking on new ventures to spread the risk of any one failing. The

development of products which require little adjustment of machinery or skills is **horizontal diversification. Concentric diversification** concerns the widening of the use of one product in order to penetrate new markets. **Conglomerate diversification** is the growth of industry into new areas as a result of changes in markets, technology, and products. *Multinationals diversify as they buy up new firms producing different products.

In declining areas, there are problems of overdependence of the labour force on one industry, especially in those areas which developed a high degree of specialization in the nineteenth century. Here, regional diversification of employment is seen as the answer to overdependence and may also foster economic growth. Governments and local authorities are the usual agents of regional diversification.

**diversification curve** A diagrammatic technique used to compare *diversification with the minimum and maximum, and to compare diversification between regions. For each type of industry, employment is calculated as a percentage of total employment. The percentages are then ranked in ascending order and cumulated (i.e. each percentage is added to the total of percentages before it). The cumulative percentage of the labour force is plotted against the percentage of industrial groups ranked in ascending order. A 45° line represents maximum possible diversification.

**diversification index** For a *diversification curve, a measure of the difference between a given distribution of diversification and a perfect diversification line showing at 45°. The area between the curve and 45° is expressed as a percentage of the total area beneath the 45° line. The higher the index, the more evenly diversified a region is.

**diversity** The abundance of species within an *ecosystem. **Alpha diversity** or **between-habitat diversity** refers to the range of organisms within a habitat. If an ecosystem is very crowded, species may only survive in the most favourable habitats for them. This is **beta diversity** or **within-habitat diversity**.

**diversivore** An organism with a wide range of diet, from plants to other animals. Since the food eaten varies from time to time and place to place, it is difficult to fit a diversivore into the *food web.

**divided circle** See *pie chart.

**division of labour** The partitioning of a production process into separate elements, with each part assigned to a different worker or set of workers. In a multinational company different elements of production may take place in different countries or in different continents. This is **spatial division of labour**. It is based on the idea that workers can attain a high degree of efficiency if they are restricted to one particular process. Division of labour is one of the hallmarks of the factory system, but can lead to the alienation of the work force as the workers lose touch with the creative process.

**doldrums** These regions of light, variable winds, low pressure, high temperature and humidity occur in tropical and subtropical latitudes.

Doldrums occur over the east Pacific, the east Atlantic, and from the Indian Ocean to the west Pacific. They are bounded to the north and south by the *trade winds, and their extent varies greatly with the seasons.

**doline, dolina** A steep-sided and flat-floored depression in *karst country. The sides are 2–10 m deep and the floor is 10–1000 m in width. **Alluvial streamsink dolines** form when a stream enters the doline and runs down through the rock to form a trough. **Collapsed dolines** form when a cave roof falls in. **Solution dolines** form when solution enlarges a point of weakness in the rock into a hollow. **Subsidence dolines** form when limestone caves develop below insoluble deposits. These superficial deposits may collapse into the cavern below.

**dome** An uplifted section of rocks. The highest part is at the centre, from which the rocks dip in all directions.

**Volcanic domes** may be formed from slow-moving, *viscous lava. These domes may be rounded as the result of pressure from lava below. A **plug dome** is a small, irregular dome within a crater. Plug domes may have spine-like *extrusions projecting from them.

**Domesday Book** A survey of England, with the exception of Cumbria, County Durham, and Northumberland, made at the behest of William I (the Conqueror), between 1086 and 1087. It covers the ownership, size, and value of estates together with details of the households, and local customs.

**domestic** Within one country, as in **domestic industry** and **domestic trade**.

**domestication** The taming and breeding of previously wild animals and plants to human use.

**domestic industry** An industry based in the home. Manufacturers supply materials to workers in their homes, pay them for the finished goods, and sell the products. This is **homeworking**. Remnants of the system still exist in Britain, notably in knitwear. Domestic industry can belong to those in whose home it takes place, especially historically. The term may also cover any industry established in the state under discussion.

**domino theory** The view, held by many US administrations and politicians, that if one small nation were to 'succumb' to communism, then its neighbours would surely follow. This view has been acted on in a military sense, most tragically in the Vietnam war.

**donga** A steep-sided gulley resulting from severe soil erosion. The term is generally used in South Africa.

**dormant volcano** A volcano which is inactive but not extinct.

**dormitory town** A settlement made up largely of day commuters who are employed elsewhere in a larger centre. These commuters have displaced the original residents or live in new housing at the edge of the town or village. Dormitory towns are characterized by a relative paucity of retail outlets since the commuters will use services in the centre of the city or in out-of-town shopping centres.

**dot map** A map displaying the distribution of some phenomenon by the location of dots of uniform size. Each dot represents a certain value of the phenomenon. Dots may be evenly spread over the map or concentrated in areas where the phenomenon is thought to occur; dots representing population numbers are located at cities or towns. The siting of the dots in this case is somewhat subjective.

**downs, downland** In South-East England, gently rolling chalk hills where natural grassland has largely been replaced by arable crops.

**downthrow** In geology, the distance of downward movement along a *fault.

**downtown** A term used in the USA to denote the heart of the city; the *CBD.

**downward transition region** In Friedmann's *core-periphery model, a region on the periphery characterized either by depleted resources, or by low agricultural productivity, or by outdated industry.

**down warping** A slow, even, downward movement of part of the earth's crust under pressure from above. The pressure may be exerted by a continental *ice sheet or by the deposition of sediment. If the weight is removed, for example, when the ice sheet melts, the crust may slowly spring back up again. See *isostasy.

**downwearing, declining slope retreat** A model of hillslope retreat where the slope angle decreases over time due to a combination of soil *creep, rain splash, and *sheet wash which causes slope convexities and concavities at the expense of straight hillslope segments. It is now generally accepted that no single model of slope evolution can explain all the features of hillslopes.

**drain** A channel cut in a naturally wet site constructed to remove excess water.

Porous clay pipes are buried beneath the surface to form **tile drains**, and **mole drains** are unlined channels in the subsoil, formed by pulling a bullet-shaped plug through the soil.

**drainage** The naturally occurring channelled flow formed by streams and rivers which removes water from the land surface.

**drainage basin** The area of land drained by a river and its tributaries. The term is synonymous with river basin.

**drainage basin geometry** Using Strahler's classification of *stream order, the following relationships hold:

1. The number of streams of each order falls in an inverse geometrical progression as the stream order rises.

2. The average slope of a stream falls in an inverse geometrical progression as the stream order rises.

3. The total length of streams in a drainage basin is linked logarithmically with the *drainage basin order.

4. The *discharge of a stream is linked logarithmically with the area of the drainage basin feeding that stream.

5. The average area of a drainage basin rises in direct geometrical progression as the order of the basin rises.

6. The average length of streams of each different order rises in direct geometrical progression as the order of the drainage basin increases.

Many of these 'laws' are true of most branching systems and are therefore not notably edifying.

**drainage basin order** Just as *stream order can be quantified, so can the order of a drainage basin. Thus, a basin serving only a first order stream is a first order drainage basin, and so on.

**drainage basins, laws of** See *drainage basin geometry.

**drainage density** The total length of streams per unit area. Any attempt to calculate drainage density is impeded by the difficulty of calculating total stream length, as the exact point at which a stream starts is problematical.

**drainage network evolution** The drainage basin can increase its area and extend its channels by landslides at the edge of the network, by *headward erosion, by the extension upslope of underground *pipes, and by the formation of *rills.

There are two main theories to account for the nature of drainage network evolution:

1. That the drainage system develops at random, but that random development will bring about a coherent network.

2. That stream networks develop by the growth of new, first order channels at a rate which is proportional to the size of the drainage basin.

**drainage patterns** The pattern of a drainage network. This pattern is strongly influenced by geological structure. **Anastomotic drainage** shows a division of rivers into channels, and develops on nearly horizontal, coarse sediments. **Annular drainage** shows the major rivers radiating out from a centre with the tributaries arranged along a series of nested arcs. Annular drainage develops on domes, particularly where belts of resistant rock are separated by belts of weaker rock. **Centripetal drainage** shows a movement into a centre created by a crater or depression. **Dendritic drainage** shows a branching network similar to that of a tree, and is most commonly found on horizontally bedded or crystalline rocks where the geology is uniform. **Parallel drainage** develops in slopes of moderate angle. **Rectangular drainage** shows the tributaries running at right angles to the major river and occurs on rocks which have intersecting, rectangular joints and faults. **Contorted drainage** is a form of rectangular drainage on complex metamorphosed rocks. **Trellised drainage** resembles a trained fruit tree. It usually occurs on dipping or folded sedimentary or weakly metamorphosed rocks. **Angulate drainage** is a form of trellised drainage where tributaries meet streams at an acute angle.

**dreikanter** A stone with three clearly cut faces, like a Brazil nut, formed by sand-blasting in desert environments.

**drift** 1. A horizontal tunnel driven into the hillside for mining purposes; an *adit.

2. In geology, superficial deposits which were derived elsewhere.

**drifter** A fishing vessel which operates by lowering weighted nets at night and drifting with the winds until morning, when the nets are drawn up again.

**dripstone** In *karst scenery, underground streams carry calcium carbonate in solution. If the water pressure of the stream falls as it enters a cave, or if the amount of dissolved carbon dioxide decreases, the carbonates will be deposited to form dripstone in hanging *stalactites or in stubbier cave-floor *stalagmites.

**drizzle** Rain made up of very small droplets, that is, up to 1 mm in diameter. Drizzle can be very dense, but is not to be confused with light rain, where the droplets are at least 3 mm across.

**drought** A long, continuous period of dry weather. Major causes of drought in Britain are the persistence of warm *anticyclones and the displacement of *mid-latitude depressions by blocking anticyclones.

**drove road** A broad, unmetalled track used by herders walking their animals, usually cattle or sheep, to market. Drove roads were used in Britain for hundreds of years until superseded by the railways.

**drowned valley** A river valley now occupied by an arm of the sea after a rise in sea level. Also known as a *ria.

**drumlin** A long hummock or hill, egg-shaped in plan and deposited and shaped under an ice sheet or very broad glacier while the ice was still moving. The end facing the ice—the *stoss—is blunt while the lee is shallow and its point is in the direction of the ice flow.

Most drumlins result from the reworking of *lodgement *till. It may be that, under high pressure, ice squeezes the till, making it stiffer so that it lodges on the valley floor forming a stoss slope. At points of low pressure, down-glacier, the till is less viscous and may be streamlined, as at the lee of the drumlin.

**drumlinoid** See *false drumlin.

**dry adiabatic lapse rate, DALR** See *adiabatic.

**dry air** Strictly speaking, air with a *relative humidity of less than 60%.

**dry bulb thermometer** A simple mercury thermometer which is usually housed in a Stevenson screen. See *wet bulb thermometer.

**dry farming** Farming without irrigation in arid areas, using techniques which conserve water for the crop. Strategies include mulching, frequent fallowing, working the soil to a fine tilth, and weeding.

**dry point settlement** In a marshy, damp, or frequently flooded area, raised sites such as low mounds or gravel terraces attract settlement. The 'ey' portion of names such as Hackney in London refers to the dry island upon which these settlements were founded.

**dry valley** A valley, usually in chalk or *karst scenery, which has no permanent watercourse along the valley floor. The theories of dry valley formation are many. Although present-day processes such as river *capture and *superimposed drainage can account for the formation of some dry valleys, most researchers believe that these valleys were cut during *periglacial phases in the Quaternary period. Under these conditions, the *permafrost would prevent the river water from soaking through chalk or limestone and would allow *dissection by *meltwater channels.

The periglacial origin of dry valleys seems to be borne out by field work, but there are arguments for falling sea levels and tidal scour as being causal factors.

**dry weather flow** A synonym for *base flow.

**dual economy** An economy comprising two very different systems, and found in many developing countries where an advanced economy coexists with a traditional economy and the two have very little contact with each other. This is a result of *uneven development. The concept also applies to core regions with large-scale, thriving industries by comparison with their less developed peripheries.

**dualism** An existence of two distinct parts. For example, dualism occurs in many Third World economies: the traditional sector and the 'modern' sector.

**dual labour market** The labour market has two sectors: primary and secondary. The **primary labour market** is typified by high incomes, fringe benefits, job security, and good prospects for upward mobility. This sector may be subdivided into upper primary workers—long-term workers who advance their position as their years of service increase—and lower primary workers. These are usually blue-collar workers in stable, skilled labour.

The **secondary labour market** is typified by low incomes, little job security, and little training. There are no rewards apart from wages. Mobility between the primary and secondary markets is very low. These differences are held to derive from the structures of capital. This analysis tends to oversimplify a complex reality.

**dumping** The off-loading of goods at below cost, usually as exports.

**dune** See *sand dune or *coastal dune.

**duricrust** A hard capping found at the surface of the soil in tropical uplands. This is thought by some to be a *plinthite *horizon, originally formed in the B horizon, but now revealed by erosion since plinthite hardens on exposure to the air. The duricrust would therefore be the remains of a fossil soil. Other processes in the formation of duricrust include evaporation of a lake, of *ground water, or of sub-surface and surface waters moving across *alluvial fans and *pediments.

**dust devil** A small whirlwind, perhaps only metres in height, which has picked up soil, silt, or sand and which moves as a seeming pillar across the landscape. Dust devils are most common in dry, sparsely vegetated areas.

**dust storm** Desert dust storms form when the wind picks up small, light particles such as silt. Many tonnes of light soil can be transported in storms some 500 km in diameter. *Accelerated erosion caused the dust storms and **dust bowl** of the Great Plains of America.

**duyoda** In a *periglacial landscape, a steep-sided, shallow depression formed as *baydzharakhs collapse. A duyoda is smaller than, but can develop into, an *alas.

**dyke** See *dike.

**dynamic** Moving, or causing movement. **Dynamic metamorphism** is the alteration of existing rock by the pressure attending earth movements.

**dynamic equilibrium** In a landform, a state of balance in spite of changes taking place. Thus, a *spit may appear to be unchanging although it is fed by deposition from its landward end and subject to erosion at its seaward end.

# E

**earth fall** See *fall.

**earth flow** See *flow.

**earth movement** A movement of the earth's crust caused by activity beneath it. This movement may reveal itself in *faults, *folds, *earthquakes, *volcanoes, and *orogenies.

**earth pillar** An upstanding, free column of soil that has been sheltered from erosion by a natural cap of stone on the top.

**earthquake** A sudden and violent movement, or fracture, within the earth followed by the series of shocks resulting from this fracture.

Earthquakes occur in narrow, continuous belts of activity which correspond with the junction of *plates.

The scale of the shock of an earthquake is known as the magnitude; the most commonly used scale is the *Richter Scale.

Earthquake waves are of three basic types: **P, primary, push waves** travel from the *focus by the displacement of surrounding particles and are transmitted though solids, liquids, and gases. **S, secondary** or shake waves travel through solids. **L, long or surface waves** travel on the earth's surface. The monitoring of these waves indicates that the earth's core is molten since S waves do not pass through it.

**Earth Resources Technology Satellite, ERTS** See *LANDSAT.

**earth's magnetic field** See *geomagnetism.

**earth tremor** A small, slight *earthquake.

**easterlies** Winds blowing *from* the east, like the north-east and south-east *trade winds.

**easting** A reference line drawn across a map from north to south. Eastings increase in number from west to east, and form the first component of a *grid reference. See also *northing.

**ebb** A flow of water back to the sea, as in an **ebb tide**. An **ebb channel**, also known as a tidal stream, is the location of the strongest tidal outflow.

**EC, EEC** The European Community, also known as the European Economic Community or Common Market, is a free trading area comprising Belgium, the Netherlands, Luxemburg, France, West Germany, Italy, Great Britain, Denmark, Eire, Spain, Portugal, and Greece. Designed initially as an economic unit, the European Community is now attempting uniformity in social as well as economic unity.

**echo sounder** An instrument to measure the depth of the water by noting the time taken for a sound emitted at the surface to bounce back from the sea floor to the surface. It can be used to measure the thickness of ice.

**eclipse** The total or partial blocking out of light from the moon, sun, or other celestial body as another celestial body passes between it and the earth.

**ecological balance** The 'balance of nature'; the quality of a stable *ecosystem. This balance is increasingly upset by human actions: pollution, removal of natural vegetation, the introduction of foreign species, and so on.

**ecological dominance** The predominance of one or a few species within an *ecosystem such that they have more importance than is possible in a purely random process.

**ecological efficiency** The ability of the organisms at one *trophic level to convert to their own use the potential energy supplied by their foodstuff at the trophic level directly beneath them.

**ecological energetics** The study of the flow of energy from the sun through and up the *trophic levels, expressed in calories. This energy may be fixed in the form of food. With movement up each trophic level, there is a very great loss of the energy available as food. The study of energetics highlights the importance of micro-organisms within ecosystems and stresses the danger of destroying these minute forms of life.

**ecological explosion** The sudden and dramatic increase in the numbers of a particular species. This may be due to unusually favourable conditions or may happen when an organism is introduced to a new habitat where there is no natural predator, for example, cane toads in Queensland.

**ecological fallacy** The danger of making an analysis at one level apply at other levels. For example, Robinson showed that there was a correlation between the number of black people in American states and literacy levels. He then showed that the assumption leading from this—that black people were inclined to illiteracy—was by no means certain.

**ecological psychology** The study of the psychology in a behaviour setting, such as a school, which gives rise to common or regularized forms of behaviour.

**ecology** The study of animals and plants in relation to each other and to their habitats. Life forms, including man, are intimately linked with their environment. An **ecological factor** is one which affects a living organism. **Production ecology** is the study of the structure of *communities in terms of the throughput of energy and chemical compounds.

**economic base theory** The view that economic activity in a city can be broken down into two components: that which meets local, internal demand and that which meets non-local demand. The former is non-*basic, serving the city but not causing it to grow, and the latter is basic and city-forming; it is the demand from beyond the city which causes the city to grow. The effect of basic activity may be calculated. The relationships are:

$$E = S + B$$
$$P = \alpha E$$
$$S = \beta P$$

where $B$ = the basic sector, $S$ = the non-basic sector, $E$ = total employment, $P$ = the population, $\alpha$ and $\beta$ are coefficients which can be obtained by *regression. A unit increase in $B$ gives rise to $\dfrac{\alpha}{1 - \alpha\beta}$ units of additional population.

It is difficult to define and establish the numbers engaged in basic employment.

**economic determinism** The thesis, as advanced by Marx and Engels, that economic factors underlie all of society's decisions.

**economic distance** The distance a commodity may travel before transport costs exceed the value of the freight. Because of lower unit transport costs, a small valuable commodity can be transported profitably further than a bulky commodity of the same value.

**economic efficiency** The ratio by value of input to output. The higher the ratio, the greater the efficiency.

**economic geography** The study of the creation of wealth and income as it affects the geography of the landscape; the analysis of the spatial distribution of the transportation and consumption of resources, goods, and services.

**economic growth** An increase in *GDP or *GNP, often expressed as a per capita figure.

**economic man** A theoretical being who has perfect knowledge of an economy and has the ability to act in his or her own interests to maximize profits. The idea of economic man has proved a useful tool in *neoclassical economics but other writers suggest that the concept of the *satisficer is more realistic.

**economic overhead capital** Investment in the *infrastructure which should encourage new industrial growth. This is often a major part of a development programme.

For example, the Appalachian Development Plan of the 1960s and 1970s was centred on road construction.

**economic rent** Economic rent is not synonymous with profit, since built into the concept is the notion of opportunity cost: the real cost of choosing one alternative good or service in terms of the sacrifice of the next best alternative. A singer may work regularly for £10 000 per annum or may sing only in starring roles for £20 000. Let his/her total transport costs for each type of work be £5000. The net income for starring concerts is £15 000 but the economic rent is £10 000, i.e. the extra profit over and above the second choice. Economic rent is all about choices, particularly of land use in agricultural geography.

The term is often used more loosely. If opportunity costs are ignored, economic rent is the difference between revenue and costs.

**economics** The study of the relation of available scarce means to supply, for a proposed end. **Micro-economics** explains how demand and supply affect prices, wages, rentals, and interest rates. **Macro-economics** focuses on the aggregate demand for goods and services, and notably upon the relationship between unemployment and the economy. **Marxist economics** sees the economy as a reflection of the history and sociology of a society. In particular, it focuses on the historical evolution of, and the conflict between, classes.

**economic system** The organization of activity to produce goods and services for given consumers. Any such system should be able to determine the needs of society for goods and services, ensure the correct allocation of the factors of production to industry, provide and maintain investment, distribute goods and services by matching supply to demand, and utilize resources efficiently.

**economies of scale** The benefits of large-scale production. As the volume of production increases, the cost per unit article decreases. It is suggested that this decrease will be halted as *diseconomies arise, but only at very high levels of production, if at all. **Internal economies of scale** arise from within a plant and include *indivisibility, specialization, and *division of labour. Furthermore, overheads like research and development cost less per unit article when production levels are high. Increases in plant size can be important; doubling the capacity of a machine does not necessarily double its cost. In a larger production system, specialist machines can be used to advantage. Buying in bulk reduces costs. These different factors operate with differing force in different industries. See also *external economies.

**economies of urbanization** Those savings brought about by *urbanization. These include the provision of an *infrastructure, the supply of labour, and a large potential market.

**economy** A system of the production, distribution, and consumption of those goods and services deemed necessary for the needs of a region, nation, or society.

**ecosphere** The parts of earth's atmosphere and crust fostering living organisms, together with the ecological factors influencing them.

**ecosystem** A community of plants and animals within a particular physical environment. There are relationships between all three categories. Ecosystems range in size from the whole earth to a drop of water.

**ecotone** A region of rapidly changing species between two overlapping ecosystems. An ecotone usually marks a change in soil, in water supply, or in exposure to the elements.

**ecotope** A defined *niche or niche space within a habitat.

**ecumene (oecumene)** The inhabited areas of the world, as opposed to the **non-ecumene**, which is sparsely or not at all inhabited. The ecumene of a nation is its more densely inhabited core. These very simplified classifications pose difficulties of delimitation.

**edaphic** Of the soil; produced or influenced by the soil.

**edaphic climax** The final stage in the development of vegetation as a response to the soil type.

**edaphic formation** The vegetation which develops in response to soil, rather than to climate.

**eddy** A roughly circular movement within a current of air or water. Eddies may have the circular and intermittent motion of a vortex, the continuous corkscrew motion termed helicoidal flow, the cylindric motion of rollers, or surge phenomena, which are short-lived outbreaks of greater velocity in any flow.

**edge** 1. In *network analysis, another term for the *link between two *nodes.

2. In behavioural urban geography, the edge is an informal boundary imagined by an individual or group separating one clearly identifiable *district from another. The definition of such boundaries is frequently problematic.

**EEC** See *EC.

**effluent** The flow into a river, stream, or lake of sewage, fertilizers in solution, or liquid industrial waste.

**effluent stream** A small *distributary. This expression is not to be confused with the term 'effluent' as in pollution.

**EFTA** The European Free Trade Association, an economic union of Norway, Sweden, Switzerland, Austria, Portugal, and Iceland, with Finland as an associate.

**EIA** See *environmental impact assessment.

**elastic** Describing a substance which will return to its original form and dimensions after it has been pulled or pushed out of shape. An **elastic rebound** is the moving back of a rock or rocks into the original shape. Ice has an **elastic flow** at depth, where it is not as powerful an erosive agent as ordinary ice.

**elasticity** In economics, a measure of the responsiveness of supply and demand to changes in price. Elasticity is calculated as the change of supply or demand, related to a 1% difference in price. Where the percentage change in demand is greater that the percentage change in price, the demand is said to be elastic. Where the opposite applies, demand is said to be inelastic. The same terminology is used for supply.

**elasticity of substitution** An indication of how easily one of the *factors of production can be substituted for one of the others.

**elbow of capture** See *capture.

**electoral geography** The geographical analysis of elections. The study includes the drawing of constituency boundaries, the influence of sociological factors on voting, and the influence of voting decisions upon the environment.

**electromagnetic radiation** Waves of energy propagated through space at the speed of light. *Solar radiation is of this type as is the energy measured by *remote sensors.

**electromagnetic spectrum** The entire range of frequencies of waves of energy in the form of electricity and magnetism. The highest frequencies are gamma rays, followed by X-rays, ultra-violet radiation, visible light, infra-red radiation, radar waves, and radio waves.

**ellipsoid** A figure shaped like a sphere, not perfectly spherical but with an oval form.

**El niño effect** The upwelling of warm water off the coasts of Chile, Ecuador, and Peru which replaces the usual nutrient-rich cold currents. Deprived of sustenance, many organisms die. This effect, which occurs about fourteen times per century, also brings rain to the dry Peruvian coast.

**eluviation** The lateral or downward movement in suspension of clay or other fine particles. The clay-depleted horizon thus formed is an **eluvial horizon** and is found either below or in place of the A *horizon.

**emergent coast** A coastal area which is experiencing uplift. Such coastlines are characteristically staright and are often associated with off shore bars.

**emigration** The movement of people from one country to another. Hence **emigrant**, the person who moves.

**emission standard** The level of pollution which is allowed, by law, into the environment.

**empirical** Based or acting on observation or experiment, not on theory. An empirical view regards sense-data as solid information and strives for objectively verifiable measurements so that knowledge can be derived from experience alone.

**empiricism** The theory that all concepts emanate from experience and that all statements claiming to express knowledge must be based on experience rather than on theory. Valid statements must be based on what can be proved to exist, not on what appears to exist. This is known as ontological privilege since *ontology relates to the being or essence of things. Such statements must be able to be declared true or false without reference to theoretical statements. This is epistemological privilege since *epistemology is the study of knowledge. Knowledge is held to be substantiated by justification derived from observed facts. Empiricism is the basis of scientific knowledge, in geography as in many other disciplines, and many human geographers search for general principles and laws in the light of the data which they have accumulated.

**enclave** A small area within one country administered by another country. Between 1945 and 1990 West Berlin was an enclave within East Germany.

**enclosure** The fencing of once common land into private ownership, most significantly in England in the sixteenth and eighteenth centuries.

**enculturation** The inculcation of a person or persons with the culture in which they grow up.

**endemic** Occurring within a specified locality; not introduced.

**end moraine** See terminal *moraine.

**endogenetic, endogenic** Meaning 'from within'.
1. In geomorphology, this refers to those forces operating below the crust which are involved in the formation of surface features.
2. In human geography, it is those forces acting from within.
Compare with *exogenetic.

**endoreic** Flowing inwards, particularly to an inland drainage basin.

**energy** The physical capacity for doing work. Nearly all our energy derives from the sun, and technical progress has reflected more and more sophisticated uses of energy, from wind and water, through fossil fuels, to nuclear power. World demand for energy has increased so much that an energy crisis has now been identified and conservation of fuel reserves is recommended.

Energy resources are commonly divided into non-renewable—fossil fuels—and renewable—wind, water, and solar power.

**enforcement notice** A notice requiring the perpetrator of unpermitted development to comply with planning regulations.

**englacial** Within a glacier, as in englacial *moraine.

**enhancement** The processing and sharpening of an image received by a *remote sensor, such as a satellite. Contrasts between tones are heightened. The operator can choose to enhance each *band differently or to base the enhancement on only part of the area, for example, cropland only.

**Enterprise Zone** In Britain, an area of a declining economy or of derelict land which is chosen for *rejuvenation. Private enterprise is attracted by such inducements as tax concessions, the provision of buildings, subsidized consultancy advice, and a relaxation of planning regulations.

**entisol** In *US soil classification, a young soil, high in mineral content and without developed soil *horizons. See *ranker.

**entrainment** The picking up and setting into motion of particles, either by wind or by water. The main entrainment forces are provided by impact, *lift force, and *turbulence. Collision between particles is an important process where the lifting agent is air.

**entrepôt** A point of transhipment between nations where goods are held without incurring customs duties.

**entrepreneur** An organizer, singly or in partnership, who takes risks in creating, investing in, and developing a *firm from its inception through to hoped-for profitability as goods and services are marketed. The enterprise of the entrepreneur can be seen as a fourth *factor of production, but other writers would classify it as a form of labour.

**entropy** A measure of the disorder within a system. Left to itself, an initially ordered state is virtually certain to randomize as time passes. Thus, it is the tendency of a system to move from a less probable to a more probable state.

**entropy maximization procedure** A method of making the best estimate of a probability distribution from the limited information available. Entropy may be seen as a measure of a system's disorder, and maximum entropy is maximum disorder within a system. Maximum entropy can be thought of as the most probable state within a system subject to constraints. Maximum entropy is the most likely state since everything tends to disorder.

The entropy maximization procedure is held to be superior to the *gravity model because it lacks the *determinism of that model and because it can be applied to more complex situations. The procedure has not been without its detractors who note that, as in the gravity model, no attention is paid to individual evaluation.

**environment** The surroundings. The **natural environment** includes the nature of the living space—sea or land, soil or water—, the chemical constituents and physical properties of the living space, the climate, and the assortment of other organisms present. The **phenomenal environment** includes changes and modifications of the natural environment made by man. The effect of the environment on man is modified, in part, by the way the environment is perceived and human geographers distinguish this—the **subjective environment**—from the **objective environment**—the real world as it is. The objective environment is of less importance to the individual than his perceived image of it. A division may also be made between the man-made **built environment** and the **social environment** which is made up of the various fields of economic, social, and political interactions.

**environmental air** In meteorology, the stationary air surrounding a 'parcel' of air moving vertically.

**environmental determinism** The view that man's activities are governed by the environment, primarily the physical environment. Man is held to build up his knowledge by encountering the world through his senses and to be unable to transcend his responses to the environment. He is at the mercy of environmental stimuli. This rather crude view of human behaviour has come under fierce criticism and has been, in part, displaced by *environmentalism, *possibilism, and *probabilism.

**environmental hazard** Sources of danger which arise in the environment. Most of these are natural hazards such as hurricanes, floods, droughts, earthquakes, and volcanoes. It has been noted that human beings consistently underrate natural hazards; the growth of San Francisco did not halt after the earthquake of 1902, nor, for that matter, after the minor shocks of 1989. Other hazards are man-made—pollution, oil spills, and pesticides for example.

**environmental impact** A change in the make-up, working, or appearance of the environment. These changes may be planned, like afforestation, or accidental, like the introduction of Dutch elm disease into Britain. Most accidental impacts bring about undesirable change, and deliberate actions may have an unexpected impact, as when the construction of a sea wall leads to the destruction of a beach. Sometimes the damage is irreversible, like the introduction of DDT into food webs.

**Environmental impact assessment, EIA**, seeks to consider the probable consequences of human intervention in the environment so as to restrict environmental damage. The US National Environmental Policy Act of 1969 required such an assessment to be drawn up for all major federal developments, giving information about the technology and location of the development, an appraisal of the likely environmental effects, both positive and negative, an outline of possible alternatives, and an estimate of any irreversible commitment of scarce resources.

**environmentalism** A concern for the environment, and especially with the bond between man and the environment, not solely in terms of technology but also in ethical terms—we are reminded of the necessity for sharing and conservation. Man is seen as having a responsibility for his environment.

The term may also be used as a synonym for *environmental determinism, but stressing the influence of the environment rather than control by the environment.

**environmental lapse rate** The fall in temperature of stationary air with height, averaging 6 °C per 1000 m.

**environmentally sensitive area** A fragile *ecosystem which will be maintained only by conscious attempts to protect it.

**environmental perception** The way in which an individual perceives the environment. This is the basis of a person's attitude to daily life and of any decisions made. It is suggested that environmental perception can be seen as a five-stage model:
1. An emotional response.
2. An orientative response with the construction of *mental maps.
3. A classifying response as the individual sorts out the incoming information.
4. An organizing response as the individual sees causes and effects in the information.

5. A manipulative response as the individual seeks to change the environment.

**environmental psychology** A study concerned with the ways in which man perceives his environment. Man can interact with the environment by interpretation, evaluation, operation, and response. Much of *behavioural geography is concerned with the first two processes as in the description of *images, *milieus, and *mental maps.

**environmental studies** Those studies, such as ecology, meteorology, or urban geography, where the links between such subjects are stressed and which aim to make people aware of their environment.

**eolian** *aeolian.

**epeirogeny** Broad vertical movements of the earth's crust which do not involve much alteration in the structure of the rock.

**ephemeral** Short-lived. *r-selected plants are ephemeral in that they grow and reproduce rapidly when conditions are favourable, dying within a short space of time. **Ephemeral streams** flow only during and after intense rain. Such streams are typical of arid and semi-arid areas.

**epicentre** The point of the earth's surface which is directly above the *focus of an earthquake.

**epidemic** A rapidly spreading outbreak of disease in a particular location. **Epidemiology** is the study of those factors which influence the spread of disease.

**epilimnion** The upper layer of a body of water. Light penetrates the epilimnion so that *photosynthesis can occur. This zone is generally warmer, and contains more oxygen, than the layers below.

**epiphyte** A plant growing on another plant but using it only for support and not for food. Epiphytes are most common in areas of *tropical rain forest.

**epistemology** The philosophical theory of knowledge. One view is that justification distinguishes genuine knowledge. Different types of knowledge may be recognized: knowledge-how, knowledge-of, and knowledge-that. In geography, the term is used to indicate the examination of geographical knowledge—how it is gained, sent, changed, and absorbed.

**epochs** The subdivisions of the units of geological time known as *periods. Thus, the Pleistocene epoch is part of the Quaternary period.

**equator** The imaginary *great circle around the world at latitude 0°. The equator is equidistant between the North and South Poles. It has a length of 40 076 km—about 2500 miles. Hence, **equatorial**—pertaining to the equator—and, for example, **equatorial air mass**.

**equatorial current** The surface movement of an *ocean current near the equator. In the Northern Hemisphere the north equatorial current flows from the west or northwest. The southern equatorial current, south of the equator, flows from the south-east or east.

**equatorial rain forest** See *tropical rain forest.

**equatorial trough** A narrow zone of low pressure, between the two belts of *trade winds, arising from high *insolation, especially in the midst of continents in summer. It is also known as the *Inter-Tropical Convergence Zone (ITCZ). The equatorial trough, also known as the equatorial front, is not constant in position, breadth, or intensity; from time to time it disappears completely. This zone also includes the *doldrums.

**equifinality** In the study of systems, the recognition that different initial states can lead to similar end states.

**equilibrium** A state of balance. In *dynamic equilibrium, inputs are balanced by outputs so that the status quo remains.

**equilibrium line** In glaciology, the point at which expansion of the glacier by accumulation is outstripped by losses of ice through *ablation. Snow does not remain below the equilibrium line throughout the warmer season.

**equilibrium species** These species show characteristics which are consonant with a stable *niche. Persistence of individuals enables the species to survive. Dispersal is less important and perseverance is more significant than recovery from adverse conditions. The survival of the young is more important than high fecundity. Large desert plants exhibit these properties. They grow rapidly in the rains and, unlike *opportunist species, put most of their energy into growth and conservation of resources. Reproduction is a rare event; some species may set seed only once in several years, as with cacti. See *$r$-selection, $k$-selection.

**equinox** Having a day and night of equal length. In Britain, these conditions prevail at the spring (vernal) equinox—21 March—and the autumnal equinox—22 September. Strong winds associated with the equinox are **equinoctial gales**.

**era** The largest unit of geological time. The approximate datings of the eras are shown in the table.

| Era | Duration in millions of years BP |
|---|---|
| **Precambrian** | 4 600–570 |
| **Paleozoic** | 570–225 |
| **Mesozoic** | 225–65 |
| **Cainozoic** | 65–0 |

**erg** Arid, sandy desert.

**erosion** The removal of part of the land surface by wind, water, gravity, or ice. These agents can only transport matter if the material has first been broken up by weathering. Some writers have claimed that erosion refers only to the transport of debris; *denudation includes the weathering as well as the transport of rocks. This is a narrow interpretation of the word.

**erosional neck** See *neck.

**erosion surface** A relatively level surface produced by erosion. Not all erosion surfaces are flat, and the term *planation surface is reserved for level erosion surfaces.

**erratic** A large boulder of rock differing from the *lithology of the *country rock on which it rests. The boulder has been moved on the surface of a glacier.

**ERTS** Earth Resources Technology Satellite. See *LANDSAT.

**eruption** The movement, whether gently or explosively, of gases, liquids, or solids from a vent or fissure in the earth's crust, forming a volcano.

**escarpment** A more or less continuous line of steep slopes, facing in the same direction and caused by the erosion of folded rock. Some writers use the term as a synonym for *cuesta.

**esker** A long ridge of material deposited from *meltwater streams running, subglacially, roughly parallel to the direction of ice flow. In many cases, mounds occur along the length of the feature, perhaps where a temporary delta has formed. Such a feature is a **beaded esker**.

**estancia** A large farming estate in Spanish-speaking Latin America, particularly in Argentina.

**estuary** That area of a river mouth which is affected by sea tides, hence **estuarine**. An estuary differs from a *delta in that the former debouches into the sea whereas the latter *progrades seaward.

**eta index, η** An expression of the relationship between a network as a whole and its *edges:

$$\eta = \frac{C}{e}$$

where $C$ = total length of all the edges in the network, $e$ = number of edges in the network.

**étang** A shallow lake separated from the sea by a bar or ridge of shingle or sand.

**etchplain** A tropical *planation surface where deep weathering has etched into the bedrock. The removal by streams of this weathered rock may lay the etchplain bare.

**ethnic group** A group within a larger society which has its own distinctive culture and customs. Ethnic groups usually formed originally as a result of migration—forced or voluntary—or by conquest. **Ethnocentricity**, is the awareness of one's own ethnic group, hence **ethnocentrism**, thinking one's own ethnic group to be more important or superior.

**ethnography, ethology** In some classifications, these are synonyms for anthropology. In English either term denotes descriptive anthropology.

**euphotic zone** The upper layer of a body of water receiving light and thus where *photosynthesis is possible.

**European Community** See *EC.

**European Free Trade Association** See *EFTA.

**eustasy** A world-wide change of sea-level, which may be caused by the growth and decay of ice sheets (**glacio-eustasy**), by the deposition of sediment, or by a change in the volume of the oceanic basins.

**eutrophic** Fertile, productive, usually of lakes. **Eutrophication** is the process by which *ecosystems, usually lakes, become more fertile environments as detergents, sewage, and agricultural fertilizers flow in. The response to this enhanced fertility in a lake is *algal bloom.

**evaporation** The changing of a liquid into a vapour, or gas, at a temperature below the boiling point of that liquid.

Evaporation occurs at the surface of a liquid, and energy is required to release the molecules from the liquid into the gas. The use of this energy, known as latent heat, causes the temperature of the liquid to fall.

**evaporite** A deposit formed when mineral-rich water evaporates. The most common evaporites are gypsum (calcium sulphate) and halite (sodium chloride).

**evapotranspiration** The release of water vapour from the earth's surface by evaporation and **transpiration**. Transpiration is the biological process whereby plants lose water vapour, mainly through pores in their leaves. This water is usually replaced by a continuous flow of water moving upwards from the roots. Rates of evapotranspiration vary with factors such as the temperature and humidity of the air, wind speed, plant type, and the nature of the land surface. Since evapotranspiration is so variable, physical geographers prefer to use the concept of **potential evapotranspiration** (**PET**). This is the greatest amount of water vapour which could be diffused into the atmosphere given unlimited supplies of water.

*Lysimeters may be used to measure PE, and various formulae have been devised to predict it.

**everglade** In Florida, a wetland with small islands and with trees covered by moss. The term may be extended to similar regions elsewhere.

**evergreen** A plant which keeps its leaves throughout the year instead of losing them seasonally. Most evergreens have some defence against water loss in the winter in the form of needle-like or waxy leaves.

**evolution** The change in attributes of a species over a long period of time such that a different species emerges. See *natural selection.

**evorsion** The erosion of rock or sediments in a river or stream bed. *Hydraulic action and *fluid stressing are the predominant processes in this form of erosion.

**exclave** A portion of a nation which lies beyond national boundaries as with West Berlin between 1945 and 1990. This type of territory is also an *enclave in terms of the host country.

**exfoliation** The *sheeting of rocks and their disintegration. This is also known as onion weathering. An **exfoliation dome** is a single, dome-shaped body of massive rock revealed through sheeting, probably as a result of *pressure release.

**exhumation** The removal of young deposits to reveal the underlying structure of older rocks.

**existentialism** A doctrine which emphasizes the difference between human existence and that of inanimate objects. Later proponents of the concept saw man as a self-created being who is not initially endowed with characteristics but chooses his own characteristics by 'leaps'. Thus a person may be said to believe in God because he has chosen to do so. Other existentialists see that the only certainty for man is death and the individual must live in the knowledge of that certainty. Human beings have paradoxical relationships with other people. In geography, existentialism sees man as striving to build up a self which is not given, either by nature or by a culture. Human beings are thus not rational decision-makers but the subjects of their experiences. Landscapes are seen through the eyes of the beholder.

**exogenetic** 1. Applying to processes which occur at or near the earth's surface.

2. In human geography, as a result of outside, environmental influences.

Compare with *endogenetic, endogenic.

**exoreic** Of drainage, flowing to the sea.

**exotic** Introduced from a foreign country, like rhododendrons in North Wales, or rabbits in Australia.

**expanded foot glacier** A small *piedmont glacier, formed when a valley glacier spreads out from the mouth of the valley making a broad mass of ice stretching out on to the lowland.

**expanded town** A town which has agreed to house *overspill population from large cities in order to relieve pressure on housing there. Expanded towns were introduced in Britain in the Town Development Act of 1952 so that local authorities with housing problems could co-operate with the receiving towns in rehousing some of their people. The rationale was that the receiving town would also benefit from the operation in that the new supplies of labour would stimulate its economy. Certain government grants were available to help with the building programme.

**expatriate** A person living, and possibly working, for some time in a foreign country.

**exponential growth model** This presupposes that population will grow exponentially through time until it reaches a ceiling beyond which population exceeds resources. At this point population growth becomes a problem, as it is highly unlikely that *zero population growth will occur. More likely are the checks proposed by *Malthus including famine, disease, and war. It is possible that society, becoming aware of the approaching crisis, will make a progressive adjustment and population growth will slacken.

**exposure** In geology, an outcrop of bare rock, either revealed naturally or by human agency.

**extended family** A family unit which consists of relatives by blood and by marriage as well as two parents and their children.

**extending flow** The extension and thinning of a glacier, often marked by an ice-fall. Extending flow can transmit material from the surface of a glacier to its base, thus increasing its powers of *abrasion. It is typical of the zone of accumulation of ice.

**extensive agriculture** Farming with low inputs of capital and labour, generally with low yields per acre. It is associated with regions of cheap available land where high revenues are unimportant.

**external economies** The benefits of locating near factors which are external to a firm, such as locally available skilled labour, training, and research and development facilities.

**externality** A side-effect on others following from the actions of an individual or group. This effect is not brought by those affected and may be unwished for. Thus, while the acquisition of a car may benefit one household by improving mobility, it generates pollution and is an obstruction to the detriment of others. Externalities may be positive or negative and two types are recognized: **public behaviour externalities** covering property, maintenance, crime, and public behaviour, and **status externalities** resulting from the social and ethnic standing of the household.

**extinct volcano** A volcano no longer liable to erupt.

**extractive agriculture** Any farming method adopted for short-term benefit rather than for long-term conservation.

**extractive industry** The extraction of *non-renewable resources; *primary industry, with the exception of agriculture. Forestry is sometimes excluded from this classification.

**extrapolation** The prediction of a value made by projecting into the future the trend that a set of data exhibits.

**extra-tropical cyclone** An area of low pressure outside the tropics; a *mid-latitude depression.

**extremes** Of temperature, the highest and lowest *shade or mean temperatures. An **extreme climate** has a large temperature range over the year.

**extrusion** A formation of rock made of *magma which has erupted onto the earth's surface as lava and has then solidified. The crystals in **extrusive rocks** are small, since the lava solidifies rapidly, giving little time for crystal growth.

**extrusive rock** See *extrusion.

**ex-works pricing** See *f.o.b. pricing.

**eye** The calm area at the centre of a *hurricane (tropical cyclone).

**eyot** In England, an old term for a small island. The term survives in many English place names, such as Hinksey.

# F

**fabric** In geomorphology, the physical make-up of a rock or sediment. **Fabric analysis** may be carried out to determine the *dip and orientation of particles in the sediment and thus to derive information about its origin.

**facies** The characteristics of a rock which distinguish it from other formations and give some indication of its mode of origin.

**factor** Anything that partly, or entirely, influences an outcome.

**factor analysis** A *multivariate statistical technique. Original, unique data are replaced by a smaller number of more fundamental, uncorrelated, hypothetical components. Factor analysis ignores the aspects of each variable which are not correlated with any other. It attempts to determine a possible underlying pattern of relationships so that the data may be reordered and reduced to a smaller set of factors from which it is possible to select the *dependent variables.

**factors of production** The requirements for production, usually represented as capital, labour, and land. Fixed capital includes the physical plant, buildings, and machinery, while circulating capital includes raw materials and components.

Labour may be unskilled, semi-skilled, or skilled, and local labour markets vary in the size and nature of the pool of labour. Cheap unskilled and semi-skilled labour may be an important locational factor for *multinational corporations while skilled labour is significant in high-technology industries. Industries may be capital- or labour-intensive. Management skills can be a vital factor of labour or can be seen as a separate factor of production under the heading of *entrepreneurship.

Land may be a source of raw material, as in mining, and is an increasingly important factor as modern factories extend on one level and require space for storage and parking.

**factory farming** A system of livestock farming in which animals are kept indoors throughout the greater part of their lives in conditions of very restricted mobility. Pigs, laying hens, broiler chickens, and veal calves are the animals most often kept under these conditions. Factory farming leads to a standardized product raised *en masse*.

**factory system** A concentration of the processes of manufacturing under one roof such that there is a substantial output of standardized products. Specialized machines are used, and the labour force, directed by the management, is deployed for a variety of distinctly different processes.

**fall** A form of *mass movement in which fractured rock and soil separates into blocks and falls away from the parent slope. **Debris falls** and **earth falls** occur on cliffs as joints weaken or as the slope is undercut. **Rock falls** occur on high and steep rock slopes and are of major importance in rock slope erosion.

**fall-line** A line of a scarp down which a number of rivers fall. The term applied originally to the eastern scarp of the Appalachian Mountains.

**fallow** Agricultural land which is not used for crops but is left in order to restore its natural fertility. **Summer fallow** is the practice of leaving the ground uncultivated during a long, dry spell. **Three-year fallow** is part of the *three-field system. See also *bush fallow.

**false bedding** A synonym for *current bedding.

**false colour** In *remote sensing, the colour on an image assigned to *bands normally invisible to the human eye such as infrared radiation.

**false drumlin** A drumlin-shaped hill formed when a rock outcrop is coated with a layer of *till.

**false origin** The arbitrary point from which a grid system is imposed upon a map. See *true origin.

**fan** See *alluvial fan.

**FAO** See *Food and Agriculture Organization.

**farm fragmentation** The division of a farmer's land into a collection of scattered lots. Fragmentation is usually the result of inheritance but may also reflect present processes like *bush fallowing and past processes like the *three-field system. Farms may be composed of as many as twenty different plots, restricting mechanization. Consolidation programmes have been initiated by many central governments.

**farm rent** Regular payments from a tenant farmer to a landlord. Rent varies with the quality of the land, the size and location of the holding, and the length of the tenancy.

**fast ice** Sea ice which is firmly joined to the coast.

**fast reactor** A nuclear reactor fuelled by plutonium which has been produced as a by-product from a *nuclear power station. The reactor is cooled by liquid sodium, which transfers the heat from the reaction to boil water. The resulting steam drives a turbine to create electricity.

**fathom** A measurement of water depth; 6 ft or 1.829 m.

**fault** A fractured surface in the earth's crust along which rocks have travelled relative to each other. The slope of the fault is know as the *dip. Where rocks have moved down the dip there is a **normal fault**; where rocks have moved up the dip, there is a **reverse fault**. A **thrust fault** is a reverse fault where the angle of dip is very shallow and an **overthrust fault** has a nearly horizontal dip. A **fault plane** is the surface against which the movement takes place. A **tear fault** is where movement along the fault plane is lateral.

Regions that are split by faults into upland *horsts or depressed *rift valleys are said to be **block faulted**.

**fault block** A section of country rock demarcated by faults and which has usually been affected by *tectonic movement.

**fault breccia** A rock composed of shattered fragments, broken when movement occurred along a fault.

**fault plane** The face over which movement occurs during faulting.

**fault scarp** A steep slope resulting from the movement of rock strata down the *dip of a normal fault.

**fault spring** A spring emerging at a fault where *impermeable rock is found below or beside a *permeable rock.

**fauna** Animal life.

**faunal realms** The simplest groupings of the animals of the world. The **holarctic** realm covers two subdivisions: the **nearctic** (almost all of North America, with Greenland) and the **palearctic** (Asia north of the tropics, Europe, and Africa north of the Sahara). The **neo-tropical** realm covers Central and South America, and the **ethiopian** embraces Africa south of the Sahara and Arabia. The **oriental** realm is Asia south of the tropics with an ill-defined boundary between it and the **australian** realm, which includes New Zealand, Australia, Oceania, and some of South-East Asia.

**favela** In Brazil, a *shanty town, usually found just beyond the city.

**fazenda** In Brazil, a very large estate originally granted to early Portuguese settlers.

**fecundity** The potential of a woman or of women in a society to bear live children. Fecundity in a population is, thus, closely linked to the proportion of women of child-bearing age.

**federalism** A two-tier system of government. The higher, central government is concerned with matters which affect the whole nation such as defence and foreign policy, while a lower, regional authority takes responsibility for local concerns such as education, housing, and planning.

Federations are designed to preserve regional characteristics within a united nation.

**feedback** The response to an action or process. **Negative feedback** causes the situation to revert to the original. For example, as population expands, its food supply per individual is diminished; the result is that the level of the population begins to fall. **Positive feedback** causes a change in the status quo; thus as medical practices improve, population increases.

**feldspar** A white or pink crystalline mineral, largely formed of alumino-silicates of barium, calcium, potassium, and sodium. Feldspars are abundant in *metamorphic rocks.

**fell** In northern England, a rocky upland of *moors or rough grazing.

**felsenmeer** A surface of broken rock fragments found in *periglacial environments. The fragments are the result of the *frost shattering of exposed bedrock.

**feminist geography** A geography which emphasizes the oppression of women and the inequality of men and women. For example, men see their homes as completely separate from their workplace such that they design suburbs as places to relax in, rather than to work in each day. It is argued that women's access to a range of goods and services is more restricted than men's, and that gender affects *environmental perception—there is no doubt that women's views of safe and unsafe environments are different from men's.

Other themes concern the geography of women's issues, like abortion laws, women as wage-earners, and women's access to education, income, health care, and day care.

It is maintained that an understanding of the social concepts of femininity and masculinity help us to understand changes in, for example, the location of paid employment. It is also argued that in social research the gender of the researcher may influence the result.

**fen** A waterlogged lowland with alkaline or slightly acid soil and colonized by water-loving plants. It takes its name from the low-lying Fens of eastern England around the Wash. See *bog.

**feral** Wild. The term is particularly applied to a plant or animal which was once *domesticated.

**ferrallitization** The combined effect on a soil of the strong *leaching and intense weathering found in the tropics. **Ferrallitic soils** are a characteristic of the tropical rain forest. Destruction of organic residues is very rapid, so that there is little *humus. Most of the bases and some of the silica is leached away. The B2 *horizon is massively impregnated with *sesquioxides which form a hard pan rich in clays. This pan is often exposed by erosion of the upper horizons. In *US soil classification, ferrallitic soils are oxisols.

**Ferrel's law** This states that a body moving over the earth will be deflected to its right in the Northern Hemisphere and to its left in the Southern Hemisphere. This occurs as a result of the earth's rotation and applies particularly to movements of the atmosphere.

**ferric, ferriferous** Containing iron.

**ferricrete** A soil *horizon made up of the *cementation of iron oxides at or near the land surface. Ferricrete forms a very hard layer which has been used as building bricks.

**ferromagnesian minerals** Dark, heavy minerals high in iron and magnesium.

**ferruginous** Of or containing iron or iron rust. A **ferruginous soil** is a *zonal soil developed in warm temperate climates without a dry season, or in the tropical *savanna or bushlands. These soils develop to a great depth because of the intensity of tropical weathering. The A *horizon is a dark red-brown with a weak crumbling structure. The B horizon is stained red by the ferruginous gravel present. In *US soil classification, a ferruginous soil is an ultisol.

**Fertile Crescent** The area of land between the Tigris and Euphrates rivers which saw the very early development of *irrigation and *drainage systems.

**fertility** The ability to bear live children. *Birth rate is the simplest and commonest measure but it does not indicate the number of women of childbearing age. The **general fertility rate** gives the number of births in a year per 1000 women of reproductive age, generally given as being between 15 and 45. Sometimes this is given as 15 to 49. Fertility rates vary because of a number of factors which include availability of land in rural societies, death rate, public health programmes, access to birth control, income, female employment opportunities, industrialization, *modernization, and customs of age at marriage, celibacy, and inheritance.

**fetch** The distance that a sea wave has travelled from its initiation to the coast where it breaks.

**feudalism** A system, common in Europe in the Middle Ages, where access to farm land was gained by service to the owner—the feudal lord. Initially, no money was involved in transactions between the serf and the lord, although the payment of cash in lieu of service became common in the later Middle Ages.

**fiard, fjärd** An inlet of the sea with low banks on either side. These are not to be confused with fiords, since they lack the characteristic steep walls.

**field capacity** The volume of water which is the maximum that a soil can hold in its *pores after excess water has been drained away; the state of a soil in this condition.

**field drainage** See *drain.

**field system** The layout and use of fields. Different communities have given rise to different systems. The extent and use of fields varies with the natural environment, the nature of the crops and livestock produced, and aspects of the culture of the farming community such as inheritance rights and available technology. A major element of field system study has been the pattern and evolution of medieval field systems with the distinction between communally organized common fields and open fields which were not available to the community.

**filling** In meteorology, the movement of air into a *low so that the *atmospheric pressure rises and the depression dies away.

**fill-in migration** As an individual moves from a small to a large city, a vacuum is created in the smaller centre which is filled by someone moving out of an adjacent rural area.

**filter-down process** In the early stages of an industrial development specialist skills are usually required, and consequently activity is concentrated in places of industrial sophistication. As the production process is rationalized and made into a routine, less skill is needed. Wage rates are now too high for the low levels of skill needed and industries therefore seek out industrial backwaters where the cheaper labour can handle the lesser demands of the simplified process. Thus, innovation filters down from the more advanced to the less sophisticated regions. Some writers believe that the evidence for a filter-down process does not appear to be very strong.

**filtering down** The movement of progressively less affluent individuals into housing stock. It is suggested that the rich move away from the city to newly built houses because their old houses are out of date, difficult to maintain, or surrounded by types of land use which are not appealing. The next social and occupational class moves into the houses vacated by the rich. Homes are subdivided and passed on to successively poorer groups.

It is by no means true that only the rich move into new homes, as public housing schemes have attested. Many higher-status housing areas have managed to withstand infiltration by poorer social groups. It is also the case that the well-off invade run-down areas in the reverse process—*gentrification.

**finger lake** A long, narrow lake in a *glacial trough.

**finger plan** The development of new towns or suburbs along routes, road or rail, radiating from the city centre. Planners see commuting as a fact of life, which should be made as efficient as possible.

**fiord, fjord** A long, narrow arm of the sea which is the result of the 'drowning' of a glaciated valley. Fiords are distinctive both because of their great depth and because of the overdeepening of their middle sections, which are deeper than the water at the mouth. The shallow bar at the seaward end of the fiord is thought to represent the spreading and lowering of ice as it was released from its narrow valley and spread out over the lowland.

**fire ecology** The study of the effects of fire on *ecosystems. These are not always deleterious; it is suggested that some ecosystems, like those of the *coniferous forests, depend on fire to evolve fully. Many ecosystems like *savanna or *garigue have resulted from fire, usually man-made, although fires do occur naturally from lightning strikes.

**firm** An independent unit which utilizes the *factors of production to produce goods and services. Revenue is kept high enough to cover costs and to generate profit. It should be noted that whereas the creation of profit is the key objective of a firm, businessmen have other motives in addition to profit, such as increased managerial satisfaction. It should also be noted that in a purely capitalist society it is numbers of individual firms who make decisions rather than an industry as a whole.

**firn** Ice formed when falls of snow fail to melt from one season to another. As further snow accumulates, its weight presses on earlier snow, compacting and melting it to a mass of globular particles of ice with interconnecting air spaces. Further snow fall, and further compaction, drives out the air spaces and turns the firn to pure ice. Where temperatures are around 0 ˚C, snow can turn to firn within five years. The process takes much longer in very cold conditions. An alternative term for firn is névé.

**firn line** The *equilibrium line in a glaciated upland.

**First World** Before 1990, those countries in Western Europe, Australasia, North America, and Japan which have some version of a capitalist, free-market economy. With political change in Eastern Europe, once part of the *Second World, the First and Second Worlds may become increasingly less distinct.

**firth** In Scotland, a narrow arm of the sea, as in an *estuary or a *strait.

**fish farming** The rearing of fish in man-made pools or tanks. Fish farming has been practised for thousands of years using ponds and fenced-off enclosures of rivers to rear fish. Manuring has traditionally taken place by raising ducks and allowing their droppings to fall into the water. Careful control of the fish is required to prevent losses from disease which would spread rapidly in the confined conditions of the tanks. Recently this has been achieved by routine dosing of the water with antibiotics and other chemicals.

**Fission** A nuclear reaction in which a heavy nucleus (such as uranium) splits into two parts which subsequently emit either two or three neutrons, releasing energy. Nuclear fission can be used to make electricity.

**fission track dating** Minerals and glasses of volcanic origin contain traces of a radioactive *isotope of uranium. This isotope decays by spontaneous fission and the resulting fragments tear into the surrounding material, leaving tracks of about 10 micrometres in length. The number of such tracks indicates the age of the volcanic matter.

**fissure** A long, narrow opening made by cracking or splitting.

**fissure eruption** A volcanic eruption where *lava wells up through fissures in the earth's crust and spreads over a large area. Fissure eruptions are usually of very fluid *basic lava.

**fixation line** Certain controls to the growth of a town which stucture the plan of the town. Old town walls act as very influential fixation lines. Growth of the town then spreads out in a radial pattern based on the fixation lines.

**fjeld** A rocky upland, specifically in Norway.

**fjord** *fiord.

**Flandrian** The time succeeding the most recent glacial stage. During this time, there has been a global rise in sea level known as the **Flandrian transgression** due to the melting of *ice sheets and *glaciers.

**flash flood** Usually in a semi-arid area, a sudden and very violent flood, often caused by unusually heavy rain.

**flashy** In hydrology, applied to a natural water course which responds rapidly to a storm event.

**F-layer** Part of the *ionosphere, about 250 km above the earth's surface; this layer can reflect high-frequency radio waves.

**flexure** The bending of rock strata under pressure.

**flocculation** In soil science, the process whereby very small particles aggregate to form *crumbs. The term is usually applied to clays. In certain *subsoils of arid areas, downward *translocation of soluble salts leads to the breakdown of these crumbs in the process of **deflocculation**.

**flood control** The averting of the chance of a dangerous flood—a **flood hazard**—by, for example, deepening existing channels and digging new ones, erecting dams or *barrages, and *afforestation.

**flood frequency analysis** The calculation of the statistical probability that a flood of a certain magnitude for a given river will occur in a certain period of time. Each flood of the river is recorded and ranked in order of magnitude with the highest rank being assigned to the largest flood. The *return period here is the likely time interval between floods of a given magnitude and can be calculated as:

$$\frac{\text{number of years of river records} + 1}{\text{rank of a given flood}}$$

**flood plain** The relatively flat land stretching from either side of a river to the bottom of the valley walls. Flood plains are periodically inundated by the river water; hence the name. The flood plain may be thought of as an area of *alluvium which is introduced to the valley, stored, subjected to weathering, and then transported downstream.

**flood stage** A stage of a river when it overflows its banks.

**flood tide** The landward movement of the tide from low to high tide.

**flora** Plant life.

**floral, floristic realms** These may be recognized and mapped as areas characterized by the indigenous plant species and not by the *biome. Thus, the Brazilian rain forest is part of the Latin American floral realm.

**flow** 1. The movement of goods, people, services, and information along a *network. This movement can be mapped, routing the flow along the path used and constructing the thickness of the line in proportion to the volume of traffic along it. This is a **flow line graph**.
2. The *mass movement of material held in suspension by water. Flows are classified by the size of the particles: **debris flow** refers to coarse material; **earth flow** to soil; and **mud flow** to clay. Flows may be the result of very high water pressure in the *debris and can occur in clay if the particles have absorbed a great deal of water before they are *entrained.

**flowage** The movement of solids such as ice or rock without fracturing. In such cases, the term *plastic flow is equally applicable.

**flow chart** A diagram showing the route and volume of any movement. On the diagram, the width of the route varies with the volume of the movement.

**fluidization** The cracking of a fine-grained rock as hot gas moves through it. The gas also enlarges existing cracks. The crack may be filled with other substances, such as the diamond-bearing kimberlite.

**fluid stressing** The erosion of weak, cohesive rocks, such as muds, by the force of water in a river. The effect of this force depends, among other factors, on the strength of the bed, the percentage of clay in the bed, the velocity of the water, and the *turbulence of the water.

**flume** A man-made channel which conveys water for some specific purpose. In practical hydrology, a flume is an apparatus placed across a watercourse in order to measure its *discharge.

**fluting and grooving** Those small ridges and hollows caused by the *differential erosion by wind or water of rock strata of varying resistance.

**fluvial** Of, or connected with, rivers.

**fluvial erosion** Erosion by streams or rivers. This involves the destruction of bedrock on the sides and bottom of the river, the erosion of channel banks, and the breaking down of rock fragments into smaller fragments.

**fluvio-glacial** Of, or concerned with, streams and rivers formed from melting glaciers. Hence **fluvio-glacial deposition**.

**flysch** A series of alternating sediments: clays, shales, and sandstones.

**f.o.b. (free-on-board) pricing** Pricing a commodity to include the cost of loading on to freight vehicles at the point of sale but excluding the cost of transporting the goods from the point of sale to the buyer. Ex-works pricing is a synonym.

**focus** The point of origin of an earthquake.

**foehn, föhn** When moist air rises over a mountain barrier, it experiences *adiabatic temperature changes, and cools at the slow Saturated Adiabatic Lapse Rate. Precipitation is common. Once past the mountains, the air, now much drier, descends. It warms at the Dry Adiabatic Lapse Rate (see *adiabatic), higher than the saturated rate by some 3 °C per 1000 metres. A dry, warm, and gusty wind results. See also *chinook.

**fog** A cloud of water droplets suspended in the air, limiting visibility to less than 1000 m.

Fog occurs when vapour-laden air is cooled below *dew point. In **advection fog**, this cooling is brought about as warm, moist air passes over cold *ocean currents, such as the Labrador current. **Radiation fog** forms during cloudless autumn nights when strong *terrestrial radiation causes ground temperatures to fall. Moist air is chilled by contact with the ground surface. The fog lingers until it is dispersed by warm sunlight.

Where cold air streams cross warm seas, **steam fog** such as Arctic smoke forms. **Frontal fog** forms when fine rain falling at a warm front is chilled to *dew point as it falls through cold air at ground level.

**foggara** In North-West Africa, a gently sloping underground channel bringing water from the uplands.

**fold** A buckled, bent, or contorted rock. Folds result from complex processes including fracture, sliding, *shearing, and *flowage.

An arch-like upfold is an **anticline** which may be symmetrical or asymmetrical. Hence **anticlinal ridge** and **anticlinal valley**, features which follow the course of the anticline. This is also true of downfolds or **synclines**. A complex anticline is an anticlinorium; a complex syncline is a **synclinorium**. In an **overturned fold** the upper limb of the syncline and the lower limb of the anticline dip in the same direction. In **recumbent folds** the beds in the lower limb of the anticline and the upper limb of the syncline are upside down. See also *nappe.

**fold mountain** An upland area formed by the buckling of the earth's crust. Many fold mountains are associated with destructive or collision margins of *plates.

**foliation** The wavy bands and layers stretching through some *igneous and metamorphic rocks (see *metamorphism).

**Food and Agriculture Organization, FAO** A United Nations organization which supports national programmes designed to increase productivity and conditions in agriculture, fishing, and forestry.

**food chain** A linear sequence representing the nutrition of various species from the simplest plant through to top *carnivores, as in rose → greenfly → ladybird → sparrow → sparrow-hawk. This direct pathway is too simplified. Plants and animals are usually linked together in a *food web. Plants, primary *producers, and *consumers at various *trophic levels are interconnected in their diet and in their role as sources of food.

**food conversion ratio** The ratio of the number of calories of a prey required to produce one calorie for a predator.

**food web** A series of interconnected and overlapping *food chains in an *ecosystem.

**footloose industry** An industry whose location is not influenced strongly by access to either materials or markets.

**foraminifera** Usually marine microorganisms of plankton and *benthic animals with calcite skeletons, found over much of earth's ocean beds. Foraminifera are very sensitive to temperature, and their presence in the fossil record may be used to reconstruct past environments.

**fore-arc basin** A zone at a convergent *plate margin lying seaward of the *volcanic arc and where sediments from adjacent continental masses may accumulate.

**foredeep** A deep, steep-sided ocean trench running roughly parallel to a mountain range or *island arc. A foredeep may become infilled with sediment and may, through *tectonic activity, form part of the land.

**foredune** On a sandy beach, the dune nearest to the sea. Foredunes may form a line along the beach.

**foreland** An area of land jutting out into the sea; a *headland, or cape.

**foreset bed** A bed of sediments laid down at the seaward, inclined edge of a delta or an advancing sand dune.

**foreshore** A vernacular term denoting that part of the seashore between the low- and high-water marks.

**forest park** An area of forestry which, as well as supplying timber, may be used for recreation. Forests provide excellent cover for car parks and picnic sites and may be used for camping and pony trekking. It may be that some areas of forestry are more important for recreation than for their economic value.

**forestry** The management of woodland to provide timber for sale. New areas are ploughed and planted while cut over forests may be replanted. The trees are given fertilizer and are protected from pests, diseases, and major fires. They are felled when the trees are mature, when there is overcrowding, or when the trees die. Most forests in Britain are planted with fast-growing, softwood conifers although *hardwoods may be planted at the periphery to soften the *environmental impact.

**formal game** An exercise in *game theory, as opposed to an informal game which simulates real-world events. See *game theory.

**formal region** A region marked by relative uniformity of characteristics. The variations within the region are less than variations between the region and other areas.

**formation, great plant formation** A major vegetation system, determined by climate e.g. tropical grassland. Thus, a formation is the plant community of a *biome.

**form line** A contour sketched on a map by eye, rather than one based on accurate survey.

**fossil** The *petrified remains, or the imprint of the remains, of a plant or animal, preserved within a rock, usually *sedimentary, but sometimes metamorphic.

**fossil fuel** Any fuel which is found underground, buried within sedimentary rock. Reserves of fossil fuels are dwindling and some writers suggest that all fossil fuels will be used up by 2800 AD.

**fossil water** See *connate water.

**fractile diagram** A plot of a distribution on probability paper to compare it with the *normal distribution which will appear as a straight line.

**fracto-, fractus** Of a cloud, shredded and ragged due to strong winds in the upper atmosphere.

**fracture** In geology, a clean break, caused by compression or *tension, in a layer of rock.

**fragmentation** See *farm fragmentation.

**free** In chemistry, not contained in a compound, as in free oxygen, free nitrogen.

**free face, fall face** An outcrop of rock which is too steep for the accumulation of soil and rock debris.

**freehold** The complete and unrestricted title to land.

**free market** A market which responds to supply and demand and with minimal or no government intervention.

**free port** A port, or part of a port, where customs duties are not payable. Costs are therefore lower, as is insurance and administration.

**free trade** Trade between countries which takes place completely free of restrictions. Such trade allows specialization in member states of free trade areas, and lowers costs because, together with competition, the markets are increased. Within a **free trade zone** there are no barriers, such as *tariffs and *quotas. However, there is not necessarily a common policy on trade with countries outside the free trade zone.

**freeway** In the USA, a multi-lane interstate motorway.

**freeze–thaw** See *frost shattering.

**freezing front** The edge of frozen or partially frozen ground. In areas of seasonal freezing, with no *permafrost, the freezing front moves downward through the earth. In areas of permafrost, the front can also move upwards from the frozen layer below.

**freight rate** This cost of transporting goods (**freight**) reflects a number of factors besides basic transport costs such as the nature of the commodity. Non-breakable, non-perishable items, like coal, are carried most cheaply as they can be carried in bulk on open wagons. The more careful the handling required, the more expensive is the freight rate. Sophisticated manufactured goods can bear high freight rates because of their greater value. Raw materials are carried for less so that they can be moved over greater distances.

Competition between alternative modes of transport can also cut freight rates. Thus, because of competition with the New York State Barge Canal, rail freight rates from Chicago to New York are less than from Chicago to Philadelphia although the latter journey is slightly shorter.

**frequency** The number of times a phenomenon occurs in a given space of time.

**frequency distribution** The range of values of any data set shown by the number of occurrences in a series of classes. The distribution may be shown as a *histogram or the mid-points of each class may be joined up with a line to make a **frequency curve** or **frequency polygon**.

**friable** Easily crumbled; usually referring to soils.

**friction** The force which resists the movement of one surface over another.

Friction between the surfaces of two mineral grains is related to the hardness of the mineral, the roughness of the surface, and the number and area of the points of contact between the grains. Friction is of major significance in any study of the movement of sediment since the forces moving the sediment must be greater than the resistance provided by friction.

**frictional force** In meteorology, the roughness and irregularity of the earth's surface which reduces wind speeds. The **friction layer**, where this effect is strongest, roughly comprises the lowest 100 m of the atmosphere.

**friction of distance** As the distance from a point increases, the interactions with that point decrease. See *distance decay.

**Friedmann's core–periphery model** See *core–periphery model.

**fringe belt** A zone of varied land use at the edge of a town or built-up area. Many of the functions of the fringe belt have been squeezed out from the town centre due to congestion, high land prices, the need for a special site, or disturbances in the central area.

**fringing reef** *Coral reef.

**front** The border zone between two *air masses which contrast, usually in temperature. A **warm front** marks the leading edge of a sector of warm air; a **cold front** denotes the influx of cold air. Fronts are, therefore, *baroclinic zones.

In *mid-latitude depressions, the fronts develop as part of a horizontal wave of warm air enclosed on two sides by cold air. These **frontal wave forms** move from west to east in groups known as **frontal wave families**.

The basic classification into warm fronts, where the boundary is at a low angle of 0.5–1°, and steeper cold fronts is further divided by the type of air movement at the front. In *ana-fronts, the warm sector air is rising, and a succession of cloud types and precipitation results. In *kata-fronts, the warm sector air is descending. Cloud development is restricted and precipitation is reduced to a drizzle.

Traditionally, much weather forecasting has been based on the correct interpretation of fronts. However, recent research would indicate that divergences in the upper air are probably more important than the convergence of air masses in the lower atmosphere.

**frontal** In meteorology, related to a *front, as with **frontal fog** or **frontal rain**.

**frontier** That part of a country which lies on the limit of the settled area. It differs from a boundary because the term frontier indicates outward expansion into an area previously unsettled by a particular state. Some frontiers have occurred where two nations advance from different directions leading to boundary disputes. A **settlement frontier** marks the furthest advance of settlement within a state while the **political frontier** is where the limit of the state coincides with the limit of settlement.

**frontier thesis** A theory put forward by Turner, who held that the westward expansion of the USA was due to the existence of 'free' land in that direction. Expansion was seen as a series of waves moving to the west: the Indian, the fur trader, the hunter, the rancher, and the arable farmer. Each wave moved further away from Europe and contributed to a new society. It is claimed that the process of expansion led to the evolution of an individualism which promoted democracy. This theory has been severely criticized.

**frontogenesis** The development of *fronts and frontal wave forms. Frontogenesis occurs in well-defined areas; for example, Atlantic Polar fronts form off the east coast of North America, while the Arctic front occurs across Canada at around 50 °N. Fronts are less common in the tropics where contrasts between *air masses are less marked.

The change and decay of fronts is known as **frontolysis**.

**frost** Frozen dew or fog forming at, or near ground level. **Black frost**, as the name suggests, is a thin sheet of frost without the white colour usually associated with frost.

Air below 0 °C is **air frost**. **Hoar frost**, or **rime**, is a thick coating of white ice crystals on vegetation and other surfaces. **Ground frost** occurs when the air at ground level is chilled below freezing point.

**frost action** See *congelifraction, *congeliturbation, *frost shattering, *frost cracking, *frost heaving, *frost thrusting.

**frost cracking** This can occur within seasonally thawed ground, but is more a feature of permanently frozen areas. When the frozen ground reaches very low temperatures, it contracts, splitting up to form a pattern of polygonal cracks. The edges around the polygon are lifted when the ground expands, perhaps as the result of slightly warmer temperatures. These polygonal areas are known as sand-wedge or ice-*polygons according to the nature of the material within the crack.

**frost creep** The downslope movement of debris, firstly through the growth of needle-like ice which lifts a thin surface crust at right angles to the ground, followed by thawing which washes the loosened debris downslope. Opinions vary about the efficacy of this process.

**frost heaving** The upward dislocation of soil and rocks by the freezing and expansion of soil water. **Frost push** occurs when cold penetrates into the ground. Large stones become chilled more rapidly than the soil. Water below such stones freezes and expands, pushing up the stones. **Frost pull** can alter the orientation of a large stone, causing it to stand upright. This occurs when ice creeps downwards from the surface. The growth of ice crystals on the upper part and the drying of the soil around the lower part causes the stone to be pulled into a more vertical inclination.

**frost pockets** Concentration of cold air in hollows and in valley floors. This occurs when night-time *terrestrial radiation is greatest on valley slopes. Air above these slopes is colder and hence denser; therefore it flows downslope.

**frost shattering** Also known as freeze–thaw, this is the weathering of rock which occurs when the water which has penetrated the joints and cracks, freezes. Water expands by 9% when it freezes, and it has been suggested that this expansion causes the rock to shatter. Some writers suggest that this force is insufficient to break up all but the softest rocks and what has been called frost shattering is really *hydrofracturing.

**frost smoke** *Arctic sea smoke.

**frost thrusting** The lateral dislocation of soil and rock by the freezing and expansion of water.

**Froude number** The ratio of the velocity ($v$) of a river to its *celerity where celerity is the product of the acceleration due to gravity ($g$) and the mean depth of flow ($d$). The Froude number ($F_e$) is calculated from the equation:

$$F_e = \frac{v}{\sqrt{gd}}$$

where $F_e$ is less than 1, deeper flow is tranquil. Where $F_e$ exceeds 1, the flow is turbulent.

**fugitive species** See *opportunist species.

**fumarole** A vent in a volcano through which steam and volcanic gases are emitted.

**fumigation** In meteorology, polluted air may be trapped beneath an *inversion. Plumes of air may then rise because of *convection, causing downdraughts which return the polluted air to ground level.

**functional classification of cities** A categorization of cities according to the functions they discharge: administration, defence, culture, provision of goods and services, communications, and recreation. In reality, any one city may fulfil a number of functions.

**functional linkage** The link between industries or between an industry and the public. Links create the chains which bind firms together so that the difficulties faced by one firm may have severe repercussions on others. Functional linkages are at the heart of *agglomeration economies.

**functional region** A type of region characterized by its function, such as a city-region or a drainage basin.

**functionalism** Basically, an anthropologist's view of society as an expression of its biological and social needs. The way in which things function must be studied in order to understand their effects.

**fungi** Important in soil science, fungi are a group of simple parasitic plants. Fungi are lacking in chlorophyll and therefore cannot photosynthesize. They attack a wide range of organic residues, such as the woody tissue of plants, and are a major element of the soil-forming processes.

**funnel cloud** A spiral of cloud descending from a low-lying cloud base and meeting the sea.

**fusion** In nuclear fusion, light atomic nuclei are fused with heavier nuclei, giving off energy without losing mass. In 1991, scientists at Culham, in the UK achieved nuclear fusion for the first time.

# G

**gabbro** A coarse-grained, basic igneous rock composed chiefly of calcium-rich plagioclase and pyroxene. Gabbro is formed through the crystallization of basaltic *magma, usually as a large *igneous intrusion deep within the earth's crust.

**Gaia hypothesis** The theory advanced by Lovelock that the earth, its rocks, oceans, atmosphere, and all its forms of life are part of a single organism—Gaia—which has evolved over the span of geological time. It is the health of the planet that matters, not that of some individual species.

**gale force** Of a wind, a speed above 62 km per hour.

**gallery forest** The forest bordering the banks of rivers in an area otherwise treeless.

**game** Not to be confused with formal *game theory, this is the technique of mimicking real-life processes in a game in order to teach the participants an understanding of a particular aspect of reality.

**game theory** This deals with the question of making rational decisions in the face of uncertain conditions by choosing certain strategies in order to outwit an opponent in a **formal game**. In geography, this strategy is often to overcome or outwit the environment and when the environment is unpredictable man has only highly probabilistic notions based on past experience.

Consider a very simplified case. Farmers in the Middle Belt of Ghana can choose either hill rice or maize as a staple crop. The climate may be wet or dry. A pay-off matrix can be set out, showing the likely yield of the crops (Table 1).

TABLE 1

|         | wet | dry |
|---------|-----|-----|
| maize     | 61  | 49  |
| hill rice | 30  | 71  |

The difference between each pair is calculated and, regardless of sign, is assigned to the alternate strategy (Table 2).

TABLE 2

|           | wet | dry |                                        |
|-----------|-----|-----|----------------------------------------|
| maize     | 61  | 49 =12; | $\dfrac{41}{12-41} = 77.4\%$       |
| hill rice | 30  | 71 =41; | $\dfrac{12}{12-41} = 22.6\%$       |

The pay-off matrix shows that more maize than hill rice should be grown but does not say whether the percentages indicate areas of both crops each year or whether maize should be planted in preference to hill rice in seven years out of ten. A further source of difficulty for all pay-off matrices lies in the assigning of values for each cell of the matrix.

**gamma index, γ** In *network analysis, a measure of the *connectivity in a network. It is a measure of the ratio of the number of *edges in a network to the maximum number possible— $\frac{1}{2} n(n-1)$.

$$\gamma = \frac{e}{\frac{1}{2} n (n-1)}$$

where $\gamma$ = gamma index, $e$ = number of edges, $n$ = number of nodes (vertices).

The index ranges from 0—no connections between nodes—to 1.0—the maximum number of connections, with direct links between all the nodes.

**gap town** A town located in a pass through an upland area which benefits from being a focus of routes.

**garden city** A planned settlement, as conceived by Ebenezer Howard, which would offer the benefits of urban living in a spacious environment without the crowded and squalid conditions of the nineteenth century city. Housing densities were to be low and broad roads were to radiate from the city centre. Parks, open spaces, and allotments were to be plentiful. Once the maximum size of the city—about 30 000 inhabitants—was reached there would be no further growth; another city would be developed. In 1903 work began on the building of Letchworth, the first garden city, and in 1919 Welwyn Garden City was founded.

**garden suburb** A planned suburban development with open spaces and low-density housing inspired by the ideas of Ebenezer Howard. Garden suburbs were built in the late nineteenth and early twentieth centuries as in Bedford Park in 1875, and Hampstead Garden Suburb in 1907.

**garigue, garrigue** Xerophytic and evergreen vegetation, found as the result of grazing, browsing, and burning in areas of *Mediterranean climate.

**GATT** The General Agreement on Tariffs and Trade is an arrangement between the states of the free world to encourage the gradual abolition of trade barriers, although each state reserves the right to protectionism if it seems to be necessary.

**gavelkind** The equal distribution of inherited land amongst the male heirs. Land may be left equally to daughters if there are no male heirs.

**GDP, gross domestic product** The total value of the production of goods and services in a nation measured over a year. Components for a finished product are not taken into account; only the finished articles are recorded. The decision as to what constitutes a finished product varies from one country to another.

**geanticline** A very large up-fold, often many hundreds of kilometres across, caused by the compression of sediment in a *geosyncline.

**geest** A heathland area of glacial sands and gravels, especially in north-central Europe.

**gelifluction** The downslope flow of soil in association with ground ice. This occurs in *periglacial environments, where water cannot percolate downwards because of the *permafrost. Spring melts of ice and *ice lenses provide enough lubricant to cause downslope flow. Gelifluction occurs only in areas of permafrost, in contrast to *solifluction.

**gemeinschaft society** A community bound together in a tightly knit pattern which is socially homogeneous and based on a clear-cut piece of territory. Gemeinschaft society is said to be a feature of villages and small towns.

**General Agreements on Tariffs and Trade** See *GATT.

**general circulation of the atmosphere** The world-scale systems of pressure and winds which persist throughout the year or recur seasonally. Such winds transport heat from tropical to polar latitudes, thus maintaining the present patterns of world temperatures.

This **global circulation** is driven by intense differences in *insolation between the tropical and polar regions, and is strongly influenced by the *Coriolis force. Air moves vertically along the *meridians and horizontally with the wind systems, both at ground level and in the upper atmosphere.

**General Systems Theory** See *GST.

**gentrification** The rebuilding, renewing, and *rehabilitation of depressed areas of the inner city as more affluent individuals and families move near to the city centre. Earlier inhabitants move out as leases fall in, houses are sold, or landlords harass their tenants into moving.

**geode** A nodule of rock, hollow at the centre, and with crystals projecting inwards.

**geodesy** The science which deals with the shape and size of the earth.

**geodetic distance** The shortest distance between two points on the earth's surface.

**Geographic Information System, GIS** A store of geographical data in digital form on a computer. Being in numerical form, it is easy to update, and many forms of *remote sensing data can be combined as an information layer in a GIS. GISs are constantly being improved.

**geoid** An earth-shaped body.

**geological inversion** Rock strata which occur in reversed order from geological time because of intense overfolding.

**geology** The study of the rocks of the earth's crust: their formation, development, nature, and landforms.

**geomagnetism** The magnetic field of the earth, also known as terrestrial magnetism. The axis of this field emerges from the earth's surface at the *magnetic poles. The position of these poles varies over time, and sometimes the positions of the north and south magnetic poles switch places. The pattern of the magnetic field at any one time will be preserved in any contemporary *extrusions of volcanic rock. The study of past magnetic fields, **paleomagnetism**, can yield information about the creation of new material at the oceanic ridges, about *continental drift, and about the dating of certain deposits.

**geometric progression** A series of numbers where each number is multiplied by a constant to produce the next, as in 1, 2, 4, 8, . . .

**geomorphology** The study of the nature and history of landforms and the processes which create them.

**geopolitics** The view that location and the physical environment are important factors in the global power structure; the state may be seen as a realm in space. Geopolitics must not be confused with *geopolitik.

**geopolitik** A view of *geopolitics developed in Germany in the 1920s. Individuals are subordinate to the state, which must expand with population growth, claiming more territory—*Lebensraum*—to fulfil its destiny. These ideas were used as a quasi-science by the Nazis to justify their territorial demands.

**geosophy** The study of geographical knowledge. One aspect may be the development of geography as a branch of knowledge; the other relates to human beings as a whole. All human beings have some geographical knowledge although the standpoint of this knowledge may be different from that of a professional geographer. This knowledge may be false but may be acted on in any case. The mind may erect barriers to certain places even though there are now no unexplored parts of the earth. See *mental maps.

**geostationary satellite** A satellite whose speed of orbit matches that of the rotating earth so that it is stationary with regard to the earth. Geostationary satellites are used, for example, for communications, or meteorological *remote sensing.

**geostrophic wind** A theoretical wind, occurring when the force exerted on the air by the *pressure gradient is equal to the opposing *Coriolis force. The net result is a wind blowing parallel to the *isobars. Except in low latitudes, where the *Coriolis force is minimal, the wind direction is the same as that of the geostrophic wind.

**geosyncline** A thick, rapidly accumulating body of sediment formed within a long, narrow belt of the sea which is usually parallel to a plate margin and is where *ophiolites form. The sediments may form gently tilted strata of uniform *dip in which case it is a **geocline**. Recent thinking indicates that ophiolites are transported from a mid-oceanic ridge; thus the concept of the geosyncline has been abandoned by some.

**geo-tectonic imagery** Mapping used to reconstruct the history of *plates based on data gathered by satellites equipped with a radar *altimeter capable of measuring the sea surface to within 5 cm. Higher sea surface levels are associated with *gravity anomalies which, in turn, reflect the presence of large topographic features such as *seamounts.

**geothermal heat** The internal heat of the earth arising from the formation of the planet and from radioactivity within rocks. Temperatures increase with depth and the rate of increase is the **geothermal gradient**.

**gerrymander** A relocation of constituency boundaries in order to gain a political advantage. One method concentrates most of the opposition's vote into a few electoral districts so that major support results in only a few successful candidates. Alternatively, opposition votes may be spread over a large area where they will have little electoral impact.

**gesellschaft society** A society characterized by formal and aloof relationships. In such a society, people merely reside in their neighbourhoods and are free from social bonds and ties. Gesellschaft society is said to be a feature of the city.

**gestalt theory** In human geography, the suggestion that between stimulus and response lies perception, which intervenes between the two. Thus, observed objects are organized into patterns, and behaviour is based on the perceived, rather than the actual, environment. The same environment may have very different meanings to individuals coming from culturally different backgrounds.

**geyser** A jet of hot water and steam issuing from beneath the earth, usually as a result of volcanic activity. Geysers often erupt at regular intervals.

**ghetto** A part of a city, often but not always a slum area, occupied by a minority group. The term was first used for the enforced residential area of Jews in Europe from the Middle Ages but has now spread to include other groups in unofficial ghettos, particularly with reference to black minorities in the USA. Within the ghetto there are distinctly different ways of life from that of the 'host' population and the prejudices of the host enforce the limitation of the subgroup in particular locations. Most ghettos display a spread of socio-economic groups and the better-off may move to the affluence of the 'gilded ghetto'.

**gibber** A large piece of rock. A **gibber plain** is a desert surface covered with pebbles, stones, and boulders.

**Gini coefficient** In a *Lorenz curve, a measure of the difference between a given distribution of some variable, like population or income, and a perfectly even distribution. The coefficient, also known as **Gini's concentration ratio**, may be calculated as the ratio of area between the diagonal and the Lorenz curve to the total area beneath the diagonal. The lower the Gini coefficient, the more evenly spread the variable.

**GIS** See *Geographic Information System.

**glacial** 1. Of or relating to a *glacier, as in **glacial age**, **glacial *diffluence**, **glacial *drainage channel**, **glacial *drift**.
2. An extended length of time during which earth's glaciers expanded widely.

**glacial erosion** Glacially eroded landscapes are moulded by *abrasion, the incorporation of debris, the 'conveyor belt' transport of *moraine on top of a glacier, rock fracturing, *plucking, plastic moulding, *pressure release, and the action of *meltwater.

The features of glacially eroded uplands are striking, but glaciers can erode huge areas of lowland, removing the soil and creating a *knock and lochan topography. Furthermore, it should be noted that glacial erosion is very selective. *Ice streams may flow in part of an otherwise stationary valley glacier.

**glacial margin channel** A stream running between the side of the glacier and valley sides. The stream may undercut the side of the valley.

**glacial movement** Glacier ice will move if the temperature at the base is above the *pressure melting point. The temperature at the base of a glacier is a function of the thickness of the ice, friction, the input of *firn, and the altitude. If these combine to give a *warm glacier, and there is a gradient, the ice will move downslope.

Ice moves by *compressive and *extending flow; these two forms may alternate down the valley profile. It also moves when the ice crystals change into a series of flat platelets, i.e. it becomes plastic and then creeps downslope. Further movement takes place by *basal slipping.

**glacial surge** The swift and dramatic movement of a glacier. Glaciers may surge at up to 100 m per day. Surging occurs for a short period of time only and is associated with the growth of ice up-glacier to unstable proportions and with severe *crevassing.

**glacial trough** Once termed a U-shaped valley, this is a wide valley floor with steep sides formed by *glacial erosion. The harder the rock which the glacier has cut through, the steeper the valley walls. The shape of a glacial trough more resembles a parabola than the letter U.

The long profile of a glacial trough is frequently irregular and marked by basins and steps. Explanations for this over-deepening and reverse flow vary: that deeper sections are formed where two glaciers meet, that *plucking is more effective in the weaker or closely jointed rocks, that flow alternates between *compressive and *extensive, or that glaciers may pass through naturally occurring narrows. In this last case, the power of the glacier would be intensified as it pushes up against the valley walls.

**glaciated valley** *Glacial trough.

**glaciation** The covering of part of the earth's surface by a *glacier or *ice sheet, together with the action of the ice on the rocks they travel over.

**glacier** A mass of ice which may be moving, or has moved, overland. Glaciers are classified by their location (*cirque glacier, *expanded foot glacier, valley glacier, *niche glacier), by their function (*diffluent glacier, *outlet glacier), or by their basal temperature (*cold glacier, *warm glacier). Features of glaciers include the **glacier snout** at the end of a valley glacier and the **glacier tongue** as ice advances into the sea.

**glacier budget** The balance in a glacier between the input of snow and *firn and the loss of ice due to melting, evaporation,

*sublimation, and *calving. A glacier grows where the budget is positive and decreases where it is negative.

**glacier retreat** The stage in a glacier when the downward movement of the ice is outstripped by *ablation. See *glacier budget.

**glacio-eustasy** See *eustasy.

**glaciofluvial** See *fluvio-glacial.

**glacio-isostasy** A change in the shape, structure, or volume of part of the earth's crust brought about by the weight of a large ice sheet. If the ice subsequently melts, the land surface may rise in compensation.

**glaze** See *hail.

**glen** In Scotland, a narrow, steep-sided valley, as opposed to a *strath.

**gleying** Where soils are waterlogged, air is excluded and the supply of oxygen is reduced. Under these conditions, *anaerobic micro-organisms flourish by extracting oxygen from chemical compounds. This is most conspicuous when the *sesquioxide of iron, ferric oxide, is reduced to ferrous oxide by the removal of oxygen. This imparts a greenish-blue-grey colour to the soil. The clay soil, rich in organic material and mottled with grey and yellow, is a **glei** or *gley soil.

**gley soils** Soils with mottled grey and yellow patches caused by intermittent waterlogging. See *gleying.

**global circulation** See *general circulation of the atmosphere.

**global energy balance** The difference between the total influx of *solar radiation to the earth's surface and the loss of this energy via *terrestrial radiation, evaporation, and the depletion of sensible heat into the ground.

**GMT** See *Greenwich Mean Time.

**gneiss** A highly metamorphosed rock of a granular texture and with a banded appearance known as **gneissose structure**.

**GNP, gross national product** The *GDP of a nation together with any money earned from investment abroad less the income earned within the nation by non-nationals. **GNP per capita** is calculated as GNP/population and is usually expressed in US dollars. It may be used as an indicator of *development.

**Gondwanaland** A 'supercontinent' which occurred as a continuous region of land formed of the now separate units of Africa, Madagascar, Antarctica, Australia, and India. See also *continental drift.

**good** This term may relate to anything which will satisfy a want, but is more strictly used to denote an object, rather than a *service.

**gorge** A deep and narrow opening between upland areas, and usually containing a river. Gorges occur in *karst scenery partly as a result of the collapse of caves. A further cause occurs when the downcutting power of the river is greater than the processes of valley wall erosion. The latter may be less effective because the water permeates the side walls rather than flowing over and eroding them.

**government incentives** Measures taken by a government to attract the development of industry in specified areas. These include grants for building, works, plant, and machinery, assistance in encouraging sound industrial projects, removal grants to new locations, free rent of a government-owned factory for up to five years, taxation allowances against investments, loans, and contract preference schemes. These last give preferential treatment to companies in *assisted areas in Britain when tendering for government contracts.

**graben** A *rift valley.

**gradation** The levelling of a land surface by erosion and deposition.

**grade** In geomorphology, a state of *equilibrium in a system such as a hillslope or river.

**graded river** A stable stream where slope and channel characteristics are such that the *discharge is enough to provide trans-

port for the *load, but where there is no energy for erosion. A graded river is in a state of *equilibrium. If any of the factors controlling discharge change, the river would respond in such a way as to re-establish *grade. A river may establish grade over one section of its course; this is a graded reach.

**graded slope** A slope of such inclination and character that output, throughput, and input remain in equilibrium. No change will be detected unless the balance of forces alters.

**gradient** The slope of some feature of the human or physical environment, usually expressed as the horizontal distance divided by the height change, and given as a percentage.

**granite** A coarse-grained igneous rock that consists largely of quartz, alkali feldspar, and plagioclase feldspar. Granite is formed by the slow crystallization of deep igneous intrusions but may also be formed by *metasomatism.

**granitization** See *metasomatism.

**granular disintegration, granular disaggregation** A form of weathering where the grains of a rock become loosened. Grains fall out to leave a pitted, uneven surface. Granular disintegration may be the result of *frost-shattering, *hydro-fracturing, *thermal expansion, or *salt weathering.

**graph** A diagram using, usually, two axes at right angles to each other, and expressing a relationship between variables. Each variable is scaled along one of the axes. **Graphicacy** is the quality of expressing relationships on a graph.

**graph theory** The mathematical study of graphs and topological maps; the nature of the links between points, and the location of the points themselves.

**gravel** A loose deposit of rock fragments rounded by river erosion. The lower size limit of gravel is 2 mm but the upper limit is either 10 mm, 20 mm, 50 mm, or 60 mm according to different authorities.

**gravity** The attractive force exerted by one body on another. This force decreases with distance. **Gravitation** is movement under the force of gravity. In geomorphology, processes and features which are brought about by this force include **gravity \*slumping** and down-moving water through the soil— **gravity water**.

**gravity anomaly** An unexpected variation in the gravity of the earth's crust. It was a difference between the expected and the observed gravity exerted by the Himalayas which led to the concept of mountain 'roots' extending deep into the magma. The gravity anomaly of the central Pacific seems to be linked with \*hot spots which increase the elevation of the surface.

**gravity model** A model of the interaction between two population centres based on Newton's Law of Universal Gravitation: two bodies in the universe attract each other to the product of their masses and inversely as the square distance between them. Thus, expected interaction between city $i$ and city $j$ is shown as:

$$k \, \frac{P_i \times P_j}{d_{ij}^{\,2}}$$

where $P_i$ = the population of town $i$, $P_j$ = the population of town $j$, $d_{ij}$ = the distance between them, and $k$ = a constant.

This original equation has been changed to accommodate features like wages, employment opportunities, and so on, and has been widely criticized, but is still used to predict future interactions. The gravity model may be applied to fields of influence of settlements, trade, traffic flows, telephone calls, and migration. Perhaps the most severe criticism of the model is that it has no theoretical basis but is based on observation only. Furthermore, planning on the basis of the model will only reinforce differences between places; people will interact more with larger towns if planners are geared to that assumption and plan for it accordingly.

**gravity slope** On a hillside, the steep slope above the gentler \*haldenhang.

**great circle** An imaginary line on the earth's surface which, if projected underground, would pass through the centre of the earth. Any great circle route between two points will represent the shortest line between the two.

**great soil groups** The primary classification of global soils into groups; a classification similar to the \*formations of vegetation. See \*soil classification.

**green belt** An area of undeveloped land encircling a town. An early green belt, about 15 km wide, was set up in the 1950s around Greater London in order to limit the spread of suburbs. Other cities have followed this example by restricting development in the semi-rural areas beyond the built-up zone. The amount of new building is restricted although by no means completely banned. In some cases, development has been switched to areas beyond the green belt, which is then sandwiched. Later motives for creating green belts have been the provision of open areas for recreation and the preservation of agricultural land. Some planners advocate the establishment of green 'wedges' which project into the city rather than a green belt.

**green fallow** \*Fallow land planted with a fast-growing green crop.

**greenfield site** Areas beyond the city where development can take place unfettered by earlier building and where low density, high amenity buildings can be constructed.

**greenhouse effect** The warming of the atmosphere as some of its gases absorb the heat given out by the earth. These include carbon dioxide and the gases used in making some aerosols and some forms of plastic. Other gases concerned include water vapour and \*ozone. Without this absorption, which is also known as **counter-radiation**, the temperature of the atmosphere would fall by 30–40 °C.

As a result of human activities such as the clearance of rain forest and the burning of fossil fuels, the volume of carbon dioxide in the atmosphere is rising. This rise is possible because the rate at which oceans can take up carbon dioxide is low, since the oceans mix slowly. Some scientists believe that with the increasing emission of carbon dioxide the earth's atmosphere will become warmer.

The analogy with a greenhouse is not perfect, since a greenhouse retains heat through lack of movement in the air as well as by absorbing *counter-radiation. It is argued that the increased carbon dioxide will, in time, be absorbed by the oceans.

**green manure** A leguminous crop not harvested but ploughed into the fields after it matures. Leguminous crops fix nitrogen from the air and thus improve the fertility of the soil.

**green revolution** The development and use of high-yielding crops in conjunction with improved agricultural technology. New breeds of crops have been developed to increase yields two to four times, to shorten the time required for growth such that more than one crop a year can be produced, and to produce a plant which can withstand extremes of climate or disease. The use of Mexican wheat has doubled yields in the Punjab and IR-8 rice has been used to such effect in the Philippines that imports are no longer necessary.

There have been drawbacks, however. The grain may not be as palatable or as attractive in appearance as the grain it replaces and more energy may be used up to process it. Heavy applications of expensive fertilizers and insecticides are required and these are often made from *non-renewable resources. The high yields and reliance on artificial fertilizers can lead to impoverished soils. Traditional rice exporters, like Burma, have seen the collapse of their markets. Increased yields mean that landowners can use their holdings more profitably and this often means that tenants are dispossessed. Copious, but strictly regulated, irrigation is required.

The green revolution has benefited the most prosperous farmers in the most prosperous areas and its price is too high for many of the peasants who need its benefits. None the less, it cannot be accounted a failure.

**green village** A settlement with houses and a church gathered around a common or village green.

**Greenwich Mean Time, GMT** The time at longitude 0° which passes through Greenwich, England. It is the *standard time for the UK, and from it many other world times are calculated.

**greywacke** A sedimentary rock consisting of angular fragments of quartz, feldspar, and other minerals set in a muddy base.

**grèzes litées** Deposits down a hillslope of *imbricated rock fragments bedded parallel to the slope. It is suggested that the debris is broken up by *frost shattering and that larger fragments roll downwards under the influence of gravity. With thawing, the finer debris washes downslope, forming a fairly smooth layer of sediment on top of the coarser material.

**grid plan** An urban area in which the basic street pattern is planned as a grid with regular spacing between blocks. Many American cities were built to this pattern.

**grid reference** A system used to pinpoint a spot on a map by reference to a grid on the map of numbered *eastings and *northings.

**grike** The joints on an exposure of limestone which have been widened through solution by *carbonation.

**grit** An extremely coarse *sandstone.

**gross domestic product** See *GDP.

**gross national product** See *GNP.

**gross reproduction rate** The number of female babies born per thousand women of reproductive age. The **net reproduction rate** also takes into account the number of women who cannot or do not wish to have children.

**ground frost** See *frost.

**ground ice** Ice found at the bed of a body of water, or fossil ice, usually in an area of *permafrost.

**ground information** In *remote sensing, information recorded by remote sensors.

**ground moraine** See *moraine.

**ground rent** A rent paid by a *leaseholder to the freeholder (the owner of the land), for the right to use the land on which his building stands.

**ground truth** In *remote sensing jargon, observations made at ground level which may then be used to classify data from a sensor. This classification can then be used to investigate an unsurveyed area.

**ground water** All water found under the surface of the ground which is not chemically combined with any minerals present, but not including underground streams.

**grouped data** Data which have been arranged in groups or classes rather than showing all the original figures.

**growing season** The time of the year during which plants will grow. This will depend on temperature, rainfall, numbers of frost-free days, hours of daylight, and the precise requirements of the plants.

**growth pole** A point of economic growth. Poles are usually urban locations, benefiting from *agglomeration economies, and should interact with surrounding areas, spreading prosperity from the core to the periphery. Observation of naturally occurring growth poles has inclined planners to create new growth poles; artificially created growth poles, as in France, have not stimulated regional development as much as was hoped. See also *metropoles d'équilibre.

**groyne** A breakwater running seawards from the land, constructed to stop the flow of beach material moved by *longshore drift.

**GST, General Systems Theory** A general science of organization and wholeness. Bertalanffy, the founder of the science, dated its inception from 1940, but it did not influence geographical thinking until the late 1960s. It introduced the applica-

tion of the *system to geography and claimed that any phenomenon cannot properly be understood until it is seen as a system of many associated parts.

**guest workers** Temporary immigrants who do not plan to, or are not allowed to, settle permanently in their work place. The German *Gastarbeiter* are the classic example: they are predominantly male, and work in low-skilled, poorly-paid, repetitive work. They have no job security, and most live in very poor housing. If the economy declines, the 'guests' are less welcome.

**Guinea current** A warm *ocean current off the coast of West Africa.

**gulch** In the USA, a steep-sided, rocky, and deep *gorge.

**gulf** A very large inlet of the sea, perhaps hundreds of kilometres long, extending far into the landmass.

**gully** A water-made cutting, usually steep-sided with a flattened floor. **Gullying** usually occurs in unconsolidated rock and rarely cuts through bedrock. Gullies usually form quickly as a result of destruction of the plant cover. **Gully erosion** is the removal of topsoil and the creation of many steep-sided cuttings in a hillside. It can be stopped by restoring a vegetation cover, by *contour ploughing, and by making terraces and small dams across the hillside.

**gust** A temporary increase in wind speed, lasting for a few seconds. A typical ratio of gust speed to wind speed in rural areas is 1.6 : 1, increasing to 2 : 1 in urban areas due to the effects of high buildings and narrow streets.

Gusts may also be associated with heavy rain, as downdrafts sweep earthwards from *cumulo-*nimbus clouds. The repeated hammer blows of gusting winds do more damage than does the persistent pressure of steady wind.

**Gutenberg discontinuity** That region of the earth's interior, between the base of the *mantle and the upper surface of the core, where the material is changing from a solid to a plastic state.

**guyot** A truncated sea-floor volcano occurring as a flat-topped mountain which does not reach the sea surface. Guyots are thought to be associated with *hot spots.

**gypcrete** A *duricrust composed of calcium sulphate.

# H

**habitat** The area in which an organism can live and which affords relatively favourable conditions for existence.

**haboob** See *local winds.

**hachure** On a map, short lines drawn at right angles to the contours and giving an indication of gradient. The closer the lines, the steeper the slope, although this is not quantified.

**hacienda** In Spanish-speaking countries, a large farm, usually a ranch.

**Hadley cell** A vertical *atmospheric cell made up of warm air rising from equatorial regions and moving polewards, transporting heat energy. In 1735, Hadley postulated the existence of such cells, extending from equator to pole in each hemisphere. In real terms, this simple pattern is complicated by the *Coriolis force, the shape of the earth, relief barriers, ocean currents, and the distribution of land and sea. Hadley-type cells do exist, however, in the tropics. Warm air rises and moves poleward, losing energy as it travels away from its heat source. Because the latitudinal expanse of the earth shrinks with distance from the equator, the moving air must converge. The combination of cooling and convergence, together with the deflection caused by the Coriolis force, causes the air in the cell to sink at around 30 °N. and S. The subsiding air is compressed and sustains an *adiabatic rise in temperature, thus generating the *subtropical high-pressure zones.

**haff** A coastal lagoon on the southern Baltic coast partially separated from the sea by a *nehrung, or long *spit.

**hail** A form of snow, consisting of roughly spherical lumps of ice, 5 mm or more in diameter. Hailstones often show a roughly concentric pattern of alternating clear ice (**glaze**) and opaque ice (**rime**).

A hailstone forms when a frozen raindrop is caught in the violent updraughts found in warm, wet *cumulo-*nimbus clouds. As it rises, it attracts ice. As it falls, the outer layer melts, but refreezes when the drop is again carried upwards by the moving cloud.

The onion-like structure of a hailstone shows that it must have passed up and down several times. A hailstone will descend when its fall-speed is enough to overcome the updraughts in the cloud.

**haldenhang** The lower, gentle slope of a hillside below the *gravity slope.

**half life** The rate of decay of a radioactive *isotope. The half life is the time taken for half the original, parent isotopes to decay. At the end of the first half life, half of the parent isotope is left; at the end of the, equally long, second half life, one-quarter of the parent isotope remains, and so on. Hence the amount of residual radiation in a rock can be used to determine the age of the rock.

**halo** In meteorology, a ring of light around the sun or, more rarely, the moon. It is caused by the refraction of light by ice crystals, thus, in popular lore, a halo round the moon foreshadows snow. A coloured halo is a **corona**.

**halophyte** A plant which can grow in saline conditions.

**ham** 1. In Anglo-Saxon place names, a village or homestead as in Birmingham.

2. A water-meadow of rich pasture.

**hamada** The level, rocky desert of the Saharan uplands, smoothed by *abrasion.

**hamlet** A small settlement without services or shops and usually without a church.

**hanging glacier** A glacier high on a plateau or mountainside but not extending into the lowlands.

**hanging valley** A high-level tributary valley from which the ground falls sharply to the level of the lower, main valley. The depth of the lower valley may be attributed to more severe glaciation because it contained more ice.

**hardness** The indication of the hardness of a rock may be indicated by comparing it to the rocks on the Moh's scale. On this scale hardness was indicated by the ability of the specimen to scratch the rocks of the scale. A rock which could scratch quartz (7 on the Moh's scale) but is scratched by topaz (8 on the Moh's scale) would have a hardness of 7–8. Mohs's qualitative scale is now being replaced by more quantitative tests.

**hard pan** A resistant layer in the soil encountered at or below the surface and usually caused by *illuviation after leaching of the upper *horizons. Hard pans may be formed of clay, *humus, or compounds of calcium, iron, or silica.

**hard water** Water containing dissolved carbonates of calcium and magnesium which inhibit the formation of a lather with soap or detergent. When hard water boils, the carbonates are deposited out as 'lime scale'.

**hardwood** Wood obtained from temperate deciduous trees such as oak, or from tropical evergreens such as teak, mahogany, and ebony.

**harmattan** See *local winds.

**Hawaiian eruption** A volcanic *fissure eruption where large quantities of *basic lava spill out with very little explosive activity.

**hazard** See *natural hazard.

**hazard perception** The view which an individual has of a natural or man-made hazard. A person will have a high perception of a hazard which occurs often, but still may suppress knowledge of such occurrences because of desire to remain in a particular location. It is not the hazard as such which influences behaviour but the assessment of its likelihood and extent. San Francisco was rebuilt after 1906 partly because buildings were then constructed which could survive earthquakes to some extent and because of a desire not to think of the risks. Later events have shown that the risks are very real.

**haze** A suspension of particles in the air, slightly obscuring visibility. These particles may be naturally occurring, e.g. sea salt or desert dust, or may be man-made, like the smoke formed from the burning of fossil fuels.

**headland** An area of high land jutting out into the sea.

**headwall** The steep back wall of a *cirque.

**headward erosion** The lengthening of a river's course by erosion backwards from its source. *Sapping is an important process in headward erosion.

**heartland** A term suggested by Mackinder to indicate the wealthy interior of Eurasia. Mackinder maintained that whoever controlled the heartland would eventually control the world as political units became larger and larger. He did not live to see the rise of *nationalism in the late twentieth century.

**heathland** An uncultivated, open area of land with a natural vegetation of low shrubs such as the family Ericaceae (heathers). Heathland tends to develop on poor soils such as *outwash sands and gravels.

**heat island** In a city, air temperatures are often higher than over open country. These higher temperatures are generated both by the combustion of fuels and by the release at night of heat stored during the day in the fabric of the city. A heat island is developed during calm conditions; winds disperse heat.

**heave** In a normal *fault, the forward, lateral displacement of the strata.

**Heaviside layer** A zone of the atmosphere between 100 and 200 km above the earth's surface which reflects long and medium radio waves.

**heavy industry** Manufacturing industry which needs large quantities of often bulky raw materials. These are usually transported by water or rail as in iron smelting or shipbuilding. These industries have a high *material index. Productivity per worker is generally low and heavy industries are often dirty and noisy.

**hectare** 10 000 m$^2$ or 2.471 acres.

**hegemony** Originally, leadership, especially by one state of a federation, in terms of power and politics. More recently, within *Marxist geography the term has been applied to the ruling class.

**helicoidal, helical flow** A continuous corkscrew motion of water as it flows along a river channel.

**henge** A British circular earthwork dating from the late Neolithic having an encircling bank with a ditch inside.

**herbivore** Any animal which eats only plant material.

**Hercynian** An *orogeny of the upper *Carboniferous to the *Permian.

**heritage coast** Stretches of unaltered coastline which are outstandingly attractive and are protected from development.

**hermeneutics** The art, skill, or theory of understanding and classifying meaning. It is often applied to the interpretation of human actions, utterances, products, and institutions. A hermeneutic interpretation requires the individual to understand and sympathize with another's point of view.

**heterotrophe** An organism which has to acquire its energy by digesting food which has been manufactured by other organisms. Thus all organisms are heterotrophes except the *primary producers which can manufacture their own food, usually by *photosynthesis.

**hide** In Britain, an area of land equal to the ploughing capacity of eight oxen in a day. This area varies from 40 to 50 ha but was smallest where the population was most dense.

**hierarchy** Any ordering of phenomena with grades or classes ranked in sequence. *Central place theory posits a hierarchy of settlements from regional capitals to hamlets. The same grades of settlement in the hierarchy are held to be spaced evenly. Research suggests, however, that settlements occur in a continuum rather than a hierarchy. It seems unlikely that the presence of a hierarchy can be established, partly through the difficulty of *ranking towns.

**high** A region of high atmospheric pressure. In Britain, the term is generally applied to pressures of over 1000 *millibars.

**high farming** A time in eighteenth- and nineteenth-century Britain associated with buoyant farm prices which stimulated new techniques, such as enclosures and scientific breeding. It also encouraged the owners of estates to engage in cultivation themselves rather than to let farms for a fixed return from their tenants.

**Highland Clearances** The eviction of inhabitants of the Scottish Highlands from their land, accompanied by the destruction of their dwellings for the creation of *deer forests. The clearances were intense from 1790 and reached a peak in 1800.

**high latitudes** Polewards of 60° latitude.

**high-order goods and services** Goods and services with a high *threshold population and a large *range. Examples include furniture, electrical goods, and financial expertise. The goods are usually *shopping goods.

**high technology** The use of advanced, sophisticated, and often complex techniques and equipment.

**high tide** The maximum encroachments of the sea within a day.

**hill farming** The extensive farming of an upland area, usually rearing sheep, although some cattle may be kept more intensively. Numbers of cattle are restricted by a lack of winter fodder, and the sheep grazing at about 2 ha per sheep must be brought to the lowlands for fattening. Hill farming has been supported by government subsidies since the 1940s, but now receives subsidies from the *EC. Traditional hill farming has given way in places to improved, sown pasture and reclaimed moorland so that sheep can be stocked at one sheep per 0.25 ha.

**hill fog** Low cloud enveloping a hill.

**hill fort** A fortified site on a hilltop, usually with a ditch and ramparts. The earliest date from the Iron Age but some British examples were created as late as the Dark Ages. Favoured sites for such structures in southern England seem to be chalk uplands.

**hillslopes** *Escarpments and valley sides. Slope studies are generally concerned with hillslopes and are not concerned with *flood plains, *river terraces, or submarine slopes.

**hinterland** The hinterland is the area serving and being served by a settlement. The term was originally applied to ports and one port may share part of its hinterland with another.

**histogram** A graph showing, by means of rectangles, the frequency of certain classes of values within a data set. The widths of the rectangles are proportional to the class intervals and the heights are proportional to the frequencies of occurrence within each class.

**historical geography** The study of past geographies and of past landscapes. This is usually achieved by teasing out *cross sections or by making a series of successive sections through time.

**histosol** See *US soil classification.

**Hjulström diagram** A diagram showing the relationship in a channel between particle size and the mean fluid velocity required for *entrainment. It shows that an entrained particle can be transported in suspension at a lower velocity than that required to lift the particle initially. When the stream velocity slows to a critical speed, the particle is deposited.

**hoar frost** See *frost.

**hobby farmer** A part-time farmer who is not wholly dependent on farming for a livelihood.

**hogback** A nearly symmetrical ridge with *dip and *scarp slopes of the same value. Hogbacks form where the dip of the beds has been tilted such that the dip is almost vertical.

**holding** In agriculture, farmed land under one owner or tenant.

**holism** The view that the whole is more than its parts. In earlier geographies, the region has been seen as having a distinct identity which does not come entirely from its separate parts. A holist looks at the workings of concepts like 'culture' or 'society' rather than the workings of individuals.

**hollow frontier** When the agricultural frontier moves forward it may leave behind a tract of worked-over farmland with a shrinking population—the hollow. Such hollows may then be used for different forms of cultivation which may support higher population densities.

**Holocene** The most recent geological *epoch, stretching from 12 000 years ago to the present day. This epoch has seen the development of early man.

**homeostasis** In ecology, the process whereby constancy is achieved in an organism or community.

**homeostatic theory** The contention that a population level remains constant in a pre-industrial society. When there is an imbalance between population growth and resources, there is a corrective response. *Malthus was one exponent of this theory.

**homestead** In the USA, under the **Homestead Act**, 1862, a unit of land thought to be enough to support a family: 65 ha in the Mid-West, but 260 ha in the semi-arid West.

**homocline** One of a regular series of hills from a large area of rock *strata of uniform thickness and *dip.

**homoiotherm** An animal which maintains an almost constant body temperature; a warm-blooded animal. **Homoiothermy** is the process whereby such a constant is maintained, despite variations in the *ambient temperature.

**homoseismal line** *Co-seismal line.

**honeycombe weathering** See *weathering pits.

**horizon, soil horizon** A distinctive layer within a soil which differs chemically or physically from the layers below or above. The **A horizon** or topsoil contains *humus. Often soil minerals are washed downwards from this layer. This material then tends to accumulate in the **B horizon** or subsoil. The **C horizon** is the unconsolidated rock below the soil. These three basic horizons may be further classified. Thus, Ah horizons are found under uncultivated land, Ahp horizons are under cultivated land, and Apg horizons are on *gleyed land. The B horizons are also subdivided by means of suffixes. Thus, Bf horizons have a thin iron pan, Bg horizons are gleyed, Bh horizons have humic accumulations, Box horizons have a residual accumulation of *sesquioxides, and Bs horizons are areas of sesquioxide accumulation. Bt horizons contain clay minerals and Bw horizons do not qualify for any of the above. Bx horizons, or **fragipans**, contain a dense but brittle layer caused by compaction. C horizons are also subdivided: Cu horizons show little evidence of gleying, salt accumulation, or fragipan; Cr horizons are too dense for root penetration; and Cg horizons are gleyed. Additional suffixes may be used. Some soil scientists use the term **D horizon** for the consolidated parent rock.

In addition to these soil horizons, other layers are distinguished. Thus, the layer of plant material on the soil surface is classified as the **L horizon**—fresh litter; the **F horizon**— decomposing litter; the **H horizon**—well-decomposed litter; and the **O horizon**—peaty. A *leached A horizon is termed an **E horizon** or *eluviated horizon.

**horn** A mountain peak formed when three or four *cirques have cut into it, back to back, leaving a *pyramidal peak.

**horse latitude** Those latitudes stretching from 30–35 °N. and S. of the equator where winds are light and weather is stable and dry. The origin of this term is uncertain.

**horst** A block of high ground which stands out because it is flanked by normal faults on each side. It may be that the block has been elevated or that the land on either side of the horst has sunk.

**horticulture** Originally garden cultivation, this now refers to the intensive production of fruit, vegetables, and ornamental plants.

**Hortonian overland flow** An overland flow of water occurring more or less simultaneously over a *drainage basin when rainfall exceeds the *infiltration capacity of the basin. Horton maintained that such overland flow was a major contribution to the rapid rise of river flow levels, and was the prime cause of soil erosion. Hortonian flow is distinct from *return flow since it involves no movement of underground water back to the surface. Recent research indicates that the Hortonian model is not widely applicable.

**Horton's Law** That the number of streams of a *stream order decreases as the order increases. A typical ratio would be 9 first order streams : 3 second order streams : 1 third order stream. It might be said that any branching system will follow this Law.

**hot desert** Located on the west coasts of tropical and subtropical climes, these have average temperatures of over 25 °C and rainfall of less than 250 mm per year. Deserts are too dry for most plant species except for *xerophytes. Xerophytic strategies for survival include the development of succulents to store water, the growth of ephemeral plants after rains, and the development of spines to ward off animal attack. Desert insects, reptiles, mammals, and birds are all adapted to drought. This is an extremely fragile *biome.

**Hotelling model** A model of the effect of competition on locational decisions. The model is usually based on two ice-cream salesmen, A and B, on a mile of beach. The cost and choice of ice-cream is the same for each distributor. Buyers are evenly distributed along the beach. The first pattern of market share has the two salesmen positioned so that each is at the centre of his half of the beach and the market is split up evenly. If A now moves nearer to the middle of the beach, he will increase his market share. The logical outcome of this will have both salesmen back to back at the centre of the beach, as long as some customers are willing to walk nearly half a mile for an ice-cream, i.e. that the consumer provides the transport. This analogy indicates that locational decisions are not made independently but are influenced by the actions of others.

**hot spot** Also known as a *plume, this is an area of localized swelling and cracking of the earth's crust due to an upward welling of *magma. The cause of hot spots is not known; indeed, some writers deny their existence.

**hot spring** A flow of hot water, rising naturally from the ground, and warmed by *geothermal heat.

**Hoyt's sector model** *Mann's model.

**huerta** An intensely cultivated, irrigated landholding along the eastern coast of Spain.

**human ecology** The study of the interrelationships and interactions between man and the environment, or the study of interrelationships between humans.

**human geography** A generalized term for those areas of geography not dealing exclusively with the physical landscape or with technical matters such as *remote sensing. It is concerned with the relationships between man's activities and the physical environment, with *spatial analysis, and with those processes which lead to *areal differentiation. The term covers a number of fields; see also *cultural geography, *behavioural geography, *economic geography, *agricultural geography, *industrial geography, *political geography, *population geography, *regional geography, *social geography, *urban geography.

**humanistic** Concerned with human interests and with the human race as opposed to the purely physical world. It is an approach which stresses distinctly human traits such as meaning, feeling, and emotion.

**humanistic geography** A view of human geography centred on human perception, capability, creativity, experience, and values. It maintains that any investigation will be subjective inasmuch as it reflects the attitudes and perceptions of the researcher who may also be an influence on the very field of his study. Two main strands may be distinguished. The first focuses on human experience and human expression and is concerned with the unique and the particular. The second takes constructions, like *existentialism, from the social sciences and explores the relationship between these and the time and space settings of ordinary life.

**humic acid** A complex acid formed when water passes slowly through *humus. Humic acid is an example of an **organic acid** in that it is formed from carbon-based compounds. It is significant in chemical weathering and in the formation of soil.

**humid** In climatology, describing air with a *relative humidity of over 65%. In the **humid tropics**, other climatic features include mean monthly temperatures of over 20 °C.

**humidity** The amount of water vapour in the atmosphere.

It is more exactly defined as the mass of water vapour per unit volume of air, usually expressed in $kg\ m^{-3}$. This is *absolute humidity. **Relative humidity** is the moisture content of air expressed as the percentage of the maximum possible moisture content of that air at the same temperature and pressure.

**humidity mixing ratio** The ratio of the mass of water vapour in a sample of air to the mass of dry air associated with that water vapour.

**humus** Material of vegetable or animal origin found in the soil. More exactly, humus is fully decomposed and finely divided organic matter. This decomposition is **humification**: the process whereby the simple mineral compounds released by weathering combine with the organic residues to form large, stable organic molecules which act as bonding agents in the structure of the soil. Humus is also important for its great ability to absorb *cations.

**hundred** An Anglo-Saxon term for a portion of a *shire or county, perhaps indicating an area of 100 *hides.

**hundredweight** In Britain, 112 lb (50.8 kg), in the USA 100 lb (45.36 kg).

**hunting and gathering** An early form of society with no settled agriculture, or domestication of animals, and which has little impact on the environment. The hunting of animals and the collection of edible plants depends on the environment rather than changing it.

**hurricane** Also known as a **typhoon**, or **tropical cyclone** with winds over 140 km per hour, this is a disturbance about 650 km across spinning about a central area of very low pressure. The violent winds are accompanied by towering clouds, some 4000 m high, and by torrential rain; 150 mm (6 inches) frequently fall within the space of a few hours. There is, as yet, no complete understanding of how these storms develop; they can begin when air spreads out at high level above a newly formed disturbance at low levels. The upper level outflow acts rather like a suction pump, drawing away the rising air at height and causing low-level air to be pulled in. The winds spiral into the centre because they are affected by the earth's rotation. The intense energy of these storms comes from the warmth of the tropical seas over which they develop. Thus, an extensive ocean area with surface temperatures of over 27 °C is necessary for hurricane formation.

The source regions must be far enough away from the equator—5° at least—for the *Coriolis force to have an effect. The removal of air at height may be along the eastern limb of an upper air trough. Moisture-laden air spirals into the centre and rises, condensing to form a ring-like tower of *cumulo-*nimbus clouds. With this condensation, *latent heat is released which causes the air to rise further and faster. The condensation also causes torrential rain. In the upper *troposphere water droplets freeze and form *cirrus clouds which are thrown outwards by the spin of the storm.

At ground level, the temperature at the centre, or eye, of the storm is only slightly warmer than that at the margins, but at heights of around 5000 m, the centre can be 18 °C warmer than the margins. This warm core maintains the low pressure which drags in the winds.

**husbandry** In geography, the farming of animals.

**hydration** The incorporation of water by minerals. Hydration often causes swelling and is believed to be a major cause of the crumbling of coarse-grained igneous rocks which are disrupted by the expansion of their hydrated minerals.

**hydraulic action** In geomorphology, the force of the water within a stream or river.

**hydraulic conductivity** The ability of a soil or rock to conduct water. The conductivity of dry soil or rock is low (**dry hydraulic conductivity**); little water is conducted since water entering a soil must form a film of water surrounding the soil particles. Until these films are formed, little conduction occurs. **Saturated hydraulic conductivity** refers to the maximum rate of water movement in a soil.

**hydraulic force** The force of water including *cavitation and fluvial *plucking.

**hydraulic geometry** The study of the inter-relationships exhibited along the course of a river. *Discharge is linked with the mean width of the channel, the mean depth and slope of the channel, the suspended *load, and the mean water velocity. Further links are thought to exist within meanders where the wavelength of the meander is related to the *radius of curvature.

**hydraulic gradient** The rate of change in *hydraulic head with distance.

**hydraulic head** The pressure exerted by the weight of water above a given point.

**hydraulic hypothesis** The view that the practice of large-scale irrigation stimulated urban development as the need for organized labour and supervisory authorities arose. Equally well, it might be that urban settlement stimulated irrigation.

**hydraulic radius** Also known as **hydraulic mean**, this is the ratio of the cross-sectional area of a stream to the length of the wetted perimeter. The wetted perimeter is the cross-sectional length of a river bed. The hydraulic radius is a measure of the efficiency of the river in conveying water. If the value of the hydraulic radius is large, a large area of water in the cross-section is affected by each metre of the bed, and there is thus little friction.

**hydro-electricity** Energy produced as generators are turned by the power of running water. The necessary conditions are a constant supply of water from rivers and lakes, steep slopes to aid the fall of water, and stable geological conditions for the construction of dams. However, recent research indicates that the construction of dams may trigger off earth movements. The energy generated is a function of the height of falling water as well as of the mass of water concerned. A high proportion of energy is converted into electricity.

**hydro-fracturing** A form of weathering whereby water enters minute fractures in a rock. If the water freezes and expands at the open end of the fracture, the rest of the water may be pushed downward. The pressure thus exerted may then deepen the crack.

**hydrograph** A graph of *discharge or of the level of water in a river throughout a period of time. The latter, known as a **stage hydrograph**, can be converted into a discharge hydrograph by the use of a stage-discharge rating curve. Hydrographs can be plotted for hours, days, or even months. A **storm hydrograph** is plotted after a rainstorm to record the effect on the river of the storm event.

**hydrography** The surveying and mapping of water, usually marine.

**hydrological cycle** Also known as the **water cycle**, these terms refer to the movements of water and its transformation between the gaseous (vapour), liquid, and solid forms.

The major processes are condensation, by which precipitation is formed, movement and storage of water overland or underground, evaporation, and the horizontal transport of moisture.

**hydrology** The study of the earth's water, particularly of water on and under the ground before it reaches the ocean or before it evaporates into the air.

This science has many important applications, such as flood control, irrigation, domestic and industrial water supply, and the generation of hydro-electric power.

**hydrolysis** The chemical reaction of a compound with water. Hydrolysis is an important component of chemical weathering and of soil formation.

**hydromorphic** Denoting areas with water-logged soils. *Gley soils form in such conditions.

**hydrophyte** An aquatic plant. See *hygrophyte.

**hydrosere** A successional sequence of plants originating in water.

**hydrosphere** The sphere of water—rivers, lakes, and seas—which forms a discontinuous layer over the earth's surface.

**hydrostatic pressure** The pressure exerted by stationary water.

**hydrothermal** Applying to hot water. **Hydrothermal deposits** are rocks and minerals formed by the action of heat and water.

**hygrophyte** A water-loving, but not aquatic, plant.

**hygroscopic** Relating to a substance which will attract and hold water. **Hygroscopic nuclei** are those *condensation nuclei, such as salt, which are thought to bring about condensation in the air.

**hypabyssal rock** An igneous intrusion which has consolidated near the earth's surface above the base of the crust.

**hypermarket** A huge complex with generous free parking offering a very wide range of goods. Out of town hypermarkets divert traffic from the city centre, simplify shopping, and can lower prices as costs of land are lower than at the city centre. However, they are designed for the more affluent and are difficult of access for those who do not own cars. They represent a serious threat to city centre stores and neighbourhood shops.

**hypolimnion** The lower layers in a body of water which are marked by low temperatures and insufficient light for photosynthesis. Levels of dissolved oxygen are low.

**hypothesis** A general supposition made as a basis for reasoning but not held to be true until proven by reference to empirical evidence.

**hythergraph** A plot of monthly rainfall against monthly temperature over a year. See *climograph.

# I

**ice age** A length of time during which ice sheets are found on the continents. Thus, an ice age is occurring at the present day. Ice ages last for some tens of millions of years with intervals of about 150 million years between them.

The term is used more loosely (with capital letters) to identify the last time that ice sheets covered much of Europe and North America.

**iceberg** A huge mass of ice, floating in the sea and usually broken off from a glacier. The depth of an iceberg is often far greater than that of an *ice floe.

**ice cap** A flattened, dome-shaped mass of ice, similar to an *ice sheet, but under 50 000 km² in area.

**ice cap climate** A climatic regime where the average yearly temperature is below 0 ˚C. Ice and snow are permanent and precipitation is very light.

**ice contact feature** Any landform developed in contact with a glacier. An **ice contact terrace** is a synonym for a *kame terrace.

**ice dam** A body of ice cutting across a glacial trough beyond the *snout and therefore impeding the movement of glacial meltwater. A lake will form behind it.

**ice fall** An area of *extending flow where the gradient of a glacier steepens and the ice, marked by crevasses, begins to split up.

**ice floe** A flat section of ice which is floating in water and not attached to ground ice. See also *iceberg.

**ice front** The floating vertical ice cliff at the seaward end of an *ice shelf, or of a glacier extending over the sea.

**ice lens** An area of ice often having convex upper and lower surfaces which exists underground in *periglacial environments.

**ice segregation** The disintegration of frozen ground as the soil moisture freezes and expands.

**ice sheet** An area of ice spreading over more than 50 000 km². The snow line is low, and the ice creeps towards the edges with a slow, massive movement.

**ice shelf** A sheet of ice extending over the sea from its land base. It is fed by snow falling on it or from glaciers on the land surface.

**ice stream** Within a glacier or ice sheet, a stream of ice moving more quickly than, and not necessarily in the same direction as, most of the ice.

**ice wedge** A near vertical sheet of ice tapering downwards. When soils are cooled below −15 ˚C, the ice contracts, causing the ground to split into vertical, polygonal cracks. When the *active layer melts in spring, these cracks fill with water. As this water refreezes and expands, the cracks widen. This process is repeated many times. Wedges grow less than 10 mm a year. These wedges create a system of polygons with raised margins. When the ice wedge finally melts, due to climatic change, debris will fall into the crack. This filled wedge is then called an **ice wedge cast**. See also *polygon, *frost cracking.

**iconography** In geography, the study of the way in which images of the landscape reveal symbolic meaning.

**idealism** The view that human activity may be explained only in terms of the thought processes that bring them about. Reality is based on, or evolved by, the mind; this is **metaphysical idealism**, free from control by material objects or processes. No material things exist independently of the mind. **Epistemological idealism** maintains that human understanding is limited to perception of external objects. The concept is used in geography in any study of how the *cultural landscape depends on the way in which people perceive their environment.

**ideographic** Concerned with establishing the uniqueness of a phenomenon. This approach has been the underlying basis of *regional geography, which is concerned with the distinction between places.

**ideology** A manner of thinking. It is a set of beliefs and values often forming the basis of an economic or political theory or system.

**igneous rock** A rock which originated as molten *magma from beneath the earth's surface. As *intrusions of magma slowly solidify, enough time elapses for large crystals to form whereas *extrusions cool quickly leaving little time for crystal growth. Thus, a coarse-grained intrusive igneous rock has a fine-grained extrusive counterpart; granite is coarse rhyolite and gabbro is coarse basalt.

**illuvial horizon** The B-*horizon of a soil; the horizon in which there is redeposition or entrapment of matter brought down from above.

**illuviation** The redeposition in a lower soil *horizon of materials *leached out from an upper horizon.

**image** A picture built up by an individual from information arising from the social and physical *milieus experienced from birth. The image of a city, for example, is made up of meeting places, paths, landmarks, limits, and areas and this image fosters a sense of belonging. This image is also a way of organizing knowledge and is a source of ready reference for movement around the city. Similar individuals in similar milieus are likely to have similar mental images and hence exhibit similar forms of behaviour.

**imageability** The extent to which an object or set of objects makes a strong impression on individuals.

**imbricated** Of deposits, laid down in overlapping sheets, as in the orientation of tabular blocks lying parallel to the slope in *periglacial environments.

**immature soil** A soil of recent formation and not fully developed. Synonymous with *azonal soil.

**immigration** The movement of a person into a foreign country as a permanent resident. The term is also used in ecology for the movements of plant seeds and animals.

**imperfect competition** In economics, a state of affairs in which the necessary conditions for *perfect competition are not met. In the real world, competition is generally imperfect.

**imperialism** The control of one or a number of countries by a dominant nation. This control may be political, economic, or both, and indicates a degree of *dependence in the subordinate nations. This is fostered by monopolizing the external trade of the colony. The imperial power takes raw materials from the colony and sells finished goods in return, discouraging the development of any manufacturing industry which might compete with its own. There now exist few relics of political empires but **economic imperialism** is alive and well.

**impermeable** Not allowing the passage of a fluid; in *hydrology, the fluid is water.

**impervious** *Impermeable.

**imports** Goods which originate from a foreign country and are bought by a nation in trade. **Invisible imports** are services, like insurance, bought from outside a country. **Import penetration** indicates the extent to which the country is dependent upon its imports; in 1982, for example, 49% of electrical goods sold in Britain were imported.

**import substitution** The production of goods by a nation in order to avoid costly imports.

**inceptisol** See *US soil classification.

**incidence matrix** A square or rectangular table used to indicate relationships between two sets. The rows and columns display the elements of these two sets. The intersections of each row or column are the cells of the matrix. Where a relationship exists between the two sets, the cell is marked with a 1; where no relationship exists, it is marked with a 0.

**incised meander** A *meander formed when a *rejuvenated river cuts deeper into the original meander. An **intrenched meander** is an incised meander with a symmetrical *cross-valley profile; an **ingrown meander** has an asymmetrical cross-section.

**inclination** A slant. In surveying, the **angle of inclination** from the horizontal of a feature may be determined by the use of a *clinometer. **Inclination-dip** is the angle of *dip of a fault, rock stratum, or mineral vein.

**inclosure** *Enclosure.

**incompetent** Of a rock, weak and liable to distortion under pressure.

**independent variable** The *causal factor in a set of variables.

**index numbers** Figures which show the relative change in one or more variables over time. The value of the variable for one particular year is chosen to be the base value, expressed as 100. The figures for the other years are then expressed as a percentage of the figure for the base year.

**index of circulation** See *Rossby waves.

**index of decentralization** An index of the degree to which an activity, such as manufacturing industry, is centrally located within an area—region, conurbation, city, or town. An index of 0 represents maximum concentration at the centre while a value of 100 indicates maximum location at the periphery.

**index of dispersion** An index of the degree to which a distribution is grouped around a central point; the mean centre. This index is the mean of the distances of all the points to the centre. The lower the index, the less the dispersal. The indices of two dispersions can be compared with each other in an **index of relative dispersion**.

**index of dissimilarity** This is often used in the study of residential differentiation in urban areas. For each district, the percentage of those working in a given group is calculated. The index of dissimilarity between two occupational groups is one half of the sum of the absolute differences between the respective distributions taken district by district. The values range from 0—complete similarity—to 100—complete segregation.

**index of level of living** An assessment of living standards using indicators such as access to health care, standard of education, house ownership, car ownership, take-home pay, employment rates, access to *amenity, and so forth. Fifty-three indicators may be used, and are analysed so that areas of high living standards have a low composite index and vice versa. The spatial analysis of these data may be set out for a region or for a nation. In Britain, standards of living are best in South-East England and worst in the North and West.

**index of primacy** An index of the importance of the largest town in a country:

$$\text{Index of primacy} = \frac{P_1}{P_2}$$

where $P_1$ is the population of the largest town and $P_2$ is the population of the second largest town.

**index of segregation** A measure of the extent to which a subgroup differs from the wider population.

**index of variability** The *quartile deviation of a data set expressed as a percentage of the *arithmetic mean. It is useful for comparing two apparently similar data sets.

**index of vitality** An index to indicate the growth potential of a population:

$$I_v = \frac{\text{fertility rate} \times \% \text{ aged } 20\text{--}40}{\text{crude death rate} \times \text{old--age index}}$$

where $I_v$ = index of vitality. See *old-age index.

**Indian summer** Calm, dry, sunny, and sometimes misty weather occurring in Britain in the autumn.

**indicator species** A species whose presence in a location points to a particular quality in its environment. For example, lichens are indicators of clean air.

**indifference curves** In economics, a model in the consumer's mind as a series of contour lines around a mountain of *utility. The object of the consumer is to select purchases within income limitations so as to touch the highest of these contours on his or her mental map.

**indigenous** Belonging naturally to a region, native.

**indirect contact space** That part of an urban area perceived indirectly through, for example, the media, or other people's experience.

**individual data** Items which are listed separately for depiction or analysis.

**indivisibility** The difficulty of using only part of a plant for profitable production. For example, if a plant has a set of machines with different capacities, they will only be used economically if they are used to the full.

**induction** The use of facts to prove a general statement; the inferring of a general law from particular instances. It differs from deduction, which is an inference of the particular from the general.

**induration** The hardening of a rock, or a soil *horizon, brought about by pressure, heat, or *cementation.

**industrial complex** A large concentration of manufacturing industry in a relatively small area. Such a complex gains from *agglomeration economies and is usually well served by transport and financial provisions.

**industrial complex analysis** A technique, developed by Isard, of studying the linkages between the industries in an *industrial complex. It is a technique combining elements of *input–output analysis and *comparative cost analysis.

**industrial crop** A non-food crop used as an industrial raw material.

**industrial diversification** The spreading of employment and investment over a wide range of industrial activities. Diversification is not always easy to recognize; a firm may be described as a food manufacturer—one product—or as a manufacturer of many types of food—several products.

**industrial estate** A district of purpose-built workshops with supporting services, often located in suburbs or at the edge of a town or city.

**industrial geography** The study of the spatial arrangement of manufacturing industry. Manufacturing industry is specifically chosen for this definition since, it is argued, it is the basis upon which regional economies are built. Explanations of industrial patterns may be based on *location theory and on models with costs as the predominant locational factor. Other approaches are concerned with the nature of decision-making, and an understanding of change: where and why some regions grow while others, like inner cities and *depressed areas, decline. Strategies may then be suggested to aid ailing industrial areas and under-developed countries.

**industrial inertia** The survival of an industry in an area even though the factors which led to its location there no longer apply. It is often advisable to update and expand a factory rather than to relocate because of existing *agglomeration economies and *external economies and because of the difficulty of moving a skilled labour force.

**industrialization** The process by which manufacturing industries develop from within a predominantly agrarian society. Mechanization is of major significance in the change from *cottage industry to a factory system. Industrialization is generally accompanied by social and economic changes. Urbanization is encouraged and groups of manufacturing towns may form. Initially there is an emphasis on primary and secondary *industry, but as industrialization continues, there is a shift to tertiary industry.

Although industrialization is often seen as a solution to problems of poverty in the

Third World, its effects may well not benefit any but a small sector of society. Furthermore, the pollution associated with industrial activity may cause serious difficulties.

**industrial linkage** See *linkage.

**industrial location policy** There are different views of the role the state should play in economic activities. One is that the state should set a minimum number of rules to ensure that the market economy functions successfully. Another sees government intervening, especially for those areas that are in industrial decline. The latter type of government may attempt to attract industry by providing any or all of the following: land, buildings, financial incentives, and advice. Industrial development officers may be appointed to attract industry. Such policies may be carried out by local authorities as well as by central government. Industrial location policy may be adopted by less developed countries in an effort to industrialize.

**industrial location theory** Theories of the forces leading to the location of industrial activity. One choice might be the *least-cost location. Another is the *locational independence approach which stresses the influence of other enterprises, especially under conditions of imperfect competition. A third is the profit maximization approach, although it is by no means certain that firms do maximize profits.

**industrial organization** The make-up of an industrial unit, especially as it concerns decision-making. This is a major component of *industrial location theory. Organizations range from the owner-operated small firm to the *multinational corporations. In the latter, the low-level functions may take place in the Third World but decisions are taken in countries with advanced economies.

**industrial overspill** The movement of industry from *conurbations to new locations outside the built-up area because of constricted sites.

**industrial park** A planned area with small, purpose-built factory units and often located near motorways or railways. See *science park.

**industrial retention policy** A policy which is developed to help maintain industrial activity by taxation incentives, subsidies, and government contracts.

**industrial revolution** Although there is some discussion about its timing, the industrial revolution is generally accepted as having occurred in Britain in the late eighteenth and early nineteenth centuries. The revolution was in technology—new techniques involving new machinery and new processes—but was accompanied by social and political changes. These changes, beginning in Britain, took place over a long period of time but their effects transformed society.

**industrial specialization** The domination in a region of a limited range of industries. Such a region will have a high *location coefficient in a few industries. Specialization may be advantageous as *functional linkages are facilitated and *external and *agglomeration economies can be made, but an overdependence on a narrow range of industries can be dangerous and industrial diversification may be necessary.

**industry** This term is now often used to cover any form of economic activity, such as the music industry, and hence covers a very broad sweep. More specifically, industry is divided into **primary industry**—the acquisition of naturally occurring resources like coal and fish; **secondary industry**—the manufacture of goods; and **tertiary industry**, which serves the public as well as primary and secondary industry and includes distribution, transport, warehousing, and retailing. Some writers suggest the term **quaternary industry** to cover administration, finance, research, and the processing and transfer of information.

**infant mortality** The number of deaths in the first year of life per 1000 children born. See also *mortality.

**inferential statistics** Statistics which may be used to predict events, such as *probabilities. See also *descriptive statistics.

**infield–outfield farming** A type of farming, now generally superseded, whereby the infield—the land nearest to the farmhouse—was cropped continuously and manured heavily while the outfields were less heavily cropped and left fallow for long periods of time in order to recover their fertility.

**infiltration** The process of water entering rocks or soil. **Infiltration capacity** is the rate at which water can infiltrate the soil. The basic mechanism is that the upper soil surface receives precipitation so that existing soil moisture is displaced downwards by newly infiltrated water. Infiltration may be controlled by factors including cracks, cultivation, freezing, the intensity and type of precipitation, and the *porosity of the soil. The last factor is probably the most important. Infiltration may not occur if the speed of the water is too great or if the rock or soil is saturated.

**inflation** An increase in the cost of goods and services, possibly caused by too much money and credit chasing too few goods.

**informal sector** Employment which is not formally recognized. No figures reveal its existence and it is untaxed. Also called the black economy or moonlighting, it can be a source of cheaper labour as no allowance need be made for tax. In the Third World, much of the work done by women is in the informal sector; this includes such activities as petty trading, small-scale agriculture, and crafts.

**information theory** One, mathematical, view of the problem of conveying a message from one point to another. The meaning of the information does not signify; what is important is the capability of the engineering to code, transmit, and decode the message. Its success depends on the carrying capacity of the technology. In geography, this approach has been used to describe the distributions of populations.

**infra-red radiation** That part of the *electromagnetic spectrum which is perceived as heat.

**infrastructure** The framework of communication networks, health centres, administration, and power supply necessary for economic development.

**ingrown meander** A *meander which cuts sideways into the bank so that there is a slight overhang above the stream. See also *incised meander.

**inland** Having no access to the open sea, as in an **inland drainage basin** or an **inland sea**.

**inlier** An exposure of rock completely surrounded by younger rock.

**inner city** An area at or near the city centre with delapidated housing, derelict land, and declining industry. The inner city is often home to those with low wages, living in multi-occupied housing.

**innovation** The introduction of a new feature or the new feature itself.

**innovation wave** The diffusion of an *innovation from its point of origin. Initially a very few, near to the point of origin, accept the innovation so that the wave peaks close to the focus. At this stage, there is a strong contrast between the area of innovation and the rest of the country. The peak of the wave moves away from the source through time as locations at a greater distance from the point of origin adopt the innovation. Next there is a period of consolidation across the whole of the region concerned, and, finally, as the innovation saturates the region, diffusion slows down until the stage of maximum acceptance, when it ceases. See also *diffusion.

**input–output analysis** A view of the economy which stresses the interdependence of different sectors. The output of one sector is often the input of another. **Primary inputs**, like land or labour, come from outside the system while **intermediate inputs** originate within the system. **Final outputs**

pass out of the system. The quantities, expressed in money values, are displayed in a matrix; the rows record the destination of the outputs while the columns show the origin of the inputs. The coefficients indicate the linkages between inputs and outputs. It is possible to predict the amount each sector must produce for a given requirement but the calculation is very large and very time-consuming because of the high number of sectors found in real life.

**inselberg** A steep isolated peak rising abruptly from a *pediment. There is some debate about the origin of this feature. Some writers invoke *parallel slope retreat for the formation of inselbergs; others believe that they are the revealed remnants of the deeply weathered rock typical of tropical climates.

**insolation** From *in*coming *sol*ar rad*iation*, this is the *solar radiation received at the earth's surface. The amount of insolation varies with latitude, since the angle of the sun's rays and the duration of daylight change with latitude and season. Other contributory factors include the *solar constant, the slope and aspect of the surface, and the amount of cloud in the *atmosphere. Global variations in insolation are a prime factor in the *general circulation of the atmosphere.

**insolation weathering** See *thermal expansion.

**instability** The condition of a 'parcel' of air which is likely to rise. Air is **unstable** if it cools more slowly than the surrounding, stationary air. It rises because it is warmer, and therefore less dense, than the surrounding atmosphere. This is *absolute instability. The rise will be checked when the temperature of the parcel is the same as that of its surroundings.

When otherwise *stable air is forced to rise, for example, over a mountain barrier, or because of *turbulence, a state of *conditional instability is said to exist.

**instrumentalism** A philosophy of science which judges the worth of a theory by its fit with empirical evidence but requires no understanding of causal correlation.

**insular** Relating to an island. An **insular climate** has a small annual and *diurnal range of temperature, and rainfall is generally high.

**integration** 1. **Social integration** is the process whereby a minority group, particularly an ethnic minority, adapts to the host society and where it is accorded equal rights with the rest of the community. *Assimilation is integration such that the immigrants' culture is lost.

2. **Economic integration** can be the breaking down of trade barriers between nations in order to set up a common market. The term is also applied to a firm which takes control of all the stages of production. A major example is an integrated iron and steel works comprising coke ovens, blast furnaces, steel forges, and a strip mill. **Horizontal integration** is the central organization of all units at the same stage of production, while **vertical integration** is the integration of units at all stages of production.

**intensive agriculture** Agriculture with a high level of inputs—capital and labour—and high yields. Outputs are valuable and often perishable. Intensive agriculture is usually found in regions of dense population and high land values.

**intentionality** A philosophy that recognizes that all consciousness is consciousness of something. Intention should be understood as a relationship of being between man and the world that gives meaning. Places are focuses of intention, having a fixed location and possessing features which persist in an identifiable form. Marcel claimed that an individual is not distinct from his place; he is that place.

**interaction** Also known as spatial interaction, this is the action between two points upon one another. An **interaction model** describes the reactions of two or more processes or systems as they affect each other.

**interbed** A stratum of rock laid down in sequence between two other beds.

**interception** The holding of raindrops by plants as the water falls on to leaves, stems, and branches. When the plant can hold no more, the water will drip from the plant (**throughfall**) or run down the stem (**stemflow**).

**interdependence** The interlocking of parts within a system. Within human geography, it views a system as a whole, stressing the role of each part of the system. For example, an advanced economy may depend on the raw materials of a less advanced economy just as much as the latter depends on the finished goods and technology of the former.

**interface** A common boundary between two systems, processes, regions, or other phenomena.

**interflow** Movement of water through soil, but at a greater depth than *throughflow. It is difficult to separate the two processes in the field.

**interfluve** An area of land between two rivers.

**interglacial** A long, distinct period of warmer conditions between *glacials when the earth's glaciers have shrunk to a smaller area.

**interlocking spurs** A series of ridges of land projecting out on alternate sides of a valley and around which a river winds its course.

**intermediate** Of rocks, containing 52–65% silica; intermediate between *acid rocks and *basic rocks.

**intermediate technology** Agricultural or industrial processes using basic skills that are available in developing countries and that require a simple, easily learned and maintained technology. Industries can be developed to suit the technology of the workers, to serve local needs, and to use plentiful supplies of labour. Where available capital is limited, it may be more effective to spread it over a number of projects rather than to concentrate on one high-technology industrial development.

**intermittent** Impermanent, occurring from time to time, as in an **intermittent spring** or an **intermittent stream**.

**intermontane** Lying between mountains.

**International Date Line** Any place just west of 180° is twelve hours ahead of Greenwich Mean Time; points just east of it are twelve hours behind. To reconcile these facts, an imaginary line—the International Date Line—has been established. The line follows 180° longitude except where it crosses land so there are some departures from the meridian. As the traveller moves from east to west over the International Date Line he gains an extra day. The traveller moving in an opposite direction keeps gaining time so that a day must be lost.

**international division of labour** The separation of the different components of industry and the allocation of each component to a different location world-wide. Research and development, manufacturing, assembly, and administration, for example, may each take place in a different country according to local considerations and costs.

**international region** Also known as a geo-strategic region, this is an association of all, or parts of, nations with a common interest. The *heartland as defined by Mackinder is an example.

**interpersonal space** The linear distance separating one individual from others. The closest distance will be shown by couples, the next by family and friends, and the furthest by strangers.

**interpluvial** A time of increased aridity in deserts; the time between *pluvials.

**interpolation** Forming an estimate of a value with reference to known values either side of it. This method is used for contour lines or other *isopleths.

**interquartile range** If the number of values of ranked data is divided into four equal parts, then the lines marking each division are **quartiles**. The interquartile range is the difference between the values of the upper and lower quartiles. The closer the clustering of values around the *median, the smaller the interquartile range. The value of the interquartile range is important when two sets of similar data are compared.

**interstadial** A warmer phase within a *glacial which is too short and insufficiently distinct to be classed as an *interglacial.

**Inter-Tropical Convergence Zone, ITCZ** That part of the tropics where two wind systems, the north-east *trade winds and the south-east trade winds, converge. Where these winds meet, pressure is low, humidity is high, and rain is spasmodic. This zone moves north and south with the seasons; it occurs in the summer season of each hemisphere. The movements of the ITCZ are impossible to predict. When it moves well away from the equator it brings unusually heavy rainfall; this caused floods in Khartoum in August 1988. If the ITCZ does not move far from the equator, droughts occur, as in Ethiopia in 1984.

The position of the ITCZ is affected by the apparent movement of the overhead sun, the relative strengths of the trade winds, and the changing locations of maximum sea-surface temperatures. It is these variations which mean that the movements of the ITCZ are highly unpredictable. The ITCZ can draw in moist air from the sea, bringing rain, and is more active in mountainous regions. However, in the dry interiors of continents it may not even bring cloud. Over the oceans, the ITCZ is broad, and often loses its identity. Winds are then absent, and such windless regions are known as *doldrums.

**interval level measurement** Measurements made such that it is possible to assess the size of the differences between them. For example, if there are three plants 18, 12, and 9 cm high, the difference between the first two may be reckoned and that could be compared with the interval between the second and third values.

**interval scale** A scale which can show the actual quantities of the variables. Either exact measurements are used or the occurrences of the phenomenon are counted.

**intervening opportunities theory** This states that the number of people travelling a given distance is directly proportional to the number of opportunities at that distance and inversely proportional to the number of intervening opportunities, that is, the number of chances of finding satisfaction in work or residence, for example, which may be encountered along the journey. The concept was advanced by Stouffer, and indicates that opportunities nearby are more attractive than slightly better opportunities further away. One drawback of this theory is the difficulty of measuring 'opportunities'.

**intervention price** A guaranteed minimum price, set by a government, for agricultural produce. Should prices fall below this minimum, the government must buy the produce at this price. The intervention price is usually a percentage of the target price—the price hoped for in the open market.

**intrazonal soil** A soil affected more by local factors than by climate, unlike a *zonal soil. Thus, waterlogging gives rise to *gley soils and a parent rock of pure calcium carbonate will produce a *rendzina.

**intrenched meander** A deeper watercourse cut into an original *meander such that the banks steepen very suddenly above the stream. See also *incised meander.

**intrusion** A mass of igneous rock which has forced its way, as *magma, through pre-existing rocks and then solidified below the surface of the ground. Intrusions can occur along the *bedding planes as **concordant intrusions** or across them as **discordant intrusions**. The crystals in intrusive rocks are large since the subterranean magma cools slowly, giving time for crystal growth. Some major forms of igneous intrusions are shown below.

**invasion and succession** A model of change used in *urban geography to represent changing land use within a neighbourhood. For example, a few in-migrants who are content with multiple dwelling invade a neighbourhood to the discontent of the residents who will eventually leave. Succession is the end of the process when the area has changed completely.

**inverse distance law** Formulated by Zipf; it states that the movement of people between two towns is inversely proportional to the distance between them.

**inversion** In meteorology, a situation in which air temperatures *rise* with height. (This is the reverse of the more common situation in which air cools with height.)

Inversions occur

when strong nocturnal *terrestrial radiation cools the earth's surface and therefore chills the air which is in contact with the ground;

when cold air flows into valley floors, displacing warmer air (see also *frost pockets);

where a stream of warm air crosses the cool air over a cold *ocean current;

where warm air rises over a cold front;

when air from the upper *troposphere subsides in a warm *anticyclone, is compressed and *adiabatically warmed.

The boundary between the top of the cold air and the beginning of the inversion is an **inversion lid**. Inversions are very *stable and damp or polluted air is often trapped below them.

**inverted relief** Relief no longer corresponding with *lithology and structure, as when a *syncline occurs at the top of a mountain. Inverted relief usually indicates that erosion has been operating for a very long time.

**invisible exports** Services like shipping and insurance which can earn foreign exchange without the transfer of goods from one country to another.

**involution** 1. The refolding of two *nappes differing in age so that parts of the younger nappe lie below older rocks.

2. A synonym for *cryoturbation.

**ion** An atom or group of atoms that has either lost one or more electrons, making it positively charged (*cation), or has gained one or more electrons thereby becoming negatively charged. Hence **ionization**, the production of ions.

**ionosphere** That part of the atmosphere, more than 100 km above the earth, which is ionized by cosmic radiation, solar X-rays, and ultraviolet radiation. To some extent, positive and negative ions move independently in this zone.

**Iron Age** After the *Bronze Age, that stage of human development which saw the smelting and use of iron, probably dating in Britain from 500 BC.

**iron band, iron pan** See *podzol.

**Iron Curtain** Between 1945 and 1989, the imaginary barrier between the West and the Eastern bloc countries: USSR, Poland, Czechoslovakia, Hungary, Rumania, Bulgaria, and Albania.

**irradiance** The amount of radiant flux per unit area falling on a surface (see *radiant excitance).

**irrigation** The supply of water to the land by means of channels, streams, and sprinklers in order to permit the growth of crops. Without irrigation *arable farming is not possible where annual rainfall is 250 mm or less and it is advisable in areas of up to 500 mm annual rainfall. To some extent, irrigation can free man from the vagaries of rainfall and, to that end, may be used in areas of seemingly sufficient rainfall because irrigation can supply the right amount of water at the right time.

Large-scale irrigation schemes may encounter difficulties if they cross national boundaries; the Punjab irrigation scheme of North-West India and Pakistan is a source of conflict between the two nations since the original scheme was set up before partition. Even within a nation, there may be disputes about water supply; Arizona and California both use the water of the Colorado, which acts as a frontier between the two states.

In its simplest form, irrigation is achieved by devices such as the *sakia and the *shaduf to lift water but, increasingly, modern pumps are used. Irrigation is not suited to saline soils since the salt will move to the surface and be so concentrated there as to inhibit the growth of most plants. Similarly, the use of *brackish water for irrigation is unwise since the salts remain in the soil after the water has been lost through *evapotranspiration.

Irrigated lands show regular and intricate systems of intensively cultivated fields dependent on water through canals, cuts, and irrigation channels.

**island** A body of land completely surrounded by water.

**island arc** An island chain, mostly of volcanic origin, in the form of an arc. According to *plate tectonic theory, the arc is formed when *oceanic crust plunges into the *mantle where it undergoes *subduction. The *magma thus formed creates a chain of submarine volcanoes which are eventually built up into islands.

**island biogeography** The number of species living in an isolated space, such as an island, can be seen as a balance between the immigration of new species and the extinction of established ones. While the population is low, the balance will be non-interactive, i.e. different species multiply without interference. However, when populations are large enough, they interact and immigration and extinction are affected.

Distant islands will receive immigrants at a slower rate than the islands near the mainland, but extinction rates will be the same for both, so that distant islands will hold fewer species.

On large islands, immigration is high since the 'target' is large. Extinction is also lower because there is more cover. Thus, large islands will have more species than small ones.

The concepts of island biogeography may be extended to any community in an isolated habitat—even to an enclosed lake, which is an island of water in a sea of land.

**iso-** Prefix meaning equal to.

**isobar** A line on a map or chart that joins places with the same atmospheric pressure. By reading the isobars over a large area it is possible to gain a visual impression of any *anticyclones or *depressions that may be present. **Isobaric areas** are parts of the atmosphere having uniform pressure.

**isochrone** A line drawn on a map connecting places of an equal journey time to the same location.

**isocline** An overfold of such intensity that both limbs dip by the same amount and in the same direction.

**isodapane** A line drawn on a map joining up places of equal *total* transport costs for industrial production and delivery between the points where the raw materials are located and the markets.

**isohel** A line drawn on a map connecting places experiencing equal amounts of sunshine.

**isohyet** A line drawn on a map connecting points of equal rainfall.

**isolated state** In *von Thünen's model, a state made up of an *isotropic plain, completely cut off from outside influence and served by a single city.

**isoline** See *isopleth.

**isophene** A line drawn on a map connecting places with the same timing of similar biological events such as the flowering of a crop.

**isopleth** A line drawn on a map connecting places with an equal incidence of any feature. Also known as an **isoline**.

**isostasy** The continental crust of the earth has a visible part above the surface and a lower, invisible one. The balance between these two is isostasy. If part of the upper surface is removed by erosion, the continental crust will rise to offset this erosion, at least in part. Where sections of the continental crust have been pushed down by the weight of glacial ice, they will rise again if the ice melts. An adjustment as a result of glaciation is *glacio-isostasy. These spontaneous alterations within the crust are **isostatic adjustments**.

**isosteric** Of part of the atmosphere having uniform density.

**isotherm** A line drawn on a map or chart joining places of equal temperature; **isothermal,** having the same temperature.

**isotim** A line drawn on a map about a source of raw materials or a market where transport costs are equal.

**isotope** One of two or more alternative forms of an element that have the same number of protons in their nucleus, but have different numbers of neutrons.

**isotropic** Having the same physical properties in all directions. The featureless **isotropic plain** is the basis of many location theories such as those of *Weber, *von Thünen, and Christaller.

**isthmus** A narrow strip of land connecting to large areas of land; the isthmus of Panama connects the Americas.

**ITCZ** See *Inter-Tropical Convergence Zone.

# J

**jet stream** A meandering band, some hundreds of kilometres across, of strong westerly winds, blowing at 100 km per hour or more, in the upper air between 9000 and 15 000 m. The major jets in each hemisphere are located around the latitudes of 50°, but their paths zigzag. These jets mark strong horizontal shifts in temperature and pressure (see *baroclinic) since they mark the boundaries between cold polar air and warm tropical air. They control, in part, the development and movement of depressions and anticyclones. The subtropical westerly jets do not appear to affect surface weather to any great extent.

In summer, an easterly jet blows over the Indian Ocean to Africa. It carries away the influx of air over the Indian subcontinent caused by the *monsoon.

**joint** A crack in a rock without any clear sign of movement either side of the joint.

**jökulhlaup** A sudden flood of glacial meltwater released when volcanic activity heats the ice.

**junction** In geomorphology, the meeting point of two rivers.

**Jurassic** The middle *period of *Mesozoic time stretching approximately from 190 to 136 million years BP.

**juvenile water** Water contained within *magma and which is emitted during volcanic eruptions.

# K

**Kamchatka current** A cold *ocean current.

**kame** An isolated hill or mound of stratified sands and gravels which have been deposited by glacial meltwater. Some kame deposits show slumping on a side which previously had been held in position by a wall of ice. Many kames seem to be old deltas of subglacial streams.

**Kame terraces** are flat-topped, steep-sided ridges of similar fluvio-glacial origin, running along the valley side. They are *ice contact features, formed between the side of a decaying glacier and a valley wall. **Moulin kames** form below *moulins.

**karaburan** A strong north-easterly wind, often carrying *loess, blowing over central Asia.

**kärez** In much of the Arab world, a man-made, underground, and very gently sloping channel carrying irrigation water from the foothills to the plain.

**karre, pl. karren** A collective name for the channels, up to 5 cm in depth, caused by solution on exposed limestone. **Kluftkarren** are the enlarged joints also known as *grikes. **Rillenkarren** are the small radiating grooves which are the overflow of surface solution pans. **Rinnenkarren** develop as a result of coalescence of small channels. Their walls are sharp, in contrast with the large rounded hollows known as **rundkarren**.

**karroo** A scrub-covered plateau land in southern Africa.

**karst** An area of limestone which is dominated by underground streams and hollows and pits usually caused by subsidence into underground channels.

Karst is most strongly developed in humid uplands where very thick, strongly jointed limestones occur. Typical karst features include *blind valleys, *sink holes,

caves, *dolines, *karren, and springs. The term **karstic** is used for karst scenery; **karstification** is the formation of karst scenery, and **karstland** is an area of karst scenery. See also *labyrinth karst, *tower karst.

**kata-** From the Greek, *kata*, 'down'—sinking of air at a *kata-front or in a *katabatic wind.

**katabatic** Referring to downslope winds. Descending *adiabatically warmed katabatic winds are *foehn winds. Cold katabatic winds result from the slumping down of very cold, and hence dry, air.

**kata-front** A *front characterized by the descent of warm air.

**kettle hole** Large masses of ice can become incorporated in glacial *till and may be preserved after the glacier has retreated. When one of these bodies of ice finally melts, it leaves a depression in the landscape; a kettle hole.

**key, cay** In the Caribbean, a very low island, perhaps only metres above sea level, formed of sand and coral.

**key village** A village designated to be developed in terms of goods and services. Key villages are to be expanded while other centres are run down, with their residents encouraged to leave. Key villages have been developed successfully in rural counties such as Norfolk and Devon but little has been done in the running down of small villages.

**khamsin** See *local winds.

**kibbutz** An Israeli rural settlement where all the agricultural land and resources are communally owned and all farming strategies are decided jointly.

**knick point, nick point** A point at which there is a sudden *break of slope in the *long profile of a river. In areas of uniform geology, the presence of a knick point may be evidence of *rejuvenation; the river is forming a new, lower profile cutting first from the mouth of the river and working upstream as *headward erosion takes place.

**knock and lochan topography** A glacially scoured lowland landscape. *Roches moutonnées alternate with eroded hollows, often containing lakes.

**knock on effect** A *multiplier effect that operates in reverse to the detriment of a region. Thus, unemployment in a key industry leads to unemployment in associated industries and therefore to unemployment in service industries.

**knoll** A low, round hill.

**knot** A unit of speed; one nautical mile (1.85 km) per hour.

**kolkhoz** A large-scale farming unit in the USSR where the state-owned land is leased to a collective. Decisions are made by an elected committee and profits are shared between the members. See *collective farm.

**Kondratieff cycles** A series of long waves of economic activity. Each cycle lasts 50–60 years and goes through development and boom to recession. The first cycle was based on steam power, the second on railways, the third on electricity and the motor car, and the fourth on electronics and synthetic materials. Kondratieff argued that one of the forces which initiates long waves is the large number of important discoveries and inventions that occur

during a depression and are usually applied on a large scale at the beginning ot the next upswing. Each cycle leaves its mark on the industrial landscape.

**Köppen's climatic classification** A system of categorizing climates of the world based on the climatic needs of the varying vegetation types. The zones are as follows: A, tropical, with mean temperatures over 20 °C throughout the year; B, subtropical, having 4–11 months with mean temperature over 20 °C; C, temperate, with 4–12 months of temperatures between 10 and 20 °C; D, cold, having 1–4 months of temperatures between 10 and 20 °C; E, polar, with 12 months of temperatures below 10° C. Further subdivisions are made on the basis of rainfall and more detailed temperature data.

**kum** A sandy desert of central Asia, similar to the *erg of the Sahara.

**Kuro Shio** A warm *ocean current in the Pacific Ocean.

**kurtosis** This applies to the degree to which the *frequency distribution is concentrated around a peak, that is, it describes the sharpness of the central peak of the curve.

**k-value** In *central place theory, the k-value expresses the number of central places of the same order in the hierarchy served by their own central place one order higher, plus that higher centre itself.

**kyle** In Scotland, a narrow arm of the sea between two islands or between an island and the mainland.

# L

**labour** The manual or intellectual work which is one of the *factors of production. The quantity of labour is the amount of work done in terms of production or time whilst the quality indicates the degree of skill and intelligence required. Labour costs are a major part of the *cost structure of many firms; in such cases they should focus on labour as the key to locational comparative advantage. In times of employment decline, high-cost labour can bring about failure in small firms and a closure of some plants in multi-site enterprises. Some employers see labour as being unreliable where trade unionism is strong, or where *absenteeism is high.

**labour-extensive** Of an enterprise, needing only a small workforce.

**labour-intensive** Of an enterprise, needing a large workforce.

**labour market** The exchange of work for *capital. In *neoclassical economics, market forces acting on *economic man are held to bring about an equilibrium between the supply of capital and the supply of labour. This takes no account of differences caused by gender, race, or location, and state intervention is not considered.

**labour theory of value** The *Marxist contention that the value of a product reflects the amount of labour time needed to make it. If the capitalist pays low wages which do not reflect the labour expended, he will obtain surplus capital. This may be seen as exploitation which can lead to class conflict.

**Labrador current** A cold *ocean current in the North Atlantic Ocean.

**labyrinth karst** The deep canyons of limestone formed by *carbonation. Initially the limestone shows *bogaz; these widen and deepen into long gorges known as karst streets with other, cross-cutting, lines

of erosion. The remnant of this carbonation is *tower karst.

**laccolith** An *intrusion of igneous rock which spreads along *bedding planes and forces the overlying *strata into a *dome.

**lacustrine** Relating to a lake. For example, a **lacustrine delta** is a delta formed when a stream enters a lake.

**lag fault** A low-angled fault with more displacement of the rocks at the top than of the rocks at the bottom.

**lagged time** The interval between an event and the time when its effects are apparent.

**lagoon** A bay totally or partially enclosed by a *spit or reef running across the entrance.

**lahar** A downslope flow of volcanic debris, either dry or mixed with water as a mud flow.

**lake** An expanse of water lying in a depression on the earth's surface. Lakes are generally only temporary features of the landscape. They may be classified according to their origin, as in an ice-dammed lake.

**lake dwelling** A house built on piles driven into a shallow lake or marsh.

**Lamarckism** The doctrine that acquired characteristics are inheritable. This has been applied to the development of theories of social evolution and to varieties of *environmental determinism. However, the theory has now been discredited.

**lamina** Any thin layer. **Lamination** is very fine *stratification.

**laminar flow** A type of non-*turbulent flow where the movement of each part of the fluid (gaseous, liquid, or plastic) has the same velocity, with no mixing between adjacent 'layers' of the fluid.

**land breeze** A wind blowing from land to sea (an **offshore wind**) which develops in coastal districts towards nightfall. See also *sea breeze.

**land bridge** A dry land connection between continents.

**land capability** The potential of land for agriculture and forestry depending on its physical and environmental qualities. The main factor investigated is soil type, but climate, gradient, and aspect are also considered. Present land use is not taken into account.

**land classification** The evaluation of land into categories with regard to the potential agricultural output. Soil quality is a major factor but any assessment should also take into account drainage, elevation, gradient, susceptibility to soil erosion, temperatures, and rainfall. Economic classifications may also be used, concerned with the layout of the farm, its workings, and prices and markets. Economic factors may change and so might the physical evaluation; chalklands are more extensively cropped than they were in the 1950s. Land classification maps have been produced but, given their intricacy, it is difficult to make useful generalizations. Furthermore, classification of land into a particular category tends to be somewhat subjective.

**land consolidation** A type of *land reform which aims to give each farmer one relatively large plot of land rather than scattered, small parcels of land.

**land economics** The study of land use and of the factors which influence and shape it. Land values are a central part of this study as the patterns of land uses and land values are interlinked.

**landform** A physical feature of the earth's crust brought about by natural processes such as *erosion, *deposition, and *tectonic activity.

**land-locked state** A nation with no access to the sea. There are 26 land-locked states ranging in size from the tiny Vatican City to Mongolia. One important preoccupation of a land-locked state is access to the sea. This may be achieved along a river like the Danube, by the creation of a *corridor, or simply by negotiating a right of passage through a maritime neighbour.

**landlord capital** In an agricultural tenancy, the landlord supplies certain assets such as land, roads, drains, and buildings. See also *tenant capital.

**landmass** A very large area of *continental crust.

**land reclamation** The winning or recovering of land, usually for agricultural use. Methods include *afforestation, chemical treatment, clearance, drainage, embanking, filling in, rainwash, *irrigation, and *terrace cultivation.

**land reform** A sweeping change in land tenure. It usually involves the breaking up of large estates and the widespread redistribution of the land into smallholdings, but may also be *land consolidation. Another variation is the policy of certain revolutionary regimes of collectivizing the land, taking it out of private ownership.

**land rent** The profit a farmer makes from the sale of his produce after all costs have been deducted. See *von Thünen's model.

**land rotation** See *rotation of crops.

**LANDSAT** A *remote sensing device; an unmanned, American satellite orbiting the earth at a distance of 12 km and recording features by means of cameras and other scanners.

**landscape** An area of the earth's surface with a distinctive appearance, natural, man-made, or both. See, for example, *cultural landscape and *natural landscape.

**landscape architecture** Originally the design of gardens, this term now also covers the planning and management of a landscape in order to meet aesthetic standards while also fulfilling some functions. An adventure playground may be laid out in a pleasing fashion or a motorway may be designed to clash as little as possible with the landscape.

**landscape evaluation** An attempt to assess the landscape in objective terms. Sometimes a consensus of views of the landscape is sought so that particular landscapes may be chosen as being outstandingly beautiful. Landscape description studies try to identify important items such as topography or buildings. Some kind of ranking method may be attempted to compare one landscape with another. Using this idea, Leopold attempted to calculate how close a landscape was to being unique. Personal preferences may also be used.

**landscape preference** It is argued that most cultures have a preferred landscape: the Dutch are said to be attracted by order and neatness while Americans are said to value a wilderness where landscape elements are very large. A knowledge of the preferred landscape might enable planners to modify the landscape with a minimum of protest.

**Landschaft** A German concept of landscape which attempted to classify landscapes, usually distinguishing between the natural and the *cultural landscape.

**landslide** Used very loosely, the term landslide covers most forms of *mass movement.

**land tenure** The nature of access to land use. Common forms of land tenure are as follows. Owner-occupied farms range from large farms using hired labour to peasant plots. Tenancies vary very widely but all involve payment, in one form or another, to the landlord from the tenant. This payment can be in the form of labour, in the form of a portion of the crop (*sharecropping), or in the form of cash. The plantation is owned by an institution and uses paid labour. Collectives may own land together and work together to an agreed strategy, sharing any profits which may accrue. There may even be land which is owned by nobody but is used by an individual or group. This last is typical of *shifting cultivation.

**land use** Any use made by man of the land surface of the earth's crust.

**land use classification** The analysis of land according to its use: agricultural, industrial, recreational, and residential. Comparisons are very difficult to make between different countries which may have different classifications. On occasion, the land may have more than one use, as in upland areas used for sheep farm ing and for recreation.

**land use survey** In the UK, the First Land Utilization Survey was carried out between 1931 and 1939. It used seven categories of land, and the original maps are kept at the London School of Economics where they may still be studied. The maps were also published, at a scale of six inches to the mile.

The Second Land Utilization Survey was carried out between 1961 and 1969 using base maps of the same scale but having 256 categories. These maps can be consulted at the Land Use Research Unit at King's College, London. Some of these maps were published at 1 : 25 000, using 70 categories, but they cover only 15% of the area of England and Wales.

**land use zoning** The segregation of land use into different areas for each type of use: agricultural, industrial, recreational, and residential. The 1947 Town and Country Planning Act required local authorities to zone land use in the future.

**lapié** The French term for *karre.

**lapili** See *pyroclast.

**lapse rate** 1. In meteorology, the rate at which stationary or moving air changes temperature with a change in height. See also *adiabatic and *environmental lapse rate.
2. In human geography, the decline of interactions between a central place and its surroundings, with distance from the central point. Towns gradually shade into countryside and industrial areas can merge into areas of rural land use.

**latent heat** The quantity of heat absorbed or released when a substance changes its physical state at constant temperature, e.g. from a solid to a liquid at its melting point, or from a liquid to a gas at its boiling point.

**lateral accretion** In geomorphology, the build-up of sediments at the *slip-off slope of a river or during *braiding.

**lateral dune** A small *sand dune, in the *lee of some obstacle and near to a larger dune.

**lateral erosion** Usually of rivers, erosion of the banks rather than the bed.

**lateral fluvial migration** Both *braided and meandering rivers change their course over time and move from side to side of the valley. Lateral movement within a braided river occurs when the water inundates the flood plain and a new course is established. Meanders migrate when the outside of a bend is undercut.

**lateral moraine** See *moraine.

**laterite** Thick, red, and greatly weathered and altered strata of tropical ground. Laterites are red because silicates have been leached out, and iron and aluminium salts now predominate. *Horizons are unclear and the nutrient status of the soil is low. Laterite is soft but hardens rapidly when exposed to the air until it has a brick-like hardness.

**lateritic soils, latosols** Soils of humid tropical or equatorial zones characterized by a deep weathered layer from which silica has been *leached, a lack of *humus, and an accumulation or layer of aluminium and iron *sesquioxides. The reddish colour of these soils is imparted by the iron compounds. See *laterization.

**laterization** The formation of *lateritic soils. Laterization takes place in warm climates where bacterial activity takes place throughout the year. Consequently, little or no *humus is found in the soil. In the absence of *humic acids, iron and aluminium compounds are insoluble and accumulate in layers in the soil. Silica is *leached out.

**latifundium, pl. latifundia** A large farm or an estate particularly in Latin America

and Spain. The estate is farmed with the use of labourers who sometimes lease very small holdings from the land owner.

**Latin America** In Central and South America, the territory discovered and settled by the Spanish and the Portuguese; the Spanish-speaking islands of the Caribbean plus all of the Americas south of the USA except for Belize, French Guiana, Guyana, and Surinam.

**Latin America Free Trade Association (LAFTA)** An organization of certain South American states formed in order to foster trade between them, and to lessen their dependence on more advanced economies. Members are Argentina, Bolivia, Brazil, Colombia, Ecuador, Mexico, Paraguay, Uruguay, and Venezuela.

**latitude** Parallels of latitude are imaginary circles drawn round the earth parallel to the equator. The parallels are numbered according to the angle formed between a line from the line of latitude to the centre of the earth and a line from the centre of the earth to the equator.

Those regions lying within the Arctic and Antarctic circles, having values of 66.5° to 90°, are termed **high latitudes**. **Low latitudes** lie between 23.5 °N. and S. of the equator, i.e. within the tropics. **Mid-latitudes**, also known as **temperate latitudes**, lie between the two.

**Laurasia** One of the two original continents which broke from the supercontinent, Pangaea, by *continental drift.

**lava** *Magma which has flowed over the earth's surface. The *viscosity of lava depends on its silica content, pressure, and temperature. The latter is the most important factor. **Basic lavas** have a low silica content and flow freely; **acid lavas** are more viscous. Water in lava also makes it more fluid. When the water in the underground magma chamber vapourizes, it expands instantly causing explosive eruptions.

**law** A theory or hypothesis which has been confirmed by empirical evidence. It generally indicates a relationship between cause and effect.

**leaching** The movement of water down the *soil profile. This results in the movement of *cations, *sesquioxides, *clay colloids, and *humus to the lower soil *horizons. Specific types of leaching include **lixiviation**—the removal of the soluble salts containing metallic cations; the removal of *chelates; *lessivage; and *desilication.

**lead–lag model** A statistical model which identifies differences of timing of fluctuations through regions and city systems.

**leading stroke** See *lightning.

**league** A more or less informal association of states for a particular purpose, such as the Organization of Petroleum Exporting Countries. *OPEC is a particularly strong league in comparison with, for example, the British Commonwealth which is more a cultural than political league.

**leasehold** The legal ownership of land or buildings, or both.

**least cost location** A site chosen for industrial development where total costs are at their theoretical lowest, as opposed to location at the point of maximum revenue. See *Weber's theory of industrial location.

**least squares method** See *regression line.

**Lebensraum** Literally, 'living space', the room needed for a nation's expansion. The concept was used by the Germans to justify their territorial growth. The term was introduced after 1870 and became a central concept in the propaganda literature of the Nazis.

**lee** The side (**lee-side**), sheltered from the wind. Somewhat confusingly, a **lee shore** is the shore *towards* which the wind is blowing.

**lee depression** These occur when troughs in *lee waves develop into lows. Such depressions are frequent in winter where mountains block low-level air streams, as in areas east of the Rockies or south of the Alps.

**lee wave** A wave-type motion in a current of air as it descends below an upper layer of stable air after its forced rise over a mountain barrier. The typical wavelength is 5–15 km with an amplitude of some 500 m. Also known as a **standing wave** or **rotor**, this type of air flow is often disclosed by the presence of *lenticular clouds which form at the crest of the wave if air reaches *condensation level.

**legend** The key to the symbols used on a map.

**leguminous** Describing a group of plants, such as beans or clover, most of which 'fix' nitrogen from the air in nodules on their roots. This fixing makes nitrogen compounds available to other plants, and thus increases soil fertility.

**leisure** That time left over after time taken for work and other obligations. The term indicates that this time is spent on activities which are worth while in themselves to the individual. The **geography of leisure** studies the spatial patterns of people's behaviour in their free time.

**lenticular cloud** In upland areas, a lens-shaped cloud produced by *eddies in the air.

**less developed country** A country with low levels of development. Indicators of lack of development include high birth, death, and infant mortality rates; more than 50% of its workforce in agriculture; and low levels of nutrition, secondary schooling, literacy, electricity consumption per head, and *GDP per capita.

**less favoured land** As identified by the *EC, a type of land of little agricultural potential, and often characterized by *rural depopulation.

**lessivage** The *translocation of *clay colloids in a soil with no change in their chemical composition.

**levante** A moist, usually rain-bearing, and easterly wind of the western Mediterranean, blowing especially between July and October.

**leveche** A hot, dry, and often dusty southerly wind blowing northwards from the Sahara to Spain.

**levée** A raised bank of *alluvium flanking a river. The bank is built up when the river dumps much of its *load during flooding.

**level** An almost flat area of land, especially in the *fens of eastern England.

**levelling** In surveying, establishing the differences in height between two points by instruments such as the *Abney level.

**ley** Within a rotation, the seeding of a field to grass or clover. **Ley farming** as a system uses grass- or clover-leys to maintain fertility.

**liana** A creeper of the equatorial rain forest which winds and climbs around trees for support.

**lichen** A flat, and sometimes circular, organism composed of a fungus associated with an *alga. See *indicator species.

**lichenometry** A method of establishing the relative age of a deposit, especially one of glacial origin. These deposits are free from lichen when first formed so that the diameter of the largest rosette of lichen on such a deposit is assumed to be an indication of the time the deposit was formed. Lichenometry can only supply relative dates of formation.

**life expectancy** The average number of years which an individual can expect to live in a given society. Life expectancy is usually given from birth but may apply at any age. It is normally derived from a national *life table. Mainly because of very high infant mortality rates, life expectancy is much lower in Third World countries than in developed nations. By the age of 70, the years of life remaining to an individual are similar in both types of society. Thus, the strong correlation between *GDP per capita and life expectancy becomes weaker as the age of an individual increases.

**life space** The limited time and space which an individual has in which to pursue a necessarily limited range of opportunities. Life space is the interaction of the individual with his behaviour setting.

**life table** A summary of the likelihood of living from any one age to any other. In a life table, a hypothetical *cohort of 100 000 births is set up and then the loss by deaths is shown for each year of life. Averages of losses are calculated for a given year, and from this the actual diminution of the cohort is shown.

**life world** The day-to-day world in which the individual lives out life and which is generally taken for granted.

**lift force** The upward force produced when fluid rises over a particle. In rivers and streams, the particle moves up from the bed into the flow when the lift force exceeds the gravitational force provided by the mass of the particle.

**light** That section of the *electromagnetic spectrum which can be seen by the eye.

**light industry** A type of manufacturing industry producing goods that are light in weight, high in value, and often very intricate.

**lightning** An emission of electricity from cloud to cloud, cloud to ground, or ground to cloud. It is accompanied by a flash of light, and is the result of variations of electrical charge on droplets within the cloud and on the earth's surface. This variation may be due to the breakup of raindrops, to the splintering of ice crystals, or to differing conditions between the splintered ice crystals and pellets of soft hail.

As a *cumulus cloud develops, the frozen upper layer becomes positively charged. Most of the cloud base is negatively charged, with patches that are positively charged. These negative charges are attracted to the earth, which has a positive charge. The result is a **leading stroke** from cloud to ground, which creates a conductive path between the two. The **return stroke**, from earth to cloud, follows the same path. This return stroke may be of the order of 10 000 amps, carried through a pathway of air which is only millimetres across. The intense heat of the stroke engenders light, and the violent expansion of the air causes shock waves which are heard as thunder.

Where the path between ground and cloud is clearly visible, **forked lightning** is seen. The illumination of other clouds by a concealed fork is **sheet lightning**. **Ball lightning** has been described as a sphere of glowing light meandering through the lower air. Little is known about it.

**limb** The section of a *fold on each side of the central axis.

**limestone** A general term for a sedimentary rock which consists mainly of calcium carbonate. Limestones vary in texture; oolitic limestone consists of tiny, rounded grains, pesolitic of larger grains, whereas other limestones are of a crystalline texture. Limestones also vary in mineral content, as with dolerite and magnesian limestone, and in modes of origin. Different limestones are classified according to geological age, as in Carboniferous or Jurassic limestones. *Chalk is a soft limestone.

**limestone pavement** A more or less horizontal bare limestone surface, cut into by *grikes—deep fissures—running at right angles to each other leaving *clints—the slabs of limestone between them.

**limiting factor** The success of an organism is limited by the presence or absence of the factors necessary for survival. Often growth of a *population is limited by an apparently minor factor in the environment, such as the presence of *trace elements in the soil.

**limnology** The scientific study of freshwater ponds and lakes. Limnology covers all biological, chemical, meteorological, and physical aspects of lakes.

**limon** In northern France, a fine-grained deposit giving rise to fertile *loams. It may have the same origin as *loess.

**linear** Of, or along, a line. In maths, a **linear model** shows the relationship between variables as a straight line, or *regression line, on a graph.

**linear eruption** *Fissure eruption.

**linear growth** *Arithmetic growth.

**linear scale** On a map, the diagram or ratio which shows the length in real life of a distance on the map.

**linear settlement** An elongated settlement. A **linear city** is a planned city developed along a single high-speed line of transport. Industry is developed along one side of the link, while shops and offices are located on the other side, with housing beyond them. The 1965 plan for Paris is based on the concept of a linear city as development was planned along two motorway routes. A **linear village** is an elongated *ribbon of settlement usually formed along a routeway such as a road or canal. Linear villages may reflect the pattern of *land tenure or may have developed as clearings were cut along the road through a forest as in the German *Straßendorf.

**line-haul costs** Costs incurred in transporting goods over a route but not including costs of loading and unloading. Line-haul costs vary directly with distance.

**line of best fit** *Regression line.

**line squall** A line of very strong winds, often associated with rain for perhaps 500 km; a feature of West African climates.

**link** The route or line joining two *nodes.

**linkage** A flow of an input or output to or from a manufacturing plant in association with other plants. Movements of matter are **material linkages** as opposed to machinery and **service linkages** such as information, advice, and maintenance. Individual plants are also tied together by **forward linkages**—supplying customers—and **backward linkages** with their suppliers. **Horizontal linkages** occur between plants which are engaged in similar stages of a manufacturing process.

**linked industry** A manufacturing industry dependent on several factories for its components.

**listed building** In Britain, any building of such architectural or historical quality that permission must be granted before it may be changed or demolished.

**lithification** Processes by which loose sediments are converted into hard rock. These processes include the expulsion of air from the sediments or the suffusion into the rock of *cementing agents, like quartz, in solution.

**lithology** The character of a rock; its composition, structure, texture, and hardness.

**lithomorphic soil** A shallow, well-drained soil such as a *ranker or *rendzina, lying on largely unweathered *parent rock.

**lithosphere** The crust and that upper layer of the *mantle which lies above the *asthenosphere.

**litter** Dead plant material which reaches the ground. In soil science, the **litter layer** is the layer of dead and dying vegetation found on the surface of the soil. Some soil nomenclatures assign the litter layer to the A*horizon, shown as $A_{00}$.

**little climatic optimum** The time period, roughly between 750 and 1200 AD, when warmer conditions obtained in Europe and North America.

**little ice age** The phase between 1550 and 1850 AD when temperatures were generally lower in Europe and North America than they are at present, and glaciers advanced.

**littoral** Of, or along, the shore, hence **littoral current**, **littoral deposit**, **littoral drift**. See *longshore drift.

**littoral zone** 1. A synonym for *foreshore.
2. In ecology, that zone at the top of a body of water which receives enough light for *photosynthesis.

**livestock** Domesticated animals in an *agricultural system. The rearing of livestock solely as food is costly because of the position of animals high in the *food chain, but such is the demand for animal protein that livestock products account for two-thirds of agricultural output in the developed world.

**lixiviation** See *leaching.

**llano** The tropical grassy plains of the Orinoco basin in South America, and from this an alternative term for *savanna.

**load** The matter transported by a river or stream. **Solution load** is dissolved in the water. **Suspension load** refers to undissolved particles which are held in the stream. On the river bed, the material of the *bedload jumps by *saltation, or rolls along the bed. The deposits forming a channel bed are known as **bed-material load**.

**loam** A fertile soil, easily worked, of clay, silt, and sand, roughly in a ratio of 20 : 40 : 40. A **clay loam** has a clay content of 25–40%, a **silt loam** has more than 70% silt, a **sand loam** has between 50 and 70% sand.

**local climate** The climate of a small area such as a moorland or city—a mesoclimate—falling between a *microclimate and a *macroclimate. At this scale, such variables as local winds and aspect are of considerable significance.

**localization** The concentration of an economic activity in one or more places. The **localizational coefficient**, or *location coefficient, can be calculated to quantify the degree of localization.

**localization economies** Advantages arising from the localization together of a number of firms in the same type of industry.

**local time** The time in any location based on the time of noon in that location.

**location** **Absolute location** is expressed with reference to an arbitrary grid system as it appears on a map. **Relative location** is concerned with a feature as it relates to other features.

**locational interdependence** The response of a plant to its competitors in a given location. Plants may be attracted or repelled by the presence of rival plants and plan their locational strategies with regard to their competitors. Irregular arrangements may be made to locate so as to split the market between two firms.

**location-allocation model** A mathematical model used to establish the optimal location for larger central facilities such as hospitals, factories, and schools. The model takes account of the location and demand of the customers, the capacity of the facilities, and operational and transport costs. These factors are used to calculate the number of facilities to be developed together with their size and location.

**locational triangle** A model devised by Weber to establish a *least cost location. Two sources of raw material are at two corners of a triangle, the other corner representing market pull. Weights hang from each corner in relation to the locational pull. Strings from each corner are joined at the centre. Assuming equal transport costs in all directions, the least-cost location, P, where the centre knot is located, is derived from the amounts of 'pull' from each of the three locations.

**location coefficient** Also known as the **location quotient**, this expresses the relationship between an area's share of an activity and the national share. For example the locational coefficient for a given region =

$$\frac{\% \text{ employed in a field in a given region}}{\% \text{ employed nationally in that field}}$$

A location coefficient of 2.0, for example, indicates that twice the percentage of workers are employed in a specific industry than the percentage employed nationally for that industry. It should be noted that a high location quotient for an industry in a region does not necessarily indicate high employment levels.

**location theory** A group of theories which seek to explain the siting of economic activities. Various factors which affect location are considered such as *localized materials and *amenity, but most weight is placed on transport costs. Early location theory was concerned with *industrial location theory, and with agricultural land use, as modelled by *von Thünen. Modern location theory has been concerned with the real individual, rather than with rational *economic man, reflecting the influence of *behavioural geography. Attention has been shifted from the single factory producing a single product to the interrelationships within an organization or agglomeration, usually as part of a *capitalist economy.

**loch, lough** In Scotland and Ireland, respectively, a lake or narrow arm of the sea.

**locked zone** An area along a rift where *plates remain attached to each other. In this zone no new crust develops, so that the locked zone stretches and the crust thins. Ultimately, the plates will separate and the locked zone becomes a deformation at the edge of each continent.

**lode** A long, narrow vein of a mineral running through a rock.

**lodgement** The release and consolidation of debris from a glacier if the basal ice reaches its *pressure melting point as the ice moves. The moving ice aligns fragments of this **lodgement till** in the same direction as the flow of the glacier.

**loess, löss** Originally referring to a loose, fine-grained soil occurring in the Rhine Valley, this term has been extended to refer to any unconsolidated, non-stratified soil composed primarily of silt-sized particles. It is a very fertile agricultural soil. The origin of loess is in dispute. Some writers believe the deposit to be wind-borne, others note the occurrence of the soil in *periglacial environments, and stress the importance of glacial grinding in the production of silt-sized particles. The loess may be derived from *outwash sands and gravels. A further school of thought points to the frequency of dust storms in deserts and postulates the importance of processes such as *salt weathering in the production of loess particles.

**logical positivism** See *positivism.

**logistic curve** A curve on a graph which shows relatively slow movement initially, becoming steeper through time and then slowing down. The curve has a characteristic S-shape and may depict features like restricted population growth or the innovation of new ideas in a community.

**longitude** The position of a point on the globe in terms of its *meridian east or west of the prime meridian, expressed in degrees. These degrees may be subdivided into minutes and seconds, although decimal parts of the degree are increasingly used.

**longitudinal** 1. Of a line of *longitude.
2. Running lengthwise, along. A **longitudinal coast** lies along the grain of the country (*concordant coast); a **longitudinal dune** forms along the direction of the *prevailing wind; a **longitudinal** valley runs along the *strike of the rocks in which it formed.

**long profile** A side-view section of a river valley along its length. Ideally, the heights are taken from the centre of the stream (*thalweg). Any meanders or bends along the course are ignored.

**long-range weather forecast** An attempt to predict the weather which will be experienced more than five days in the future. It depends heavily on the use of models by computers.

**longshore drift** The movement of sand and shingle along the coast—**longshore**. Waves usually surge on to a beach at an oblique angle and their *swash takes sediment up and along the beach. The *backwash usually drains back down along the beach at an angle more nearly perpendicular to the coast, taking sediment with it. Thus there is a zigzag movement of sediment along the coast.
**Longshore currents**, initiated by waves, also move beach material along the coast. The term **littoral drift** is synonymous.

**long wave** See *earthquake.

**loop, the loop** The central business district of Chicago; from this comes the use of the word for any *CBD.

**loose-knit village** A settlement where buildings are scattered at random but are not far enough apart to be deemed isolated. The village extends over a fairly large area without a clear nucleus.

**lopolith** A large *intrusion which sags downwards in the centre, forming a bowl-shaped mass.

**Lorenz curve** A *cumulative frequency curve showing the distribution of a variable such as wealth or population against an independent variable such as income or area settled. If the distribution of the dependent variable is equal, the plot will show as a straight, 45° line. Unequal distributions will yield a curve. The gap between this curve and the 45° line is the inequality gap. Such a gap exists everywhere, although the degree of inequality varies.

**low, low pressure system** A region of low atmospheric pressure. In Britain, the term low is generally applied to pressures of below 1000 *millibars.

**lowest bridging point** The point on a river's course which is nearest to the sea and crossed by a bridge. Such a point is favoured since it is served by road, by river, and by sea.

**low-order goods and services** Goods and services with a low *range and a low *threshold population like daily newspapers, bread, and hairdressing. The goods are often *convenience goods. See *central place theory.

**Lowry model** A model of the evolution and distribution of urban land use—residential, industrial, and service—and the urban qualities of total population and *primary, *secondary, and *tertiary industry. It is based on the assumption that activities can be predicted from a given level of *basic employment. The model uses *economic base theory to determine the total population and employment in service industries. The population is assigned to zones of the city in proportion to their *population potential. Service employment is allocated in proportion to the market potential of each zone. These allocations have to meet land use constraints, notably housing densities, and threshold populations for the various services. The model is run several times while allocations are determined until the system reaches equilibrium.

**low technology** Simple equipment and/or manufacturing methods, often using local, easily available materials.

**lumbering** The extraction of timber from forests. Hence **lumberjack** and **lumberman**.

**lunar** Of the moon. The earth rotates in one **lunar day**—24 hours and 50 minutes—and the **lunar month** is the period of time between new moons—roughly 29 days.

**lunette** See *sand dune.

**lynchet** Small terraces, perhaps dating from prehistoric times, when belts of uncultivated land were sometimes left between ploughed areas. These terraces could be due to geomorphological processes; their origin is a matter of debate.

**lysimeter** A block of soil, covered with vegetation, placed in a container and replaced in the site from which it came. The input of precipitation is measured with a rain gauge and the drainage from the base of the block is also recorded. The block of soil is repeatedly weighed. With the aid of these measurements, estimates of the loss of water by *evapotranspiration may be made.

# M

**maar** A shallow, circular crater of volcanic origin, usually filled with water.

**macchia** The Italian *maquis.

**machair** The white, shelly sand found along the western shores of Scotland. **Machair soil**, derived from this deposit, is a light soil suitable for arable farming.

**mackerel sky** See *cirro-, cirrus.

**macro-** Large-scale, as in **macroeconomics**—the study of an economy as a whole.

**macroclimate** The general climate of a region which extends for several hundred kilometres, such as the Great Plains of North America.

**macrogeography** The application of *centrality in order to identify patterns in observed phenomena. At its centre lies the concept of *population potential which, it is alleged, is related to many patterns in social and economic geography.

**macrometeorology** The study of large-scale meteorological phenomena which can cover hundreds of kilometres or may encompass the whole globe; from *monsoons to the *general circulation of the atmosphere.

**maelstrom** A whirlpool. The name comes from a whirlpool near the Lofoten islands, Norway.

**maestrale** The Italian *mistral.

**magma** The molten rock found below the earth's crust which can give rise to igneous rocks. Molten magma may pick up pieces of existing rock—xenoliths—and is also charged with gases. It may dissolve and absorb the surrounding rocks in **magmatic stoping**.

**magmatic water** *Juvenile water.

**magnesian limestone** Limestone with between 5 and 15% magnesium.

**magnetic** Of a magnet. The earth emanates the magnetic forces which make up its **magnetic field**. A **magnetic meridian** is any line joining magnetic north and magnetic south, and a compass needle will align itself along such a meridian. The angular distance between *true north and *magnetic north is the **magnetic declination** or **magnetic variation**.

**magnetic anomaly** As new, hot crust arises at the mid-*oceanic ridge, it takes on the magnetic alignment of the earth at that time. At each side of the rift, there will be a band of newly magnetized crust. When the earth reverses its polarity, this magnetic alignment becomes anomalous. Successive episodes of *sea-floor spreading give rise to a pattern of magnetic anomalies. The bands thus formed can be correlated with the periods between reversals of the earth's magnetic field and thus can be dated.

**magnetic poles** The earth's magnetic field resembles that of a bar magnet located at the earth's centre. The axis of the imaginary bar magnet emerges from the earth's surface at the magnetic poles.

The north and south magnetic poles have repeatedly changed places and the magnetic axis has also moved. The timing of the intervals between such **magnetic polarity reversals** seems to be irregular. See also *geomagnetism.

**magnetic quiet zone, MQZ** Areas of crust where bands of *magnetic anomalies are wide and of a low order of magnetism. Their origin is not fully understood.

**magnetosphere** The full extent of the earth's magnetic field up to and including the *ionosphere.

**Magnox reactor** Magnox is an alloy of magnesium which can be used to clad the uranium fuel in a nuclear reactor. It is used because it does not react with carbon dioxide, which can thus be used to carry the heat from the reactor to the generator.

**malapportionment** A device used by some politicians to improve their chances in an election by drawing up particular electoral units. The most successful ploy is the establishment of small constituencies for one's own party while creating large constituencies for the opposition. In this way, votes for one's own party will go further. See also *gerrymander.

**mallee** A shrubby evergreen plant in southern Australia, forming **mallee scrub**.

**Malthusianism** Malthus (1766–1834) put forward the theory that the power of a population to increase is greater than that of the earth to provide sustenance. He asserted that population would grow geometrically (1, 2, 4, 8, and so on) while food supply would grow arithmetically (1, 2, 3, 4, and so on). When population outstrips resources, **Malthusian checks** to population occur:

    misery—famine, disease, and war;
    vice—abortion, sexual perversion, and infanticide;
    moral restraint—late marriage and celibacy.

Malthus's predictions were not borne out in eighteenth-century Britain, perhaps because of the opening up of new lands for agricultural output and migration. However, in 1972 the *Club of Rome put forward Malthusian-type predictions of disaster due to population increase.

**mammatus cloud** A breast-shaped thunder cloud associated with strong *convection.

**mammilated** Smooth and rounded in appearance. The term can be used for landforms of different sizes from a rock to a landscape.

**mandate** A territory, once part of the German or Ottoman Empires, governed by a member of the League of Nations between the World Wars. The territory was held in a mandate until it was deemed to be capable of self-government.

**mangrove swamp** The term **mangrove** is applied to a number of types of low trees and shrubs which grow on mud flats in tropical coastal areas where the tidal range is slight. The roots trap silt which accumulates to form the swamp. Mangroves are significant agents of *progradation along tropical coasts.

**Manning roughness coefficient** The resistance of the bed of a channel to the flow of water in it. Representative values of the coefficient are 0.010 for a glassy surface to 0.020 for alluvial channels with large dunes. The coefficient is expressed as $n$ in **Manning's equation**:

$$Q = \frac{A \, (R^{2/3} \times S^{1/2})}{n}$$

where $Q$ = discharge, $A$ = cross-sectional area, $R$ = hydraulic radius, $S$ = slope, measured as a fraction.

If the Manning coefficient is known from tables, $Q$ may be calculated. This is useful during times of flood.

**Mann's model** This model of British urban development combines the *sector theory with the *concentric zone model. Four basic sectors are postulated: middle class, lower middle class, working class, and lower working class. Each sector displays four zones. In each case, there is the *CBD, the *transitional zone, a zone of smaller houses, and the outermost zone made up of post-1918 housing.

**manor** The smallest area of land held in the Middle Ages by a feudal lord. It usually covered one single village, and consisted of the lord's holding together with *open fields farmed on the *three-field system. It had its own court for dealing with minor offences.

**mantle** The middle layer of the earth with a thickness of some 2800 km. The mantle lies between the crust and the core of the earth. The upper layer is rigid, and forms the lower part of the *lithosphere. The lower layer of the mantle is the *asthenosphere.

**manufacturing industry** The mechanized method, usually on a large scale, of processing materials into partly finished or finished products.

**map** A representation on a flat surface of all or part of the earth's surface, or all or part of the stars. **Diagrammatic maps** include *choropleths, *dot maps, *flow charts, plans, and *topological maps.

**map projection** A method and result of mapping a large area. The earth is a sphere, a map is flat; it is impossible to produce a map which shows true shape, true bearings, and true distance. The term projection comes from Mercator's projection, which was drawn as the shape and size of landmasses as they would throw shadows, lit from the centre of the earth, onto a cylinder of paper encircling the earth and touching it at the equator. No projection is perfect: Mercator's exaggerates the size of the earth in high latitudes; Mollweide's and Peters' are correct in area but distort shapes, and so on. **Azimuthal projections** show true direction: **gnomic projections** show the shortest straight line distance between two points; **orthographic projections** convey the effect of a globe. **Interrupted projections** show the earth as a series of segments joined only along the equator. Details of the projection used are given below most maps in a good atlas.

**maquis** The evergreen brushwood and thickets of Mediterranean France.

**marble** A crystalline, metamorphic *limestone (see *metamorphism) shot through with veins of other minerals such as *mica.

**march** A frontier zone, often debated, between two nations.

**mares' tails** Wisps of *cirrus cloud teased out by strong winds in the upper atmosphere.

**marginal analysis** In economics, a concentration on the boundaries, or margins, of an activity rather than looking at it in its entirety. It may be concerned with, for example, the *utility or costs of an extra unit of production.

**marginal costing** The expenditure incurred by producing a further unit of a product or service or the expenditure saved by not producing it. **Marginal cost pricing** is the fixing of the price of all units at the cost of producing the last unit.

**marginal land** Land which is difficult to cultivate and which yields little profit.

**marginal propensity to save** The proportion of an increment of income that is saved. An MPS of 0.5 indicates that the worker will save half of the increase paid.

**margin of cultivation** The distance from a market where the revenue received for a product exactly equals total cost. Given that production costs are the same whatever the distance from the market, transport costs rise with distance, and are, therefore, the determining factor of the location of the margin of cultivation.

**marina** A harbour with moorings for pleasure yachts.

**marine** Of, or concerned with, the sea.

**maritime** Near the sea coast. **Maritime climates** have smaller extremes of temperature, both diurnally and seasonally, than their continental counterparts. **Maritime air masses** are moist.

**market** In economics, the demand for a product.

**market area analysis** The analysis of the way in which the market area of a firm is established. Lösch postulated an *isotropic plane with settlements regularly spaced. As one settlement develops manufacturing, its trade area can be represented by a demand cone. At its centre, the point of production, demand is high since the price need not include transport costs. With movement away from the point of production, the cost of the product will rise as transport costs are added. Transport costs may be incurred by movement of goods to the customer or by the customer in travelling to the point of production. Either way, buyers will be paying more than they would at the point of production. The market area will extend to the point where costs are enough to make the product prohibitively expensive.

Beyond this point, a competitor may locate. In time, a hexagonal pattern of market areas will arise since the hexagon represents the most efficient shape of trade area. Thus, *locational interdependence determines the pattern of market areas. The market will be supplied by a system of regularly spaced plants, and the density of these plants increases as industry develops.

In reality, the evolution of market areas is far more complex than the analysis given above.

**market cycle** A series of periodic—usually one-day—markets such that a trader moves from one location to the next in a weekly cycle.

**market economy** An economy in which the major parts of production, distribution, and exchange are carried out by private individuals or companies rather than by the government, whose intervention in the economy is at a minimum. It is characteristic of *capitalism.

**market gardening** The intensive production of fruit, vegetables, and flowers.

**marketing geography** The geographical application of the way that production of goods is linked with their marketing. Retail functions are at the heart of the study, especially as they affect the internal planning of the city, but all the marketing functions such as consumer behaviour, information flows, and the role of transport are also studied.

**marketing principle** The principle upon which Christaller based his k = 3 hierarchy of central places (see *central place theory). It is that the supply of goods and services from a central place should be as accessible as possible to the next lower centre that it serves.

**market orientation** The tendency of an industry to locate close to its *market. Industries locate near the market if the cost of transport of the finished goods to the customers is a major part of the selling price. One example is the brewing industry where large, bulky quantities of water are used to make the finished product.

Industries may also locate near the market in order to benefit from *agglomeration economies. An industry may be market orientated at regional scale but material orientated at subregional scale. Compare *material orientation.

**market potential** The intensity of possible contacts with markets. The market potential is the sum of the ratios of the market to distances to the point under consideration. Thus:

$$P_i = \sum_{j=1}^{n} \frac{M_j}{d_{ij}} = \frac{M_1}{d_{i1}} + \frac{M_2}{d_{i2}} + \frac{M_3}{d_{i3}} \cdots + \frac{M_n}{d_{in}}$$

where the market potential ($P_i$) at point i is the summation ($\Sigma$) of $n$ markets (j) accessible to the point i divided by their distance ($d_{ij}$) from that point. $M$ is usually a measure of actual retail sales, and transport costs may be substituted for $d$.

**market-system firm** A firm which operates as a response to changes in demand, not having a large enough part of the market to influence the price of its product. Most small manufacturing firms fall within this category, producing a limited range of products from a single plant.

**market town** Any town which has a trading market. In earlier times in Britain, permission was granted by the monarch to hold a market.

**Markhov chain** An unfolding of events where each happening is partially determined by previous occurrences and partly by chance.

**marl** A mixture of clay with lime (calcium carbonate). **Marling** is the addition of marl to a light soil to increase its water-retaining capacity and to improve its texture.

**marriage rate** The number of marriages per thousand population.

**marsh** An ill-drained area of land, frequently flooded. Strictly speaking, the soil in a marsh is low in organic matter, as opposed to that in a *bog.

**Marshall Plan** A programme, running from 1948 to 1952 for the recovery of post-war Europe, funded by the USA and vital to European reconstruction.

**Marxism** A view of world events based on the work of Karl Marx and Friedrich Engels. Marx saw man's history as a natural process rooted in his material needs. The historical evolution of mankind is seen as the outcome of the *modes of production which finally determine the nature of each historical epoch, the specific forms of property prevailing in it, and its class structure. The struggle between the classes is limited by the mode of production which determines the social struggle. This struggle provides the impetus for change. All history is the history of the class struggle. Marx believed that the outcome of this struggle was revolution.

Capitalism fosters large-scale economic and social development but produces conditions which hamper its development (see *Marxist geography). Through systematic impoverishment of the masses, it creates a proletariat of exploited industrial workers who sell their labour as a marketable commodity. It is suggested that the proletariat will eventually rebel to emancipate mankind as a whole. This rebellion will put an end to all class distinction and all forms of exploitation. The sense of depersonalization and powerlessness felt by the working class will cease as the means of production become common property.

**Marxist geography** Marxist geography attempts to explain the world and also to change it. Marxism sees human beings gradually transforming themselves from stage to stage until they reach social perfection, and this transformation is seen as an aim towards which societies should be moving. This change is brought about by 'dialectical' processes—conflict between opposing forces—bringing forth a new synthesis which again is contradicted, and so on. The forces shaping society are seen as entities having direction and power over men and women. These entities include capital, *labour, *capitalism, *modes of production, the state, class, society, and the market.

Marxist geography highlights the dialectical relationships between social processes, the natural environment, and spatial relationships. It is concerned with the modes of production which underlie the superstructure of society. It sees spatial and environmental problems, such as the destruction of habitats or uneven development, originating deep within the social formations of capitalism. It is aimed at changing the fundamental operations of social processes by changing the workings of production.

Marxist geography is the study of the inherent contradictions of capitalism as they appear in the landscape and as they relate to each other.

Examples may be given of the changing structures and contradictions of capitalism. There is an inherent contradiction in a capitalist state which seeks to generate better conditions funded by taxation. Higher demand for raw materials generates higher costs. More output leads to more pollution and, in an environment where the authorities require strict controls on pollution, costs again rise. The result of these contradictions is the movement by multinational firms from established industrial regions in search of new environments to develop (despoil) and of new, politically virgin, labour to hire (exploit).

These views have been criticized. Many writers object to the passive role acted out by individuals. Man has been robbed of his decision-making powers. Furthermore, in Marxist geography, parts of the system like class, capitalism, and modes of production are seen as things that have substance and causal efficiency, not as concepts.

**Marxist theory of rent** Concerns that part of surplus value paid to landowners. Different rents may reflect the quality of the land or the amount of capital invested. **Monopoly rent** is the rent paid to the landowner when he leases the land to produce goods which are sold in a *monopoly. **Absolute** rent is extracted when the landlord can regulate the supply of land and force up prices.

**massif** A rather uniform area of higher land, clearly distinct from the surrounding lowland.

**massive** In geology, of a rock with little or no *cleavage, *jointing, or *stratification.

**mass movement, mass wasting** The movement downslope of rock fragments and soil under the influence of gravity. The material concerned is not incorporated into water or ice, and moves of its own accord, but slides are often triggered by increase in water pressure on rocks and soil.

A widely used classification of mass movement uses the combination of types of movement (*falls, *topples, *slumps, *slides, and *flows) with the nature of the material (bedrock, *debris, and fine soil). In this classification, the term *creep is synonymous with *flow. Many cases of mass movement include more than one type of movement.

**mass production** The making of goods in very large numbers using a standardized process.

**mass strength** The strength of a rock in its resistance to erosion. Mass strength will vary according to the innate strength of the rock, but other factors are important, such as the jointing and bedding of the rock and its state of weathering.

**matched samples** In two sets of measurements, where one measurement from the first set can be paired with one and only one measurement from the other set. An example would be the rates of evapotranspiration for different temperatures.

**material index** The ratio of the weight of *localized materials used in the manufacture of a product to the weight of the finished product. A material index of much greater than 1 indicates that the factory should have a *material orientation, while a material index of less than 1 would suggest a *market orientation. Such an index could be achieved by an industry using largely ubiquitous materials, like water in the brewing industry.

**materialism** The doctrine that matter is the only kind of reality. Mental states are purely neurophysical events in the brain.

**material orientation** The tendency of an industry to locate close to its raw materials. Industries with a high *material index locate near their raw materials as do industries where the costs of raw materials are a major part of the selling price. Industries may be material orientated at sub-regional scale but *market orientated at a regional scale.

**mathematical geography** The study of the earth's size and shape, of time zones, and of the motion of the earth.

**matrix** In statistics, an ordered array of numbers. The $y$-axis shows units of observation in columns, such as locations, while variables are shown across the $x$-axis (as shown in the example).

| Nationality | Number of children in family (%) | | | | |
|---|---|---|---|---|---|
| | 1 | 2 | 3 | 4 | 5 |
| A | 20 | 40 | 20 | 10 | 10 |
| B | 10 | 15 | 25 | 30 | 20 |
| C | 20 | 25 | 35 | 15 | 5 |

Each row of the matrix gives an inventory of the variable for a given area whilst each column shows variations of one characteristic.

**maximum–minimum thermometer** A thermometer which records the highest and lowest temperatures in a given period. One version uses a tube of mercury to push small needles along a column. When the mercury moves away, the needles remain at the furthest extent of the mercury. A **maximum thermometer** records only the highest temperature; a **minimum thermometer** only the lowest.

**maximum sustainable yield** The greatest yield of a renewable resource while keeping steady the stock of that resource.

**mean** See *arithmetic mean.

**mean centre** The 'centre of gravity' of a distribution such as population or industry over an area. It is determined by imposing an arbitrary grid on a map of the distribution. The coordinates for each point are recorded, and the means of the $x$ and the $y$ coordinates are calculated. Plotting these averaged coordinates gives the mean centre of the distribution.

**meander** A winding curve in the course of a river. The wavelength of a meander is about ten times the channel width. No satisfactory cause has been advanced for the formation of meanders, but there may be some link with *helicoidal flow.

The **meander belt** is the total width across which the river meanders and the **meander core** is the piece of land in the centre of an *incised meander. See also *ingrown meander, *intrenched meander.

**meander bar** *Point bar deposit.

**meandering valley** A winding valley, floored with *alluvium.

**meander neck** The strip of land separating one side of a meander from another.

**meander scar** An infilled *ox-bow lake.

**meander scroll** *Point bar.

**meander terrace** A terrace formed on one bank of a river where the river undercuts the alluvium at the *bluff.

**mean deviation** The mean of the sum of the deviations from the mean of all the values in a data set. The deviations are summed regardless of sign and the total is divided by the number of observations.

**mean information field, MIF** In *diffusion, the field in which contacts can occur. It generally takes the form of a square grid of 25 cells, with each cell being assigned a probability of being contacted. The possibility of contact is very high in the central cells from which the diffusion takes place, becoming markedly less so with distance from the centre, that is, there is a *distance decay effect. The probability values for the field may be based on observation, on a pre-existing theory, or arbitrarily. The model can then be used to simulate the dif-

fusion of an innovation from a central point. To use the model, the MIF is placed with the centre over the source. A random number is then used to find the cell containing the destination of the innovation. From this receiving cell a random number is again used to find the receptor of the second generation of diffusion. This model can be run through a computer to foresee complicated diffusions, but the workings of the model are based on many assumptions which do not apply in the real world.

**mean sea-level, MSL** The average level of the surface of the sea taken from recordings made over a long period of time. British MSL is based on data from Newlyn, Cornwall, and is used as the *Ordnance Datum from which heights on an *Ordnance Survey map are taken.

**mean solar day, mean solar time** Since the time of the rotation of the earth varies slightly, a mean time is usually calculated from a series of observations.

**mechanical erosion** Erosion by physical means, such that the eroded material undergoes no chemical change. The main agents of such erosion are wind, water, and ice.

**mechanical weathering** The splitting up *in situ* of rock without chemical change. Processes include *exfoliation, *thermal weathering, *frost shattering, *granular disintegration, and spalling.

**mechanization** A change from work by hand to the use of machinery, both in agriculture and in industry.

**medial moraine** See *moraine.

**median** In a set of data ranked according to size, the median is the central value, having an equal number of values above and below it, and is expressed as

$$\frac{n+1}{2}$$

where $n$ is the number of ranks. If there is an even number of ranks, the median lies midway between the two central values. For *grouped data, the median is found by plotting the data on a *cumulative frequency curve. The median value occurs halfway along the *y*-axis of cumulative frequency—at 50%.

**medicinal geography** The application of geographical methods to medical problems. For example:

1. The relationship of the distribution of disease due to geographical variables, such as the incidence of bilharzia and the spread of irrigation schemes.

2. A statistical analysis to discover whether patterns of disease are due to chance or causal factors.

**Mediterranean climate** A climate of hot, dry summers and warm, wet winters. This climate is not only characteristic of Mediterranean lands, but is also found in California, central Chile, and the extreme south of Africa.

In summer, the climate is dominated by *subtropical anticyclones, and *trade winds prevail. Daily weather is greatly influenced by *sea breezes and *land breezes. In winter, *mid-latitude depressions bring rain. *Local winds, such as the mistral of southern France and the Santa Ana of California, are of great significance.

**Mediterranean soils** Soils formed in *Mediterranean climates. In the wet winters, there is *leaching of clays and carbonates and the release of iron which imparts a red colour to the soil. Leaching is slight during the dry summers so that there is often a buildup of a carbonate *horizon in the soil.

**megalith** Any large stone which has been sited by humans and which may have been erected as a monument, hence **megalithic**. Most megaliths date from between about 3000 to 2000 years BC. Megaliths may be arranged in rows or circles.

**megalopolis** Originally designating the eastern seaboard of the USA from Boston to Washington, this is now any continuous built-up area of more than 10 million inhabitants. It is usually formed by the coalescence of *conurbations.

**meltwater** Water given out when snow or ice melts. Most snow and non-glacial ice melts in spring, often causing widespread flooding. Glacier ice may cause an increase in river levels later in the year.

Glacial meltwater is produced by melting at the surface or by pressure and *geothermal heat at the base. Some surface meltwater may percolate through the ice to emerge at the base. A **meltwater channel** cuts through *drift or rocks in a once glaciated area. It may be completely unrelated to the present drainage pattern.

**meltwater erosion** Meltwater derived from glaciers can be a powerful agent of erosion. Water flows on, within, and at the base of decaying ice, often under pressure. Because of this pressure, meltwater can carry large quantities of debris; this load promotes *abrasion. For the same reason, meltwater can flow upslope.

Four major types of meltwater can be distinguished. **Ice margin meltwater** follows the edge of the glacier when drainage routes have been cut off by ice. **Tunnel valleys** occur below the ice and can cut steep-sided, flat-floored valleys. **Spillways** are channels cut by streams overflowing from *proglacial lakes. **Coulees** are canyons formed by the sudden and violent release of water from ice-dammed lakes when the barriers which impound them are breached.

**menhir** A single standing *megalith.

**mental map** A map within the mind of an individual which reflects the knowledge and prejudices of that individual. Such a map reflects the individual's perceptions of, and preferences for, different places and is the result of the way in which an individual acquires, classifies, stores, retrieves, and decodes information about locations. Thus, for much of South-East England, the North is compressed into Yorkshire and Lancashire. The North extends much further in reality than is generally recognized in the South. Mental maps may also include images of locations—the South may still be perceived as an area of privilege, of white-collar workers and sleek financiers. Thus, different locations may be ranked in order of attractiveness as perceived by an individual or group and this may affect decisions about relocation or recreation, for example.

Mental maps are conditioned by the way in which individuals organize the space available and in turn reflect an individual's perspective. Recent studies have shown that an industrialist's conception of the location of assisted areas may be wildly inaccurate.

**Sequential mapping** focuses on links between places while **spatial mapping** concentrates on landmarks and areas rather than on paths.

**Mercalli scale** An early scale used to register the strength of an earthquake and now replaced by the *Richter scale.

**mercantilism** The view that one nation's gain is only achieved by another nation's loss. According to this, the trading nation can prosper only if it encourages exports and discourages imports, the latter through the erection of *tariff barriers.

**mercantilist model** The view, propagated by Vance, that the most important urban function is wholesaling. Cities in the 'New World' developed because of trading contacts with the 'Old World' and are more affected by their external markets than by internal markets.

**mere** A large, shallow lake, especially in *till.

**meridian** An imaginary circle along the world's surface from geographic pole to geographic pole. Meridians are described by the angle they form west or east of the **prime meridian** which has a value of 0° and runs through Greenwich, England.

**meridional** 1. Pertaining to the south.
2. Pertaining to a *meridian, hence **meridional circulation**: in meteorology, air flowing longitudinally, across the parallels of latitude. Also known as **Meridional flow**, it occurs in *atmospheric cells and results in part from changes in temperature along lines of longitude.

**meridional temperature gradient** The change in temperature experienced by movement north or south along a *meridian.

**mesa** A steep-sided plateau or upland which is formed by the erosion of nearly horizontal *strata. This landform resembles a *butte but is much more extensive. Mesas and buttes are held to be evidence of *parallel slope retreat.

**meseta** The high plateau of central Spain.

**mesic** Well, but not excessively, watered.

**mesoclimate** See *local climate.

**Mesolithic** The middle period of the *Stone Age between the *Palaeolithic and the *Neolithic.

**mesometeorology** The study of middle-scale meteorological phenomena, between small features, like *cumulus clouds, and large features, like anticyclones. Mesoscale features are up to 100 km across and last for less than a day. **Mesoscale precipitation areas (MPAs)** are small-scale clusters of *convection cells arranged into bands 50–100 km wide, in association with a low-level *jet stream. A further example of a mesoscale feature is the **polar low** which, in a British winter, brings an hour or two of falling pressure followed by some three hours of snow.

**mesopause** The boundary, some 80 km above the surface of the earth, between the *mesosphere and the *thermosphere.

**mesophyte** A plant which requires a moderate climate in terms of temperature and precipitation.

**mesoscale** The middle tier of a rough hierarchy of scales. Thus, mesoclimate is concerned with phenomena larger than a local climate but smaller than the *general circulation of the atmosphere.

**mesoscale precipitation area, MPA** See *local climate.

**mesosphere** A zone of the atmosphere extending from the *stratopause, some 50 km above the earth's surface, to the *mesopause.

**Mesozoic** The middle *era of earth's history stretching approximately from 225 to 190 million years BP.

**metalled** Of a road, covered with hard stone, cement, or tarmac to make an all-weather surface, free from dust.

**metamorphic** See *metamorphism.

**metamorphic aureole** That area of rock altered in composition, structure, or texture by contact with an igneous *intrusion.

**metamorphism** The change in a rock from its original form by heat or by pressure beneath the surface of the earth, hence **metamorphic rock**: a rock thus changed. When *magma forms an *intrusion, it heats and alters the surrounding rocks by **contact metamorphism**, which forms a ring of altered rocks—the *metamorphic aureole—around the intrusion.

**Dislocation metamorphism** occurs through friction along fault planes or *thrust planes. **Regional metamorphism** (also known as **dynamic metamorphism**) occurs during an *orogeny.

**metasomatism** The change in *country rock brought about by the invasion of fluid into that rock. Granites are formed at great depths by invasion of granitizing fluids.

**meteor** A solid body moving from space into the earth's atmosphere, where it may glow because of the friction encountered there. What is left of the meteor, a **meteorite**, reaches the earth's crust. Disintegrating meteors may produce **meteoric dust** in the atmosphere.

**meteoric water** Water precipitated from the atmosphere, as opposed to *juvenile water.

**meteorological screen** *Stevenson screen.

**meteorology** The study of the character of the atmosphere and the events and processes within it, together with the interaction between the atmosphere and the face of the earth.

**métropoles d'équilibre** Eight metropolitan areas chosen to be *growth poles in the Fifth French Plan between 1966 and 1970. The aim was to promote regional development and to shift economic activity away from Paris.

**metropolis** A very large urban settlement usually with accompanying suburbs, hence **metropolitan**, pertaining to a city. The term is used rather loosely as no precise parameters of size or population density have been established.

**metropolitan city** In the USA the equivalent of a *conurbation.

**mica** A transparent mineral made of silicates and easily split into very fine, flexible sheets.

**micelle** A cluster of molecules in a colloid. See *clay micelle.

**micro-** Small. A **micro-nutrient** is one which is needed by an organism in small quantities only; a **micro-organism** is too small to be seen with the naked eye.

**microclimatology** The study of small-scale climates such as those beneath standing crops, within forests, or in built-up areas. See *urban climates.

**microfauna** Any animals, such as bacteria, too small to be seen individually by the naked eye.

**microflora** Any plants, such as algae, too small to be seen individually by the naked eye.

**microgenetic** Concerned with human adaptation to environmental change.

**micrometeorology** The study of small-scale meteorological phenomena operating near the ground surface, such as the investigation of climates within a field of grain or in a forest.

**microplate tectonics** The process by which the edge of a continent is modified by the transport, accretion, and rotation of *terranes.

**Middle East** Syria, the Lebanon, Israel, Jordan, Egypt, Saudi Arabia, Yemen, Oman, Bahrain, Iraq, Iran, Kuwait, the United Arab Emirates, Qatar, Palestine, and, possibly, Turkey.

**mid-latitude** The zones between 40° and 60° in each hemisphere. Hence **mid-latitude depression**, an area of low atmospheric pressure occurring in this zone, shown on a weather map as a circular pattern of *isobars with the lowest pressure at the centre. This low is some 1500–3000 km in diameter and is associated with the removal of air at height and the meeting of cold and warm *air masses in the lower atmosphere. At the fronts between the air masses, a horizontal wave of warm air is enclosed on either side by cold air. The approach of the warm front is indicated by high *cirrus cloud. With the approach of the front, the cloud thickens and lowers. Rain falls. As the warm sector passes over, skies clear and the temperature rises. The cold front is marked by heavier rain and a fall in temperature.

The air behind the cold front moves more rapidly than the warm sector air and eventually pinches out the warm air, lifting it bodily from the ground to form an *occlusion.

Mid-latitude depressions move at around 30 km per hour in summer and 50 km per hour in winter and last between four and seven days. See also *cyclogenesis.

**midnight sun** A night without darkness occurring around the summer *solstice north or south of latitude 63° 30″ N. or S.

**mid-oceanic ridge** *Oceanic ridge.

**MIF** See *mean information field.

**migration** The permanent or semi-permanent movement of people from one place to another. A simple classification considers scale and separates internal migration, where no national boundaries are crossed, from international migration. Such movements may be voluntary, or involuntary, as when minorities are expelled from their country of birth by governments. Further aspects of this classification break down migrations as temporary and permanent. In the case of commuting, migration is a daily act; a purist would not call commuting a migration because there is no change of residence. Temporary migrations are seasonal, as migrant workers

move in search of work, or periodic, as when a worker, usually male, moves to an industrial, urbanized area and sends remissions back to the women and children, perhaps over a period of a year or two. A good example of periodic migration is the movement of males from their homes in Botswana and Lesotho to work in the gold and diamond mines of South Africa.

Other classifications are based on the natures of the point of origin and arrival, such as rural–rural or urban–rural. Rural–rural migration may be seen in the movement of *nomadic people while urban–rural might include the movement of elderly people when they retire or when richer people move from the city to suburbs. *Rural depopulation covers rural–urban migrations.

Further classifications are concerned with the motive for migration. Compulsory movements, such as the repatriation of Ghanaians from Nigeria, are seen to be entirely due to *push factors. Other cases include **innovative migration** where people move to achieve something new, like settlement of new lands, **economic migration** where people move from a poor to a richer area, and **betterment migration** where people move simply to better themselves. See also *Ravenstein's 'Laws' of Migration.

**Milankovitch cycle** The position of the earth with regard to the sun varies, and thus the *insolation at the earth's surface varies. The orbit of the earth changes in a cycle of 9600 years, the time of the year when the earth is nearest to the sun changes in a 21 000-year cycle, and the angle between the plane of the earth's orbit and the plane of the rotational cycle changes in a 40 000-year cycle. These cycles were built into a model which may be used to explain climatic change.

**mile** A **statute mile** is 5280 ft—about 1.609 km. A **geographical mile** is the extent of one *minute along the equator—6080 ft or 1.852 km.

**milieu** The sphere in which each individual lives and which he is affected by. This sphere includes the tangible objects and people, the social and cultural phenomena, and the *images which influence human behaviour.

**millibar** A unit of atmospheric pressure, measured by a barometer. Each rise of 1 $cm^3$ of mercury in a barometric column represents a rise in air pressure of 1000 dynes.

**million city** An urban area with a population in excess of one million. Most lie in Europe and North America but the number of million cities in the Third World is rising rapidly.

**mineral** A naturally formed, usually inorganic (although petrol is a mineral), unmixed, and often crystalline substance. **Mineral soils** are low in humus as are the **mineral horizons** of a soil. **Mineral springs** have a high content of dissolved mineral salts.

**mineralization** 1. In soil science, the breakdown of organic residues, by oxidation, to form soluble or gaseous chemical compounds which may then take part in further soil processes or be utilized by plant life. Mineralization is an essential process in the formation of *humus.
   2. The fossilization of buried plant and animal matter as the organic parts are replaced by other minerals.

**minifundio** In Latin America, a very small farm, some few hectares in extent.

**minimum efficient scale (m.e.s.) of production** The least possible size of a plant which is compatible with profitable production. Below this size, *economies of scale do not apply. This minimum can be defined in terms of production or, less often, in terms of employment. Minimum sizes vary with the nature of different industries and may be so large that there is insufficient capital for production.

**minimum requirements method** A technique for assessing the number of *non-basic workers within a city. Specific size groupings are established for settlements of over 10 000. The percentages of labour forces are established for each occupation in each size group. Within the groupings the lowest number of workers in each employment group is noted. These lowest numbers are the minimum requirements for the relevant occupation and city group. The minimum requirements are compared with occupational groups in centres of similar size. Any workers in excess of the minimum requirement are assumed to be non-basic workers. The formula for establishing the number of non-basic workers is:

$$S = e_i \frac{e_t}{E_t} \times E_i$$

where $S$ = the minimum requirement for that industry, $e_i$ = the employment total for that industry, $e_t$ = the total employment for that area, $E_i$ = the national employment figure for that industry, $E_t$ = the total national employment.

**minor intrusion** A small-scale *intrusion, such as a *dike, *laccolith, or *sill.

**minute** One-sixtieth of a degree of latitude or longitude.

**Miocene** An *epoch of the Cainozoic period from 26 to 7 million years BP.

**miogeoclinal deposits** Unbroken sequences of nearly flat strata which have accumulated in shallow water at the margins of a continent.

**mirage** When air near ground level is heated strongly by contact with the hot earth, it becomes less dense. Incoming rays of light are bent when entering this layer, so that a patch of sky is mirrored in the hot air. This often gives the appearance of water.
   Occasionally, when air at ground level is very cold, rays of light from regions beyond the horizon are bent downwards. As a result, features usually beyond the horizon become visible.

**misfit stream** A stream which appears to be too small to have made the valley in which it is flowing. The valley may have been cut by a former glacier or by a larger stream which has been *captured.

**mist** A suspension of water droplets in the air which restricts visibility to between 1 and 2 km.

**mistral** See *local winds.

**mixed cultivation** The growing of two crops in alternate rows in a field, often to reduce soil erosion or for one to provide shade for the other.

**mixed economy** An economy where many of the activities of production, distribution, and exchange are undertaken by central government, and where there is more government intervention than in a free *market economy.

**mixed farming** A type of commercial agriculture concerned with the production of both crops and animals on one farm. Stock on a mixed farm used to be grazed on fallow land, but many modern mixed farms produce some, or all, of their fodder crops.

**MNC** See *multinational corporation.

**mobile** Capable of moving or of being moved; hence **mobility**. A **mobile dune**, although partly fixed, is still liable to movement by *deflation. For **mobile industry**, see *footloose industry.

**modal centre** See *centrality of population.

**modal split** The varying proportions of different transport modes which may be used at any one time. The choices of modes may be determined by the costs, destinations, capacities, and frequencies of the modes together with the nature of the goods carried and their destinations. Modes of transport may be seen as competing services and particularly so in the rivalry between the private car and public transport systems. In many cases the travelling time and comfort of a car journey outweigh costs so that non-cost factors play an important part in determining the modal choice.

In the transport of freight, water transport and pipelines are most suited to high volumes of freight over a long haul while small-scale local movements are best served by road.

**mode** The figure in a set of data which occurs most often. The mode is often used to indicate a class grouping rather than an individual value so that the **modal class** is indicated. However, the modal class will fluctuate according to the size of the value range for each class and a change of class limits may well give a different distribution.

**model** A representation of some phenomenon of the real world made in order to facilitate an understanding of its workings. A model is a simplified and generalized version of real events. An **iconic model** represents reality on a smaller scale, an **analogue model** shows reality in maps and diagrams, and a **symbolic model** uses mathematical expressions to portray reality. **Probabilistic models** take into account the fact that human behaviour cannot be predicted with absolute certainty, while **simulation models** use mathematic laws of probability to simulate the consequences of human behaviour.

**model township** A planned settlement, first conceived in late nineteenth-century Britain by philanthropic industrialists to house their workforce. Bourneville, built in suburban Birmingham by Cadbury in 1879, is one example.

**mode of production** The way in which society organizes production. Marxists claim that this organization reinforces and reproduces the status quo. In the primitive mode of production, land and raw materials are communally owned and labour requirements are shared. In the slave mode of production, the labourer is a chattel who may be bought and sold. Under a *feudal system the proprietor owns the land and most of the produce, but the peasant, who is tied to the land, may own some of the *factors of production. Under *capitalism, the worker may sell his labour for a wage but does not own the other factors of production.

**moder** A type of *humus which is less acid than *mor but more acid than *mull. The degree of mixing of this humus with the mineral content of the soil is greater than that of mor, but it still shows as a stratified layer.

**modernization** The change in society towards a more efficient government and control, better provision for health and social security, increased educational opportunities, and, possibly, increased social mobility.

**modifiable areal units** Areas studied in geography which may be arbitrary units with no link with spatial patterns which have developed. The use of large units may increase *correlation coefficients and may mask changes within the area. Thus census boundaries may hide smaller-scale patterns. Analyses using different units may produce different results. In many cases the investigator has to use the units for which data are available rather than the units which are more suited to the investigation.

**moho, Mohorovičić discontinuity** The boundary in the earth's interior between the crust and the upper *mantle. It occurs at about 35 km below the continents and at around 10 km beneath the oceans.

**Moh's scale** See *hardness.

**moist coniferous forest** Some writers include this area with *coniferous (boreal) forest but it is found only on the west coast of Canada and the USA where the climate is cool and moist throughout the year. Very large evergreens such as redwoods and Douglas fir grow. It is difficult to know why evergreens, rather than broad-leaved deciduous trees, abound. Undergrowth is sparse.

**moisture index** A measure of the water balance of an area with regard to gains from precipitation (P) and losses from *potential evapotranspiration (PET). The moisture index (MI) is calculated thus:

$$MI = \frac{100(P - PET)}{PET}$$

See also *lysimeter

**molecule** The smallest group of combined atoms which have the properties of their element; hence **molecular**. **Molecular attraction** is the attraction of molecules of water for each other or for molecules on the surface of a rock or mineral. By this attraction, *capillary action can take place, and ground water can be held in fine-grained rocks.

**mollisol** In *US soil classification, soils with a rich *humus content, developed under grassland. *Chernozems, *rendzinas, and *chestnut soils fall into this category.

**monadnock** An isolated peak standing above the level of a *peneplain.

**monocline** A one-sided fold.

**monoculture** A farming system given over exclusively to a single product. Its advantages are the increased efficiency of farming and a higher quality of output. Disadvantages include a greater susceptibility to price fluctuations, climatic hazards, and the spread of disease.

**monopoly** Theoretically, the provision of a good or service by a single supplier. In practice, a monopoly occurs where one firm controls most of the output of a particular industry. Legal opposition to monopolies is common in capitalist economies so firms have to seek new products if they wish to continue to grow in the domestic market. *Industrial diversification of this type is prudent since a single-product firm is vulnerable to a fall in the demand for its product.

**monsoon** The original usage of this word (from Arabic *mausim*—meaning seasonal wind) has now been superseded and the term is used to describe a sudden wet season within the tropics. The Asian monsoon was thought to be a large-scale system of *land breezes and *sea breezes, due to the intense heating of southern Asia in summer time. It is now known that upper air movements play a large part in the development of the monsoon.

In winter, pressure is high over central Asia. Winds blow outwards. Some depressions, guided by upper air westerlies, move from west to east, bringing rain. During the spring, a *thermal low develops over northern India. Early summer rains are related to a trough in the upper air. In early summer the direction of the upper air changes from westerly to easterly. With this change, the monsoon 'bursts', giving heavy rain. The sequence and causes of these changes are unclear.

During summer, pressure is low and rainfall at a maximum. The now easterly jet steers *monsoon depressions. Subsiding upper air prevents rainfall in the Thal and Thar deserts of the north-west of the subcontinent. By autumn, the westerly jet is re-established. *Trade winds dominate, and *hurricanes are common in the Bay of Bengal.

**monsoon depression** A low pressure system occurring in summer and affecting southern Asia. It is 1000–2500 km across with a *cyclone circulation up to 8 km. It lasts 2–5 days and occurs roughly twice a month, bringing 100–200 mm of rain per day.

**monsoon forest** A type of tropical forest found in regions showing a marked dry season followed by torrential rain, a monsoon. The vegetation is adapted to withstand the drought so that trees are semi-deciduous or evergreen. The forest is more open and has more undergrowth than *tropical rain forest.

**montane** Of a mountain, as in **montane forest** which is found in the uplands of the tropics and which often supports moss.

**Monte Carlo model** A method of representing reality in an abstract form which incorporates an entirely random element and describes a sequence of events from one state to another in terms of probability. It is impossible to predict any outcome as one process may give rise to any number of events. Change is represented by random sampling from a number of probabilities and though each stage of the model is dependent on the stage before, it is also subject to chance factors.

**moon** A natural satellite of a planet. The earth's moon revolves around the earth in approximately 28 days. It is seen from earth when illuminated by our sun. At **new moon**, it is not visible, but it waxes until a **full moon** is seen, after which it wanes. The gravitational pull of the moon gives rise to *tides.

**moor** Open upland of plants such as heather or bracken, used, if at all, as *rough grazing.

**mor** An acid *humus developed from the tough, acidic leaf litter of conifers and heathland vegetation. The activity of soil fauna, such as earthworms, is slight, and mor remains unmixed with the mineral content of the soil.

**moraine** Any landform deposited by a glacier or ice sheet. Certain moraines are deposited at the side of the glacier as **lateral moraines**. Where two lateral moraines combine, a central, **medial moraine** may be formed. Moraine beneath a glacier may exist as a blanket covering the ground. This is **ground moraine**, also known as a till sheet. Other moraines have been moulded by ice parallel to the direction of ice movement. These include **fluted moraines** which are long ridges, possibly formed in the shelter of an obstruction. *Drumlins are streamlined moraines.

**End** or **terminal moraines** mark the end of a glacier and **recessional moraines** mark stages of stillstand during the retreat of the ice. A moraine running across a glacier is not an end moraine if the up-glacier surface shows streamlining. Such streamlined transverse moraines are **rogen moraines**. These are ridges, up to 30 m in height and crescentic in shape, with the 'horns' of the crescent pointing in the direction of the ice flow. Other transverse moraines form where a glacier meets its *proglacial lake. These are **de Geer moraines** and consist of *till, layered sand, and lake deposits.

At the margin of a glacier is an **ice-dumped moraine**. **Push moraines** occur when a glacier is retreating in the melt period but re-establishing itself in the cold season when the advancing glacier pushes up last year's moraine.

**morbidity** Ill health, disease.

**more developed countries, MDC** The countries of Europe together with Australia, Canada, Japan, New Zealand, the USA, and the USSR.

**morphogenetic region** A region in which a distinctive complex of land-forming processes are determined by climate and give rise to a distinctive set of surface features.

**morphological mapping** A technique of mapping landscape features using standardized symbols. For example, slope elements may be displayed—convex, free face, concave, break of slope. Recognition of such features is not objective, however, and some landforms lie more in the eye of the beholder.

**morphology** The study of form. However, the term is now used as a synonym for the form itself as in the morphology of the landscape or of the city.

**mortality** Death; a low mortality rate indicates a long life expectancy. Mortality rates are higher in the Third World than in developed nations. Rates differ within countries; in Britain, mortality is higher in the 'old' industrialized regions of the North and North-West than in the more recently industrialized areas of the South. Regional variations hint that life expectancy is lower in soft water regions than in areas of hard water. There are indications that country dwellers live longer than town dwellers. Mortality also varies between socio-economic classes; mortality rates increase down the scale. This is thought to be a reflection of lifestyles rather than affluence. *Infant mortality also increases down the social register and from developed to less developed countries.

**mosaic** A composite photograph of an area made by assembling all or part of a number of prints.

**moshav** An Israeli agricultural co-operative where each family controls its own farm but holds machinery and services in common.

**mother of pearl cloud** Also known as nacreous cloud, this is a rare and slightly rainbow-tinted cloud of the upper *stratosphere.

**motorway** In the UK, a road of restricted access, reserved for certain specific types of vehicle and designed for the movement of heavy volumes of traffic at high speed. Gradients are slight and curves are gentle. Because of this ease of transport, many motorways have attracted industrial development.

**mottled soil** With variously coloured patches, as in a *gley soil.

**moulin** Also known as a glacier mill, this is a rounded, often vertical hole within stagnating glacier ice. Meltwater, heavily charged with debris, swirls into the hole. Some of this debris settles out at the base of the moulin. After the retreat of the ice, a mound, known as a **moulin kame**, is left behind.

**mountain** In Britain, a hill exceeding 600 m. A **mountain chain** is made up of a series of roughly parallel mountain ranges.

**mountain building** The creation of uplands by movements of the earth's crust. This is often, but not necessarily, associated with an *orogeny. Possible causes of the uplift of mountains are:
a decrease of the density of the crust causing it to rise, possibly above a *hot spot;
thickening of the crust at *collision margins;
*subduction below continents, causing them to rise;
overthrusting of sedimentary rocks during collision;
compression at *converging or at *conservative plate margins.

**mountain ecology** A change in altitude up a mountain is equivalent to a latitudinal shift away from the equator, and vegetation types accordingly change with height.

Thus, in the San Francisco mountains there is a change upslope from hot desert cactus at 200 m to oak scrub at 800 m. By 2000 m, the forest is coniferous shading into spruce and Douglas fir. At 4000 m, the tree line ends and Alpine tundra is encountered. Since each stage is of limited area, the full range of each *biome is not represented.

**mountain meteorology** Mountains give rise to distinctive climates. Upland areas are cooler than lowlands of the same latitude, since temperatures fall by 1 °C per 150 m. Heating of the valley floor to a higher temperature than the valley sides may lead to *anabatic mountain winds. Equally, colder and heavier air at the peaks may spill down into the valley floor as a *katabatic wind.

Warmer, moist air will be forced to rise over mountain barriers. As the air is chilled with height, *orographic rain falls. When such air has passed over the barrier, it descends and is *adiabatically warmed. This may bring warm winds, like the *chinook. Since the warmed air is now capable of holding the remaining moisture, a 'rain shadow' of drier air develops in the lee of mountains.

On a larger scale, mountain barriers affect low pressure systems as they pass over and *lee depressions may also develop. The location of major mountain barriers such as the Rockies and Himalayas affects the formations of air in the upper atmosphere.

**mountain wind** A wind which occurs when heavier, cold air flows downslope from mountain peaks or from a glacier. See *katabatic wind and *bora.

**movement minimization theory** The view that consumers choose the shortest journey to buy goods and services whatever the cost. However, consumers may be more attracted by lower prices than by short journeys, and many consumers are motivated by quality, service, and ease of parking.

**moving average** A method of calculating *central tendency over time. The average is calculated, for example, over five years. For each year after this, the earliest value is dropped from the calculation and the most recent one is added in, again to make an average over five years.

**MPA** See *mesoscale precipitation area.

**MQZ** See *magnetic quiet zone.

**MSL** See *mean sea-level.

**mud** Unconsolidated silt and/or clay. In estuaries and sheltered coastal areas, it forms **mud flats**. When partly consolidated, it forms **mudstone**, a soft *shale.

**mud flat** An accumulation of mud in very sheltered waters. Mud from the shore is carried into *estuaries and sheltered bays and settles at low water.

**mud flow** The *flow of liquefied clay. Debris of all sizes, including large blocks of rock, may be transported by mud flows.

**mud volcano** When volcanic gas moves upwards through soft clay, it beats the clay into an eruption of soft, cold, bubbling mud which may form a cone. Alternatively, hot mud may be ejected from a volcanic *vent.

**mulga** A spiny shrub or tree of the acacia family forming **mulga scrub** over large arid areas of Australia.

**mull** 1. In soil science, a mild *humus produced by the decomposition of grass or deciduous forest litter. Earthworms and other soil fauna mix this humus thoroughly with the mineral content of the soil.

2. A promontory or headland in Scotland.

**multinational corporation, MNC** A very large business with offices, factories, subsidiaries, and branches in many countries. See *international division of labour.

**multinational state** A state which contains one or more ethnic minorities as identified by religion, language, or colour. If the minority is concentrated in a particular area or is associated with an historic homeland, pressure may build up for the minority to achieve a measure of autonomy.

**multiple land use** The use of land for more than one purpose as when an area of forestry contains nature trails and picnic or camping facilities.

**multiple nuclei model** A model of town growth advanced by Harris and Ullman, based on the fact that many towns and nearly all large cities grow about many nuclei rather than around a simple *CBD. Some of these nuclei are pre-existing settlements, others arise from urbanization and *external economies. Some activities repel each other; high-quality housing does not generally arise next to industrial areas, and other activities cannot afford the high rates of the most desirable locations. New industrial areas develop in suburban locations since they require easy access, and outlying business districts may develop for the same reason.

**multiplier** The economic consequence, intended or otherwise, of an action, whether in terms of the number of jobs created or the extra income. Basically, if a given amount of money is injected into a region, the income of that region increases not by the amount of cash injection but by some multiplier of it. In a closed system, the multiplier may be calculated if the *marginal propensity to save is known for the population.

Thus, if the government builds a factory giving each worker £1000 half is spent on, say, food and half is saved. Of that £500, the food supplier might spend £250 on clothes and save £250, and so on. The value of the multiplier for a closed system is shown as:

$$k = \frac{1}{MPS}$$

where k is the multiplier and $MPS$ is the *marginal propensity to save. In reality, much of any increment may well be spent outside the region. This draining away of money is known as leakage. Thus:

$$k = \frac{1}{MPS + P}$$

where $P$ is the percentage of additional income spent on leakages. A low regional multiplier makes very remote the possibility of rejuvenating a problem area.

The multiplier can work in reverse if a source of income is cut.

**multiracial** Of a society made up of a number of ethnic or cultural groups.

**multispectral** Of a *remote sensor which uses a number of wavebands when recording images; hence, **multispectral scanner** and **multispectral sensing**.

**multivariate analysis** Any statistical technique analysing the relationship between more than two variables.

**municipal** Relating to local government, especially that of a town or city.

**muscovite** Brown or green *mica.

**muskeg** A term used in Canada to describe spring bogs.

**mutualism** See *symbiosis.

# N

**nadir** In *remote sensing, the point on the ground vertically below the centre of the sensor.

**nanoplankton** *Phytoplankton together with *zooplankton.

**nappe** A sheet of rocks which has been moved forward over the formations beneath it and in front of it, finally covering them.

**narrows** A *strait.

**natality** The production of a living child; birth.

**nation** A large number of people of mainly common descent, language, and history, hence **national**, a member of a nation, or of a nation. A nation need not be a *state, as in a *multinational state.

**national grid** 1. The series of reference lines used on *Ordnance Survey maps.
2. The system of generating stations which supplies electricity to the consumer.

**nationalism** The feeling of belonging to a group linked by common descent, language, and history, and with a corresponding ideology which exalts the nation and expects loyalty from its citizens.

**nationalization** The bringing of a system or type of production into state ownership.

**National Park** An area little affected by human exploitation and occupation, with sites of particular scenic or scientific interest and which is protected by a national authority. This protection is limited in Britain by the need for farmland, forestry, and other commercial uses but there are fairly strict controls on development. New roads should be hidden under cut-and-cover tunnels or within cuttings, camping and caravan sites are meant to be hidden behind trees, and new buildings should be made of the same stone and to the same design as were traditionally used.

National Parks are generally sited in areas of low industrialization and the purpose of the Park may conflict with local demands for employment. Furthermore, the attraction of an area to visitors may diminish as the Park becomes overcrowded. One solution is to concentrate visitors in a few points served by car parks, gift shops, and information centres, such that the open countryside remains thinly populated by tourists.

The first National Park was Yellowstone, designated in 1872 by the US Congress. British National Parks were first planned in 1949 with the National Parks and Access to the Countryside Act. As a result of this Act, some 20% of the total land area of Britain is officially protected.

**nation state** A *nation which is also a *state. The two do not always go hand in hand.

**native** Of a plant or animal, originating in the area in which it is now found.

**NATO** See *North Atlantic Treaty Organization.

**natural** Formed without the influence of man, as with **natural gas** as opposed to gas manufactured from coal.

**natural area** A spontaneously arising and individual area of an urban society with common social, economic, and cultural characteristics. Cities contain numbers of natural areas delimited by informal boundaries such as canals, parks, railways, rivers, and main roads.

**natural change** A net change in total population due to a lack of balance between births and deaths. **Natural decrease** occurs when deaths exceed births; **natural increase** when births exceed deaths.

**natural hazard** A hazard is an unexpected source of danger to the environment. By this definition, the Indian monsoon is not a hazard, but its failure is. The impact on the human environment is greater when it is unprepared for; small decreases in rainfall afflict Britain much more than summer droughts afflict the Mediterranean. Some hazards are unavoidable; Bangladesh is unable to forestall the catastrophic effects of a tropical cyclone because of poverty and because of the lack of higher ground on which to evacuate the population at risk. See also *hazard perception.

**natural increase** The growth of a population as births exceed deaths. The **natural increase rate** is calculated by subtracting deaths from births and then dividing the result by the number of the total population.

**naturalization** 1. The introduction of an organism to a new habitat in which it can thrive and reproduce.
2. The granting of citizenship to a foreigner.

**natural landscape** The landscape unaffected by human agency. Most landscapes at present are *cultural landscapes.

**natural region** A region unified by its physical attributes. Three general facts have a great bearing on the character of any region: latitude, relief and structure, and location. These work together to form regions which may be characterized according to topography, climate, and vegetation.

**natural resource** Any naturally occurring material which man chooses to use. See *resource.

**natural selection** The theory proposed by Charles Darwin which is popularly summarized as 'the survival of the fittest'. Organisms produce numbers of offspring, some of which are successful. The characteristics of these 'fittest' offspring are then reproduced in the next generation.

**natural vegetation** In theory, the grouping of plants which has developed in an area without human interference. Most landscapes have been changed by man through forest clearance, agriculture, and industry. It is argued that there are relatively few areas of truly natural vegetation left.

**nature conservation order** An order designed to protect certain plant or animal species or to conserve features of national importance. If development of a site is banned by an order, the landowner may be compensated.

**nature reserve** An area of land, usually enclosed and of restricted access, set aside for the protection of plants, animals, or the landscape.

**nautical mile** Theoretically, the length of one minute of arc on a *great circle drawn on a sphere of equal area to the earth. In Britain it is taken to be 1853.18 m.

**neap tide** A tide with a low range, occurring twice a month when the gravitational force of the moon is opposed by that of the sun.

**nearest neighbour analysis** The study of settlements in order to discern any regularity in spacing by comparing the actual pattern of settlement with a theoretical random pattern. The straight line distance from each settlement to its nearest neighbour is measured and this is divided by the total number of settlements to give the observed mean distance between nearest neighbours. The density of points is calculated as:

$$\frac{\text{number of points in the study}}{\text{size of area studied}}$$

The expected mean in a random distribution is calculated as:

$$\frac{1}{2\sqrt{\text{density}}}$$

The expected mean is compared with the observed mean.

$$R_n = \frac{\text{observed mean}}{\text{expected mean}}$$

where $R_n$ is the nearest neighbour index. An index of 0 indicates a completely clustered situation. 1 shows a random pattern,

2 a uniform grid, and 2.5 a uniform triangular pattern. The interpretation of index values can be difficult since these values are not part of a continuum.

**nebkha** See *sand dunes.

**neck** A mass of lava which has solidified in the *pipe of a volcano. Erosion of the material surrounding the neck may reveal a steep tower or an **erosional neck**.

**negative change of sea level** A fall of sea level in relation to the land, perhaps caused by a decline in the volume of the sea, or by a change in the configuration of the oceanic crust.

**negentropy** The extent of organization in a system. See *entropy.

**nehrung** A spit found along the southern coast of the Baltic Sea.

**neighbourhood** A district forming a community within a town or city, where inhabitants recognize each other by sight. It has been claimed that neighbourhoods evolve their own distinctive characteristics although the evidence for this is not strong.

**neighbourhood business district, neighbourhood centre** A rank in the hierarchy of business districts below the *CBD and regional business centre. Neighbourhood centres offer frequently needed *low-order goods and services and serve populations of 5000 to 10 000.

**neighbourhood effect** It is claimed that individuals are affected by the mores of the neighbourhood in which they live, and that the social environment of the neighbourhood conditions people's behaviour. If the neighbourhood is very run down, inhabitants may not treat it with respect, while the peer pressure in a high-class residential district may encourage the residents to maintain their property. The concept is attacked by those who maintain that the neighbourhood is less important than other social and economic factors.

**neighbourhood unit** The concept of the neighbourhood as a distinctive residential area was advanced by Perry in 1929 and has been used in the planning of *new towns. The town is planned to contain units of about 5000 people, each unit having its own low-order centre supplying convenience goods, medical facilities, and primary education. Through traffic is discouraged. The aim is to foster a sense of community in each neighbourhood unit, but such schemes have not always proved to be successful.

**nematodes** Roundworms, sometimes called threadworms or eelworms. They are important in the breakdown of soil *microflora into *humus.

**neoclassical economics** Classical economists held that the price of goods was determined by competition in the market and not by the producing firms. Furthermore, the workings of the market alone should regulate the economy; the best government policy was *laissez-faire*. To this, neoclassicists added the concept of marginal utility. This is the added satisfaction (utility) which comes from acquiring extra (marginal) goods or services. Consumers are held to spend money on extra goods and services to maximize the satisfaction received.

The neoclassical approach to industrial geography sees all firms or individuals acting in a manner similar enough to make generalizations possible.

**neocolonialism** The control of the economic and political systems of one state by a more powerful state, usually the control of a developing country by a developed one. The means of control are usually economic, including trade agreements and investment. It is argued that the imposition of Western business methods on a developing country creates a new, alien, class structure.

**neoglacial** A time of increased glacial activity and extent during the *Holocene. Glaciers expanded during this phase; the *Little Ice Age may represent one such advance.

**Neolithic** In Britain, the period approximately between 3000 and 2000 BC during which time more sophisticated techniques such as grinding and polishing were applied to the making of stone implements. This era also saw the beginnings of the domestication of animals and the planting of crops.

**neotectonics** The study of the causes and effects of the movement of the earth's crust in the **neogene**, i.e. the late *Cainozoic era. Some restrict the term to studies since the Miocene: others use it to refer to *Quaternary movements alone.

**neritic** Pertaining to shallow waters.

**ness** A *headland, as in Dungeness, Kent.

**nesting** The way in which one network fits into a larger one. An example is taken from *central place theory where a smaller market area fits into a larger one.

**net migration balance** The figure arrived at when *natural increase is subtracted from the total change in population. It is the balance of immigration and outmigration.

**net primary productivity** In ecology, the amount of energy which primary *producers can pass on to the second *trophic level. This represents the amount of carbon dioxide taken in by a plant minus the carbon dioxide it emits during respiration. Respiration rates can be measured if the plant's carbon dioxide output in the dark is recorded. **Gross primary production** may be calculated since gross primary production = net primary production + respiration.

**net radiation** The balance of incoming solar radiation and outgoing terrestrial radiation. Net radiation is generally positive by day and negative by night.

**network** A system of interconnecting routes which allow movement from one centre to the others. **Network connectivity** is the extent to which movement is possible between points on a network. **Network density** is the total area covered by the network divided by the total length of the links between points. A **planar network** can be represented on a flat surface; a **nonplanar network** exists in three dimensions.

**network analysis** A method of studying networks in terms of *graph theory.

**neutrality** Some states, such as Sweden and Switzerland, have chosen to be permanently neutral except when their territory is at risk, while others, like Eire in the Second World War, have been neutral in particular conflicts. Austria is bound to neutrality under the terms of the Allied peace treaty of 1955. **Neutral zones** are often established between rival states, and are usually policed by United Nations forces.

**nevados** A cold wind coming off the Andes in Ecuador; a *katabatic wind.

**névé** An alternative term for *firn.

**New Commonwealth** The former colonies of the British Empire from the Caribbean, Africa, and Asia.

**newly industrialized country, NIC** A hitherto underdeveloped country of the Third World which is increasing its industrial base.

**new town** A newly created town, either on a greenfield site or around a pre-existing settlement, planned to relieve overcrowding and congestion in the major conurbations by taking in the *overspill population. The aim was to create a town which would be economically viable, with light industry, services, and shops. The Greater London plan of 1944 laid down proposals for ten new towns, and after the New Towns Act of 1946, work started on the development of the first group of new towns such as Bracknell and Crawley. Housing densities were low—about five houses per ha—and housing was arranged in *neighbourhood units of around 5000 people with their own facilities such as shops, schools, and medical centres.

The second generation of new towns, such as Redditch and Telford, designated between 1955 and 1965, also used the neighbourhood unit but less rigorously, and greater emphasis was placed on the development of centralized functions and on solving the problems caused by mass ownership of cars. To cut down the length of journey to work, industries were not as rigidly zoned and separated from residential areas.

The third generation of new towns such as Milton Keynes and Peterborough were more individual in their plan and were more often created around pre-existing settlements. All British new towns were planned to give a balance of social groups, and while the first new towns were planned to house up to 80 000 people, the third and last group may house up to 500 000.

The development of new towns began in Britain but they may be found in countries as different as the USSR and the USA.

**new village** As villages expand, they may be swamped by new developments. It may be better to build new villages rather than to spoil existing villages. To this end, new villages have been built at Bar Hill in Cambridgeshire, Studland Park in Suffolk, and New Ash Green in Kent.

**New World** North, South, and Central America together with the islands of the Caribbean.

**NIC** See *newly industrialized country.

**niche** A set of ecological conditions which provides a species with the energy and habitat which enable it to reproduce and colonize. A niche is usually identified by the needs of the organism.

**niche glacier** A small patch of glacier ice found on an upland slope. Niche glaciers differ from *cirque glaciers in that their ice has little effect upon the topography.

**nick point** See *knick point.

**nimbo-, nimbus** Referring to clouds bringing rain, as in nimbo-*stratus clouds.

**nitrification** The conversion of organic compounds of nitrogen to nitrates, which can be absorbed by plants.

**nitrogen cycle** The cycling of nitrogen and its compounds through the *ecosystem. Micro-organisms living in the root nodules of leguminous plants can 'fix' atmospheric nitrogen, that is, they can assimilate atmospheric nitrogen into organic compounds. Fixing can also occur via blue-green algae, from lightning strikes, and by industrial processes. The ammonia and nitrates resulting from fixing are picked up by plants and animals and changed into proteins and amino acids. These are returned to the soil as faeces or as dead tissue. 'Denitrifying' bacteria then act upon these wastes to release free nitrogen into the air.

**nitrogen fixation** The conversion by some soil bacteria and some blue-green algae of atmospheric nitrogen into organic nitrogen compounds. This comes about mostly by bacteria in the root nodules of *leguminous plants.

**nivation** The effects of snow on a landscape. These include *abrasion and *frost-shattering. Furthermore, melted snow triggers mass movements such as *solifluction and *slope wash. These processes may produce the shallow pits known as **nivation hollows**. In time, these hollows may trap more snow and may deepen further with more nivation so that *cirques or *thermocirques are formed. Snow has the greatest effect on a landscape where it is thin and melting.

**noctilucent cloud** A high, glowing, silver cloud, probably made of ice crystals and found in the *stratosphere.

**nodal** At, or like, a *node.

**nodes** 1. In *network analysis, destinations or intersection points which are part of a *network. These are also known as vertices.

2. In behavioural urban geography, the strategic points in a built-up area around which the individual plans his movements.

**nodule** A small, rounded concretion of minerals.

**nomadism** A form of social organization where people and animals move from place to place in search of pasture. The itinerary of movement may take the form of a routine pattern but as rainfall varies, there may be movement away from this routine. True nomads have no fixed abode and no *sedentary agriculture. **Semi-nomads**, like some Australian Aborigines, wander for some of the year and grow crops for the rest of the year.

As international boundaries are increasingly well defined, with border guards, nomadism will decline. Governments try to immobilize nomads as an attempt to bring them in line with more advanced societies for the purposes of taxation as well as for health and literacy. However, many researchers now consider that nomadism represents the best use of fragile ecosystems.

**nominal scale** A scale with data grouped in such a way that it precludes quantitative description, such as soil classification or the recognition of various cultural groups. All the categories are different from each other and have no relative order.

**nomothetic** Concerned with finding similarities between places or phenomena. Thus, for example, models of urban morphology are derived by looking for resemblances in cities—this is a nomothetic approach.

**non-aligned** Of a nation-state which does not necessarily support either the USA or the USSR.

**non-basic worker** A worker concerned with serving the city in which she or he lives and who is thus not bringing wealth into the city.

**non-conformity** A series of sedimentary strata overlying an igneous or metamorphic rock.

**non-ecumene** The uninhabited or very sparsely populated regions of the world. It is not easy to draw boundaries between the *ecumene and the non-ecumene as regions of dense occupation merge into sparsely populated regions. If there is a boundary, it is not static.

**non-parametric statistics** Statistical tests which are not based on a *normal distribution of data or on any other assumption. They are also known as distribution-free tests and the data are generally ranked or grouped. Examples include the *chi-squared test and *Spearman's rank correlation coefficient.

**non-renewable resource** A finite mass of material which cannot be restored after use, such as natural gas. Some nonrenewable resources may be sustained by *recycling.

**Norfolk rotation** A four-year crop *rotation of wheat, then a root crop, then barley, followed by a *leguminous crop.

**normal distribution** The line graph showing the expected frequency of occurrences in each class of any set of data for a given variable. The normal distribution is shown as a bell-shaped curve which is symmetrical about the mean. The laws of probability state that between $+1\sigma$ (*standard deviation) and $-1\sigma$ 68.27% of the items in the data set will be found, between $+2\sigma$ and $-2\sigma$ 95.45% of all the items in the data set will be found, and between $+3\sigma$ and $-3\sigma$ 99.97% of all the items in the data set will be found. In other words, a difference of more or less than 3 standard deviations from the mean is only to be expected once in every 300 observations. So, if in a sample data set of 50 items, one value exceeds $+/-3$ standard deviations from the mean, the data may be suspect and should be checked.

**normal fault** A fault with a plane between 45 and 90° and with a *downthrow which has slid down the fault plane.

**normative theory** Any theory which seeks to explain or predict what would happen under theoretical constraints. In geography, normative models, like the *von Thünen model of land use, generally rely heavily on assumptions and pre-conditions and most *spatial analysis is normative. Many normative models are wildly unrealistic since they ignore the complexity of the real world, concentrating on idealized concepts such as rational, *economic man, and *isotropic plains.

**norte** A cold northerly wind of Central America.

**North Atlantic drift** A warm *ocean current, driven by the prevailing south-westerlies from Florida to north-west Europe, at velocities of 16–32 km per day.

Onshore winds transfer heat from this current to coastal areas, thus bringing warmer conditions than would be expected at high latitudes in north-west Europe.

**North Atlantic Treaty Organization, NATO** A defence alliance, founded in 1949, by Belgium, Canada, Denmark, France, Iceland, Italy, Luxemburg, the Netherlands, Norway, Portugal, the UK, and the USA. Greece, Turkey, and West Germany joined later.

**north-east trades** See *trade winds.

**norther** A cold northerly wind of Texas and the Gulf of Mexico, often bringing thunder and hail.

**Northern Lights** *Aurora Borealis.

**northing** On a map, a reference line running east–west and numbering up from south to north. It is used for the second part of a *grid reference; the first part is the *easting.

**North Pacific current** A cold *ocean current.

**North Pole** The northern end of the earth's axis. **Magnetic North** is the direction a compass points towards. The two rarely coincide.

**North–South** See *Brandt report.

**northwester** A strong, hot, and dry wind of New Zealand.

**nuclear family** Husband, wife, and children.

**nuclear fission** See *fission.

**nuclear fusion** See *fusion.

**nuclear power** A form of energy which uses nuclear reactions to produce steam to turn generators. Naturally occurring uranium is concentrated, enriched, and converted to uranium dioxide—the fuel used in the reactor. This fuel readily undergoes nuclear fission which produces large amounts of heat. Some of the highly radioactive spent fuel may be reprocessed while the bulk must be disposed of. Both are costly and hazardous undertakings. The main advantage of nuclear power is the relatively small amount of an abundant fuel which is required. The major disadvantages are very high construction and decommissioning costs, highly technical operations, the problem of waste disposal, and the major problems which may arise with any accident. Furthermore, nuclear power stations have a short lifespan.

The locational requirements of a nuclear power station include very large amounts of water as a coolant, stable and firm geological conditions, and distance from large centres of population because of the radiation hazard.

**nuclear winter** A series of nuclear explosions would produce large quantities of smoke and dust. These particles might intercept incoming solar radiation and reflect it back into space. If this were to occur, very much lower temperatures would obtain at the earth's surface, giving severe wintry conditions.

**nucleated settlement** A settlement clustered around a central point, such as a village green or church. **Nucleation** is fostered by defence considerations, localized water supply, the incidence of flooding, or rich soils so that farmers can easily get to their smaller, productive fields while continuing to live in the village.

**nuée ardente** A glowing cloud of volcanic ash, *pumice, and larger *pyroclasts which moves rapidly downslope. The material from a nuée ardente consolidates to form ignimbrite, also known as welded tuff.

**nullah** In India, a dry stream bed.

**null hypothesis** A hypothesis, to be tested statistically, that no difference is to be seen within the groups tested or that no correlation exists between the variables. If the null hypothesis can be rejected, the existence of a difference or a relationship can be proved.

**nunatak** A mountain peak which projects above an ice sheet. Nunataks are generally angular and jagged due to *frost shattering and, after the ice has retreated, contrast with the rounded contours of the glaciated landscape below.

**nuptiality** The frequency of marriage within a population, usually expressed as a *marriage rate. It is a major factor in *fertility, although less so now in Britain with a large proportion of children born out of wedlock. The most basic rates express the number of marriages per thousand population, or the number of people per thousand marrying in a given year.

**nutrient cycle** The uptake, use, release, and storage of nutrients by plants and their environments. In temperate *ecosystems, far more nutrients are stored in the soil than can be used immediately by plants. The soil then acts as a reservoir for nutrients. In tropical ecosystems, almost all the nutrients are stored in the plants and the soil is impoverished. The living parts of the ecosystem fulfil a number of functions in the nutrient cycle such as regulation of nutrients in outgoing water, the storage of combined nitrogen, and the control of water loss through *transpiration.

**nutritional density** See *physiological density.

# O

**oasis** A fertile, watered spot in a desert.

**OAU** *Organization of African Unity.

**obduction** The reverse of *subduction.

**oblique fault** A fault with its *strike at an oblique angle to the strike of the bed it cuts through.

**obsequent** Of a stream or river, flowing in the opposite direction to the *dip of the strata it flows over.

**occlusion** A stage which may occur in a *mid-latitude depression where the cold front to the rear catches up with the leading warm front, lifts the wedge of warm air off the ground, and meets the cold air ahead of the warm front. If this overtaking air is colder than the cold air which is ahead of it, it will undercut it, forming a **cold occlusion**. If, on the other hand, it is warmer than the cold air which is ahead of it, it will ride over it forming a **warm occlusion**.

**occupancy rate** The number of people dwelling in a house per habitable room. A rate of one person per room is taken as acceptable; more than one person per room represents overcrowding.

**occupational mobility** The ability of the individual to change jobs after the acquisition of a new skill.

**ocean** The water which covers some 70% of the earth's surface. Although there is no strict difference between the two, an ocean is generally understood to be larger than a sea. Its bed is the **ocean floor**, and an ocean occupies an **ocean basin** which is often blanketed with coarse **oceanic mud**.

**ocean current** A permanent or semipermanent horizontal movement of unusually cold or warm surface water of the oceans, to a depth of about 100 m. The global system of winds is the most important cause of these currents, which are also affected by variations in the temperature, and hence density, of the water, and by the *Coriolis force. Currents are an important factor in the redistribution of heat between the tropics and the polar regions.

Cold currents originate in high latitudes and can greatly modify the temperatures of coastal areas as far inland as 100 km. As tropical air streams move over these currents, advection fog forms over the sea and the air streams are stripped of most of their moisture; onshore winds are therefore dry. Cold currents thus contribute to desert conditions. Conversely, warm currents originate in tropical waters, and bring unusually warm conditions to the higher latitudes affected by them.

**oceanic climate** *Maritime climate.

**oceanic crust** That portion of the outer, rigid part of the earth which underlies the oceans. The oceanic crust seems to be mostly underlain by a basalt layer, 5–6 km thick. Its average density is around 2.9, more than the *continental crust, but less than the *mantle.

**oceanic ridge** A section of oceanic crust where *magma rises up through a cracking and widening ridge, creating new crust which is then pushed away from the ridge. Some magma cools below the crust, some of it forces into fractures, and much flows out to form new crust. By this mechanism, the oceanic plates are areas of sea-floor spreading and the oceanic crust is moved away from the ridge. The term mid-oceanic ridge properly refers to the Atlantic Ocean; other ridges are not at the centre of the oceans.

**oceanography** The study of the oceans. This covers the shape, depth, and distribution of oceans, their composition, life forms, ecology, and water currents, and their legal status.

**ocean trench** A long, narrow, but very deep depression in the ocean floor where, at the junction of two *plates, one plate dives steeply beneath another and penetrates the *mantle.

**OD** See *Ordnance Datum.

**ODECA** *Central American Common Market.

**OECD** See *Organization for Economic Co-operation and Development.

**OEEC** An earlier form of the *Organization for Economic Co-operation and Development, formed in 1947 with the particular aim of overseeing the distribution of US aid under the *Marshall Plan.

**office park** A planned area developed to provide the buildings and *infrastructure needed for offices.

**offshore** 1. In meteorology, moving seawards from the land, as in **offshore wind**.
2. In geomorphology, the zone to the seaward side of the breakers as in **offshore bar**.

**ogive** In the shape of a pointed arch.
1. Bands of dark and light ice stretch across glaciers in this shape because the central ice of a glacier moves more rapidly than the sides. The term has been extended to refer to such bands.
2. *Cumulative frequency curve.

**O horizon** A soil *horizon containing half-rotted organic matter and/or *humus.

**oil dome** A gentle dome within sedimentary rocks containing mineral oil. This accumulation of oil may be called an **oil-pool**.

**oil refining** The processing of crude oil into petrol, paraffin, diesel oil, and lubricants. Oil refineries require stable, firm geological conditions, large sites, and easy access to oil supplies. Countries without sufficient domestic oil supplies will refine oil imported by tankers; a coastal location is, therefore, generally used.

**oil sand** A porous oil-filled sand or sandstone at or just below ground level. Although oil sands are rich in oil, they are costly to exploit.

**oil shale** A *shale from which oil and natural gas may be distilled.

**okta** In meteorology, a measure of the extent of cloud cover. This runs from 1 okta (scant cloud cover) to 8 oktas (complete cloud cover). Oktas are shown on *synoptic charts by a circle which is progressively shaded in as cloud cover increases.

**old-age index** The number of old people in the population as a percentage of the total adult population.

**Old Commonwealth** Australia, Canada, and New Zealand.

**Old World** Europe, Africa, and Asia.

**oligopoly** The domination by a few firms of a particular industry. In order to maintain their share of the market, such firms are forced to imitate each other's behaviour. A classic example was the introduction of unleaded petrol by both Shell and Esso almost at the same time. Elsewhere, more dubious examples are price-fixing between competing firms and the sharing out of the market.

**oligotrophic** Poor in nutrients, usually of lakes, soils, and peat bogs.

**omnivore** An animal which eats plant and animal matter.

**onion weathering** See *exfoliation.

**ontogenetic** Concerned with the development, notably of intellectual development, of human beings, especially of the individual.

**ontology** The study of the nature of being, of what exists or what can be known. See also *empiricism.

**Oolite** A form of limestone made of small, round particles.

**oolith** A grain of rock, between 0.25 and 2 mm in diameter, made up of a fragment of shell or mineral with a hard mineral coating. Ooliths form a large portion of **oolitic rocks**, such as **Oolitic Limestone**.

**ooze** A deep, sea-floor deposit either of tiny organisms such as diatoms (a type of algae) or of fine inorganic sediments.

**OPEC** The Organization of Petroleum Exporting Countries, a central body which, at regular intervals, fixes the price of oil on the international markets. Although a supplier of oil, Britain is not among the OPEC countries since they are all at odds with the old colonial powers who controlled the oil industry in its early stages. OPEC increased petroleum prices very dramatically in 1973 and 1974 to the great discomfort of most Western nations.

The founder members are Iran, Iraq, Kuwait, Saudi Arabia, and Venezuela. Later members include Algeria, Ecuador, Gabon, Indonesia, Libya, Qatar, Nigeria, and the United Arab Emirates.

**opencast mining** A system of mining which does not use shafts or tunnels and is, hence, cheaper. The layer above the mineral is removed and the deposit beneath is extracted using earth moving machinery. The *overburden may then be replaced. Most opencast mining is permitted or licensed on the condition that this takes place.

**open field** A distribution of farm land associated with *feudalism in Europe. Each manor had two or three large open fields and each farmer was awarded a number of strips within each field. Holdings were scattered so that no one had all the good or all the poor land.

**open system** A system which is not separated from its environment but exchanges material or energy with it.

**ophiolite** An old land fragment of oceanic crust, formed at a mid-*oceanic ridge, moved across the ocean floor by *sea-floor spreading, and finally lifted above sea level. This explanation of their formation caused the rejection of the concept of a *geosyncline by some writers.

**opisometer** An instrument used for measuring distance on a map. A small wheel is pushed along the distance to be measured and its revolutions are recorded on a calibrated dial.

**opportunist species** Species which survive by the rapid colonization or recolonization of a *habitat. Such species have very good powers of dispersal in order to seek new habitats. Life is short, fecundity and reproduction are high, and these species are able to withstand difficult conditions. The term fugitive species is also used for opportunist species since they are seen as colonizing those marginal habitats, such as deserts and saline areas, which are not used by other organisms. See also *r-selection, k-selection.

**opportunity cost** A term used in *neo-classical economics to express cost in terms of the sacrifice of alternatives.

**optimization model** A model used to find the best possible choice out of a set of alternatives. It may use the mathematical expression of a problem to maximize or minimize some function. The alternatives are frequently restricted by constraints on the values of the variables. A simple example might be finding the most efficient transport pattern to carry commodities from the point of supply to the markets, given the volumes of production and demand, together with unit transport costs.

**optimizer** A decision-maker who seeks the best outcome, usually to maximize profits, especially those received from manufacturing industry. In choosing an industrial location, the profit maximizer is assumed to know all the relevant factors at given locations including the cost of assembling materials and distributing products, the price of labour, and *agglomeration and *external economies.

**optimum city size** Some writers contend that benefits accrue from urbanization up to a particular point—the optimum size. Beyond this point diseconomies operate: pollution and congestion set in, and the city is a less efficient and less pleasant place to live in.

**optimum location** The best location for a firm in order to maximize proits. It is argued that profit-maximizing firms will force less successful firms out of business and that this will result in firms moving towards optimum location patterns. In the absence of complete knowledge by the decision-maker, the point of maximum profits may not be clear.

**optimum population** A theoretically perfect situation where the population of an area can develop its resources to the best extent, and achieve maximum output while enjoying the highest possible standards of living.

**orbit** The elliptical or circular path taken by a planet as it moves around its sun, or by a satellite, natural or man-made, around a planet.

**order of goods** See *high-order goods and services and *low-order goods and services.

**ordinal scale** A scale which represents the relative importance or order of magnitude of data but not their absolute values.

**ordinate** The vertical or *y*-coordinate on a graph.

**Ordnance Datum, OD** In Britain, mean sea level at Newlyn, Cornwall. From this level, all the heights on British maps are calculated.

**Ordnance Survey, OS** The official map-making authority in Britain. The first OS maps were produced for the army, hence the term Ordnance, which means artillery.

**Ordovician** A *period of *Paleozoic time stretching approximately from 500 to 430 million years BP.

**ore** A naturally occurring deposit which contains a mineral, or minerals, in sufficient concentration to justify commercial exploitation.

**ore-dressing** Crushing an ore to separate out the minerals it contains by chemical processing, sedimentation, and flotation.

**organic** 1. In chemistry, containing carbon.
2. In biology, of a plant or animal.

3. In farming, without the use of artificial chemicals, as in **organic farming**.

**organic acid** Acid compounds of carbon, such as acetic acid, which are produced when plant or animal tissues decompose.

**organic soil** As opposed to a *mineral soil, a soil made largely from *organic material.

**organic weathering** The breakdown of rocks by plant or animal action or by chemicals formed from plants and animals. *Humic acids break down rock, and bacteria reduce iron compounds.

**Organization for Economic Co-operation and Development, OECD** A group of nation-states with the aim of promoting mutual growth and development, aiding less developed countries, and evolving common policies of social welfare. The members are Australia, Austria, Belgium, Canada, Denmark, Eire, France, Finland, Germany, Iceland, Italy, Japan, Luxembourg, the Netherlands, New Zealand, Norway, Portugal, Spain, Sweden, Switzerland, Turkey, the UK, USA, and Yugoslavia.

**Organization of African Unity, OAU** An association of independent African states designed to encourage African unity, to discourage *neocolonialism, and to promote development.

**Organization of American States** An association of Latin American states with the USA. It is designed to encourage American solidarity, to aid co-operation between members, to maintain present boundaries, and to arbitrate in disputes between members.

**Organization of Petroleum Exporting Countries** See *OPEC.

**orientation** The positioning of a map, an observer, or a surveying instrument to face north.

**orogen** The total mass of rock deformed during an *orogeny.

**orogeny** Movements of the earth which involve the folding of sediments, faulting, and *metamorphism. Two major types of orogeny are recognized: a cordilleran type in which *geosynclinical deposits are severely deformed, and a continental collision which results from the trapping of the oceanic crust and sediment between two masses of continental crust.

**orographic precipitation, orographic rainfall** Also known as **relief rainfall**, this forms when moisture-laden air masses are forced to rise over high ground. The air is cooled, the water vapour condenses, and precipitation occurs. Some authors maintain that relief merely intensifies the precipitation caused by *convection or formed at fronts. The term **orographic intensification** is, therefore, used occasionally.

**orthogonal** At right angles. Orthogonals plotted through the crests of waves in plan illustrate the process of *wave refraction.

**OS** See *Ordnance Survey.

**osmosis** The passage of a weaker solution to a stronger solution through a semipermeable membrane. In soils, the more dilute soil moisture passes by **osmotic pressure** into plant roots. In this way, soil moisture is taken up by plants.

**outback** The remote areas of Australia.

**outcrop** An uncovered exposure of rock at ground level.

**outlet glacier** A glacier streaming from the edge of a body of ice located on a plateau.

**outlier** In geology, an area of younger rock surrounded by older rocks.

**outport** With the increasing size of modern ships, some old harbours are no longer deep enough. Consequently, a new port—an outport—is built seawards of the original port, where there is deeper water.

**outwash sands and gravels** Sediments washed out by glacial meltwater and deposited beyond the ice sheet or glacier supplying the water and the debris. Such deposits are usually sorted with the coarser sediment being deposited nearer to the ice front and finer material being laid down further away. This term is synonymous with **outwash fan, outwash plain**, or *valley train.

**overbank stage** The stage of a river as it floods over its banks.

**overbound(ed) city** A city where the administrative boundary includes areas which are not *urban.

**overburden** The layer of rock and soil overlying a particular rock *stratum.

**overcropping** Growing so many crops that the soil loses its fertility.

**overcrowding** Too many people in too little space. One method of measuring overcrowding is to count each room in a house, except the kitchen and bathroom, and to divide the total by the number of people living in the house. In Britain, if the answer is less than 1, the house is overcrowded.

**overdeepening** A phenomenon found in *cirques and *glacial troughs where the middle section of the feature is lower than the mouth. It is suggested that the overdeepened section is the zone of maximum ice thickness. It is possible to find overdeepening in glacial landscapes, since ice can move upslope within the general direction of ice flow.

**overflow channel** A steep-sided and relatively narrow channel cut by meltwater from a *proglacial lake as the level of the lake rises and spills over the relief barrier which contained the water. It is suggested, however, that some features once identified as overflow channels are subglacial meltwater channels.

**overfold** An overturned, asymmetrical anticline. See *fold.

**overland flow** Water flows overland either because the rainfall intensity is greater than the infiltration capacity of the soil, or because the soil or rock which it flows over has become saturated, i.e. because the water table has come to the surface. Saturated zone overland flow occurs in small valleys in humid climates, where there are strips of land bordering streams, in hillside hollows with high water tables, and where soil moisture levels are high.

**overpopulation** Too great a population for a given area to support. This may be because population growth has outstripped resources or because of the exhaustion of resources. The symptoms of overpopulation include high unemployment, low incomes, low standards of living, and, possibly, malnutrition and famine. *Malthus was probably the first European to identify population problems but his views were discredited for some time. At present, some neo-Malthusians are supporting the same argument. Marxists, however, view overpopulation as the result of the maldistribution and underdevelopment of resources. In the developed world, some would suggest that pollution and the desecration of the countryside are indicators of overpopulation.

**overspill** The population which is dispersed from large cities to relieve congestion and overcrowding, and, possibly, unemployment. It occurs with redevelopment in the city where new building is at much lower densities so that some—the overspill—cannot be housed in the city.

**overthrust** A near horizontal fold subjected to stress such that the strata override underlying rocks.

**ox-bow lake** A horseshoe-shaped lake once part of, and now lying alongside, a meandering river. The lake was once part of a meander and erosion at the neck left only a short distance from one neck to another. When the river breaks through this narrow stretch of land, the old meander becomes a temporary lake. Ox-bow lakes quickly fill up and become hollows in the landscape.

**oxidation** In geomorphology, the absorption by a mineral of one or more oxygen *ions. Oxidation is a major type of chemical weathering, particularly in rocks containing iron. Within soils, oxidation occurs when minerals take up some of the oxygen dissolved in the soil moisture.

**oxisol** A soil of the *US soil classification. See *ferrallitization.

**ozone** A form of oxygen. The **ozone layer** stretches from 15 to 50 km above the earth's surface. It absorbs most of the harmful ultraviolet radiation from the sun. Some scientists believe that the propellant gases used in aerosol sprays are destroying the ozone layer. It is also claimed that destruction of the ozone layer increases the incidence of skin cancer. Ozone is a form of oxygen where three atoms of the gas are combined in one molecule, rather than two atoms, as in free oxygen.

# P

**Pacific Suite** A *petrographic province marked by intense folding and calcium-rich rocks.

**Pacific-type coast** A coastline where the trend of ridges and valleys is parallel to the coast. If the coastal lowlands are inundated by the sea, a coast of interconnected straights parallel to the shore may result.

**pack ice** All sea ice except for that which is attached to terrestrial ice.

**pahoehoe** A highly fluid lava which spreads in sheets. The surface is a glassy layer which has been dragged into ropy folds by the movement of the hot lava below it.

**paleoecology** The reconstruction of past environments from the evidence of fossils. It is possible to use the fossil record to reconstruct the histories of communities. The origin, development, and extinction of species may also be studied in order to test ecological hypotheses.

**Paleolithic** The old *Stone Age; a time when humans began to make simple stone tools, particularly of flint.

**paleomagnetism** See *geomagnetism.

**Paleozoic** The *era of earth's history stretching approximately from 570 to 225 million years BP.

**palsa** A permafrost peat mound which obtrudes because it is better drained and thus more subject to *frost heaving than wetter areas. Palsas contain slim ice lenses and are not to be confused with *pingos which enclose a solid ice core.

**palynology** The study of pollen grains as an aid to the reconstruction of past plant environments. One weakness of this study is that most of the pollens found come from wind-pollenated species and animal-dispersed pollen is under-represented. See also *pollen analysis.

**pampas** The natural grassland of southern Brazil, Argentina, and Uruguay. Trees were found in the river valleys, and shrubs occurred wherever hills rose above the level of the plains. Most of the pampas has now been altered by cultivation or grazing, and, probably, by fire.

**pan** Either a large, shallow, flat-floored depression found in arid and semi-arid regions or a compacted, indurated soil horizon. Pans may be flooded seasonally or permanently.

**Pangaea** A supercontinent consisting of the whole land area of the globe before it was split by *continental drift.

**pannage** The woodland diet of swine, and thence the right to feed swine in the woods of the manor.

**parabolic dune** See *sand dune.

**paradigm** The prevailing pattern of thought in a discipline or part of a discipline. The paradigm provides rules about the type of problem which faces investigators and the way they should go about solving them. Kuhn, who first used the term in this sense, contends that the evolution of a new paradigm marks a new stage in thinking. The paradigm, or shared view, persists for a while and then becomes obsolete, to be replaced by a new paradigm. In geography, the traditional paradigm of regional geography has generally been replaced by *positivist analysis.

**parallel drainage** See *drainage patterns.

**parallel retreat** *Parallel slope retreat.

**parallel slope retreat** The evolution of a hillslope where the angle remains constant for each part of the slope. Parallel retreat assumes uniform lateral erosion over the whole hillslope. The length of the slope element is also constant except for the *pediment which increases in length over time. It is now generally conceded that no single model of slope evolution can explain all the features of hillslopes.

**parametric statistics** Statistical tests which make certain assumptions about the nature of the full population from which a sample is taken; usually the assumption of the *normal distribution. Parametric tests normally involve data in absolute numbers or values rather than ranks. An example is the *Student's *t*-test.

**parasite** An animal or plant living in or on another living organism and drawing sustenance directly from it.

**parent material** The rock from and on which a soil has been formed.

**Pareto optimality** A state of affairs where it is not possible to improve the economic lot of some people without making others worse off; a *mercantilist view. A **Pareto improvement** occurs if resources can be better utilized such that one group's prosperity increases without incurring a cost to others.

**parish** In Britain, originally an ecclesiastical unit comprising a village and a church with a clergyman in charge. It is now a unit of local government which does not necessarily share the ecclesiastical parish boundaries.

**park** Originally an enclosed area used for hunting, in the eighteenth century it applied to the grounds of a country house. It now refers to open land used for recreation in a town or city.

**part-time farmer** Some smallholders supplement their income by finding a job; some workers (ouvriers-paysans) supplement their food-supply by farming; others farm as a hobby.

**passive glacier** A glacier with little *alimentation or *ablation. It flows slowly. Erosion and transport are at a minimum.

**passive system** In *remote sensing, a sensor which detects radiation from the earth's surface but which does not generate its own radiation.

**pastoralism** The breeding and rearing of animals. Sedentary pastoralism ranges from the keeping of a small herd to ranching hundreds of stock over a very large area. **Pastoral nomads** move with their flocks which supply them with food, shelter, and goods for sale.

**patch cutting** Felling trees in one specific area so that regeneration will take place from the trees surrounding the patch.

**paternoster lakes** A series of elongated lakes in a *glacial trough. The lakes are 'strung' together by rivers, giving the effect of a rosary; hence the name.

**path** In behavioural urban geography, a channel along which individuals move within a city.

**patterned ground** The arrangement of stones into polygons, circles, nets, and stripes. The cause of such patterns is not fully understood, but it is suggested that in spring thawing takes place first under large stones because they conduct heat more readily. The stones would therefore slump. Stones on surfaces where vegetation cover is sparse might tend to migrate to such depressions. Water flowing into these depressions may wash out finer particles. *Frost heaving, drying, and shrinking are also involved. Patterned ground is most common in *periglacial areas but is not restricted to them.

**pays** In France, a small distinctive *region characterized by a common natural endowment and its own culture, such as Brie in the Paris Basin. Attempts have been made to distinguish pays in other parts of the world to establish particular regions.

**peak land-value intersection** The road intersection in a *CBD where land values are at a maximum.

**peasant** A farmer whose activities are dominated by the family group. The family provides all the labour and the produce is for the family as a whole. Land holdings are small, sometimes owned by the family, but often leased from a landlord. Most of the produce is consumed by the family, but occasional surpluses are sold in the open market.

**peat** A mass of dark brown or black plant material produced when the vegetation of a wet area is partly decomposed. Peat may be dried and used as fuel because of its high carbon content.

Peat forms where the land is waterlogged and where temperatures are low enough to slow down the decomposition of plant residues.

**pebble** A small, rounded stone roughly 1–6 cm across.

**ped** In soil science, an aggregate of silt, sand, and clay of characteristic shape. Peds vary in size even within the same soil *horizon. Soils are separated into peds by plant roots, soil fauna, and alternate wetting and drying, or freezing and thawing. See *soil structure.

**pedalfer** Any soil high in aluminium and iron, and from which the bases such as calcium and magnesium carbonates have been *leached. Pedalfers generally occur in regions with an annual rainfall of more than 600 mm.

**pedestal** A pillar made of weak rock capped with a more resistant rock.

**pediment** A gently sloping plain, generally concave and generally cut across rock, at the foot of a mountain. Usually there is a clear *break of slope between the low-angled pediment and the steeper regions of the slope above it. Some cite erosion as the cause of **pedimentation**; others widen the term to include depositional features. The coalescence of neighbouring pediments is thought to be the cause of *pediplain formation.

**pediplain** A flat or low-angled plain at the foot of mountain *scarps. It is usually bare, or may have a thin layer of *alluvium. See *pediment.

**pedocal** Any soil high in calcium carbonate and magnesium carbonate because *leaching is slight. Pedocals occur in areas with an annual rainfall of under 600 mm.

**pedogenesis** The formation of soils. **Pedogenic** processes are soil-forming processes. The chief pedogenic factors are time, relief, *hydrology, parent rock, climate, fauna, and flora. These last three have a profound influence on soils. Climate affects the vertical movements of water and minerals which lead to the formation of soil *horizons. Animals, notably earthworms, are the main agents in the mixing of soil materials. Plant roots attract soil water by *osmosis and their vegetation will determine the nature of the plant litter and hence the nature of the *humus.

**pedology** The science of soils: their characteristics, development, and distribution.

**pedon** A small sample of a soil sufficiently large to show all the characteristics of all its horizons.

**pelagic** Of marine life, belonging to the upper layers of the sea, hence **pelagic division, pelagic zone**.

**peneplain** A low-lying *erosion surface, the remnants of a landscape after erosion. See *cycle of erosion.

**peninsula** A piece of land jutting into, and almost surrounded by, the sea. Hence **peninsular**.

**perception** The process of evaluating and storing information received. It is the perception of the environment which most concerns human geographers. The nature of such perception includes emotional feelings for an environment, an ordering of information, an understanding, however subjective, of the environment, and the intervention within environmental systems in order to change them.

**perched block** An *erratic.

**perched water table** A partly saturated, confined *aquifer underlain by an impermeable rock with the main *water table below the two.

**percolation** The filtering of water downwards through soil and permeable rock. A **percolation gauge** measures the quantity of water moving in this way.

**percolines** An underground network of water seepage zones. Old root channels and soil cracks are enlarged by *interflow so that a branching pattern of drainage is formed below the ground surface.

**perennial** Active throughout the year, hence **perennial irrigation, perennial stream**.

**perfect competition** A hypothetical state of affairs under which a good is sold. There are many suppliers, each of whom is responsible for only a small number of total sales, there is no collusion between suppliers, and buyers and sellers are fully aware of the prices being charged throughout the market.

**pericline** A domed structure of sedimentary rocks.

**perigean tide** A *spring tide. The term comes from **perigee**, the point in the moon's orbit when it is nearest the earth.

**periglacial** Originally, the climate, processes, and landforms of areas bordering on *ice caps, this term has been extended to refer to any area with a *tundra climate, such as mountainous areas in mid-latitudes. Here, the dominant processes of cold climatic zones occur: *abrasion, *frost shattering, *solifluction, and *nivation.

**perihelion** The point in the orbit of a comet or planet when it is nearest to the sun it encircles.

**period** 1. A unit of geological time; the subdivision of an era. Thus the Cretaceous period is part of the Mesozoic era.
2. The time taken for succesive wave crests to pass a given point.

**periodic market** A trading market held on one or more days of each week and on the same days of the week. The markets served by the traders can be seen as forming, together, the necessary *threshold values of the goods. Alternatively, the periodic market may bring more retail opportunities to the inhabitants of rural areas.

**periphery** That part of a region, a country, or the world which is isolated and away from economic development.

**permafrost** Areas of rock and soil where temperatures have been below freezing point for at least two years. Permafrost need contain no ice; temperature is the sole qualification. Any water present need not be frozen since the presence of dissolved minerals lowers the freezing point of water. The permafrost zones are of two types: continuous and discontinuous. The **permafrost table** marks the upper limit of permafrost and is overlain by the *active layer.

**permanent snow line** Above this line, the winter fall of snow exceeds the snow which is melted in summer; below it, melting is greater. This line varies with latitude.

**permeable** In geomorphology, allowing water to pass through along *bedding planes, cracks, fissures, and joints, and through rock *pores. **Permeable rocks** also have the capacity to be saturated by water.

**Permian** The latest *period of *Paleozoic time stretching approximately from 280 to 225 million years BP.

**personal construct theory** This suggests that man constructs assumptions as to how things are ordered. Man is continually constructing and testing images of reality. The actions of an individual are psychologically schooled by the ways in which events are anticipated. It is assumed that individuals seek to fulfil desired ends and to avoid undesired outcomes.

In a study investigating, say, shopping centres, a personal construct technique may be used. The respondent is given three shopping centres and asked to identify the two which are felt to be most similar and to justify this choice. The criteria on which this judgement is based are then ascertained and built into the investigation so that the qualities of the centres are constructed from people's experience rather than imposed by the preconceptions of the investigator.

**personal space** The zone around an individual which he reserves for himself.

Personal space, as opposed to intimate space, is usually reserved for a normal conversational voice and for friendly interaction. The extent of a personal space around an individual is 1–1.5 m for a north European but closer contact may be acceptable in other cultures.

**pervious** As distinct from *permeable, allowing water through cracks and fissures, but not through pores within the rock.

**PET** See *Potential evapotranspiration.

**petrification** The turning of organic remains into stone as the original tissue is replaced by minerals.

**petrographic province** A region of *igneous rocks with enough in common to differentiate them from the rocks of another region.

**phacolith** An elongated dome of intrusive igneous rock usually located beneath the crest of an anticline or the trough of a syncline.

**phenomenal environment** The natural environment together with the effects of human activity.

**Phillips curve** A negative exponential curve depicting the relationship between the percentage change in wages and the level of unemployment. As unemployment increases, the increase in wages declines, and the lower the level of unemployment, the higher the rate of inflation.

**phlogophite** Yellow *mica.

**phosphorus cycle** On the death of an organism, it will decompose, returning the phosphorus to the earth to be taken up by plants and thence to animals.

**photic zone** The upper levels of a body of water which are penetrated by light.

**photochemical smog** Nitrogen dioxide ($NO_2$) is emitted from petrol engines. Ultraviolet light splits this into nitric oxide (NO) and monatomic oxygen (O). This oxygen reacts with free atmospheric oxygen ($O_2$), forming *ozone ($O_3$) which is irritating to the lungs. The ozone also reacts with the nitric oxide to make further nitrogen dioxide in a dangerous feedback loop. Furthermore, the hydro-carbons emitted from the burning of *fossil fuels react with some of the monatomic oxygen to add to the photochemical smog. See also *smog.

**photogrammetry** The use of photographs to obtain measurements which may then be used to make a map.

**photosynthesis** The chemical process by which green plants make organic compounds from atmospheric carbon dioxide and water in the presence of sunlight. Since virtually all other forms of life are directly or indirectly dependent on green plants for food, photosynthesis is the basis for all life on earth.

**phototroph** An organism which can obtain energy from sunlight.

**phreatic** Referring to *ground water situated below the *water table. The **phreatic zone** is permanently saturated.

A **phreatic eruption** of a volcano is one in which *meteoric water is mixed with the lava. This water may be given off as a *geyser or as steam.

**phreatophyte** A class of desert plant with very long tap roots which develop to reach the *phreatic zone.

**pH scale** A scale, running from 1 to 14, for expressing how acid or alkaline a solution is. A strong acid, with a high concentration of hydrogen ions, has a pH of 1–3, a neutral solution has a pH of 7, and a strongly alkaline solution has a pH of 10–14.

**phylogenetic** Concerned with the evolution of man as an animal.

**physical geography** The branch of geography which deals with the natural features of the earth's surface. There is some difference of opinion on the scope of physical geography; soils and oceanography are often omitted from its study.

**physical weathering** *Mechanical weathering.

**physiography** The study of landforms and processes in physical geography.

**physiological density** Also known as nutritional density, this is population density in inhabited and cultivated areas. See also *population density.

**phytoplankton** The plant component of *plankton.

**pictogram** A map of distributions where pictorial symbols such as motor cars or soldiers are placed on the location of the phenomenon mapped. The symbols may be drawn to some scale to indicate the sizes of the distribution, but this can be very misleading if they are scaled to the height of the symbol since the accompanying increase in breadth misrepresents the actual dimensions.

**pie chart** A circle divided into sectors. The circle represents the total values, and the sectors are proportional to each value within the total.

**piedmont** Located or developed at the foot of mountains, as in a **piedmont glacier**.

**piggy-back principle** An integrated system of road and rail transport over distance which combines the benefits of both. Goods are packed in containers which are taken by container lorries to the railway where they are easily transferred to the rail cars for the major part of their journey. They are then taken by road to their destination. In this way, the accessibility of road travel is combined with the lower costs of long-distance railway travel.

**pillow lava** Lava extruded under water and forming a series of rounded masses.

**pingo** An isolated, roughly dome-shaped hill with a large core of ice. Pingos vary in size from 5 to 75 m in height and 30 to 600 m in diameter. Pingos are thought to have grown by *cryostatic pressure, in this case by the encroachment of ice around the water and sediment of a lake bed. As the area of water freezes it turns into an *ice lens. It is unable to expand into the frozen regions beside and beneath it, so it expands upwards, taking with it the lake deposits on top of the ice lens. This is a **closed-system pingo**. Pingos also grow by *artesian pressure where underground water cannot return to the surface because it underlies frozen or impermeable strata. Cryostatic pressure of the ice causes the movement of water upwards, again also doming up the *talik. This latter is an **open-system pingo**.

**pioneer advance** The movement of new human settlement beyond the present line of occupancy. Pioneer advance is slow, difficult, and, in modern times, expensive so it is often underwritten by governments.

**pioneer community** The earliest *sere developing on a raw site.

**pipe** 1. A volcanic channel or conduit filled with solidified *magma. Sometimes the hard pipe rock is exposed after erosion.
2. In *hydrology, a natural, subsurface channel, often near-horizontal, through which water passes. Pipes can transfer water underground as a rapid route for subsurface storm flow.

**pipeline** A steel or plastic tube used to transport gases, liquids, and slurries—mixtures of solids and water. Pipelines have a limited range of uses as they operate from one fixed point to another and can carry a restricted range of goods. Construction costs are high but running costs are relatively low.

**pipkrake** Needle ice.

**pisiculture** Fish farming.

**pisolite** A round stone, larger than an *oolite and with a diameter of 2 to 10mm.

**pixel** In *remote sensing, an element of a picture; the basic unit from which an image may be built up. Pixels can be taken from an area of 5 $m^2$ to 10 $km^2$ or more. Pixel information for *band or *brightness varies according to the sensor system used. Decreasing **pixelation**—the use of smaller pixels—produces a sharper image. A *LANDSAT scene of $185 \times 185$ km contains nine million pixels with each pixel having a brightness between 0 and 255.

**place** In *humanist(ic) geography, a place is a centre endowed with meaning by man.

**placelessness** With mass communication, and increasingly ubiquitous high technology, places become more and more similar and with increased personal mobility, people are said to identify less with one place; the pull of the home town is slackening.

**place names** The study of the early forms of present place names may indicate the culture which gave the name together with the characteristics of the site. For example, *ey* meaning a *dry point and *ley* meaning a forest, wood, glade, or clearing appear in many place names such as Bermondsey and Henley-in-Arden. Place names are used as evidence of the dating of a settlement from which a chronology of settlements may be devised. There are pitfalls; *ham*, a village, can be confused with *hamm*, a watermeadow, for example.

**placer deposit** A mineral occurring as an alluvial deposit in the sand and gravel of *alluvial fans and valley floors. Such minerals are generally resistant to corrosion by water. The most important placer deposits are diamonds, gold, and tin.

**place utility** The desirability and usefulness of a place to the individual or to a group such as the family. Factors such as housing, finance, amenity, and the characteristics of the neighbourhood are perceived by the individual or group as being satisfactory or unsatisfactory. In the latter case, stresses may be set up resulting in the desire to move away from the place. Dissatisfaction with one place may lead to *search behaviour for a more satisfactory location.

This concept is difficult to apply since assigning quantitative values to utility is problematic. However, places may be ranked in terms of utility. Changing utility rankings may reflect changes in alternatives, changes in the individual's *action space, and changes in the individual's preferences over time.

**planalto** A plateau, especially in Brazil.

**planation surface** A flattish plain resulting from erosion. Few planation surfaces survive because they have been *dissected, but they can be extrapolated from concordant peaks.

**plane table** A drawing board, mounted on a tripod, which can be kept level. It is used in conjunction with an *alidade in surveying.

**planetary winds** The major winds of the earth such as the *westerlies, *trades, etc., as opposed to local winds.

**planeze** One of a series of triangular facets facing outward from a conical volcanic peak. The planezes are separated by radiating streams which run down the flanks of the cone.

**plankton** Minute organisms which drift with the currents in seas and lakes. Plankton includes many microscopic animals and plants including *algae, various animal larvae, and some worms. The animals are **zooplankton** and the plants are **phytoplankton**.

**planned economy** An economy under the control of central government. The term is often used to denote a communist economy. See *communism.

**planning** As practised by local or national government, the direction of development. Changes are scrutinized, and **planning permission** is only given if the development does not conflict with agreed aims. Planning presupposes an ability to foresee future events and a capability of analysing situations and solving problems.

In Britain, if a developer is refused planning permission, he may make a **planning appeal** to the Secretary of State for the Environment who will consider both sides of the proposal. He may propose an altered plan.

**planning blight** The adverse effect of a proposed development such as a motorway. The value of housing may drop if a new development is planned. In Britain, if the landowner cannot dispose of his property, or cannot make as much use of it as he could, he may serve a purchasing notice on the planning department of the local authority.

**planning-system firms** Firms which can choose to plan certain courses of action. Rather than responding to the market, they can manipulate and create demand by the use of advertising. Such firms usually have many plants producing diversified goods and are multiregional if not multinational.

**plant** 1. In a system, the buildings, machinery, and land into which inputs are made and from which output issues.

2. In industrial geography, an individual factory producing power or manufactured goods.

**plantation** An agricultural system, generally a monoculture, for the production of tropical and subtropical crops. The corporately owned holdings are large and employ labour on a large scale. Early stage processing often takes place on site. Plantations are typically of tree and bush crops and were often developed by colonial powers. With independence, many Third World countries have nationalized their plantations or redistributed the land.

**plant succession** The gradual establishment of a series of plants within a given area. This series of communities occurs in a roughly predictable order while the habitat progressively changes. See *succession.

**plastic flow** Movement of material, especially rocks and ice, under intense pressure. The material flows like a very *viscous substance and does not revert to its original shape when the pressure is removed. As it moves, *shearing occurs.

**plastic moulding** Ice which moves plastically will flow around and above an obstacle. This may cause deposition in the lee of the obstruction.

**plate** A rigid segment of the earth's crust which can 'float' across the heavier, semi-molten rock below. The plates making up the continents—**continental plates**—are less dense but thicker than those making up the oceans—the **oceanic plates**.

Thus, a plate is part of the *lithosphere which moves over the plastic *asthenosphere. The boundary of a plate may be *constructive, *destructive, *conservative, or, more rarely, a *collision margin.

**plateau** An extensive, relatively flat upland area.

**plateau basalt** Very fluid lava which wells up in a *fissure eruption and covers a large area, often more than 100 km across.

**plate tectonics** The theory that the earth's crust consists of eight large and several small *plates. The movement of some plates causes earthquakes and volcanoes. This occurs when one plate plunges below another. Such a boundary is termed a **destructive margin** since the descending plate melts back into the *magma. At *oceanic ridges, plates divide and magma wells up from the earth's interior. The magma forms new crust. This is a **constructive margin**. At **conservative margins** the plates move parallel to the line of the plate boundary.

See also *earthquake, *island arc, *ocean ridge, *ocean trench, *subduction zone, *volcano.

**platform** See *craton.

**playa** A flat plain in an arid area found at the centre of an inland drainage basin. Within such an area, lakes frequently form. Evaporation from the playa is high and alluvial flats of saline mud form. The term is also used to describe a lake within such a basin.

**Pleistocene** An *epoch of the Quaternary period, stretching from the end of the *Pliocene, some 2 million years, ago to the beginning of the *Holocene. During the Pleistocene, temperatures in the Northern Hemisphere varied between the very cold *glacials and the warmer *interglacials.

**plinth** The lower, outer section of a *sand dune.

**plinthite** A hard capping or crust at the surface of an unconsolidated soil. The term is used by some to denote a surface layer of *laterite.

**Pliocene** The youngest *epoch of the *Tertiary period.

**plucking** The direct removal of loose bedrock by the impact of water or by incorporation into glacier ice. Since the tensile strength of ice is low, plucking generally occurs only when the rock is jointed and weathered. Some writers prefer to use the term *quarrying rather than plucking.

**plug** A mass of solid lava in the neck of a volcano. Sometimes, as in the French puys, the volcano has been eroded to expose the plug.

**plume** An upwelling of molten rock through the *asthenosphere to the lower *lithosphere. The *hot spot thus formed shows up in volcanic activity at the surface. As continents move over the hot spot, there is a chain of vulcanicity at the surface since the plume is stationary with respect to the *mantle.

**plunge pool** A pool at the base of a waterfall, often undercutting the sheer rock face. Plunge pools form as a result of *hydraulic action, *cavitation, and *pothole erosion.

**plunging wave** See *destructive wave.

**pluralism** This term may be used to denote any situation in which no particular political, cultural, ethnic, or ideological group is dominant. There is often competition between rival groups and the state or local authority may be seen as the arbitrator. It has been asserted that this is the way that cities are run, rather than by an élite.

The term may also be used to signify the cultural diversity of a *plural society.

**plural society** A society made up of a number of distinct groupings. These may be distinguished by race, religion, language, or lifestyles.

**pluton** A mass of igneous rock which has solidified underground. Plutons vary in size from *batholiths to *sills and *dikes.

**plutonic rock** An igneous rock which has cooled and crystallized slowly at great depth.

**pluvial** A time of heavier precipitation than normal. During the last million years, more than one pluvial has brought wetter conditions to deserts. These have helped to create many current desert landforms. Pluvials and *interpluvials have alternated many times.

**pneumatic action** Of, or acting by means of, wind or trapped air. An example of the latter is the air compressed between a wave and a cliff face. See also *cavitation.

**pneumatolysis** The process of chemical change in a rock brought about by the action of gases from the interior of the earth.

**podzol, podsol** A soil characteristic of the coniferous forests of the USSR and Canada. These soils have an ashy coloured layer just below the surface. A hard layer is often found in the lower, B *horizon.

In podzols, *translocation has meant the *leaching out from the A horizon of clays, *humic acids, and iron and *alluvial compounds. These constituents may then accumulate to form a hardpan or iron band.

**podzolization** The formation of a podzol. This occurs when severe *leaching leaves the upper *horizon virtually depleted of all soil constituents except quartz grains. Clay minerals in the A horizon decompose with reaction to *humic acids and form soluble salts. The leached material from the A horizon is deposited in the B horizon as a humus-rich horizon band or as a hard layer of *sesquioxides.

**poikilotherm** An organism which has its body heat regulated by the temperature of its surroundings; **poikilothermy** is the state of being cold-blooded.

**point bar deposit** The accumulation of fluvial sediment at the *slip-off slope.

**polar** Applying to those parts of the earth close to the poles.

Air masses originating over source regions in the mid-latitudes (40–60°) are termed **polar air masses, P**, and are characteristically cold. They are not to be confused with Arctic or Antarctic air masses.

**polar front** Over the north Atlantic and north Pacific, the *front where polar maritime air meets tropical maritime air. *Mid-latitude depressions commonly form at the polar front as above it, in the upper atmosphere, blows the **polar front jet stream**.

**polar high** An area of heavy, cold air bringing high pressure at high latitudes.

**polarization** The further workings of *uneven development, rather than a redress of the imbalance. Better locations attract capital and labour so that productivity and output increase. This has a *backwash effect on less favoured regions which become more and more disadvantaged.

**polar low** See *cold low.

**polar orbital satellite** A satellite, used for *remote sensing, which traverses the earth along the meridians of *longitude.

**polar wind** An extremely cold wind blowing from either of the poles.

**polder** The Dutch term for land which has been reclaimed from the sea, lakes, or river deltas. The land is bounded by a dike, is drained, and is maintained by pumping.

**pole** The North and South Poles are at either end of the earth's axis, around which the earth rotates. The **magnetic poles**, which are indicated by the needles of a compass, vary in their location over time. At present, magnetic north lies near Prince of Wales Island, Canada, and magnetic south is in South Victoria Land, Antarctica. See also *geomagnetism.

**Pole Star** A star in the constellation of Ursa Minor. From it, the direction of true north can be deduced for the Northern Hemisphere.

**political geography** A division of human geography concerned with the geographical analysis of political studies, including among other things, the spatial expression of political ideals, the consequences of decision-making by a political entity, and those geographical factors which influence political activities and problems.

**polje** Generally in Yugoslavia, any enclosed or nearly enclosed valley of any origin. More specifically, in *karst terminology, a large enclosed basin with a flat floor and steep sides. Streams can be ephemeral or permanent; usually the water drains into *streamsinks. Most poljes are aligned with underlying structures such as folds, faults, and troughs, and most have a long, complex history.

**pollen analysis** Also **palynology**, this is the detection of past climates from the different types of pollen grain preserved in lakes, peats, and muds.

**poll tax** See *community charge.

**pollution** An undesirable change in the physical, chemical, or biological characteristics of the natural environment. Although there are some natural pollutants such as volcanoes, pollution generally occurs because of human activity. **Biodegradable pollutants**, like sewage, cause no permanent damage if they are adequately dispersed, but **non-biodegradable pollutants**, such as lead, may be concentrated up the food chain. Other forms of environmental pollution include noise and the emission of heat into waterways, which may damage aquatic life. Present-day problems of pollution include *acid rain and the burning of *fossil fuels to produce excessive carbon dioxide.

**pollution dome** A mass of polluted air in and above a city or industrial complex which is prevented from rising by the presence of an *inversion above it. Winds may elongate the dome into a **pollution plume**.

**polygons** Through the process of *frost cracking, *periglacial surfaces may exhibit polygonal areas of ground separated by cracks. If these cracks fill with debris, when the permafrost expands, the ground rises around the wedges. These are **sand-wedge polygons**. If, in more humid environments, the cracks are filled with ice, the feature is an **ice-wedge polygon**.

**polysaccharide gum** The sticky by-product of the decomposition of roots by microorganisms which can bind soil minerals into aggregates.

**ponente** A cool, dry, westerly wind of Corsica and southern France.

**pool and riffle** The alternating sequence of deep pools and shallow riffles along the relatively straight course of a river. The distance between the pools is 5–7 times the channel width. It has been suggested that pool and riffle development is the precursor of meanders but supporting evidence is not conclusive.

**population** In ecology, a group of individuals of the same species within a *community. In statistics, any collection of individuals under consideration. These individuals need not necessarily be living organisms.

**population density** The ratio of a population to a given unit of area. **Crude density** is simply the number of people living per unit area and can be very misleading. Britain and Sri Lanka have similar crude densities but very different living standards. Accordingly, densities may be plotted using different criteria. **Physiological density** is based on the ratio between total population and inhabited areas. This is thought by some to be an indication of living standards. **Occupational density** is the density of a particular occupation, for example farmers, over the total area of the country, and **room density** is the average number of people per room in a given area.

**population dynamics** The study of the numbers of populations and the variations of these numbers in time and space. A demographer will study numbers of people; an ecologist will study the numbers of organisms of different species and their numerical relationship to each other.

**population equation** The future size of a population depends on a range of functions. Thus:

$$P_{t+1} = P_t + (B{-}D) + (I{-}E)$$

where $P_t$ and $P_{t+1}$ are the sizes of population in an area at two different points in time, $t$ and $t+1$ are those points, $B$ is the birth rate, $D$ is the death rate, $I$ is immigration, and $E$ is emigration.

**population explosion** The dramatic, almost exponential, increase in world population in the twentieth century, brought about by better hygiene and sanitation, and improved health care.

**population geography** The study of the geography of human populations, their composition, growth, distribution, and migratory movements. It is concerned with the study of *demographic processes which affect the environment, but differs from demography in that it is concerned with the spatial expression of such processes.

**population potential** The proximity of people at a given point. The population potential at one place is the sum of the ratios of population at all other points to the distances from the place in question to those points. Thus:
population potential,

$$V_1 = \sum_{j=1}^{n} \frac{P_j}{d_{ij}} = \frac{P_1}{d_{i1}} + \frac{P_2}{d_{i2}} + \frac{P_3}{d_{i3}} \dots \frac{P_n}{d_{in}}$$

where the population potential $(V_1)$ at point i is the summation $(\Sigma)$ of $n$ populations $(j)$ accessible to the point $i$ divided by their distance $(d_{ij})$ to that point. Transport costs may be used instead of distance.

**population problems** Between about 9000 years BP and about AD 1800 it is estimated that world population grew from 5–10 million to 800 million, with an average growth rate of 0.1% per annum. Between 1800 and 1980, world population grew to 4.4 billion. World population is set to double every 35–45 years. If this rate of growth is sustained, there would be standing room only in the next century. The problem is more acute in the Third World because a large proportion of the population is very young. The eventual reproductive capacity of such regions could result in an expansion of population which would end in *Malthusian disasters, though many regret such a pessimistic view.

**population projection** The prediction of future populations based on the present age-sex structure, and with the present rates of fertility, mortality, and migration. In fact, a set of projections can be calculated based on a series of assumptions.

**population pyramid** See *age/sex pyramid.

**population studies** The primary analysis and then attempted explanation of *demographic patterns and processes. Attempts are made to link spatial variations in the distribution and composition of migration and population change with variations in the nature of places.

**pore** In geomorphology, a minute opening in a rock or soil, through which fluids may pass. **Porous rocks** allow water to pass through or be stored within them.

**pore-water pressure** The pressure exerted on rock and soil particles by the water in the *pores between them.

**pork barrel effect** Government expenditure aimed at gaining votes. Government contracts can be of vital importance to employment within a region and may increase the popularity of an administration as elected members of government divert spending to the areas they represent.

**porosity** The ratio of the volume of pores to the volume of matter within a rock or soil, expressed as a percentage.

**port** This is defined as a place where ships may anchor to load and unload cargo, and may be classified by its function. **Terminal ports** are the final destination of cargo-carrying ships. Some **specialized ports** handle predominantly one particular type of traffic and include ferry ports, fishing ports, and naval ports. **Ports of call** lie between terminal ports and may handle part of the cargo of a vessel.

**portage** The overland transport of boat and/or its goods from one navigable waterway to another.

**positive change in sea level** A rise in sea level caused perhaps by melting ice caps, *eustasy, or *isostasy.

**positive discrimination** A policy designed to favour some deprived region or group

and to redress, at least in part, *uneven development. It is claimed that such a policy treats the effects of inequality rather than tackling its causes. Not all of the minority or region needs help and many deprived people are outside the catchment area. None the less, the *EC, for example, still uses schemes of positive discrimination.

**positivism** The belief that an understanding of phenomena is solely grounded on sense data; what cannot be tested empirically cannot be regarded as proven. Positivism has no value judgements, only statements which can be tested scientifically.

To this basis were added the concepts of **logical positivism**, that a tautology is a form of verifiable statement—an analytic statement—as opposed to a synthetic statement which can be scientifically tested. Positivism was accepted by the 'new' geographers of the 1950s onwards as it was argued that human behaviour followed certain 'laws' which could be used to predict events. Thus, the *gravity model is widely used in transport planning. See also *empiricism.

**possibilism** A view of the environment as a range of opportunities from which the individual may choose. This choice is based on the individual's needs and norms. It grants that the range of choices may be limited by the environment, but allows choices to be made rather than thinking on *deterministic lines.

**post-glacial** Usually, the time from the end of the *Pleistocene epoch to the present.

**post-industrial city** Cities exhibiting the characteristics of a *post-industrial society. Service industries dominate with a strongly developed *quaternary sector and *footloose industries abound, often on pleasant open space at the edge of the city.

**post-industrial society** A post-industrial society has five primary characteristics:
1. Domination of service, rather than manufacturing, industry.
2. The pre-eminence of the professional and technical classes.

3. The central place of theoretical knowledge as a source of innovations.

4. The influence of technology.

5. The existence of a new intellectual technology.

At present, the development of a post-industrial society is linked only with very advanced economies, if it exists at all.

**post-modernism** In the modernist period, buildings were largely functional with little or no ornamentation. Post-modernist buildings are designed to reflect vernacular architecture, often combining styles from different periods or places. Ornamentation is a feature. Brick is widely used even though it is usually a skin covering the concrete used primarily as the building material. It is held that post-modern architecture changes man's concept of the city, and causes less *alienation for the inhabitants of the city.

**potential evapotranspiration, PET** The maximum continual loss of water by evaporation and transpiration given a sufficient supply of water. PET often outstrips actual *evapotranspiration.

**potential instability** The condition of a parcel of air which may become unstable. See *conditional instability.

**pothole** Loosely, a vertical cave system. More precisely, a more or less circular hole in the bedrock of a river. The hole enlarges because pebbles inside it collide with the bedrock as the water swirls.

**potomobenthos** Organisms of the river bed.

**potomoplankton** *Plankton floating in slow-flowing rivers and streams.

**poverty cycle** The vicious circle of deprivation from one generation to the next. The cycle can be broken, but not without expenditure and commitment.

**power** Defined as the ability to do or act, this is also seen as the influence of an individual or group upon another. Power within a society is worked out in its economic, social, and political life; *capitalism has the control arising from a majority who dominate the *factors of production over a

minority which does not. In a *centrally planned economy it is the state which dominates, supposedly reflecting the will of the people. The power structure of a society is reflected in its social organization and in its economy. These in turn have their own spatial expression.

**pragmatism** An interpretation of the meaning and the justification of beliefs in terms of their practical effects or contents. The method of reasoning is by *induction.

**prairie** A large area, found outside the tropics, with grassland and occasional trees as natural vegetation. The term was originally applied to the prairies of North America where rainfall is low and summer temperatures are high. Similar conditions are found in the South American *pampas, the Russian *steppes, and the South African *veld.

**prairie soil** A soil of the wetter prairies, resembling *chernozem in its high *humus content and its development under grassland. However, increased rainfall means that prairie soils are *leached of calcium. This soil, therefore, has no calcium nodules and is slightly acid.

**Pre-Boreal** After the last *Quaternary glaciation, a phase of cold, dry climate which encouraged the growth of birches and pines in Britain.

**Precambrian** The oldest *era in earth's history dating from about 4600 million years BP to the start of the *Cambrian.

**precipitation** In meteorology, the deposition of moisture from the atmosphere on to the earth's surface. This may be in the form of dew, rain, hail, frost, fog, sleet, or snow.

**predator** An organism which takes other live organisms as its food and thereby removes the prey individuals from a population.

**predator–prey relationships** In theory, there should be an equilibrium between predators and prey. Thus, when predators are scarce, the numbers of prey should rise. Predators would respond by reproducing more, and, possibly, by changing their hunting habits. As the population of predators rises, more prey are killed and their numbers fall. Many of the predators then die; thus numbers of predators and prey oscillate between two extremes.

The oscillation predicted above is rarely reproduced in laboratory experiments and is not easy to find in the wild. This is because predator numbers are not solely dependent upon the number of prey available. Furthermore, there must be an opportunity for some prey to avoid attack, otherwise extinction of both species may result. **Predation** will have no effect on numbers of prey if the individuals caught are beyond reproductive age. Lastly, prey are often sought by more than one predator.

There is a suggestion that predation allows more species to survive. It is argued that predation frees some part of every *niche giving more room for more species. This suggestion has been confirmed in a number of field observations.

**pre-industrial city** A city established before industrialization with a distinct morphology, as advanced by Sjoberg. In the pre-industrial city, the élite gather at the centre because of their association with political and religious power and zones beyond the centre are marked by housing of lower-status occupants. The city is compact, often walled, and there is little separation between workplace and home. Specialized quarters exist where particular crafts or communities are found.

**preservation** Preservation has been defined as the protection of human features in the landscape, as opposed to *conservation, which is concerned with the protection of the natural landscape. This distinction is not always made.

**pressure** *Atmospheric pressure. The location of belts of high and low pressure makes up the **pressure system** of this planet.

**pressure gradient** Also known as **barometric gradient**, this is the degree of change in atmospheric pressure between two areas. On a weather map, these changes are indicated by *isobars. Where the isobars are close together, there is a steep pressure gradient, and winds are strong. Widely spaced isobars indicate a gentle pressure gradient and winds are generally light.

**pressure melting point** In glaciology, the temperature, often well below 0 °C, at which ice under pressure will melt. *Warm glaciers have bases at or above the pressure melting point of that ice.

**pressure release** The expansion of a rock formed under pressure when that pressure is released. Thus, a glacier may remove the *overburden and the revealed rock 'bursts' open. Some writers attribute the splitting of granite *tors to pressure release.

**pressure wave** Push wave. See *earthquake.

**prevailing wind** The most frequently occurring wind direction at a given location.

**price** The money for which a commodity or service is bought or sold. The **price mechanism** is the way in which supply and demand can regulate economic activities. The mechanism can be spontaneous—'in the market'—or can reflect deliberate governmental adjustments. **Pricing policies** are the arrangements whereby prices of commodities to the consumer are determined. In the past, prices could either be *f.o.b. or *c.i.f., but commodities today are increasingly sold at the *uniform delivered price. Under capitalism, producers may collaborate to maintain artificially high prices. Under socialism, prices are set centrally by the state.

**primary industry, primary activity** Economic activity, such as fishing, forestry, and mining and quarrying, concerned with the extraction of natural resources.

**primary producer** A plant which can synthesize carbohydrates using carbon dioxide and the sun's energy, with chlorophyll as the catalyst.

**primary urbanization** Urbanization which results from forces arising within a country as a spatial expression of a region's culture.

**primary vegetation** *Natural vegetation.

**primary waves** See *earthquake.

**primate city** The largest city within a nation which dominates the country not solely in size but also in terms of influence. The development of primacy is not fully understood but some researchers have suggested that the importance of the primate city tends to decline as the economy grows and that, therefore, primacy tends to occur in less developed nations. However, the rise of the primate city may be encouraged by colonialism and it occurs more often at the major port. Capital cities of past empires also tend to be over-large.

**primate rule** See *rank-size rule.

**prime meridian** The 0° *meridian, passing through Greenwich, London, from which all other longitudes are determined.

**primeur crop** A crop of fruit, vegetables, or flowers grown and sold out of season or early in the season.

**primogeniture** Inheritance of wealth, property, or title by the oldest son.

**principal components analysis** A statistical technique of changing the variables in a data matrix so that the new components are correlated with the original components but not with each other. The principal component $y_1$ accounts for relatively large shares of the original variance, $y_2$ accounts for the second largest variance, and so on.

**principle of least effort** The theory behind *movement minimization procedures.

**private sector** That part of a national economy which is not owned by the state.

**privatization** The sale, to the public, of shares in formerly *nationalized industries.

**probabilism** *Possibilism sees individuals or groups making choices within the scope of the environment. Probabilism suggests that some choices are a good deal more likely than others.

**probability** The likelihood of an event occurring. In statistics, probability is expressed as a number ranging from 0—absolute impossibility—to 1—absolute certainty. It may also be expressed as a percentage. Where p is the probability,

$$p = 0.05 \text{ is the 95\% level}$$
$$p = 0.01 \text{ is the 99\% level}$$
$$p = 0.001 \text{ is the 99.9\% level}$$

**proclimax** An arrested point of a succession which does not develop a *climax community because of repeated disturbances, for example, from fire. Overgrazing may lead to a proclimax as animals leave unpalatable plants which are then over-represented.

**producer** *Primary producer.

**producer goods** Goods, such as components, tools, and raw materials, used by manufacturers rather than by the public. See *consumer goods.

**production** In ecology, the increase of body mass as food is converted into new living material.

**productivity** The output of an economic activity seen in terms of the economic inputs such as capital, labour, and raw materials. Some writers argue that this economic view is too narrow and that social and environmental 'costs' must also be considered. Furthermore, the cost of raw materials can also be seen as the depletion of finite resources.

**productivity rating** An estimate of an area's ability to support plant growth. Productivity, as suggested by Paterson, increases with the length of the growing season, the average temperature of the warmest month, the average precipitation, and the amount of solar radiation. Paterson postulated six grades of productivity and produced a world map indicating the occurrence of these grades. This map reflects the plant life that a climatic zone could support whereas the actual vegetation may differ from this.

**product-moment correlation coefficient** A statistical test for assessing the degree of correlation between two data sets, x and y. The formula for the test is given as:

$$r = \frac{1/n \sum (x - \overline{x})(y - \overline{y})}{\sigma^x \cdot \sigma^y}$$

where $\sigma^x$ and $\sigma^y$ are the standard deviations of the respective data sets.

Coefficients run from +1—perfect positive correlation—through 0—no correlation—to −1—perfect negative correlation. A further test is necessary to determine the statistical significance of a particular correlation. This is done by expressing the correlation coefficient r in terms of the *Student's t statistic:

$$t = \frac{r\sqrt{n-2}}{\sqrt{1-r^2}}$$

and then reading off the value of t at the correct degrees of freedom from a graph.

**profile** 1. A side view, such as the *long profile of a river.
  2. The assembly of soil *horizons by which a soil can be identified.

**profit surface** Variations in profit shown as a three-dimensional surface, derived from subtracting the relevant *cost surface from the corresponding *revenue surface, a calculation of the utmost difficulty.

**proglacial** Situated in front of a glacier. A **proglacial lake** is formed between the terminus of the ice and higher ground which is often in the form of a terminal *moraine.

**progradation** The accumulation of beach material which leads to an extension of the beach seawards. When there is an excess in the supply of sediment, a beach will **prograde**.

**programming region** A region which is designed to serve a particular purpose, such as a multi-purpose river project or a depressed region which requires a regional policy as an attempt to solve its problems.

**projection** A technique for transforming the three-dimensional sphere of the earth into the two dimensions of a map. There are four aspects of the map to be considered, area, distance, direction, and shape, and it is impossible to re-create them all in the same map.

**promontory** A *headland jutting into the sea.

**propulsive industry** A vigorous, fast-growing industry characterized by a high level of technology, expert management, and an extensive market. Propulsive industries are instrumental in promoting growth in other industries to which they are linked.

**protalus rampart** At the foot of a slope, a deposit of angular rock fragments formed of material which has fallen from the permanent banks of snow found upslope.

**protection** Procedures adopted by a government to favour domestic goods by imposing *quotas or *tariffs on foreign imports. Governments adopt **protectionism** in order to help the country become self-sufficient, to protect new industries, or as a bargaining tool.

**proto-industrialization** The phase in a peasant society as rural industries develop in advance of industrialization and factory production.

**psychic income** The enjoyment, which cannot be measured in financial terms, that people derive from location in a particular place. The example usually cited is an entrepreneur who chooses his factory site near a favourite golf course in order to receive enjoyment as well as gaining profit from his industry. Although no manufacturer will readily operate at a loss, many industrialists will locate away from the optimum point in order to benefit from psychic income.

**psychologism** The explanation of social phenomena wholly in terms of the mental characteristics of the individuals concerned. Psychologism thus overlooks the economic, social, political, and environmental influences which act on the individual.

**public goods** Goods freely available, either naturally, like air, or from the state, like education. **Pure public goods**, like defence, are provided for all. However, pure public goods may be distributed impurely, as when an area with a high crime rate has a higher level of policing. **Impure public goods**, like libraries, are provided at particular locations, so that they are more accessible to some than to others.

**public housing** Houses rented to tenants by national or local governments.

**public sector** That part of a national economy owned and controlled by the state.

**pull-apart basin** Where *plates diverge in a *fault zone, the crust may be stretched and weakened so that it subsides, forming a basin, such as the Sea of Galilee.

**pull factor** A positive factor exerted by the locality towards which people move. Pull factors have included the granting of new land for farmers (the Prairies and Great Plains), assisted passages and other government inducements (Australia), freedom of speech or religion (America in the eighteenth century), and material inducements (Hong Kong). People moving for material gain are presently termed economic migrants.

**pumice** A very light, fine-grained, and cellular rock produced when the froth on the surface of lava solidifies.

**pumped storage scheme** Electricity cannot be stored, so when demand is low, at night, some can be used to pump water from a lower to a higher reservoir. At peak demand, the water is allowed to fall back to the lower level, passing through turbines which turn generators. The scheme incurs a net loss of energy.

**push factor** In *migration, any adverse factor which causes movement away from the place of residence. Examples of pushes include famine, changes in land tenure (e.g. the *Scottish Highland Clearances, 1790–1850), political persecution (Tamil separatists, Sri Lanka, 1989), and mechanization, which made agricultural workers redundant (but see *rural depopulation), and which made factory products cheaper than those of cottage industry. Relatively few migrations are spurred by push factors alone.

**push moraine** A ridge of *morainic material formed at the ice margin as an advancing glacier moves over *drift formed during a previous glacial period.

**push wave** See *earthquake.

**puy** In France, a free-standing *volcanic neck.

**P-wave** Push wave. See *earthquake.

**pyramidal peak** Synonym for *horn or aiguille.

**pyramid of numbers, ecological pyramid** A diagram of a *food chain which shows each *trophic level as a horizontal bar. The bars are centred about a vertical axis and the levels are drawn in proportion to the *biomass at each level. There is a big step between *producers and primary *consumers, thereafter the steps are smaller. Generally speaking, the animals on the higher levels are larger and rarer than animals lower down the pyramid.

**pyroclast** A fragment of solidified lava, ejected during explosive volcanic eruptions. Classification of pyroclasts is by size. Fragments less than 4 mm across are ash; compacted ash is tuff. Those between 4 and 32 mm are lapilli and fragments larger than 32 mm are blocks. Collectively, these fragments are *tephra. Pyroclasts formed from lava produce *volcanic bombs and volcanic *breccia. **Pyroclastic rock** is formed from volcanic debris.

# Q

**qanat** *Foggara.

**quadrat** A small, usually square, frame used in sampling, notably in *biogeography and *ecology. Quadrats are placed systematically or at random over the area to be studied and, for example, the vegetation occurring within the quadrat is recorded.

**quadrat analysis** A statistical technique for analysing distributions. The area to be analysed is divided into cells of equal size and the number of points occurring within each cell is determined. This distribution is then compared with a hypothetical distribution based on the theory being investigated. It should be noted that the size and shape of the cells may influence the observed distribution.

**quagmire** A *bog, also known as a **quaking bog**, which shudders when trodden on.

**qualitative** Concerned with quality, and often applied to a judgement not backed up by objective measurement.

**quality of life** The degree of well-being felt by an individual about his lifestyle. Preferences vary, but most assessments of the quality of life consider *amenity, together with social benefits such as health, welfare, and education, and economic aspects such as income and taxation.

**quantifiable** Able to be expressed in numerical terms.

**quantification** The measurement of processes or features in numerical terms. The figures thus derived are used in **quantitative analysis**. The **quantitative revolution** in geography of the 1950s and 1960s sought to use statistical analyses to investigate causal connections between events or properties. Mathematical models are also made in an attempt to investigate reality.

**quarrying** A type of erosion which removes rock which has broken up between joints to form blocks. The agents of erosion may be ice, rivers, or sea water.

**quartile** One of the four equal divisions in a *dispersion diagram of a data set.

**quartile deviation** The *interquartile range divided by 2.

**quartz** Silicon dioxide, commonly found in *sedimentary and *metamorphic rocks, often occupying joints and veins. It is a very resistant, stable, and usually white, rock, and can form large crystals.

**Quaternary** The most recent *period of the *Cainozoic era. During the *Pleistocene *epoch of this time, from about 1.8 million years BP to some 10 000 years ago, much of Britain's glacial and periglacial scenery evolved.

**quaternary industry, quaternary activity** Economic activity concerned with information: its acquisition, manipulation, and transmission. Into this category fall law, finance, education, research, and the media.

**quicksand** Unstable, supersaturated sand which will not bear the weight of any heavy material, which would be sucked down into the quicksand.

**quota** A fixed level indicating the maximum amount of imported goods or persons which the receiving state will allow in a given period of time.

# R

**radial–concentric plan** The street pattern of a settlement where a number of roads radiate from the centre and are cut through by a series of circular roads having their centre at the heart of the city from which the radial roads arise.

**radial drainage** See *drainage patterns.

**radial plan** See *finger plan.

**radiance** In *remote sensing, the distribution of radiant energy.

**radiant exitance** In *remote sensing, the measure of radiant energy emitted per unit area. **Radiant flux** (also known as **radiant power**) is the rate of flow of radiant energy in watts.

**radiation** Energy travelling in the form of electromagnetic waves. These may be X-rays, ultraviolet, visible, infra-red, microwaves, or radio waves.

**radiation fog** Fog formed as moist air comes into contact with ground which has been cooled as a result of *radiation of heat from the earth during a long and cloudless night. For this fog to form, air should be gently moving but not completely calm as in that case only a very thin fog layer will form.

**radioactive decay** The emission by some elements of charged particles from the nucleus, accompanied by electromagnetic radiation, usually at a constant rate. A method of dating has been established based on the rate of radioactive decay. See *C 14 dating and *half life.

**radiocarbon dating** *C 14 dating.

**radiometer** In *remote sensing, a device that records *radiance or *irradiance.

**radiometric age** The age given to a substance based on rates of *radioactive decay.

**radius of curvature** In a meander, the mean distance from the centre of the curve to points at the edge of the meander.

**rain** A form of precipitation consisting of water droplets ranging from 1 to 5 mm in diameter. The type of rain produced reflects the circumstances in which it formed. A mass of warm air rising at a warm front will develop layered clouds and produce steady rain. Air forced to rise quickly at cold fronts will bring heavier rain. These are both examples of **frontal rain**. **Convection rain** occurs when warm, unstable air rises rapidly. Air forced to rise over mountains may form **orographic (relief) rain**. See also *Bergeron–Findeisen theory and *coalescence theory.

**rainbow** An arch of the visible parts of the spectrum caused by the reflection and refraction of sunlight within raindrops.

**raindrop erosion** Soil erosion caused by the impact of raindrops on the ground, displacing soil particles. Raindrop impact may alternatively cause *compaction.

**rainfall intensity** The rate at which rain falls, usually measured in mm per hour. The reaction of a river to a storm event is linked to rainfall intensity; intense rain has a greater impact on the ground, but runoff is usually rapid. The intensity of rainfall is usually inversely proportional to its duration.

**rainfall runoff** The overland and downslope flow of rainwater into channelled flow when the rock or soil is saturated.

**rain gauge** An instrument used to measure rainfall. The simplest rain gauges consist of a funnel, 125 or 200 mm across, connected by a narrow tube to a reservoir. This reservoir is designed so that the water collected will not splash, run out, or evaporate. In **tilting syphon** rain gauges, a pen is connected to a float in the water collector. The pen records on to a rotating chart the amount of water in the reservoir.

**rain shadow** An area of relatively low rainfall to the *lee side of uplands. The incoming air has been forced to rise over the highland, causing precipitation on the windward side, and thus decreasing the water content of the air which descends on the lee side.

The descending air is subject to *adiabatic warming, and this increases its capacity to hold much of the remaining water vapour.

**rainsplash** The impact of raindrops on the soil may break down soil *peds, loosen soil particles, and cause *turbulence in the *sheet wash of water flowing downslope.

**raised beach** A former beach which now stands above sea level some metres inland. Where land is rising because of *isostasy, several raised beaches may be seen at different levels.

**R and D, research and development** Industrial innovation requires research which seeks to apply new discoveries to industrial processes. These discoveries are then developed as factory systems. Most large industries have R and D facilities, and often have access to independent R and D from educational establishments and government programmes.

**random** Haphazard, without a regular pattern, with an equal chance of any event or location occurring. A **random number** table consists of a series of numbers taken entirely at random, generated by chance.

**Random sampling** uses such numbers to select individual units. The numbers can be used as coordinates on a grid system of the area under consideration.

**Randstad** In the Netherlands, the *ring city made up of Amsterdám, Haarlem, Leiden, s-Gravenhage (The Hague), Rotterdam, and Utrecht.

**range** In statistics, the difference between the two extreme values in a data set.

**range of a good or service** The maximum distance an individual will travel to obtain a given good or service. An illustration is given by the distance people will travel to buy a pint of milk as opposed to the journey for an Old Master drawing. There is confusion, however, in the fact that many trips are actuated by the need to purchase more than one commodity.

**range, township, and section** The division of land west of the Appalachians adopted by the US Government in 1785. Townships are squares of 36 square miles, and a series of townships constitutes a range. Each township may be divided into sections of one square mile. All divisions are related to a base *meridian.

**ranker** An *intrazonal soil, not yet fully developed. This soil is shallow, with an A *horizon directly on top of non-calcareous rock.

**ranking of towns** Many attempts have been made to elicit a *hierarchy of towns. One approach is to rate cities by their functions, but this is difficult since a 'shop' might be a large jewellers or a corner store. A refinement of this is to attribute different scores to different functions and to make a total for each settlement. *Multivariate analysis has been used although the data are not always available and are difficult to collect. Other methods emphasize the interaction between a settlement and its field (see *centrality) and *spheres of influence may be established. *Graph theory has also been used to rank towns.

**rank-size rule** Settlements in a country may be *ranked in order of their size. The 'rule' states that if the population of a town is multiplied by its rank, the sum will equal the population of the highest ranked city. In other words, the population of a town ranked $n$ will be $1/n$th of the size of the largest city. On normal graph paper, the plot of cities and their size and rank will appear as a concave curve. When plotted on logarithmic scales, the graph may emerge as a straight line. This is the **rank-size pattern**. Other variations occur when the log-log scale is used. The **binary pattern** shows a flat upper section and a steeper lower section, giving a concave curve. This pattern is shown in federal countries such as Australia. By contrast, many developing countries show a sharp fall from the largest, *primate city to the other cities. This is the **primate rule**. A further modification is the **stepped order** where a number of settlements may be found at each level with each place resembling others in size and function.

**rapids** Areas of greatly disturbed water across a river. Unlike waterfalls, rapids are the result of a continuous and relatively gentle slope, rather than a sudden vertical drop.

**rare gases** Also known as noble or inert gases, these are uncommon gases such as neon or krypton which are chemically unreactive.

**rates** In Britain before 1989, a form of local taxation raised on all property, domestic or industrial, based on the rateable value of the property. The rateable value is assessed by the local authority and a tax has to be paid in relation to that value. Rates vary nationally and areas with low rates may attract new industrial developments although recent studies suggest that rates are only a very small part of manufacturing costs. The system of domestic rates has now been superseded by the *community charge or poll tax but businesses still pay rates.

**ratio scale** A scale which shows data which have been converted into another form. For example, an occupational group, such as teachers, may be shown as a percentage of the total workforce.

**Ravenstein's 'Laws' of Migration** These were formulated in the late nineteenth century and state that:

1. Most migration is over a short distance.

2. Migration occurs in steps.

3. Long-range migrants usually move to urban areas.

4. Each migration produces an opposite movement.

5. Rural dwellers are more migratory than urban dwellers.

6. Within their own country females are more migratory than males.

7. Most migrants are adults.

8. Large towns grow more by migration than by natural increase.

9. Migration increases with economic development.

10. Migration is mostly due to economic causes.

**ravine** A small, narrow, steep-sided valley.

**raw materials** The unprocessed substances used in manufacturing.

**reach** A straight stretch of river.

**reaction time** The time between any kind of change and the response it elicits in a system.

**realm** See *faunal realms, *floral realms.

**recession** In hydrology, the decline in river flow after a storm event has passed.

**recession limb** That part of a *hydrograph which records the fall in *discharge after the river has reached a peak of flow due to a storm event. The line of the recession limb is controlled by the amount of water stored in the basin and the way it is held in the *catchment area.

**recharge** The refilling of an *aquifer by the infiltration of precipitation into a porous rock.

**reclamation** The process of creating usable land from waste, flooded, or derelict land.

**recovery rate** The time taken for a *diffusion wave to re-form having been blocked by a *diffusion barrier. The recovery rate of a wave front is directly related to both the type and size of the barrier it encounters.

**recreation** An activity undertaken for the pleasure or satisfaction which it gives to the individual. Some would restrict the term to activity away from the home.

Geographical studies of recreation include demands for, and movement to, recreational facilities, and assessments of the impact of recreation on the landscape. **Recreation carrying capacity** is the amount of recreation which a site can take without any deterioration of its qualities.

**rectangular drainage** See *drainage patterns.

**recumbent fold** *Overfold.

**recycling** The reuse of *renewable resources in an effort to maximize their value, reduce waste, and reduce environmental disturbance. In Britain, the 1980s saw an increase in recycling, notably with regard to glass and paper. The recycling of scrap metal is a major source of metal in refineries from Ghana to the Netherlands.

**redevelopment** The demolition of old buildings and the creation of new buildings on the same site. Redevelopment can solve existing problems of congestion and poor design, but for residential areas in particular, it is seen to be wasteful of resources, destroying communities, and creating urban deserts until building takes place. Some redevelopment schemes have been built on too large a scale, and individuals are 'lost' in the concrete.

Post-war Britain has seen much city centre redevelopment. The old city centres evolved without motor vehicles, and the population of the city was smaller. Many old city centres are therefore inadequate. Redevelopment is based on the provision of *CBD functions and often segregates vehicular traffic from pedestrians.

**redlining** A demarcation of the poorer districts of a city, often the *inner city, where buildings are so much in decline that mortgages will not be granted for the purchase of property.

**red rain** The washing out of fine dust particles over *mid-latitudes. For Europe, the major sources of dust are the Sahara and the fringes of the Sahel. This dust is picked up by air streams which then rise by convection, or over relief barriers, into the upper *troposphere. The dust is carried north and west until it is washed out by precipitation. Red rain is generally alkaline because of the high calcium content of the Saharan dust.

**reduction** The loss of oxygen from a compound. For example, the *sesquioxide ferric oxide can be reduced to the monoxide ferrous oxide by bacteria. A more precise definition of reduction is that it represents a gain of electrons in a compound.

**reef** See *coral reef.

**reforestation** The planting of trees in a previously forested, but now cleared, area.

**refugee** A person seeking shelter in a foreign land because of persecution or the threat of persecution in his or her own country.

**reg** A stony *desert pavement.

**regelation** When ice is under pressure, its melting point is lower than 0 ˚C. When the pressure lessens, the melting point rises so that refreezing occurs. This is regelation.

**regime** 1. A recurring pattern, as in the seasonal pattern of climates or the yearly fluctuations in the volume of a river or a glacier.
2. A political system.

**region** Any tract of the earth's surface with either natural or man-made characteristics which mark it off as being different from the areas around it.

Many attempts have been made to distinguish regional boundaries. The French *pays were taken as a model for the demarcation of regions, but few researchers can agree to the boundaries of almost any region, such as the Great Plains, because different criteria are used to determine the extent of **multiple-feature regions**. **Single-feature regions**, like areas in the USA of covered bridges, are easier to demarcate. Many regions have clearly distinguishable cores but the regional characteristics diminish with increasing distance from the core. These are **nodal regions**.

*Regional geography, once the heart of

geographical study, has now been generally superseded by the 'new' geography which searches for the generalizations and 'laws' to be deduced from the landscape.

**regional geography** The study in geography of *regions and of their distinctive qualities. A pre-condition of this study is the recognition of a region, its naming, and the delimitation of its boundaries. One approach has been to identify 'natural' regions while another was to establish economic regions based on agriculture and/or industry. Often there was an intimation of a link between the two types of region. Once the keystone of geography, the status of regional geography has been in decline since the 1950s.

**regional inequality** A disparity between the standards of living applying within a nation. It is difficult to quantify the prosperity or poverty of a region, but there are two basic indicators. The first is unemployment, which has been used in Britain as a symptom since the 1920s. Most UK regional policy has been concerned with the alleviation of unemployment. The second indicator is per capita income which in Britain generally falls to the north and west. Other factors indicating disparity include the type of industry and its growth or decline, numbers of young people in further education, housing standards, and the quality of the environment. Some would assert that all economic development brings about regional inequality. See *uneven development.

**regionalism** A move to foster or protect an indigenous culture in a particular region. This may be a formal move, made by the state as it creates administrative or planning regions, or an informal move for some degree of independence arising from an emotional feeling, based on territory, of a minority group.

**regionalization** The demarcation of regions such that there is little variation within each region while each region is sharply distinct from the others. Different regions can be classified in different ways according to the criteria used; each criterion throws up a different region.

**regional metamorphism** The change, brought about by both heat and pressure, in the rocks of a very large area.

**regional multiplier** The stimulation of economic growth by growth itself. As secondary industries develop they create a demand for raw materials and goods. Thus, machinery is made from steel and this stimulates steel manufacturing while the development of the steel industry requires more machinery. As manufacturing industry prospers, more jobs arise in service industries.

**regional policy** A policy, adopted by government, aimed at redressing *uneven development within a country. Measures include improving the *infrastructure; building new towns to move people away from poor housing stock and to stimulate the construction industry; and providing inducements to new industry in the area in the form of tax incentives, grants, and subsidies, and the provision of purpose-built factories.

**regional science** An interdisciplinary study which concentrates on the integrated analysis of economic and social phenomena in a regional setting. It seeks to understand regional change, to anticipate change, and to plan future regional development. This study is particularly associated with the work of Isard and draws heavily on mathematical models.

**regional share** See *shift share analysis.

**register of population** A record of the major events in the lives of a population: births, deaths, marriages, divorces, and adoptions. In most European countries, registers were kept before censuses were held and are probably more reliable for historic investigations.

**Registrar General's classification of occupation, UK** A number of classifications exists but the broadest one groups occupations into five socio-economic classes with the implication that occupation is a meaningful indicator of social welfare.

I. Professional occupations—e.g., doctors and lawyers.

II. Managerial and lower professional occupations—e.g., managers and teachers.

IIIN. Non-manual skilled occupations—e.g., office workers.

IIIM. Manual skilled occupations—e.g., bricklayers, coal-miners.

IV. Semi-skilled occupations—e.g., postal workers.

V. Unskilled occupations—e.g., porters, dustmen.

**regolith** Broken rock debris at the base of a soil, overlying the bedrock.

**regression line** A 'best fit' line through a series of points on a graph, showing the form of the relationship between two sets of data. This line can be drawn by eye or calculated. In this calculation, the aim is to ensure that the sum of the squares of the deviations by the points from the line is at a minimum—the **least squares method**. In determining the position of a point, $y$ is assumed and the average value of $x$ is calculated as follows:

$$x - \overline{x} = r \frac{\sigma^x}{\sigma^y}(y - \overline{y})$$

where $\sigma^x$ and $\sigma^y$ are the standard deviations for data sets $x$ and $y$ and $r$ is the correlation coefficient.

The value of $x$ can be calculated when $y = 0$, and again for any other value of $y$. If there is a straight line relationship, these two sets of coordinates are all that is required to draw the regression line. The regression line may be used to project the value of one data set, given a value for the other.

**rehabilitation** The installation of modern amenities and the repairing of old houses which are structurally sound. Rehabilitation is a method of improving the housing stock of a city without destroying existing neighbourhoods and many local authorities give grants for the rehabilitation of individual houses. It may be that rehabilitation only postpones *redevelopment as the refurbished houses will decay over time.

**Reilly's law** The principle that the flow of trade to one of two neighbouring cities is in direct proportion to their populations and in inverse proportion to the square of the distances to those cities. For a settlement between two cities, $a$ and $b$, trade to those cities may be expressed as:

$$\frac{R_a}{R_b} = \frac{P_a}{P_b}\left(\frac{d_b}{d_a}\right)^2$$

where $R_a$ and $R_b$ are the volumes of trade to town $a$ and town $b$, $P_a$ and $P_b$ are their respective populations, and $d_a$ and $d_b$ are the distances from the place under consideration to towns $a$ and $b$.

**rejuvenation** The renewed vigour of a once active process. The term is generally applied to streams and rivers which regain energy due to the uplift of land through *isostasy or by a fall in the *base level. Rejuvenation may also apply to the resumption of movement along an old fault line.

**relative humidity** The ratio between the amount of water vapour in a given quantity of air and the maximum carrying capacity of water vapour in air of the same temperature. Relative humidity is expressed as a percentage of this ratio. Thus, saturated air has a relative humidity of 100%.

**relative variability** The mean deviation as a percentage of the *arithmetic mean. It is useful in comparing two apparently similar data sets.

**relaxation time** The time taken for any system to re-establish *equilibrium after a change in the factors which control or influence that system.

**relevance** Within geography, the degree to which its subject and methodology can make a practical contribution to the solution of environmental and social problems. In the 1970s certain geographers felt that there was not enough attention paid to the unequal distribution of goods and resources throughout the population and that geographers should address themselves to questions of human welfare, social justice, and public policy. See *welfare geography.

**relict landform** A geomorphological feature which was formed under past climatic regimes but still exists as an anomaly in the changed, present-day climatic conditions.

**relief** The shape of the earth's surface. **High relief** generally denotes large local differences in the height of the land; **low relief** indicates little variation in altitude. A **relief map** depicts the surface of an area by the use of *contours or coloured shading.

**relief rain** See *orographic precipitation.

**religion, geography of** The study of the spatial distribution of organized religions and their territorial development over time.

**remembrement** A French term for the re-ordering, consolidation, and enlargement of land holdings.

**remote sensing, remote sensor** The gathering of information about an object without being physically in touch with it. Most sensors record information from the infra-red parts of the electromagnetic spectrum emitted by the object. Remote sensors are carried by satellites as much as 36 000 km above the earth; the higher the altitude, the more of the surface can be seen at one given time.

Images from remote sensors are not photographs. All satellite remote sensing data is digital. Scanners record radiation from the surface and transmit this to a receiving station as numbers. These numbers are then used by image-processing computers which generate a picture. The computers can manipulate and present images in an enormous number of ways (*contrast stretching).

Remote sensors have advantages over conventional *aerial photography. They cover larger areas instantaneously; they gather data from a wider spectral range; they do this at frequent and consistent intervals; and the basic data is *digital, which makes for easier updating. Furthermore, data is recorded more cheaply than by aerial photography.

**rendzina** A soil rich in *humus and calcium carbonate, developed on limestone. The A *horizon is dark, calcareous, but usually thin. The B horizon is absent and the C horizon is chalk or limestone. A rendzina is an example of an *azonal soil, dominated by rock type.

**renewable resource** A recurrent *resource which is not diminished when used but which will be restored. Examples include tidal and wind energy. Renewable resources may be consumed without endangering future consumption as long as use does not outstrip production of new resources, as in fishing.

**renewal** See *urban renewal.

**rent** See *Marxist theory of rent.

**rent gradient** The decline in rents with distance from the city centre. It reflects the cost of transport from the outlying districts to the centre. It is suggested, however, that as city centres decline and as the importance of motorways as locational factors increases, the traditional gradient of rent from city centre to outer suburbs might be reversed.

**replacement rate** The degree to which a population is replacing itself, based on the ratio of the number of female babies to the number of women of childbearing age. This is the **gross reproduction rate**. The **net reproduction rate** is defined as the average number of daughters born to mothers during their reproductive years while allowing for mortality. If the number is over 1, the population will grow, if below 1, the population will diminish.

**repose slope** A slope whose angle reflects the *angle of repose of the *debris covering it.

**representative fraction** Information on a map about its scale. It gives the ratio of one unit of length on a map to the distance represented by that unit. In Britain, the most common *Ordnance Survey maps have a representative fraction of 1 : 50 000 (very roughly, one inch to the mile; one centimetre to five hundred metres) and 1 : 25 000 (roughly two and a half inches to the mile; one centimetre to two hundred and fifty metres).

**research and development** See *R and D.

**research and science park** *Science park.

**resequent drainage** A *drainage pattern where streams follow the original slope or dip of the land, as in *consequent drainage, but actually developed as *subsequent drainage following lines of weakness in rocks now long since eroded away.

**reserves** *Resources which are economically viable to develop. Reserve status thus depends on factors such as demand, cost, and available technology.

**residual** 1. In geomorphology, material, such as **residual soil**, or **residual debris** resting on the rock from which it was formed.
2. In statistics, the difference between an actual, observed, value and a value predicted by a *regression. A **positive residual** is where the observed value exceeds the computed value; a **negative residual** is the opposite.

**resolution** The quality and sharpness of an image based on information from a *remote sensor. Resolution depends on *pixel size and the angle of the incoming data.

**resource** Some component which fulfils man's needs. Resources may be manmade—labour, skills, finance, capital, and technology—or natural—ores, water, soil, natural vegetation, or even climate. The perception of a resource may vary through time; coal was of little significance to Neolithic man while flint was of great importance. Such resources depend on relevant technology. Other resources, like landscapes and ecosystems, may be permanently valued whatever the technology.

Resources can be *renewable—**flow resources**—or *non-renewable—**stock resources**.

**resource allocation** The assessment of the value of a resource or of the effects of exploiting a resource. The quantity of a resource may be determined in absolute terms, such as area, or in terms of the ability of man to utilize it. Values of resources may also be seen in social terms, although these are difficult to cost.

**resource-frontier region** A newly colonized region at the periphery of a country which is brought into production for the first time.

**resource management** The careful control of the exploitation of a resource, having regard to factors such as economic and environmental costs, future needs, and political considerations. This entails **resource development**—bringing resources into production—and **resource conservation**—the maintenance of the resource.

**resource orientation** The tendency of manufacturing industry to locate near the source of its *raw material or materials.

**restructuring** Also known as **structural adjustment**, this is a change in the economic make-up of a country. Restructuring may be necessary in a declining economy in order to promote growth. It may also be imposed by an authority, like the World Bank, to improve an ailing economy of a nation which is in debt to that authority. Restructuring in this case usually involves major cuts in the public sector.

**resurgence** The appearance or reappearance on the surface of an underground stream, perhaps because, having flowed through *permeable strata, it now reaches underlying *impermeable rocks.

**retail trade gravitation, law of** See *Reilly's law.

**retrogressive approach** A way of attempting to understand the past by studying the present; the analysis of past landscapes requires that the present landscape be studied.

**retrospective approach** The study of present-day landscapes in the light of the past landscapes.

**return cargo** If a vehicle must return empty after making a delivery, the freight rate must be high enough to cover both journeys. Any cargo utilizing the return journey can negotiate favourable freight rates.

**return flow** Water which has seeped through the soil as *interflow but which backs up the hillslope when it has reached a saturated layer.

**return period** The length of time between events of a given magnitude. This can be calculated for many natural phenomena including droughts, floods, and earthquakes. Calculation of the return period is only useful if continuous records have been kept over a number of years.

**revenue surface** A three-dimensional diagram with the horizontal axes showing distance and the vertical axis showing the spatial variation in revenue. See *cost surface.

**reverse fault** A fault, perhaps caused by *compression, where movement is up, rather than down, the *fault plane.

**Reynolds number ($R_e$)** The relationship between the size of an object passing through a fluid and the density, velocity, and viscosity of the liquid. The Reynold's number is given as:

$$R_e = \frac{lV_p}{\mu}$$

where $l$ = length of moving object, $V$ = velocity of the liquid, $p$ = density of the liquid, $\mu$ = viscosity of the liquid.

At high Reynold's numbers, flow is *turbulent and at very low numbers it is *laminar.

**rhizosphere** The immediate environment of plant root surfaces.

**rhyolite** An *igneous rock, glassy or almost glassy in appearance, and sometimes banded. It is formed from *viscous lava and is made up of *quartz, *feldspars, and *ferromagnesian minerals.

**ria** The seaward end of a river valley which has been flooded as a result of a rise in sea level.

**ribbon development** A built-up area along a main road running outwards from the city centre. Such a location combines the attraction of cheaper land away from the city centre with high accessibility and the chance of attracting trade from passing traffic. The lines of buildings on each side of the road may be only one plot deep.

**Richter Scale** A scale of the magnitude of earthquakes, ranging from 0 to 10. On this scale a value of 2 can just be felt as a tremor. Damage to buildings occurs for values of over 6, and the largest shock recorded had a magnitude of 8.9. The scale is logarithimic and is related to the amplitude of the ground wave and its duration.

**ridge and furrow** A set of parallel ridges and depressions formed during the period of strip cultivation in the Middle Ages. As the land was always ploughed to the same pattern, the plough then threw up earth to make ridges which often survive in the present landscape.

**ridge and valley** An almost parallel series of ridges and intervening valleys, such as those found in the Appalachian Mountains of the USA, where the valleys have been carved out of less resistant rock.

**ridge of high pressure** A small *high, often briefly bringing fine weather, lying between two *mid-latitude depressions.

**riegel** An outcrop of rock, forming a bar across a *glacial trough.

**riffle** A rocky or gravel section of a river bed causing ruffled flow.

**rift valley** A valley bounded by two roughly parallel faults formed when the rocks of its base moved down the fault plane.

**rills** Small channels, between 5 and 2000 mm in width, very closely spaced. Hence, **rill erosion. Shoestring rills** cut into the soil in a system of long, parallel lines. Rills are often seasonal features and a few contain enough *load to be regarded as miniature rivers. Rills are more likely to be formed by solution than by *abrasion.

**rime** See *frost.

**rime ice** Ice which forms when water droplets in the air freeze directly on to a glacier.

**ring city** A city created along the outer side of a circular routeway with open space at the centre of the ring. Such a development is seen at *Randstad Holland in the Netherlands.

**riparian** Of, or pertaining to, a river bank.

**rip current** A strong current moving sea-wards in the near-shore zone.

**ripple** A small ridge, a very few centi-metres high, formed on a beach or on a sandy river bed by the motion of water.

**rise** A broad, long, and gently sloping elevation on the deep sea floor.

**rising limb** That section of a river *hydro-graph which covers the beginning of the increased discharge until the maximum flow. See *hydrograph.

**risk** The likelihood of possible outcomes as a result of a particular action or reac-tion. Technically speaking, the likely out-comes of risks can be assessed as a series of different odds, while there is no calcula-tion of probabilities in *uncertainty.

**river** A *perennial or permanent flow of water, usually confined to a channel (the **river bed**) bordered by **river banks**. A steep, undercut bank is a **river cliff** and the land drained by the river and its tributaries is a **river basin**.

**riverain** Of, or pertaining to, a river, its banks, and its valley. See *riparian.

**river capture** See *capture.

**river terrace** A bench-like feature running along a valley side, roughly parallel with the valley walls. Most terraces form when a river's erosional capacity increases so that it cuts through its *flood plain. Many river valleys have been subject to alternat-ing phases of *aggradation and *dissec-tion such that a series of terraces has developed. These are **cut and fill terraces**, formed as erosion alternates with deposi-tion. Two similar terraces on each side of a river are **paired terraces**. These occur at times of elevation of the land surface or when downcutting is greater than *lateral erosion. **Unpaired terraces** usually form when lateral erosion dominates.

**riviera** A term taken from the Riviera coast from Marseille in southern France to Genoa in Italy, now used to describe any coastline of outstanding natural beauty.

**Roaring Forties** That area between 40 and 50 °S. where westerly winds, uninterrupted by land masses, blow strongly, often at *gale force.

**robber-economy** The exploitation of re-sources which takes no account of provi-sion for the future.

**roche moutonnée** A rock shaped by two major glacial processes. The *stoss and the central sections of the rock are stream-lined and *abrasion is the dominant process. The down-ice, lee, side is rugged and steep, and is thought to have under-gone *plucking. Roches moutonnées may be over 100 m in height and up to 1 km in length, but they are usually much smaller.

**rock** The hard material making up the earth's crust; or a piece of this material. It is a mixture of minerals which may be classified as *igneous, *metamorphic, or *sedimentary, or may be classified by age.

**rock creep** The slow, downslope move-ment of rock fragments, caused by gravity.

**rock fall** See *fall.

**rock flour** Silt- and clay-sized particles of debris formed because of grinding due to *abrasion within and at the base of a glacier. Streams arising from areas of gla-cial abrasion have a grey-green colour as rock flour is carried within them, in suspension.

**rock slide** See *slide.

**rock varnish** See *desert varnish.

**rollers** In hydrology; see *eddy.

**room density** Also known as the *occu-pancy rate, this is the number of persons in a house per unit habitable room. It is a widely used index since it is an easily cal-culated and sensitive indication of housing provision where any density of over one person per room indicates overcrowding.

**ropy lava** *Pahoehoe.

**Ro-Ro system** A drive on/drive off (roll on/roll off) ferry system, especially used on the cross-Channel routes.

**Rossby waves** Large meanders, on a global scale, of upper air flows. In the Northern Hemisphere, there are four to six such waves, most clearly identifiable in the middle *troposphere. Rossby waves are induced by large mountain barriers, such as the Rockies, by differential heating of the atmosphere, and by interaction with smaller-scale atmospheric disturbances.

Where the waves cover only a small zone of latitude, they are said to have a low *zonal index. Winds are strong and persistent and the weather is mild and damp over Europe. When the waves break down into separate cells, they have a greater latitudinal spread and are said to have a high zonal index. This can lead to the formation of persistent anticyclones which bring long periods of settled weather.

**Rostow's model of growth** Rostow saw economic growth as occurring in five stages. Initially, technology is primitive and social structures are rigid. Change is rare. This is the 'traditional society'. The second stage is a transition stage—the 'pre-conditions for take-off'. Here, possibly because of outside stimuli, investment begins in industry and the infrastructure develops. It is upon these bases that 'take-off' occurs. This is a period of very considerable growth in the economy and is accompanied by changes in society as well as in technology. Growth gives rise to the 'drive to maturity'. Industrial development now diversifies, imports fall, and investment is still high. The final stage—the 'age of high mass consumption'—is reached as consumer goods are of increasing importance and as the Welfare State develops. The Rostow model makes no attempt to explain these changes, and the terminology is somewhat vague.

**rotational slip** The semicircular motion of a mass of rock and/or soil as it moves downslope along a concave face.

**rotation of crops** A system of growing a series of different crops for each year in a cycle, in order to maintain the fertility of the soil. *Leguminous crops such as clover supply nitrates which later crops can take up. **Rotation grass** is grass sown for one year of a rotation.

**rotation of the earth** The spinning earth takes roughly 24 hours to turn around its axis. From the earth's surface it looks as if the sun, moon, and stars, are moving around the earth from east to west but, of course, it is the earth that moves.

**rotor** See *lee wave.

**rough grazing** Vegetation, such as natural grass, heather, bracken, and shrubs, used for grazing animals.

**r-selection, k-selection** Two major strategies may be adopted for the survival of a species. r-selected plants (where r stands for maximum increase) respond swiftly to favourable conditions with most of their energies devoted to rapid maturity and reproduction. (See *opportunist species.) k-selected plants survive by putting their energies into persistence. (See *equilibrium species.) If r and k are envisaged as being two ends of a continuum, most species have some of the characteristics of both to a greater or lesser extent along the continuum. It is suggested that over time an r-strategist species may develop k-strategist tendencies. As an r-strategist plant reproduces, the space available for seeding becomes less, so that rapid development is no longer important and persistence is required.

**rubification** The change of soil colour to yellow or red. This occurs in warm climates where intense weathering liberates iron. This iron attaches to clay minerals and, combined with some *lessivage, **rubifies** the soil.

**rudaceous** Coarse-grained sedimentary rock, either consolidated as in *conglomerate or unconsolidated as in *till.

**runnel** A very small stream, larger than a *rill.

**runoff** The movement over ground of rain water. Runoff occurs when the rainfall is very heavy and when the rocks and soil can absorb no more.

**rural** In, of, or suggesting, the country. In practice, it is difficult to distinguish truly rural areas because of the blurring at the *rural–urban continuum and the increase of commuting whereby rural inhabitants work in cities. Perhaps the clearest indication of rurality in society is the distance to large *urban centres.

**rural community** A group of people living in the same rural place who have common ties with each other and with their location. It is the smallest social group which caters for the daily social life of the inhabitants.

**rural depopulation** The decrease in population of rural areas, whether by migration or by falling birth rates as young people move away. It has been argued that the mechanization of agriculture leads to rural unemployment, and hence depopulation. Some writers argue that the move to the cities took place before mechanization and that machines were, therefore, needed to supplement the dwindling workforce. Others see rural depopulation as the product of wider changes in the economy, such as *industrialization.

**rural geography** The study of the rural landscapes of the developed world. It includes the origin, development, and distribution of rural settlement, *rural depopulation, the causes and consequences of agricultural change, patterns of recreational use of the countryside, tourism, planning, and the growing influence on rural areas of urban dwellers.

**rural planning** The management of rural areas with regard to some objective such as the maintenance and improvement of rural living standards, or easy access to jobs and social, economic, and welfare services. The most usual aspects of rural planning are maintenance of rural landscape, the recreational use of the countryside, and the planning of populations, settlements, and amenities. Also studied are rural problems such as lack of access to amenities and services, substandard housing, and rural unemployment.

**rural–urban continuum** Movement along a scale from the single isolated farm to *megalopolis does not elicit any clear boundaries from hamlets, villages, towns, and cities. The change is seen as a continuum. See *counter-urbanization.

**rurban** Combining the characteristics of both town and country. For **rurban fringe**, see *rural–urban continuum.

# S

**saeter** In Scandinavia, an upland pasture, usually used in summer only.

**sagebrush** A type of *xerophytic scrub in the western USA.

**Sahel** The semi-arid zone lying to the south of the Sahara and to the north of the wooded *savanna. It extends from Senegal to the Sudan. Rains are light and infrequent and drought and famine are major problems.

**sakia** A simple apparatus used for lifting water to irrigation canals by means of a circular chain of buckets set vertically. Usually a beast of burden trudges round in a circle to turn a wheel which is geared to the vertical chain.

**salina** An enclosed, salty *playa.

**saline** Salty. **Salinity** is the amount of salt present in a solution, usually expressed in parts per thousand by weight.

**salinization** The buildup of salts at or near the surface of a soil. In dry climates, surface water evaporates rapidly. This causes the soil moisture, together with its dissolved salts, to come to the surface by *capillary action. This water then evaporates, leaving behind a crust of salts on the surface. The incorrect use of irrigation in arid lands can cause salinization.

In coastal districts, salinization can occur when sea water percolates into the soil as a result of the over-pumping of ground water.

**SALR** Saturated adiabatic lapse rate. See *adiabatic.

**saltation** The bouncing of material from and along a river bed or a land surface. The impact of a falling sand grain may splash other grains upwards so that a chain of **saltating** particles may be set up. Saltation upwards is the result of *lift forces; the downward movement occurs when lift is no longer effective and the particle is subject to drag and gravity.

**salt dome** An almost circular mass of salt which has been forced upwards from its point of origin deep within the earth's crust. Under pressure, the salt becomes plastic and is squeezed towards the weakest part of the sedimentary rock above it. Salt domes are often associated with deposits of oil and natural gas.

**salt flat** The almost level, dried up bed of a salt lake.

**salt marsh** Many low-lying coasts are vegetated. It is this vegetation that traps silt particles and, to some extent, consolidates them. As the marsh develops, salt-tolerant species give way to less hardy specimens. The marsh becomes part of the coast land. In the tropics, *mangrove swamps are created by a similar mechanism.

**salt pan** A very shallow, enclosed basin of salty water, usually fed from the sea. After evaporation, deposits of salt are left behind which may be exploited for commercial or domestic use. Man-made salt pans can be constructed for the same means.

**salt weathering** A form of *crystal growth with some *hydration. As the crystals grow in fissures, they exert force on the rock. The salts concerned may come from chemical *weathering or may have been carried inland from the sea by spray, snow, or rain.

**sample** A portion of the full *population taken to be a worthwhile and meaningful representation of that population. A **systematic sample** selects survey points that are equally spaced over the area under investigation. A **random sample** selects points at random intervals, the coordinates being taken from a table of random numbers. In

**stratified sampling** the area under study is divided into different segments by the student. For example, a survey area may be divided into different geological regions or a residential area may be divided into detached, semi-detached, and terraced housing. Within each zone, the sample points are generated from a random number table and the number of points sampled in each zone correspond with the proportion of the total area that each zone represents.

The size of the sample must also be considered. If the data are widely spread, more samples are needed than if the values are clustered. A running mean can be calculated from the data, and when the addition of more measurements does not change this mean very greatly, enough data have been measured.

**samun** In Iran, a warm, dry *foehn blowing down from the mountains of Kurdistan.

**sand** Particles of rock with diameters ranging from 0.06 mm to 2.00 mm in diameter. Most sands are formed of the mineral quartz. Sandy soils are loose, nonplastic, and permeable, and have little capacity to hold water.

**sand dune** A hill or ridge of sand sorted and accumulated by wind action. Once a dune is formed, sand will settle on it rather than on bare surfaces. This is because the friction of the sandy surface is enough to slow down the wind, which then sheds some of its *load.

Dunes formed in the *lee of some obstacle are **topographic dunes**: **lunettes** are formed in the lee of a *deflation hollow, **nebkhas** form in the lee of bushes, **wind shadow dunes** form in the lee of hills and plateaus, and some dunes form windward of such topographic obstacles. **Parabolic dunes** are hairpin-shaped with the bend pointing downwind, and originate around patches of vegetation.

Wind direction is significant. Where the direction is very changeable, **star dunes** form. The linear **seif dunes** form when two prevailing winds alternate, either daily or seasonally. When the supply of sand is limited, **barchans** form with the horns pointing downwind. Barchans may be re-shaped into **dome dunes** by strong winds. **Barchanoid dunes** are undulating, continuous cross-wind dunes which may grade into long **transverse dunes**. See also *coastal dunes and *lateral dune.

**sandplain** In Western Australia, a flat and sandy desert.

**sandstone** A sedimentary rock composed of compacted and cemented sand.

**sandstorm** Usually occurring in arid or semi-arid areas, the sandstorm forms when turbulent wind picks up sand to a height of up to 30 m.

**sandur,** pl. **sandar** A sheet, or gently sloping fan, of *outwash sands and gravels.

**sand-wedge polygons** See *frost cracking, *polygon.

**Santa Ana** See *local winds.

**sapping** The breaking down and undermining of part of a hillslope such that small slips occur. Mechanisms include undercutting of a cliff by wave action, undercutting at the foot of a *bluff along a river, and *frost shattering at the base of a *bergschrund.

**saprophyte** An organism which grows on decaying plant or animal material.

**saquia** *Sakia.

**sargasso** A brown, tropical seaweed found in abundance at the surface of the Sargasso Sea of the western Atlantic.

**sarsen stone** A *megalith of hard sandstone found, for example, at Stonehenge, England. The sarsen stones of Stonehenge came from South Wales. How the stones were transported is not known; some suggest that they are erratics left at the end of the Ice Age, others that they were carried by boat and then moved on rollers overland.

**sastrugi** Ridges of ice particles, transported by wind, and lying across an ice sheet. They are orientated at right angles to the prevailing wind.

**Satellite Probatoire pour l'Observation de la Terre, SPOT** A French *remote-sensing satellite.

**satellite town** A town located well beyond the limits of a major city and which operates as a discrete, self-contained entity. Most of the early *new towns were satellites of London.

**satisficer** A decision-maker whose aim is to make a choice which is acceptable rather than optimal, possibly because of limited knowledge and ability or because maximization of profit is not the only goal. The decision-maker may be inclined to maximize *psychic income, that is the satisfaction which may come to managers from causes other than financial ones, such as *amenity. Other satisficers are loath to undertake the somewhat hazardous process of seeking the optimum because they are averse to uncertainty. Others may be guided by moral concerns.

**saturated** In meteorology, of air which cannot hold any more water vapour. If saturated air is cooled, condensation follows.

**saturated adiabatic lapse rate, SALR** See *adiabatic.

**saturated mixing ratio lines** Lines of constant *humidity mixing ratio plotted against height and pressure on a *tephigram.

**savanna** Broad belts of tropical grassland flanking each side of the equatorial forest of Africa and South America. These belts are associated with the sinking of high-level equatorial air on its return to the *Inter-Tropical Convergence Zone. Such descent leads to an *adiabatic temperature increase so that rainfall is slight. Trees are modified to minimize water loss; they have small flat leaves and are often thorny.

The boundaries of the savanna are far from clear; there is a gradual change from tall grasses, 1–3 m high with scattered trees, to grassy woodland, and finally to the rain forest. However, where savanna vegetation has been repeatedly burnt, there can be a sharp division between this

and the equatorial forest which is less easily fired.

**savanna woodland** Tropical grassland with scattered trees and *xerophytic undergrowth.

**scalded flat** In Australia, a large and level stretch of saline soil.

**scale** The relationship between a distance on a map or plan and the corresponding distance on the ground, shown as a numbered line, or as a *representative fraction.

**scarp** A steep slope. It may result from faulting, or folding and subsequent erosion.

**scarp and vale terrain** Scarps interspersed with wide valleys; common in South and East England.

**scarp-foot spring** A spring at the foot of a scarp, often where *permeable rocks are underlain by *impermeable rocks.

**scarp slope** A steep slope; the steeper ridge of a *cuesta.

**scatter diagram** A pictorial way of representing data to see if two sets of measurements may be associated with each other. Two scales, one for each type of variable, are drawn at right angles to each other and each set of data is plotted. If the dots appear to fall on to a diagonal line, an association is indicated. The statistical significance of such an association may be evaluated by using other statistical tests.

**schist** A *metamorphic rock, finer grained than *gneiss, and characteristically with broad, wavy bands, which are not *bedding planes but sorted zones of minerals such as *mica.

**science park** An area of buildings for research and development and for high-technology industries. See also *industrial park.

**scientific method** An approach to problem-solving. The first stage is identifying the nature of the problem and the second stage is the formation of a hypothesis as the potential answer. Information must then be collected and classified as the limits to the question are defined. In the fourth stage the hypothesis is tested against the real world and attempts are made to establish laws. These are easier to establish in the physical sciences than in the social sciences. A combination of laws produces a theory which defines and explains the problem.

**scoria** A volcanic rock made of sharp rock fragments, and full of air pockets once occupied by gases. **Scoria cones** may be built around the central vent of a volcano.

**scour and fill** The erosion and later filling of a water channel.

**scree** Shattered rock fragments which accumulate below and from free rock faces and summits. The term may be extended to the slope, commonly of 35°, made up of these fragments.

**scroll** A low, narrow ridge running parallel with a *meander and formed in times of flood.

**scrub** Low or stunted trees and shrubs, found in such adverse conditions as exposed hillsides, semi-deserts, and areas of poor soil. Dense patches of scrub are **scrub forest**.

**sea, law of the** A framework, agreed to by the majority of maritime nations, for administering the seas. It recognizes seven administrative zones: internal waters, the *territorial sea, the *contiguous zone, the *continental shelf, exclusive fishing zones of up to 320 km from a nation's coastline, exclusive economic zones of the same extent as the fishing zones, and the high seas.

**sea breeze** Land heats more rapidly than water. In coastal districts, this means that on sunny days the land is warmer than the sea. The air above the land is warmed, and expands. A circulatory system develops, with warm air rising over the land and descending over the sea to flow back onshore as a gentle sea breeze. At night, the land cools more rapidly, so that the air over the sea is now warmer. The situation is thus reversed, and an offshore land breeze blows.

Sea breezes greatly modify coastal climates and can bring cooler conditions in the afternoon to areas with hot, humid climates. Such breezes can move some 300 km inland before they die down in the early evening.

**sea-floor spreading** The creation of new crust as *magma rises up at a *plate margin. The magma creates new oceanic crust as the far end of the plate moves away. See also *constructive margin.

**sea-fret** In Devon and Cornwall, a salt mist coming from the sea. It is harmful to vegetation.

**sea-level** *Mean sea-level.

**seamount** A mountain on the ocean floor which does not break the water surface. A flat-topped seamount is a *guyot.

**search behaviour** The way in which an individual or entity reacts to information by selecting one of a set of alternatives to solve the problem of location. The decision-maker has an awareness of a set of places from which to choose. The choice depends on the degree to which information is available and on the decision-maker's ability to evaluate the information. Some decision-makers comb through the options thoroughly; others are not thorough and display a certain irrationality in their choice. The choice made may be incorrect if based on inexact, partial data and superficial analysis.

**SEASAT** A satellite equipped with *remote sensors, designed to investigate the oceans. Launched in 1978, it fell from orbit after a few months, but transmitted enormous amounts of data before it fell.

**seaway** A canal, such as the St Lawrence Seaway in Canada, wide and deep enough to take ocean-going ships.

**sebka** A depression in usually arid countryside which becomes marshy for a short time after an infrequent rainfall event.

**secondary air mass** An *air mass which has been modified by the passage of time or by its movement to an area differing from the source region. Some schemes of classification differentiate between a **k air mass** which is colder than the surface over which it is moving and a **w air mass** which is warmer. In general, a k air mass is inclined to *instability, with gusty, turbulent winds, while w air masses have *stable or *inversion conditions, with *stratus clouds.

**secondary depression** A small *low, moving, in the Northern Hemisphere, in an anticlockwise direction, around a *mid-latitude depression.

**secondary industry** The creation of finished products from raw materials; that is, manufacturing. This activity often involves several stages.

**secondary soil** A soil, such as *loess, transported from its place of formation.

**secondary urbanization** Urbanization which results from forces which are external to a country, such as foreign, colonial settlement.

**secondary vegetation** The vegetation that naturally colonizes an area where the *primary vegetation has been cleared, by man or by fire.

**secondary wave** See *earthquake.

**second home** A property occasionally used by a household whose normal place of residence is elsewhere. Second homes are usually found in rural areas where they are used for recreation and leisure. In some cases the purchase of second homes by outsiders can drive up house prices beyond the pockets of local residents.

**Second World** Before 1990, the communist countries of Eastern Europe together with the USSR.

**sector model** *Mann's model.

**sector principle** The principle on which claims to territory in the Arctic and Antarctic are made. The territory is shared out in the form of arbitrary sectors, each one having an apex at the poles and including an outer area bounded by the coast. The principle has worked well in establishing control of the Arctic ice, but there are disputed claims over the land mass of the Antarctic which may possibly yield mineral resources.

**sector theory** The view that housing areas in a city develop in sectors along the lines of communication, from the *CBD outwards. High-quality housing areas run along roads and also reflect the incidence of higher ground. Industrial sectors develop along canals and railways away from high-quality housing. Thus a high-status residential area will spread out along the lines of the sector by the addition of new belts of housing beyond the outer arc of the city. Once contrasts in land use have developed in a sector near to the city, these contrasts will be perpetuated as the city grows. This theory was advanced by Hoyt and Davie and was based on residential rent patterns in the USA.

**sedentary** Fixed, not moving, as in **sedentary agriculture** where the farmer and his fields are permanently settled.

**sedentary soil** A soil formed from the *parent rock which it still overlies.

**sedge** A coarse grass, triangular in cross-section, growing in *bogs.

**sediment** Material which has separated and settled out from the liquid which originally carried it. For **pluvial sediments** the ability of a river to carry sediment depends on particle size as well as the river discharge. See also *load.

**sedimentary rock** A rock composed of sediments, usually with a layered appearance. The sediments come mostly from pre-existing rocks which have been broken up and then transported by water, wind, or glacier ice.

Rocks formed from such sediments are *clastic sedimentary rocks and may be subdivided by size into three groups: *argillaceous, *arenaceous, and *rudaceous.

**sedimentation** The blocking of an aquatic system by the deposition of sediment. Sedimentation may choke reservoirs and raise the river bed by the deposition of silt.

**sediment yield** The total mass of sediment, in suspension or as *bedload, which reaches the exit of a drainage basin. High sediment yields may reflect the discharge of the river basin but the nature of the catchment area, be it of weak or resistant rock, farmed or urban land, is also important.

**seed bed** An area which contains the contacts and social ties which a newly established small firm needs. In such an area, the *infrastructure is well established together with the factors which a small firm cannot afford on its own, such as workshops and factory units, ancillary industry, financial and legal services, and specialized services. Failure in such locations is less costly than on a larger scale, while success sees the movement of the small firm to larger premises. In consequence, the turnover of firms in a seed bed tends to be rapid.

Attempts have been made to develop seed beds in order to stimulate industrial growth; one example is the *science park.

**seeding of clouds** According to *coalescence theory, for fine raindrops to become heavy enough to fall as rain, they must get bigger. Cloud seeding provides *condensation nuclei as crystals of ice, silver iodide, or solid carbon dioxide are scattered over a cloud in an attempt to cause precipitation.

**seepage** In hydrology, an oozing out of water.

**segmented economy** An economy characterized by a variety of firms ranging from multinationals to small workshops, as opposed to an **atomistic economy** which is made up of a host of small firms.

**segmented labour** A labour force made up of two or more types of worker. Movement of labour from one type to another is not easy, especially between one type of skilled labour and another. This makes changes in the industrial structure difficult.

**segregation** The separation of the subgroups of a large population particularly into distinct residential areas. This segregation may be based on grounds of income, race, religion, or language. See *index of segregation.

**seif** See *sand dune.

**seine fishing** A type of fishing where a long net is used to surround shoals of fish. When the two ends of the net meet the net is hauled on to the boat.

**seismic** Of an earthquake. The **seismic focus** or **seismic origin** is the point of origin of the earthquake within the crust. The resulting shocks are **seismic waves**, which may be recorded and measured by a **seismograph**. **Seismology** is the study of earthquakes and of other earth movements such as those that may be caused by man.

**seismic tomography** The interpretation of earthquake waves to determine the nature of the internal structure of the earth, including the patterns of flow in the *mantle. For example, seismic waves travel more rapidly through the cold regions of the earth's interior than through the warm; inferences can therefore be made about interior temperatures by timing the velocity of waves.

**selective logging** The felling, at intervals, of the mature trees in a forest of mixed age. This type of forest management mimics natural processes in that the canopy is maintained while timber is produced.

**selective migration** The migration of one part of the population. This may be spontaneous. Most countries now practise selective migration by demanding qualifications, such as skills, youth, and health, for immigrants.

**selva** The dense *tropical rain forest of the Amazon Basin.

**semi-arid** Receiving enough rain to support *scrub.

**sensible temperature** The temperature, which may be modified by wind or humidity, felt by a human being.

**sensor** A device which can detect sound, electromagnetic radiation, or gravitational force, especially one deployed on a satellite.

**separatism** The desire of a particular ethnic group—usually a minority—to form their own separate and sovereign state.

**sequential mapping** See *mental map.

**sequent occupance** The succeeding stages of human habitation over time on one site. Each stage is seen as being established by its predecessor, although the sequence will almost certainly be interrupted by outside forces.

**serac** A mass of glacier ice, formed between crevasses and most often found at a sudden increase in the slope of the glacier.

**sere** A particular and easily recognized stage of an ecological *succession.

**sericulture** The production of silk.

**service industry** Those economic activities, including wholesaling, transport, and retailing, concerned with the distribution and consumption of goods and services. To these may be added administration and, possibly, the provision of information, although some might see the latter as *quaternary industry.

**sesquioxide** A compound of oxygen with a ratio of 2 : 3. For example, iron sesquioxide, $Fe_2O_3$.

**set-aside grant** A gift of money from the government to a farmer in order to encourage him to take land out of agricultural production. Its purpose is to cut down on the production of surpluses. Commonly, farmers who do set aside land increase yields on the lands they continue to farm so that the surpluses continue.

**settlement** In human geography, any form of human habitation from a single house to the largest city.

**settlement hierarchy** The ranking of settlements, usually by size. It is suggested that settlements high up in the hierarchy have larger *urban fields than those lower down.

**settlement pattern** The nature of the distribution of settlements. Some settlement patterns may be seen as a reflection of cultural traditions. For example, the isolated farmstead is typical of North Wales, while the nucleated village is typical of lowland England. The technique of *nearest neighbour analysis may be used to test for any regularities in settlement patterns.

**shade temperature** The temperature of the air as recorded on a thermometer inside a *Stevenson screen, and therefore out of direct sunlight. Unless otherwise specified, all temperatures in climatic statistics are shade temperatures.

**shadow price** A price used in *cost–benefit analysis to value intangible items like clean air.

**shaduf** A simple apparatus used for lifting water for irrigation by means of a bucket and a lever to raise and lower it. When above the bank, the shaduf may be swung round ready to feed water on to the land or into a trough.

**shake wave** See *earthquake.

**shale** A fine-grained sedimentary rock formed when layers of clay are compressed by the weight of overlying rocks. Shales have a layered structure and are easily split along the *bedding planes. **Shale oil** may be distilled from bituminous shale.

**shanty town** An area of usually unauthorized, makeshift housing, generally at the edge of a Third World city. Shanty towns grow because demand for cheap housing outstrips supply. Houses are made from available cheap materials such as packing cases, metal cans, plywood, and cardboard. Sanitation is grossly inadequate, electricity and gas may not be available, and roads are not metalled. In addition, education and medical facilities are severely limited.

**shape index** A statistic used to quantify the shape of an areal unit. Chorley and Haggett expressed this statistic as:

$$\text{shape index} = \frac{1.27^A}{L^2}$$

where $A$ = area of shape in $km^2$, and $L$ = the length of the longest axis in km.

A value of 1.0 expresses maximum compaction where the shape is circular. As the shape is elongated, the less compact the shape, and the lower the value of the index.

**share-cropping** A type of farming whereby the tenant pays his rent to the landowner in produce rather than in cash. The landlord often provides seeds, stock, and equipment in return for a fixed proportion of the output. Share-cropping usually shows low yields in comparison with owner-occupied farms or cash tenancies since the incentives are less.

**shatter belt** A zone of fragmented rock caused by movement along a *fault.

**shear** Stress applied along only one face of a body.

**shear box** An apparatus which can determine the resistance of a rock or soil to shearing. The soil is placed into a layered box. Whilst a normal force is applied to the top layer, the bottom layer is pulled out sideways. The *shear strength of the soil is the force which needs to be applied to deform the sample.

**shearing** The deformation of a material so that its layers move laterally over each other. In geology, shearing bends, twists, and draws out rocks along a fault or *thrust plane. Such shearing is sometimes accompanied by shattering or crushing of the rock near the fault. A **shearing force** acts parallel to a plane rather than perpendicularly. **Shear stress** is the force or forces applied tangentially to the surface of a body and causing bending, twisting, or drawing out of that body.

**shear plane** The face along which *shearing occurs.

**shear strength** The ability of a rock or soil to withstand *shearing.

**sheet flow** *Overland flow.

**sheeting** The splitting of the outer layers of rock, probably as a consequence of *pressure release resulting from the erosion of overlying material. Other factors include *thermal weathering and the swelling of the outer layers of rock as they are moistened by rain or dew. Sheeting is generally parallel to the land surface.

**sheet lightning** The effect of a whole cloud, or clouds, being lit momentarily by a shaft of lightning which may not be visible.

**sheet wash** A form of erosion whereby a thin film of water transports soil particles by rolling them along the ground.

**shelter belt** A *windbreak, planted to reduce wind speed.

**shield** The very old, rigid core of relatively stable rocks within a continent. This is usually a *Precambrian nuclear mass around which, and to some extent upon which, younger sedimentary rocks have been deposited. See also *craton.

**shield volcano** A volcano formed of successive eruptions of free-flowing *lava which creates a gently sloping, broad dome tens of kilometres across and around 1 km high.

**shifting cultivation** In this agricultural system, a patch of land is cleared, crops are grown, and the patch is then deserted until the soil regains its fertility. *Bush fallowing is a practice similar to that of shifting cultivation but involves no change of residence, grows crops for longer, and has a shorter fallow.

**shift share analysis** The analysis of three components of industrial change: the national rate of change in manufacturing, the industrial structure of regions, and their locational advantages or disadvantages. The **differential share** compares the differences in a region between the employment in a particular industry and the employment it would have had if it had changed at the national rate for that industry. The difference is between the expected change, if employment follows the national pattern, and the actual change. The **regional share** indicates what would have happened if the region had maintained its share of total national manufacturing employment. The **structural shift** estimates the change expected in a region if each industry in the region has changed at its own national rate. Shift share analysis has been strongly criticized.

**Shimbel index** The number of *edges connecting any *node by the shortest possible routes to all other nodes on a *network. It is, therefore, a measure of the *accessibility of that node.

**shingle** Rounded pebbles on a beach.

**shire** An administrative district formed in England by the Anglo-Saxons, generally for the purposes of taxation. It was superseded by the Norman counties, some of which retain the term 'shire'.

**shoal** An area of shallow water within a lake, river, or sea.

**shopping goods** *High order goods which are relatively rare purchases. More time is usually taken over their selection, and the customer may travel long distances for a particular purchase.

**shore** The land adjoining a large body of water or next to the sea.

The **backshore** is the part normally above the high water mark but still influenced by the sea. The **foreshore** covers the area between the high and low tide marks and is exposed at low tide. The **nearshore** is seaward of the foreshore and ends at the breaking point of the waves. The **offshore**, in coastal geomorphology, is the zone seaward of the breakers but in which material is moved by the waves.

**shore platform** A very gently sloping platform extending seaward from the base of a cliff. Platforms widen as the cliffs retreat. They are subject to *salt weathering, alternate wetting and drying, *water-level weathering, and processes of erosion such as *quarrying, *hydraulic action, *pneumatic action, and *abrasion.

It is argued that a platform of over 800 m in width cannot have been formed by these forces alone, hence the term 'shore platform' rather than 'wave-cut platform'. Thus, changes in erosional processes and in sea level must have taken place.

**shott** In North Africa and the Middle East, a shallow, and sometimes saline, lake or watercourse which may dry out at certain seasons.

**shrub** A low, branching perennial plant with woody stems growing from its base.

**sial** The *continental crust, dominated by minerals rich in silica and aluminium.

**Siberian high** A cold *anticyclone located in winter over central and northern Asia.

**sidewalk farming** In the USA, the cultivation of a holding some distance away from the urban area where the farmer lives. It is generally restricted to cereal crops.

**significance test** A statistical test aimed at demonstrating the probability that observed patterns cannot be explained by chance. The **significance level** is the level at which it is decided to reject the *null hypothesis.

A significant result has a 1 in 20 (5%) probability of the observation occurring by chance, a highly significant result has a 1 in 100 (1%) probability, and a very highly significant result has a 1 in 1000 (0.1%) probability.

**sierra** Originally a range of jagged peaks, but now the equivalent in Spanish of the term 'mountains'.

**silage** Green crops, such as grass and clover, which are compressed, fermented, and stored for use as animal fodder.

**silcrete** A *duricrust cemented with silica.

**sill** An *intrusion of igneous rock which spreads along bedding planes in a nearly horizontal sheet. This level sheet may be up to 300 m in thickness.

**silt** Fine grains of soil minerals ranging in size between clay and sand. Silts are often laid down by rivers when the flood water is quiet. The diameter of silt particles ranges from 0.002 mm to 0.06 mm.

**Silurian** A *period of *Paleozoic time stretching approximately from 430 to 395 million years BP.

**silviculture** The study of the breeding, cultivation, and development of trees.

**sima** The lower part of the continental crust and the oceanic crust, dominated by silica and magnesium.

**simoom** In the northern Sahara, a very hot wind, heavily laden with dust, and blowing in the hottest months.

**sink hole** In limestone topography, a roughly circular depression into which drain one or more streams; a synonym for a *doline.

**sinter** A deposit of minerals, notably of silica and sulphates, precipitated in layered deposits from the gases released in an area of volcanic activity.

**sinuosity** The amount that a river meanders within its valley, calculated by dividing total stream length by valley length.

**sirocco, scirocco** A hot, dry, and sometimes dusty wind, blowing from the Sahara to the north Mediterranean coast.

**site** The position of a structure or object in physical, local terms such as a river terrace.

**Site of Special Scientific Interest, SSSI** A site in the UK which is of particular importance because of its geology, topography, or ecology. Planning permission for the development of the SSSI is granted only after consultation with the Nature Conservancy Council.

**situation** The location of a phenomenon, such as a town, in relation to other phenomena, such as other towns.

**skerry** In northern Europe, a small island.

**skewness** In a frequency curve, a lack of symmetry.

**skid row** In the USA, that section of a city whose population has a large number of males, often as drop-outs, derelicts, and petty criminals. Such areas are said to have developed from cheaper accommodation for young, male in-migrants.

**skylab** An American, manned satellite, containing *remote sensors, and launched in 1973.

**slack** A hollow in an area of coastal *sand dunes.

**slaking** In geomorphology, the disintegration of fine-grained rocks. It has been suggested that slaking is the result of alternate wetting and drying of the rock, but the mechanism is not fully understood.

**slash and burn** The clearing of land, usually tropical, where the trees are cut down, the land cleared of most of the trunks, and the rest of the vegetation is fired. It is suggested that the ash formed is a fertilizer.

**slate** A weak sedimentary rock, easily split along thin layers of bedding, formed by the compression of shales.

**sleet** Very wet snow, or a mixture of snow and rain.

**slickenside** A rock surface which has been scratched or polished by the effects of friction during structural changes.

**slide** A form of *mass movement in which material slides in a relatively straight plane. Slides usually have a length much greater than the depth of the moving material and the sliding mass generally breaks into many blocks as it moves.

**slip** The amount of movement along a *fault plane. Movement in the direction of the *strike is **strike-slip**; movement along the direction of the *dip is a **dip-slip**. The term is often used less precisely to describe a downslope movement of soil and rocks.

**slip-off slope** The relatively gentle slope at the inner edge of a meander. This is the site of *point-bar deposits.

**slope** In geomorphology, any slanting surface of the earth's crust, above or below sea level. Slope studies refer mostly to *hillslopes.

**slope elements** The differing parts of a slope. These may be convex, straight, or concave; the shape of a slope is an expression of the predominant processes acting on it.

Convex sections are generally at the top of a slope. These usually gentle slopes are formed by soil *creep and *rainsplash. Downslope from the convex sections, there may be a straight slope of bare rock. This is the *free face (fall face). Below this, the concave elements are either due to increased water erosion downslope or to the extension of larger pieces of debris rolling further than the rest. Compound slope profiles may exhibit some or all of these segments and may show a repetition of certain elements.

**slope length** The length along the ground of a slope, and not on a map where it will be represented as being shorter.

**slope wash** The downslope movement of sediment by an almost continuous film of water.

**slum** An area of poor housing, often characterized by multi-occupance, overcrowding, and poverty. Schools are poor, items sold in local shops are more expensive than those sold in a supermarket, and sanitation inadequate. Slum populations often exhibit high concentrations of drug abusers, alcoholics, criminals, and vandals.

**slum clearance** The demolition of substandard housing, usually accompanied by *rehabilitation and *redevelopment. Some schemes involve rebuilding on the same site, as in London's Barbican, while other clearances relocated the population at the edge of the city, as in the Roehampton estate in south London.

**slump** A form of *mass movement where rock and soil move downwards along a concave face. The rock or soil rotates backwards as it moves in a *rotational slip. Slumps differ from *slides in the different nature of the *shear plane.

**smallholding** In Britain, a holding of under 20.2 ha (50 acres), and of low rental value.

**smog** A combination of smoke and fog. The fog occurs naturally; the 'smoke' is introduced into the atmosphere by the activities of man. After the five-day long period of smog in London in 1952, smoke abatement measures were introduced in Britain. British cities are still estimated to lose between 20 and 55% of incoming solar radiation from November to March through smog.

Furthermore, chain reactions occur in association with exhaust gases, notably in areas of intense car use such as Los Angeles. Toxic gases are formed. See also *photochemical smog.

**SMSA, Standard Metropolitan Statistical Area** An urban area of the USA. This can be a town of 50 000 people, or two towns, each larger than 15 000 people, and together totalling more than 50 000, or a county with more than 75% of its population working in industry. In addition to these three categories are areas which seem, by employment, commuting, or population density, to be urban rather than rural.

**snout** The lower end, or terminus, of a valley glacier.

**snow** Vapour from the atmosphere frozen into minute crystals which combine together to fall to the earth as light, white flakes.

**snow belt** See *sunbelt.

**snow line** In an upland area, or at *high latitudes the level above which snow cover is permanent.

**social** In human geography, concerned with human society. **Social role** is the behaviour society expects from a person; **social status** is the esteem in which that person is held by others. **Social structure** is the framework of society, with its roles and inter-relationships, its constraints, conventions, and rules.

**social anthropology** The study of people in a social context with a strong historical bias. It tends to be concerned with the cultures and societies of the, as yet, non-industrial world.

**social area analysis** The analysis of a city to define urban areas which contain people of similar living standards, ethnic background, and lifestyle. Three constructs have been used to differentiate urban areas. First is social rank. The distribution of skills changes from manual to semi-skilled and skilled white-collar jobs. The second factor is urbanization, which weakens the importance of the family unit as it increases. Third is segregation, which sees a redistribution of population as it proceeds. Variables were chosen for the three constructs: for example, occupation, education, and rent for social rank; fertility and working women for urbanization; and isolation of racial groups for segregation. The value of these variables is then plotted orthogonally for social rank and urbanization. The results may be used to map different socio-economic groupings in the city.

**social capital** Assets, like roads, schools, and hospitals, which belong to society rather than to individuals.

**social costs** In economics, the total costs of any action. These costs are made up of private costs, which are met by the individuals concerned, and indirect costs, which are borne by third parties.

**social Darwinism** The application of the concept of evolution to the development of human societies over time. It is an idea which emphasizes the struggle for existence and the survival of the fittest. Such ideas have been used to justify naked capitalism, and have been extended to defend power politics, imperialism, and war.

**social distance** The perceived distance between social strata, as with different socio-economic, racial, or ethnic groups. This distance may have arisen spontaneously, but is often imposed on one group by a dominant group.

**social formation** The prevailing pattern of class structure which goes hand in hand with a particular mode of production. That is to say, there will be one type of class structure associated with capitalism and another, quite different, type associated with communism.

**social geography** Originally this was defined as the study of the spatial patterns of social, as distinct from political and economic, factors. The subject may now be subdivided into three categories. The first lies in the spatial expression of capitalism; the city has a social structure as an expression of class structures which are reflected in its morphology. Another aspect stresses the 'alternative' view of human geography which studies the response of the economically disadvantaged rather than the successful. A third category emphasizes *welfare geography.

**socialism** A social system based on common ownership of the *means of production and distribution. Some writers consider that socialism is achieved when the major part of the means of production is owned by the state. In communist theory, socialism is the first stage on the road to full communism. It differs from communism in that it is attached to ethical and democratic values and because it allows both common and state ownership.

**social network** The cluster of relatives, family, and neighbours to which an individual or family is connected. Such groupings often share the same values and goals.

**social physics** A view of human society which applies analogies from the world of physics to aggregate human behaviour. Perhaps the best-known example of this is the *gravity model which sees the attraction of a town for the surrounding population as being proportional to its population and inversely proportional to the distance away from the town. This is analogous to the gravitational attraction of a physical body in Newtonian physics.

**social polarization** The results of *segregation within a society such that the ends of the social spectrum consist of large social groupings very different from each other.

**social space** The combined use and perception of space by distinct social groups. Social space provides an environmental framework for the behaviour of the group.

**social statistics** Information, judged by a government to be of public interest, about people: their birth, life, and death. Social statistics include the vital statistics of birth, death, and fertility, together with wealth, income, living standards, occupation, and education.

**social well-being** A state of affairs where the basic needs of the populace are met. This is a society where income levels are high enough to cover basic wants, where there is no poverty, where unemployment is insignificant, and where there is easy access to social, medical, and educational services. Many attempts have been made to quantify social well-being. See *territorial social indicators.

**sociation** A unit of plant communities; the smallest area of ground in which the full range of plant types for that community can be found.

**socio-economic groups** See *Registrar General's classification of occupations.

**sociology** The study of societies; both the description of social phenomena and the evolution of a conceptual scheme for these phenomena. Different strands may be recognized: curiosity about how a society hangs together, theories of social evolution, and the interpretation of these theories.

**softwood** Easily worked wood obtained largely from fast-growing coniferous trees such as pine, spruce, and fir.

**soil** The upper layer of the ground consisting of weathered rock which supplies mineral particles, together with *humus.

**soil association** 1. In Britain, a group of *soil series developed on a similar parent material or on a combination of rocks.
2. In the USA, an area in which different soils occur in a characteristic fashion, or a landscape which has characteristic kinds, proportions, and distributions of component soils.

**soil classification** An ordering of soil types. The simplest arrangement distinguishes between *pedocals, rich in calcium carbonate, and *pedalfers, low in calcium but high in compounds of aluminium and iron. The **great soil groups** are *zonal, *azonal, and *intrazonal. Of the zonal soils, *podzols are found beneath coniferous forest, and latosols (see *lateritic soils) develop in warm moist conditions. *Chernozems, *prairie soils, and *chestnut soils are formed beneath grassland. Grey and red *desert soils occur in hot, arid areas, and *tundra soils form in *periglacial environments.

Intrazonal soils include *peats, saline *solonchaks, and alkaline *solonetz. Azonal soils include *alluvium and *sands. See also *US soil classification.

**soil compaction** *Compaction.

**soil creep** See *creep.

**soil erosion** The removal of the soil by wind and water and by the movement of soil downslope. **Accelerated soil erosion** is erosion increased by human activity. The causes of such erosion include the removal of windbreaks and the exposure of bare earth, either by arable farming or by overgrazing. Fire, war, urbanization, and stripmining also accelerate the erosion of the soil. See also *gully.

Wind erosion is by *deflation. Water erosion takes place in gullies, *rills, or by *sheet wash. Downslope *mass movement ranges from soil *creep to *landslides.

**soil horizon** See *horizon.

**soil moisture budget** The balance of water in the soil; this is the net result of the combined effects of *precipitation (P) and *potential evapotranspiration (PET).

When PET exceeds P, there will be a phase where soil moisture is used up, after which, with the continued excess of PET over P, there will be a **soil moisture deficit**. This deficit may be remedied if, during wetter seasons, P exceeds PET, thus inducing **soil moisture recharge**. This may then be followed by a **soil moisture surplus**. See also *moisture index.

**soil pore** Any open space within the soil framework. The **porosity** of a soil is judged by the percentage of pore spaces. Water will not drain freely from a soil with an average pore space of less than 0.03 mm.

**soil profile** A vertical series of soil *horizons from the ground surface to the parent rock. The profile results from the *translocation of soil constituents, and the horizons vary in their degree of separation. A soil is classified according to the arrangement of its horizons.

**soil series** A group of soils formed from the same parent rock and having similar *horizons and *soil profiles, but with varying characteristics according to their location.

**soil structure** The way in which sand, silt, clay, and humus bond together to form *peds. Four major structural forms are recognized: **block-like, platey, prism-like,** and **spheroidal**. Platey structures are formed of thin, horizontal layers. Prism-like structures are **columnar** where the tops are rounded and **prismatic** where the tops are level. Spheroidal structures are *crumbs if highly water-absorbent, and **granular** if only moderately so.

**soil texture** The make-up of the soil according to the proportions of sand, silt, and clay present. Twelve different textural classes are recognized, and the structure of the soil can be determined when the percentage of these three soil constituents are plotted on a *ternary diagram.

**solano** *Levante.

**solar** Of the sun. Hence, **solar day**: the average time between one noon and the next at the same location; **solar year**: the average time taken by the earth to complete one rotation; and **solar month**: one-twelfth of a solar year.

**solar constant** The rate per unit area at which *solar radiation reaches the outer margin of the earth's atmosphere. Despite its name, the solar constant probably varies slightly over time.

**solar energy** Any energy source based directly on the sun's radiation. Solar heat is trapped by an absorbent material, usually a black metal panel. The heat is then transferred to pipes which carry warmed air or water. In another method, the sun's rays may be centred on to one spot where the concentrated rays heat up a liquid in order to power a generator. The sun's radiation may be used also in solar cells which convert it into electricity. The chief advantage of solar energy is that, to all intents and purposes, it is inexhaustible. Its disadvantages include the fact that when it is most used for heating purposes, the days are short, the intensity of the rays is low, and the sun is often obscured by cloud.

**solar radiation** The electromagnetic waves emitted by the sun. These vary in wavelength from long-wave radio waves, through infra-red waves and visible light, to ultra-violet waves, X-rays, and gamma-radiation. Earth receives only 0.0005% of the sun's radiation.

**solar wind** The flow of atomic particles from the sun.

**sol brun lessivé** A type of *brown earth from which some clay has been *leached, forming an E *horizon.

**solfatara** A vent through which steam and volcanic gases are emitted. Some writers reserve the term for vents through which steam only is emitted.

**solifluction** The slow, downslope movement of water-saturated debris most notably, but not exclusively, in areas with cold climates. **Solifluction lobes** are deposits of waste which have formed bulges in the slope profile without breaking the surface. A continuous bulge across a slope is a **solifluction terrace**.

**solonchak** An *intrazonal saline soil found in hot, arid climates. Evaporation of soil moisture brings saline ground water to the surface where it, too, evaporates. The salts which have been *translocated remain as a grey surface crust.

**solonetz** An *intrazonal, formerly saline, soil. Periodic rainfall has leached the salts from the surface layer and these accumulate in the B *horizon.

**solstice** The time (21 June or 22 December) at which the overhead sun is furthest from the equator and appears to stand still before returning towards the equator. The longest day occurs at the summer solstice, the shortest day at the winter solstice.

**solum** In soil science, the layers above the parent material. This part of the earth's surface is strongly influenced by climate and vegetation.

**solution** In geomorphology, the process whereby a fluid, usually water or *carbonic acid (see *carbonation), as the **solvent**, picks up and dissolves particles of a solid (the **solute**).

**solution mining** A mining technique whereby low-grade ores are injected with a solvent. The solvent leaches out the metal in solution which is then pumped to the surface. The metal is then extracted from the solution.

**sonar** Echo-sounding; the device used in *sonic mapping.

**sonde** A *remote sensor used at relatively low levels to monitor the atmosphere.

**sonic mapping** The determination of the depth of the sea by projecting very high-frequency acoustic pulses from a ship. The depth can be calculated from the travel time of the pulse from the ship to the bottom of the sea and back.

**sorting** In geomorphology, the deposition of sediments in order of size. Wind- and water-borne sediments usually drop the larger particles first. *Varve clays are especially good examples of sorting.

**souming** In *crofting, the right of grazing on common pastures.

**sounding** *Sonic mapping.

**source** The point of origin of a stream or river when it is clearly identifiable as such.

**source pricing** *f.o.b. pricing.

**source region** The region from which an *air mass derives its properties.

**south-east trades** The *trade winds of the Southern Hemisphere.

**southerly burster** A strong local southerly wind experienced in south-eastern Australia, bringing torrential rain and a sudden drop in temperatures.

**Southern Cross** A constellation, visible in the Southern Hemisphere, which can be used to find *true south.

**sovereignty** The authority of a state which, according to international law, is autonomous and not subject to legal control by other states or to the obligations of international law.

**sovkhoz** In the USSR, a large farm owned and managed by the state. See *collective farm.

**spa** A type of resort having mineral springs which are, or have been, thought to have curative properties.

**space** The extent of an area, usually expressed in terms of the earth's surface. **Absolute space** refers to clearly distinct, real, and objective space. **Relative space** is perceived by a person or society and concerns the relationship between events and between aspects of events.

**space–cost curve** A section through a *cost surface which can relate to the costs of a single input or to total costs. If the costs rise steeply from the lowest point, locational choice is restricted. Shallow curves allow more leeway in the choice of location for a particular industry.

**space–revenue curve** A section through a *revenue surface indicating, in one dimension, the revenue to be earned from a given volume of sales.

**space–time forecasting model** A model which attempts to forecast changes in variables over time and space. This type of model is usually a *regression based on earlier values and takes into account the lag caused by *diffusion. Such models are often of the 'black box' type which does not explain changes but is, none the less, used for prediction.

**spalling** The American term for *exfoliation.

**spatial** Spread across the landscape.

**spatial analysis** A type of geographical analysis which seeks to explain patterns of human behaviour and its spatial expression in terms of mathematics and geometry. Many of the models are grounded in micro-economics and predict the spatial patterns which should occur, given a number of pre-conditions. It is based on the tenet that *economic man is responsible for the development of the landscape.

**spatial co-variation** The study of two or more geographic distributions which vary over the same area. A close 'fit' of two variations shows that the phenomena are associated by area. Statistical methods can be used to determine these associations.

**spatial diffusion** See *diffusion.

**spatial growth model** This model is based on the concepts of *Rostow and Taafe and is the spatial expression of Rostow's stages of economic growth. In stage I, most villages are untouched by change, subsistence agriculture is the rule, and only a few isolated ports have contact overseas. Stage II is analogous with Rostow's 'take-off'. Some of the ports expand while others stagnate and communications develop to the interior. These developments are the infrastructure necessary to economic growth. In stage III, 'the drive to maturity', growth takes place at the larger ports and connections are made between inland centres. The interior centres continue to grow and it is suggested that the *primate city is located inland as it reflects a shift to domestic rather than export markets.

**spatial interaction theory** The view that the movement of persons between places can be expressed in terms of the attributes, such as population or employment rates, of each place. This theory is based on the *gravity model and although it can be made to explain spatial interactions, it has no theoretical underpinning; its validity is, therefore, restricted.

**spatial mapping** See *mental map.

**spatial margin** The points at a distance from a factory where costs are equal to revenue and no profit is made. Beyond the spatial margin, costs are such that the producer would make a loss if goods were transported there. A producer may locate his factory anywhere within the boundaries of the spatial margin and operate at a profit. In some industries, spatial margins are rather meaningless because the entire country lies within them.

The industrialist may well have other factors—like *amenity—influencing his choice of location. If the benefits gained from locating near amenities but still within the spatial margin compensate for extra profits at the optimum location, an enterpreneur may choose to locate there. Other reasons for locating within the spatial margins but not at the optimum location may be the residence of the founder, the availability of factory space, sociability on the part of the entrepreneur, and the support of local authorities or central government.

**spatial monopoly** The monopoly of a good enjoyed by a supplier over a marked area where no competitor exists.

**spatial pattern** The pattern of distribution of some feature such as towns or types of plant. Three broad patterns are recognised: clustered, random, and regular. See *nearest neighbour analysis.

**spatial preference** The choice of one spatial alternative, such as a housing area, a holiday resort, or a shopping centre, rather than another. **Repressed preference** occurs where the preference cannot be acted upon. With **absolute preference**, no alternative is considered; with **relative preference**, choices need to be made. Relative preferences can be manifest, where a choice has been made, or latent, where the individual is aware of a possible choice but does not yet need to make that choice.

**Spearman's rank correlation coefficient** Also known as Spearman's rho, the meaning of this coefficient is the same as that of the *product moment correlation coefficient. The two sets of variables are ranked separately and the differences in rank, $d$, are calculated for each pair of variables. The equation is:

$$r_s = 1 - \frac{6 \Sigma d^2}{n^3 - n}$$

where $n$ is the number of paired variables.

**specialization index** A quantitative measure to indicate degrees of industrial specialization in a given area.

$$I = \sqrt{P_1^2 + P_2^2 + P_3^2 + .....P_n^2}$$

where I is the index of specialization and $P_1$, $P_2$, and $P_3$ are the percentage of total employment of each industry in turn.

An index of 70 or over indicates a high degree of specialization in comparison with 55 or below for a diversified area. See *diversification.

**species** A *population or series of populations in which the individual members can interbreed freely with each other, but not with other species.

**species–area relationship** The relationship between the numbers of different plant and animal species and the area they inhabit. Generally speaking, the number of species present increases with the increase in area of a community, although the rate of increase in species numbers slows down as tracts become successively larger.

**specific heat** The amount of heat needed to raise the temperature of 1 g of a substance through 1 °C. Water has a relatively high specific heat; it warms and cools slowly. Land, with a lower specific heat, warms and cools rapidly. Thus, in coastal areas, the more moderate water temperatures decrease the range of temperatures of the land.

**spectral signature** In *remote sensing, the spectral characteristics of the radiation emitted by a particular type of land use. Each type of plant has its distinctive spectral sign, but spectral signatures must be checked by observations at ground level.

**speleothem** A collective noun for depositional features such as *stalactites and *stalagmites. Most speleothems are made of calcareous rock, but columns of other material such as gypsum or silica may be found.

**sphere of influence** Initially a region influenced by a colonial power but not directly colonized; this is an outmoded concept. The term is increasingly used as a synonym for the *urban field of a city.

**spheroidal weathering** The weathering of jointed rocks along the joints by water, such that shells of decayed rock surround isolated, unaltered corestones of unweathered rock.

**spilitic suite** A slowly subsiding *petrographic province affected by volcanic action.

**spilling wave** See *constructive wave.

**spillway** See *meltwater erosion.

**spinifex** A sharp-pointed, tough, and tussocky grass growing in the arid lands of Australia.

**spit** A ridge of sand running away from the coast, usually with a curved seaward end. Spits grow in the prevailing direction of *longshore drift. Their ends are curved by the action of waves coming from different directions.

**spodosol** A soil of the *US soil classification. See also *podzol.

**spoil heap** A mound of waste material left over from mining or quarrying.

**SPOT** See *Satellite Probatoire pour l'Observation de la Terre.

**spot height** A point on a map showing, by numbers, the height above *mean sea level of that place.

**sprawl** *Urban sprawl.

**spread, lateral spread** A relatively rare form of *mass movement; a type of *slumping generally only found in the clayey sediment around the edge of *ice sheets.

**spread effect** The filtering through of wealth from central, prosperous areas, to peripheral, less wealthy areas. Thus, increased economic activity at the core may stimulate a demand for more raw materials from the periphery and technological advance in the core region may be applied to other regions.

**spring** The point at which water emerges at the land surface. A spring often marks the top of the *water table, or occurs where a layer of *permeable rock lies above an *impermeable rock layer.

**spring-line villages** A series of villages at the foot of a scarp through which water percolates until it emerges as a spring at the point where the rock type changes to an impermeable layer. Such springs attracted early settlement.

**spring-sapping** The undermining of the hillside immediately above a spring. With undercutting, small slips occur just above the spring. The stream then emerges from slightly higher up the hillside and, in time, the upper valley of the stream will have been extended a considerable distance upslope.

**spring tide** A *tide with its maximum range between low and high tide. Spring tides occur twice monthly when the gravitational effects of the sun and moon are at a maximum.

**spur** A finger of upland projecting out into a valley. See *interlocking spur.

**squall** A storm characterized by sudden and violent gusts of wind. See *squall line.

**squall line** A cluster of storm-bearing *convection cells, each between 2 and 8 km in width, measuring in total some 100 km.

This line of squalls may be created when cold air overruns warm sector air in an *occlusion, or along an *inversion created by an influx of maritime air over a surface cooled by nocturnal radiation. Squall lines occur in West Africa where low-level *monsoon air is overrun by dry, warmer air from the Sahara. In all these cases, conditions are gusty and rain is heavy.

**squatter** Anyone who moves into an unoccupied house without a legal right to do so.

**squatter settlement** See *shanty town.

**squatting** The illegal commandeering of housing, usually in the inner city, by the homeless.

**squattocracy** The Australian equivalent of the English *squirearchy.

**squirearchy** The small-scale landed gentry.

**SSSI** See *Site of Special Scientific Interest.

**stability, stable** In meteorology, the property of a pocket of air which is unlikely to rise far. Thus, if a parcel of air cools more on rising than the air which surrounds it, it becomes denser than its surroundings and therefore sinks.

In ecology, a stable *ecosystem is one which will maintain or return to its original condition following any disturbance.

**stabilization** An intervention in an economy to reduce fluctuations in prices.

**stabilized dune** A coastal *sand dune fixed by vegetation.

**stable population** A population where fertility and mortality are constant. This type of population will show an unvarying age distribution and will grow at a constant rate. Where fertility and mortality are equal, the stable population is stationary.

**stac** *Stack.

**stack** An isolated islet or pillar of rock standing up from the sea bed close to the shore. A stack is a residual feature formed when marine erosion attacks a cliff.

**stadial** A time of glaciation when glaciers advanced and periglacial conditions extended, but not as significantly as in a *glacial.

**stage** 1. The level of water in a channel. **Stage recorders** monitor the depth of water at a gauging station. Because there is a relationship between discharge and stage at any point, stage can be used to calculate discharge.

2. The position reached in a sequence such as *Rostow's stages of growth.

3. In geology, a *stratigraphic division of rocks formed at the same age, usually having the same fossil assemblage.

**stages of growth** See *Rostow's model.

**stalactite** A column usually of limestone hanging from the roof of a cave. It grows as an underground stream deposits its dissolved load of calcium carbonate and it may extend far enough to meet a *stalagmite and thus form a continuous column.

**stalagmite** A column usually of limestone, formed on the floor of a cave when the dissolved calcium carbonate in the underground water is deposited as the water evaporates in splashing on to the cave floor.

**stand** An area of vegetation dominated by one species, for example, an oak stand.

**standard atmosphere** The atmosphere at its average temperature and pressure at ground level. It is used as the base line in equipment measuring, among other things, altitude.

**standard deviation,** σ A measure of the spread of values on each side of the *mean in a data set; a measure of dispersion. It is calculated as the square root of the *variance of a data set. The units of the standard deviation are the same as the units used for the values. σ may be derived from the equation:

$$\sigma = \sqrt{\frac{\Sigma (x - \bar{x})^2}{n}}$$

A low standard deviation indicates a close grouping about the mean and vice versa.

**standard error of the mean** In statistics, the *standard deviation of a set of means of samples, where all samples are of the same size and selected at random from the same population.

**standard hillslope** A hillslope made up of four sections; from top to bottom: *waxing slope, *free face, *constant slope, and *waning slope.

**standard industrial classification** A grouping of industries classified by a government. The British government recognizes 27 main groups of industry—main order headings—which break down into subgroups—minimum list headings.

**standardized mortality ratio** The ratio of observed to expected deaths.

$$\text{SMR} = \frac{\text{observed deaths}}{\text{expected deaths}} \times 100$$

The expected deaths are derived from national figures, while the observed deaths reflect the real conditions. Thus a comparison is made between national and local trends. An SMR of 100 indicates that the age-standardized mortality rate in the group being studied is the same as the overall, or standard, population. A ratio less than 100 indicates a higher than average death rate; over 100 is a lower than average one.

**Standard Metropolitan Statistical Areas** See *SMSA.

**standard parallel** A line of *latitude used as the basis for a *map projection or a *grid reference system.

**standard time** The time based on the highest point of the sun in the sky; on noon.

**standing crop** The *biomass present at a given time in a given area.

**standing wave** See *lee wave.

**staple** A principle item in an economy. This may be food for domestic consumption as with the potato in early nineteenth-century Ireland, or maize in East Africa. Many Third World exports are based on a staple such as cocoa in Ghana, or sugar in Mauritius. Dependence on an export staple is seen as characteristic of a developing, rather than developed, country. The **staple export model** sees the production and export of staples as a trigger to economic growth.

**star dune** See *sand dune.

**state** A territorial unit with clearly defined and internationally accepted boundaries, having an independent existence and being responsible for its own legal system. **State capitalism** is an economic system where the government owns and directs large parts of the economy in competition with the private sector. **State socialism** is the ownership, management, and planning of virtually all of the economy.

**state farming** In a *centrally planned economy, a farm owned by the state which then employs workers to farm it.

**state intervention** Any activity of central government designed to affect the economy.

**static lapse rate** *Environmental lapse rate.

**stationary population** See *stable population.

**steady state** A system where input is balanced by output. Thus, a soil might contain a constant amount of water with the 'new' water entering the system being exactly balanced by the 'old' water leaving it.

**steam fog** Fog formed where colder air moves over a body of warm water. The evaporation of the water is chilled by the cold air and condenses into wispy fog. *Arctic sea smoke is a fog of this type.

**stem flow** See *interception.

**step faults** A series of parallel *faults each having movement in the same direction but with an increasing *throw from top to bottom.

**steppe** The wild grasslands of central Europe and Asia. The natural vegetation has by now been removed or much altered by cultivation and grazing.

**stepped order** See *rank-size rule.

**stepwise migration** A type of migration which occurs in a series of movements, for example, from a hamlet to a village, from a village to a town, and from a town to a city.

**stereoscope** A type of binocular used to create a three-dimensional image from two photographs, usually *aerial photographs, taken at different angles but of the same area.

**Stevenson screen** A white, wooden box with louvred sides, standing, on legs, about 1 m above the ground, and made to protect the meteorological instruments inside it from strong winds and radiation.

**stillstand** A time of *tectonic inactivity between phases of movement. The term is also used to indicate a time when sea level remains constant.

**stimulus-response theory** The basis of *behaviourism which sees human behaviour as a learned response to stimuli. This approach reduces the environment to a set of stimuli, ignores the way that man creates his reality, and sees the mind as a 'black box' with no need to understand it. Most stimulus-response theory is based on work with animals.

**stochastic** Governed by the laws of probability. A **stochastic model** shows probable changes through time.

**stock** 1. An irregular igneous *intrusion which cuts across the strata of the *country rock. A stock is similar to a *batholith, but is much smaller.
   2. The material components of the environment including mass and energy, and biotic or abiotic matter. A stock becomes a *resource when it is of use to man.

**stocking rate** The number of livestock per unit area.

**Stone Age** The period, in Britain, from about 25 000 years BP to around 20 000 years BP. During this time people first made implements and weapons of stone. It is the first major phase of prehistoric culture.

**stone pavement** In a *periglacial landscape, pavements of large boulders on saturated land in valley floors. It has been suggested that the larger stones have been pushed up to the surface, leaving behind a silty layer. Unlike *felsenmeer, the stones are not thought to be in their original sites.

**stoping** The assimilation at depth of *country rock by an igneous *intrusion. The heat of the intrusion melts the country rock which then mingles with the *magma.

**store cattle** Cattle bought or bred for fattening, thence to be sold to a butcher.

**storm beach** *Shingle thrown above the level of normal or *spring tides by very strong storm waves.

**storm surge** Conditions of very low pressure over the sea can cause the water to rise. When this is combined with strong onshore winds, water 'piles up' and there is an unusual, rapid rise in tide level above the normal high water mark.

**stoss** The side of a feature facing upwind, upstream, or up-glacier.

**stoss and lee topography** A glaciated landscape where the landforms facing up-glacier show erosion while their lee sides show a degree of protection from glacial erosion. See also *crag and tail.

**strait** A narrow stretch of water linking two larger bodies of water.

**strandflat** An extensive *shore platform up to 65 km in width along the coast of Norway. Its formation has been variously attributed to *frost shattering, glacial erosion, and periglacial erosion.

**Straßendorf** A *street village.

**strath** In Scotland, a broad valley.

**stratification** A sorting or arrangement into layers, hence **stratified**. In geology, stratification is a feature of most *sedimentary, and some *igneous, rocks. In meteorology, it is the formation of stable layers in the atmosphere.

**stratified society** A society marked by more or less distinct social levels, perhaps arranged by birth, occupation, or wealth.

**stratigraphy** The study of the divisions of rocks in time and of the links between similar rocks as they occur in different areas.

**strato-, stratus** Layered cloud. See *cloud.

**stratosphere** A layer of the earth's atmosphere, above the *troposphere, 50 km in depth. Within the stratosphere, temperatures remain constant until the 'ceiling' of the stratosphere, the **stratopause**, is reached.

**stratum, pl. strata** In geology, a layer of distinctive deposits with surfaces roughly parallel to those above and below.

**stream order** The numbering of streams in a network. There are many different methods; the most widely used is that of Strahler. This system classes all unbranched streams as **first order streams**. When two first order streams meet, the resulting channel is a **second order stream**. Where two second order streams meet a **third order stream** results, and so on. Any tributary of a lower order than the main channel is ignored. This system is not ideal—there are other more appropriate methods—but it is the most widely used.

**streamsink** An opening in the earth, usually produced by the solution of limestone, down which surface streams and ground water disappear.

**stream stage** The height of a stream in relation to its banks, variously described as *bankfull stage, *flood stage, and *overbank stage.

**street village** The German Straßendorf; a settlement of linear form strung out along a routeway. Most street villages grew up as Dark Age German colonists moved eastwards into the forests of Central Europe, cutting roads as they went.

**strength** In geomorphology, the resistance of a rock mass to rupture under stress. **Intact strength** is the strength of a rock with no fissures or *joints. **Mass strength** is the strength of the rock including joints and fractures.

Strength varies with the following factors, in order of importance: the spacing of joints, the cohesion and *frictional force of the rock, the *dip of any fissures, the state of weathering of the rock, the width of fissures, the movement of water in or out of the rock mass, the continuity of the fissures, and the amount of infilling of soil within the fissures.

**strength theory** The assertion that *migration occurs when individuals are economically secure, rather than weak, but the move may still be made for increased income or better *amenity.

**stress** The force applied to a unit area of a substance measured in newtons per $m^2$. Compressive stress crushes the rock which may collapse as the air pockets within it are compressed. Tensile stress is a force which tends to pull a rock or soil apart and which may cause fractures and pores to open. A *shear stress deforms a rock or soil by one part sliding over another.

**striation** A long scratch biting into a rock surface. Most **glacial striations** are a result of *abrasion by the fragments incorporated in the ice. These striations are only a few millimetres across.

**strike** Just as the *dip of a slope is the difference in inclination from the vertical, so the strike is its difference in inclination from the horizontal.

**strike fault** A *fault with a *strike parallel to the strike of the strata involved.

**strike-slip fault** A *fault with movement transverse to the *strike of the strata.

**strike valley** A valley aligned with the *strike of the rocks in which it lies.

**string bog** In a *periglacial landscape, a marshy area which contains ridges of peat, and, for most of the year, ice within the peat. Peat-forming plants tend to grow in clumps, initiating the ridges, which are separated by shallow depressions occupied by ponds and lakes.

**strip cultivation** In Britain and Western Europe, a medieval form of land use. Large fields are divided into parallel strips, each tenant or owner farming one or more strips.

**strip mining** The removal of the *overburden to expose and extract mineral deposits by the use of excavators and drag lines. Permission for strip mining is often granted only if the company replaces the overburden when mining is complete.

**strombolian eruption** Volcanic activity, relatively frequent and mild, in which gases escape at intervals, producing small explosions.

**structural adjustment** See *restructuring.

**structuralism** A methodology concerned with a logic which underlies human behaviour. This logic is based on the nature of the structures within which an individual operates. Thus, what individuals do may be what they are permitted to do by the overall circumstances—structures—in which they operate. These structures are the rules, conventions, and restraints upon which human behaviour is based. For example, within the structure of capitalism, the location of industry may be seen in terms of the maximization of revenue. However, a 'green' interpretation would look for a site where environmental damage is least. Other structures might be based on *Marxism or on the search for better *amenities.

**structural shift** See *shift share analysis.

**structure** The configuration of the rocks of the earth's surface. Structures vary from the small, as in the columnar structure of a rock, to the large, as in *basin and range structure.

**Student's $t$-test** Two versions of the $t$-test may be used. For *matched samples, the technique is used to establish whether the values come from populations with the same mean. It is used for small samples, usually less than thirty, expressed in *interval level measurements.

**stump** A *stack almost reduced to sea level by *marine erosion.

**subaerial** Occurring on land, at the earth's surface, as opposed to under water or underground.

**Sub-Atlantic** A climatic phase, lasting in Britain from 2500 BP to the present day. Temperatures are lower than in the

*Sub-Boreal but still moderate and humid. Lime trees gave way to oak, beech, and elm.

**Sub-Boreal** A climatic phase, lasting in Britain from 5000 BP to 2500 BP. Conditions were drier than in the phase before, and oak gave way to ash, birch, and pine.

**subcontinent** A land mass, such as India, which is large, but not as large as a continent, and not as distinct.

**subduction** The transformation into *magma of a *plate as it dives under another plate.

**subduction zone** A zone where rocks of an oceanic plate are forced to plunge below much thicker continental crust. As the plate descends it melts and is released into the *magma below the earth's crust. Such a zone is marked by volcanoes and earthquakes.

**subglacial** At the base of a glacier; hence **subglacial channel** formed of meltwater, and **subglacial moraine**.

**subgraph** In *network analysis, the graphs, or networks, forming an unconnected part of a whole graph or network.

**subhumid** Of a climate, wet enough to lack *xerophytic vegetation, but not wet enough for tree growth; the climate of, for example, the Great Plains of the USA.

**sublimation** A direct change of state from a solid to a gas omitting the liquid stage.

**sublittoral zone** That zone of the sea between the lowest mark of ordinary tides to the end of the *continental shelf.

**submarine** Under the surface of, or at the bed of, the sea. Hence, **submarine ridge** as an alternative to mid-*oceanic ridge. **Submarine canyons** are steep-sided valleys of the *continental shelf.

**submerged coast** A coastline formed when sea level rose and which thus may be characterized by *rias, *fjards, *fiords, or **submerged forests**.

**subsequent drainage** Drainage which results from the lines of weakness on the rocks in the area it flows over.

**subsequent streams** Rivers running down the *strike of usually weak *strata, or along the line of a fault. Subsequent streams usually run at right angles to *consequent streams of which they are frequently tributaries.

**subsidence** Sinking to a lower level; of part of the earth's crust, or of air. The latter may bring about a **subsidence inversion** as descending air warms *adiabatically to a temperature above that of the air beneath. See *inversion.

**subsistence economy** An economy with little or no cash, but possibly with bartering.

**subsistence farming** A form of agriculture where almost all the produce goes to feed and support the household and is not for sale.

**subsoil** Part of the soil below the layer normally used in cultivation to the depth to which most plant roots grow.

**subtopia** A satirical term applied by Nairn to low-density urban sprawl characterized by 'abandoned aerodromes, fake rusticity, wire fences, traffic roundabouts, [and] car parks'.

**subtropical** The term is used loosely to refer either to regions which experience some features of *tropical meteorology during part of the year, or to regions of near-tropical climate.

A more precise definition denotes those areas lying between the Tropic of Cancer and 40 °N. and the Tropic of Capricorn and 40 °S.

**subtropical anticyclones** Areas of high pressure brought about when air which has risen in the tropics subsides in *subtropical areas. The air is warmed *adiabatically as it descends; therefore rainfall is unlikely.

Some authorities think that the subtropical anticyclones are the key to the world's surface winds, as they affect both the *trade winds and the *westerlies.

**subtropical high** A belt of almost permanent high pressure around 30 °N. and 30 °S.

It is formed when equatorial air which has risen to the tropopause (see *troposphere) fans out northwards and southwards and then subsides at these latitudes.

**subtropical jet stream** A *jet stream blowing above the *Hadley cells.

**suburb** One-class communities located at the edge of the city and developed at low rates of housing per acre. The provision of open space is a characteristic feature. See *suburbanization.

**suburbanization** The creation of residential areas and, to some extent industry, at the edge of the city. The term suburb usually indicates an area of houses set apart and open spaces. Suburbanization is the result of public transport, mass car ownership, pressure on space within the city, natural increase in the city, and the freedom of *footloose industries from locational constraints.

**suburbia** The *suburbs, often used as a pejorative.

**succession, plant succession** A series of complexes of plant life at a particular site. In theory, plant succession is viewed as the growth and development of plant life, on originally bare earth, with a definite sequence of communities.

**succession and invasion** In *urban geography, a change in the nature of the residents, or in the land use, of an urban area.

**succulent** A plant which stores water in its stem or leaves; a type of *xerophyte.

**sudd** In North-East Africa, a mass of vegetation floating on water. It may cause flooding or the creation of a marsh.

**suitcase farmer** A farmer whose holdings are scattered; he or she moves from one site to another as they need attention.

**sulphur dioxide** A gas given off when *fossil fuels, especially coal and crude oil, are burned and which contributes to the problem of *acid rain. It is also produced naturally in volcanic eruptions.

**summer solstice** See *solstice.

**sunbelt** In the USA, the southern and western states which are experiencing major in-migration from the states of the north-east (the snow belt, or frost belt). Movement to the sunbelt states is based on their resources, their *amenity, and, supposedly, cheap non-unionized labour. This movement has been stimulated by federal investment in aerospace and micro-computers.

**sunspot** A dark area on the surface of the sun which emits increased *solar radiation. The numbers of sunspots vary, but they seem to be at a maximum every eleven years.

**supercooling** The cooling of a substance below the temperature at which a change of state would be expected. For example, supercooled water droplets may exist in clouds at −20 °C. When these collide with an aeroplane, they immediately freeze and become a hazard.

**superficial** At the surface. In geology, *Quaternary deposits such as *alluvium, *colluvium, *till, or *loess are classified as **superficial deposits** which have been transported from their place of origin. The term *surface deposit is synonymous.

**superglacial, supraglacial** At the surface of a glacier; hence a **superglacial stream**.

**superimposed drainage** A pattern of rivers which have been let down on to a very different underlying structure from the one on which they were formed. Thus, the radiating drainage pattern of the Lake District is thought to be one formed on a dome which has subsequently been removed by erosion, revealing very different geological structures.

**superimposition, law of** That in a series of sedimentary rocks the oldest strata are at the bottom, except in cases of severe faulting or folding.

**supermarket** A self-service shop providing most foodstuffs under one roof and with an area of at least 185 m². A **superstore** is larger and provides clothing and consumer goods as well as foodstuffs. Most superstores are located at the edge of urban areas where land is cheaper and parking is easy.

**superpowers** The USA and USSR, both characterized by very great areal extent, by large populations, and by formidable military power.

**supersaturation** Of a solution which contains more solute than it can theoretically contain when it is saturated. In meteorology, it occurs when air is more than saturated with water vapour, but when condensation does not occur because of a lack of *condensation nuclei.

**superstructure** According to Marx, the institutions of society; the legal and institutional forms of the social system. These include the state, the law, government and official power, and the body of moral, political, religious, and philosophical beliefs. Marx believed that changes in the economic base would lead to a transformation of the superstructure.

**supply and demand** The availability of goods and services and the willingness of the customer to buy. These forces determine prices in a free-market economy.

**supply curve** A graphical representation of how much of a good will be supplied at a given price. With supply on the horizontal axis and price on the vertical axis, a typical supply curve slopes upwards and to the right because supply tends to increase as the price paid to the supplier increases.

**supraglacial** *Superglacial.

**surazo** A cold winter wind of the Brazilian *campo.

**surface deposit** Also known as superficial, this is unconsolidated material such as *alluvium, *colluvium, *drift, or *loess, which has been transported from its place of origin.

**surface wash** Mostly *overland flow, with *raindrop erosion.

**surface wave** See *earthquake.

**surge phenomena** See *eddy.

**survey** A gathering of data.

**survey analysis** The different research methods used to collect and analyse data not available from other sources. These data are usually elicited from questionnaires.

**survivorship curve** A plot of population figures against time for a group born in the same year, showing how many remain after each year, starting from birth.

**suspended load** The very fine particles of silt and clay hanging in, and carried by, a stream.

**suspension** The state in which small particles of an insoluble material are evenly distributed within a fluid such as water or air. Particles may be carried upwards when *turbulence outstrips the force of gravity.

**sustainable development** A form of development based on wise management of resources and which should therefore have some long-lasting success.

**sustained-yield resource** A resource which is managed such that it may be regarded as *renewable. Forestry may be managed as a slow-growing but renewable resource of fuel and timber and a sustained-yield recreational resource. Sustaining the recreational appeal of forests as more and more visitors flock in may be more difficult than sustaining the timber flow.

**swallow hole** A vertical or near-vertical shaft down which a stream disappears in areas of limestone topography.

**swash** The water moving up a beach from a wave.

**swathe** In *remote sensing, a strip of the earth's surface scanned by an orbiting sensor.

**S-wave** Shake wave. See *earthquake.

**swell** In seas or large lakes, large, undulating waves which do not break.

**swidden cultivation** *Shifting cultivation. Despite the unstable appearance of the swidden system, since land use changes every two years, it can be said that it is a stable response to the environment as it mimics the exchange of elements occurring naturally.

**symbiosis** An association of two participants whereby both partners benefit. Thus, flowering plants rely on insects for pollination and the insects feed on their nectar. Lichens are an amalgamation of fungus and algae so close that it is difficult to separate them. Such an interdependence may be termed mutualism. Measures of interdependence vary from total to slight.

**symbiotic relationship** An association of two different organisms living together to their mutual benefit. Originally a biological term, the words have been extended to cover relationships between humans.

**symbol** In cartography, a drawing used to indicate the presence of a certain feature on a map.

**symmetry** Of a shape which may be divided into two parts, one the mirror image of the other, around a central axis. In a **symmetrical fold**, both limbs dip away from the axis at the same angle.

**sympatric** Living in the same region. The term is used by ecologists to specify separate species whose territories overlap. Different species can occupy the same geographical location and yet still have individual *niches as they use different parts of the environment.

**synchronic analysis** The study of the internal linkages of a system at a given point in time. An example from *historical geography is the taking of *cross-sections.

**synclinal valley** A valley formed by a down*fold.

**syncline** A downfold of rock *strata. See also *fold.

**synclinorium** See *fold.

**synoptic chart** A map on which are plotted the data of weather phenomena for a given area at a particular point in time. Pressure in *isobars is shown together with cloud cover (see *okta), temperature, wind speed and direction, and *precipitation. **Synoptic meteorology** is concerned with the outline of present meteorology and the forecasting of future weather.

**synoptic image** An image of a large part of the earth's surface as provided by a *remote sensor.

**system** Any set of interrelated parts. A system can consist entirely of abstract ideas, but geographers prefer to use the concept in such fields as ecology, hydrology, and geomorphology. An **open system** allows mass and energy to circulate into and out of it; a **closed system** gives and receives energy and not mass.

A system deals with inputs, throughput, and outputs. Systems usually have a negative feedback, i.e. a redress of balance such that a kind of equilibrium is maintained. An example of this is the performance of a hillslope: *increased* mass movement downslope leads to *decreased* stream erosion at the base of the slope.

Systems may be studied at all scales and it should be noted that each system is part of a larger system. Thus, an oak leaf system is part of an oak tree system which is part of an oak wood system . . . and so on. It is difficult to establish the boundaries of a system. Using this latter example, we must decide upon what constitutes an oak wood.

In a **cascading system**, a series of small subsystems are linked from one system to another.

**systematic geography** As opposed to regional geography, which is concerned with the many aspects of a region, this is the study of the earth's surface aspect by aspect; for example, settlement, industry, geomorphology, and meteorology.

# T

**tableland** A *plateau bounded by steep drops.

**tafone**, pl. **tafoni** See *weathering pits.

**taiga** The predominantly coniferous forest located south of the *tundra in northern continents.

**tail** The tapering end of those parts of a frequency distribution away from the arithmetic mean. Statistically, a **one-tailed test** investigates only one end of a distribution; a **two-tailed test** investigates both ends.

**take-off** See *Rostow's model of growth.

**talik** Within a *permafrost zone, the layer of unfrozen ground that lies between the permafrost and the seasonally thawed *active layer. The development of talik is promoted by the presence of lakes and rivers.

**talus** A *scree slope formed of *frost-shattered rock *debris which has fallen from the peaks above or crept downslope: **talus creep.** Some writers use the term talus as a synonym for scree; others use the term to indicate the origin and type of slope which is usually straight, and at an angle of 34–35°.

**tank** In Pakistan, India, Bangladesh, and Sri Lanka, a small pool made by damming a stream in order to conserve rainwater from the monsoon.

**tapering** 1. Of freight rates, the lowering of transport costs per unit distance with an increasingly long journey.
    2. The *distance decay effect where the benefits of a *public good decline with distance from the point of supply.

**tariff** A list of duties or customs to be paid on imports. **Preferential tariffs** reduce import duties on products of a certain type or origin and **retaliatory tariffs** are levied by a nation whose exports are taxed by a trading partner. Tariffs may be imposed to reduce imports or to protect domestic industry from foreign competition.

**tarn** A small mountain lake.

**tear faults** A fault characterized by lateral movement, transverse to the *strike of the rocks.

**technology** The techniques, tools, and instruments used by man in his various activities.

**tectonic** Of, or concerned with, the processes acting to shape the earth's crust. See also *plate tectonics.

**tectonostratigraphic terrane** See *terrane.

**teleconnections** Events in the atmosphere which occur simultaneously but in areas very far apart. An example is the sinking of air over the eastern South Pacific and the rising of air over Indonesia.

**teleology** The theory that events can only be explained and that evaluation of anything can only be justified by considering the ends towards which they are directed.

**temperate** Not extreme, especially of a climate. The **temperate latitudes** range from the *tropics to the Arctic and Antarctic Circles. The term mid-latitudes is often used as an alternative since these latitudes often enjoy intemperate weather.

**temperate glacier** *Warm glacier.

**temperature anomaly** A temperature much higher or lower than expected in a given location. Cold currents, for example, can produce unexpectedly low temperatures; warm currents, unexpectedly high.

**tenant capital** The equipment, such as livestock, seed, fertilizers, machinery, and cash supplied by a tenant in an agricultural system.

**tensile stress** See *stress.

**tension** A stretching force in the earth's surface which may cause faulting or jointing. Compare with *compression.

**tenure** The right to, or the holding of, an office or property. See *land tenure.

**tephigram** A graph displaying the thermodynamic properties of the atmosphere. Five properties are shown: temperature in *isotherms, pressure in *isobars, dry adiabats, saturated adiabats (see *adiabatic), and saturation mixing ratio lines. The plotting of data received from meteorological balloons can indicate future cloud levels and the likelihood of rain and fog.

**tephra** A deposit made of fragments of rock shattered by an explosive volcanic eruption.

**terminal costs** Transport costs incurred by the handling of goods at each end of a route. If these costs are a major element in the price of transport, then *line-haul costs are of minor importance. In such cases, distance is not an important part of transport costs.

**terms of trade** Within a country, the relationship between the prices of imports and exports. The trend in this century has been for cheap primary products and expensive manufactured goods. This has acted adversely on developing countries and has led to policies of industrialization, aimed at import substitution, in the Third World.

**ternary diagram** A triangular graph used to illustrate the percentages only of three components where the total percentage is 100%.

**terrace** In geomorphology, a level or nearly level narrow tract of land formed on one or both sides of a lake, river, sea, or valley. **Terrace gravel** may remain on a river terrace after the finer *alluvium has been eroded away.

**terrace cultivation** Farming a series of steps, often bordered by small walls, on a hillside. The practice may arise from a lack of level land or from an attempt to check soil erosion.

**terracette** A small terrace, about 50 cm across, and closely spaced with other terracettes. They rise above each other in steps of less than 1 m. Terracettes are held to be evidence of soil creep, but the cause of these features is uncertain.

**terrain** An area of land, often seen in terms of its distinctive relief.

**terrane** Properly known as a **tectonostratigraphic terrane**, this is a crustal block, not necessarily of uniform composition, bounded by faults, and with a history distinct from adjoining terranes. Moving at 10 cm per year, a terrane, sometimes as large as India, can circle the globe in only 400 million years. Many continents are patchwork agglomerates of terranes.

**terra rossa** A red *intrazonal soil developed in Mediterranean regions by the weathering of limestone. The soil has a clay-loam texture and its red coloration comes from the dissociation of clay to form iron oxide. *Leaching during the winter rain makes the soil acid.

**terra roxa** The deep red, rich soil of southeast Brazil.

**terrestrial** 1. On land, as opposed to water. 2. Of the earth.

**terrestrial magnetism** See *geomagnetism.

**terrestrial radiation** This is the heat radiated from the earth. The wavelength of *solar radiation reaching the earth is short and does not heat the atmosphere through which it passes. It does, however, heat the earth's surface. In turn, and particularly on clear nights, much of this heat is radiated away from the earth. It is by longwave terrestrial radiation that the earth's atmosphere is heated. About one-third of the solar radiation intercepted by earth is radiated back into space.

**territoriality** The need by an individual or group to establish and hold an area of land. In animals, territoriality is an urge, fuelled by aggression, to define a territory for mating and food supply. In human beings, on the other hand, it is more an organization of space in order to make sense of it. The individual needs security and identity and this is shown most clearly in relation to the home which provides security of mind and body and a relatively threat-free environment. The community requires a suburb or small town with which to associate, providing an identity and the means of communicating that identity.

**territorial justice** The application of ideas of social justice to an area of territory; the deliberate policy of redressing an imbalance. Since social justice varies according to the *mode of production and the nature of the *social formation, territorial justice cannot be the same universally.

**territorial production complex, TPC** A type of large-scale industrial complex identified by Soviet planners. It is part of an industrial hierarchy, below the national economy and the major industrial unit, but above specific industrial centres. The term refers to planned development and not to spontaneously arising industrial complexes.

**territorial seas** The coastal waters together with the sea bed beneath them and the air space above them, over which a state claims *sovereignty. Traditionally, this area included all the coastal waters up to 3 nautical miles from the coast. The definition of a landward baseline has been problematical for countries, such as Norway, with a deeply indented coastline. In such cases, a baseline is drawn to link the major promontories.

The extent claimed from the baseline varies. Most countries claim 12 nautical miles. In 1983, the Law of the Sea Convention proposed a 200 nautical mile Exclusive Economic Zone with rights over the sea and the resources of the sea bed. It has not been possible to demarcate such zones over most European waters since the nations are less than 400 miles apart. In such cases, a median line is drawn between the baselines of the states concerned.

**territorial social indicator** A measure of *social well-being over a given area. A set of social indicators measures the distribution and dimensions of desired social conditions. Several indicators may be used: wealth and employment, *amenity, health, social problems, social belonging, and recreation and leisure. The availability and selection of these data may vary from place to place.

**territory** 1. The living space of an animal which it will defend from the forays of other territorial animals. Animals need space in which to reproduce and their territory can be some or all of the following: a source of food, a source of mates, and a breeding area. When many individuals of a species divide an area into territories, the divisions may be spaces of relatively similar size. If all the available space is taken up, then the size of the population is at a maximum. The consequence of *territoriality is to set a limit to population, but this consequence is a side-effect; territoriality is not a population control device.

2. That area held by a soverign state.

**Tertiary** The earlier *period of the *Cainozoic era.

**tertiary industry** Economic activity concerned with the sale and use of economic goods and services, in other words, *service industry.

**Tethys** An ocean which developed during *Paleozoic and *Mesozoic times, running from the coast of southern Spain to South-East Asia. Great thicknesses of sediment were formed since the sea floor kept subsiding at the same rate as deposits were laid down. These sediments were compacted, subjected to volcanic action, and then uplifted and deformed by the earth movements which formed the Alps (the Alpine orogeny). But see *ophiolite.

**texture** The size and shape of particles in a soil or rock.

**thalweg** The line of the deepest flow along the course of a river. This usually crosses and recrosses the stream channel.

**theodolite** A surveying instrument composed of a small telescope which can rotate in a vertical plane to sight angles.

**thermal** 1. Of heat.
2. An updraught used by glider pilots to gain height.

**thermal depression** An area of low pressure caused by convection resulting from heating at the earth's surface, as above the Thar Desert, India, before the *monsoon.

**thermal erosion** If *permafrost melts, it is subject to *mass movement. A river which is above freezing point may melt and undercut its bank to form a **thermo-erosion niche**. The undercut portions of the bank, frozen in the upper parts, collapse and melt. This leads to mass movement of the bank downslope.

**thermal expansion** Also known as **insolation weathering**, this is the rupturing of rocks and minerals mainly as the result of large, daily temperature changes. The exterior of the rock expands more than the interior. The effectiveness of thermal expansion in an environment with no water is questioned.

**thermal low** An intense low pressure system caused by local heating of the earth's surface and leading to the rising of air by *convection. Heavy rainfall will result if the air rises and cools enough for condensation to occur.

**thermally direct cell** See *atmospheric cell.

**thermal metamorphism** *Metamorphism brought about by heat, generally from an *intrusion.

**thermal pollution** The contamination of cold water by adding warm water. Sources of heat include water used to cool electricity stations, the urban *heat island, and the construction of reservoirs. Many aquatic organisms cannot tolerate warm water.

**thermal sensing** *Remote sensing of the *infra-red radiation from a feature. It has the advantage of being able to pick up images through cloud and at night.

**thermal spring** A naturally occurring hot spring, heated by *geothermal heat.

**thermal stratification** Of a lake, a series of fairly well-marked layers of water at different temperatures.

**thermal weathering** The weathering of rocks, achieved by exposure to the sun. The outer zone expands on heating, pulling away from the still unheated rock below. It is doubted that thermal weathering alone can cause disintegration; water on the rocks is probably a contributory factor.

**thermal wind** Not a real wind, but the difference between the *vector of an upper-level wind and the lesser vector of a lower-level wind. It is thus an expression of the wind shear between the two layers under consideration.

**thermocirque** A large hollow on a hillside formed from the coalescence of *nivation hollows. Thermocirques are shallow because the centre of the hollow is protected from further erosion by a covering of snow.

**thermodynamic diagram** A type of graph, of which the *tephigram is an example, plotting the qualities of the atmosphere. Such diagrams are used as aids to weather forecasting.

**thermo-electricity** Power produced from a range of fuels such as coal, oil, peat, lignite, nuclear fuels, or *geothermal heat which drive steam turbines or internal combustion engines to turn over the generators.

**thermokarst** The irregular landscape typical of a *periglacial region. The term 'karst' is used to indicate a number of features formed by subsidence and does not imply the presence or development of a limestone landscape.

**thermosphere** A layer of the upper atmosphere above about 80 km from the earth's surface where temperatures increase with height.

**Thiessen polygon** A subdivision of a drainage basin, containing a rain gauge. Polygons are constructed by first siting the rain gauges. Their locations are plotted on a base map. These points are connected by drawing straight lines between the sites. The lines are bisected with perpendiculars which meet to form the polygons. The areas of the polygons are calculated and expressed as fractions of the total area. Each fraction is multiplied by the precipitation recorded by its rain gauge. The sum of these calculations represents total precipitation over the catchment area.

**thinning** The extraction of some of the young trees in a forest so that the remainder grow and develop fully. The aim is to remove as much timber as possible while maintaining output.

**Third World** All those countries deemed to be *less developed. Many indicators from per capita *GDP or *GNP to infant mortality may be used to judge the less developed status of a country, and many countries qualify for Third World status in some respects only. For example, Saudi Arabia is of developed status in terms of per capita GDP, but of less developed status in terms of infant mortality.

**thorn forest** Tropical woodland of *xerophytic thorny trees.

**Thornthwaite's climatic classification** A classification based on the usefulness of *precipitation to plants, thermal efficiency, and the moisture index, where

$$MI = \frac{100(P - PE)}{PE}$$

MI = moisture index
P = precipitation
PE = potential *evapotranspiration
Using these indices, six broad types may be distinguished:
perhumid: moisture index over 100
humid: moisture index 20 to 100
moist subhumid: moisture index 0 to 20
dry: moisture index − 20 to 0
semi-arid: moisture index − 20 to − 40
arid: moisture index below − 40.

**three-field system** A farming system, prevalent in medieval lowland Britain, whereby two of the three fields were cultivated while the third field was left fallow to recover its fertility. The crops were then rotated so that a different field was left fallow.

**threshold population** The minimum population needed to justify the provision of a certain good or service. This may be crudely expressed in population numbers although purchasing power may be a better yardstick for commercial goods or services. The threshold is demonstrated by the provision of medical services ranging from a district nurse to a GP to a hospital with consultants and finally to a specialist hospital, such as Great Ormond Street Hospital for Sick Children. Each good or service may have two limits: the inner area containing the threshold population and the outer area bounded by the *range of the good or service. The actual evaluation of the threshold population for most goods and services is difficult.

**throughfall** See *interception.

**throughflow** The movement downslope of water through the soil. Throughflow is a major factor in the hydrology of a drainage basin where the rock underlying the soil is impermeable. See *interflow.

**throw** Of a fault, the vertical displacement of strata along a fault line.

**thrust** A movement causing the formation of a reverse fault of a very low angle.

**thrust fault** A low-angled fault where the upper limb has broken at the axis and has been pushed well ahead of the lower limb.

**thrust plane** The low-angle fault face over which movement occurs.

**thufur** A low mound which forms part of a polygonal pattern in *periglacial areas.

**thunder** When a stroke of lightning passes through the atmosphere, the air becomes intensely hot, perhaps to 30 000 ˚C. The violent expansion of this heated air causes a shock wave which is heard as thunder.

**thunderstorm** A period of heavy rain with *thunder and *lightning.

**tidal** Of the tide. A **tidal current** is a strong rush of sea water associated with the movements of the tides, that is, the **tidal streams**. **Tidal flats** are areas of mud and sand uncovered only at low tide. The difference between the levels of high and low tides is the **tidal range**.

**tidal barrage** A barrier built across an estuary or arm of the sea to create a reservoir of water. The energy reflected in the tides can be used to generate electricity. See *tidal energy.

**tidal energy** Energy based on the motions of the tide. Schemes to use tidal energy have been implemented at the Rance Barrage Tidal Scheme near Saint-Malo in France and on the east coast of Canada.

**tidal wave** See *tsunami.

**tide** The twice daily rise and fall of sea level. Tides are the result of the pull exerted on the earth by the gravity of the moon and of the sun. This pull affects the land masses as well as the oceans but the reaction of the water is much greater and much more apparent. The moon 'pulls out' two bulges of water from each side of the earth. These bulges are fixed and the earth moves through them. This gives high water twice daily.

The sun also attracts water. When the effects of both sun and moon coincide, twice monthly in the second and fourth quarters of the moon, high **spring tides** occur. When the sun and moon seem to be at right angles to each other with the earth, the forces of moon and sun are opposed to each other, and lower, **neap tides** result.

The vertical distance between high and low tides is the **tidal range**. All places with a high tidal range have strong tidal currents, but swift currents can also occur in localities of low tidal range.

**tierra caliente** In much of northern Latin America and Central America, distinct climatic zones correlate with altitude. The lowest is the tierra caliente extending to 1000 m and with a humid, hot climate.

**tierra fria** A climatic zone of northern Latin America and Central America. It extends from 1000 m to 1800 m, above the *tierra caliente. Temperatures are mild to warm.

**tierra helada** One of the climatic zones of northern Latin America and Central America, stretching from 3000 m. It is the highest of the four zones and is permanently covered with snow.

**tierral templada** The climatic zone found between 1800 and 3000 in northern Latin America and Central America. Temperatures are warm.

**till** The substance of which *moraines are made. It is the sediment which is deposited directly from a glacier, and which exhibits a wide range of particle sizes, from fine clay to rock fragments and boulders.

Some tills are classified by means of their origin: *ablation, or meltwater till, *lodgement till, and *sublimation till. **Flow till** is created when saturated debris found at the top of the ice, flows into depressions within the ice, and is then deposited. A **till plain** blankets the ground, with only a few mounds and ridges poking through.

**till fabric analysis** The study of the fabric of *till to determine the movements of the glacier under which it formed.

**tilt block** A block of crust demarcated by two *faults at an angle to the rocks around.

**time–space convergence** Places are separated by absolute distance and by time. With improvements in transport systems, this time-distance diminishes. Janelle expressed the rate at which this takes place as:

$$\frac{TT_1 - TT_2}{Y_1 - Y_2}$$

where $TT_1$ and $TT_2$ are travel times in different years and where $Y_1$ and $Y_2$ are the relevant years.

**time–space geography** An approach to geography developed at the University of Lund by Hägerstrand and his associates. Time and space provide the room needed for sequences of events and Hägerstrand expressed this as a web model. This is based on four propositions: that space and time are scarce resources which individuals draw on to achieve their aims, that achieving an aim is subject to *capability constraints, *coupling constraints, and *authority constraints, that these constraints interact to demarcate a series of probability boundaries, and that choices are made within these boundaries. Time–space geography provides a method of mapping spatial movements through time.

**time–space prism** The representation of the constraints limiting the time within which the individual can act.

**time zone** A division of the earth's surface, usually extending across 15° of longitude, devised such that the standard time is the time at a meridian at the centre of the zone.

**tithe** A local tax first levied in England in the fourth century to pay for the church and its clergy. Tithes were at first paid in kind but subsequently commuted into money terms. The last tithes will lapse in 1996. In medieval England, the crops paid as tithes were stored in **tithe barns**.

**tolerance** The ability of an organism to survive environmental conditions. The prefixes *eury-* and *steno-* refer to wide and narrow ranges of tolerance respectively. An organism can be widely tolerant of one factor, such as temperature (eurythermal), but narrowly tolerant of another, such as salinity (stenohaline).

**tombolo** A spit which joins an offshore island to the mainland.

**tonne** Also known as a **metric ton**, this weighs 1000 kg, 2204.62 lb, or 0.984 of an imperial ton.

**tonnage** The carrying capacity of a ship measured by weight.

**topographic(al) map** A map which indicates, to scale, the natural features of the earth's surface, as well as human features. The features are shown at the correct relationship to each other.

**topological map** A map designed to show only a selected feature, such as the stations on the London underground. Locations are shown as dots, with straight lines connecting them. Distance, scale, and relative orientation are not important.

**topophilia** The feeling of affection which individuals have for particular places. 'Places' in this sense may vary in scale from a single room to a nation or continent.

**topple** A form of *mass movement from a rock face where top-heavy rocks with vertical or forward-leaning bedding planes are separated from the bedrock and fall. As the rock peels from the top of the free face, it turns.

**topsoil** The cultivated soil; the surface soil as opposed to the *subsoil.

**tor** An upstanding mass of rocks or boulders which rises above the gentler slopes which surround it. Tors are thought to have been formed by *frost shattering in *periglacial conditions. This theory is disputed by those who maintain that tors form underground during the deep weathering typical of tropical areas. In this case, the tors are first formed before the *overburden is eroded away to reveal the boulders. According to these theories tors are examples of *relict landforms.

**tornado** A destructive, rotating storm under a funnel-shaped cloud which advances over the land along a narrow path. Such a storm is most common in 'tornado alley', extending from northern Texas through Oklahoma, Kansas, and Missouri, with as many as 300 tornadoes a year.

The exact mechanism of its formation is not fully understood, but tornadoes are associated with intense local heating coupled with the meeting of warm, moist air from the Gulf of Mexico and cold air from the *basin and range area of the western United States. Tornadoes are often associated with hurricanes.

**tourism** Making a holiday involving an overnight stay away from the normal place of residence. This is in contrast to recreation which involves leisure activities lasting less than 24 hours. This holiday may be based on the cultural, historic, and social attractions of an urban centre, or on the appeal of a different environment. Urban tourism increases the importance of the *central place while tourism at the periphery can provide the income for economic development.

**tower karst** Limestone towers, from 30 to 200 m in height with nearly vertical walls and gently domed or serrated summits. The towers stand above large, flat *flood plains and swamps and show undercutting from rivers and swamps. Tower karsts are thought to represent the last remnant of a limestone outcrop.

**town** A relatively small urban place. No limiting figures of population or areal extent are agreed upon. Towns may be regarded as central places providing goods and services to their surroundings but without the degree of economic specialization to be found in a city. In the USA, 'town' has a particular administrative connotation.

**townscape** In urban geography, the objective, visible scene of the urban area or the subjective *image of the city. The townscape has three separate, but closely related, parts: the street plan or layout, the architectural style, and the land use.

**township** In Australia, an area of land divided into lots for potential development. In South Africa, an area of black housing.

**TPC** See *territorial production complex.

**trace element** Elements, such as manganese, zinc, copper, and cobalt, which are required in very small quantities to ensure normal development of an organism.

**trace fossil** A record in the rocks of the life of an organism but not of the organism itself, like animal tracks.

**traction** The transport of debris along a river bed by rolling and sliding, not *saltation. The load so carried is the **traction load**.

**trade** The movements of goods from producers to consumers. The classic explanation for trade is expressed in terms of *comparative advantage.

**trade gap** The shortfall of exports compared with imports.

**trade-off theory** The assertion that people balance out the cost of land and the cost of transport in choosing a place of residence. In the suburbs, land is relatively cheap but transport costs for commuters are high. In the centre of the city, land costs are higher but the journey to work is short. Any locational choice is a trading off of factors such as these.

**trade winds** The tropical *easterlies, blowing towards the equator from the *subtropical anticyclones at a fairly constant speed. In this context, the word 'trade' comes from the nautical expression 'to blow trade', i.e. to blow in a regular course.

**traffic** The movement of people and vehicles along a routeway. **Traffic capacity** is the maximum number of vehicles which can pass over a route in a given time, while **traffic density** is the existing number of vehicles.

**traffic principle** The basis of settlements about a central place such that the number of services on straight-line routes is at a maximum. The number of settlements at progressively lower levels follows the sequence 1, 4, 16 . . . This is the k = 4 hierarchy as advanced by Christaller.

**traffic segregation** The subdivision of towns and cities into certain units where road traffic is restricted and pedestrians predominate. Each of these units is linked to the rest of the town by good roads which carry most of the traffic.

**tramontana** A cold, dry wind blowing southwards from northern Italy and central Spain.

**transactional-constructivist theory** This suggests that experience and behaviour are influenced by factors acting in the transactions between the individual and the environment. The environment is seen as a complex and organized stimulus field that provides the context for human behaviour. Environmental information operates to change the mind's construction of the environment, and it is this changed mental construction that most immediately influences overt behaviour. However, transactions between man and the environment are extremely difficult to assess.

**transcurrent fault** *Strike-slip fault.

**transect** A section along a survey line used to study relationships in the landscape.

**transferability** The capacity of a good to be transported. Transferability is largely determined by transport costs and movement will take place only if the cost or *economic distance is not too great. As economic distance increases, so transferability decreases and any intervening source of goods will be used. Since economic distance and intervening opportunities vary, so transferability may change over time.

**transfer costs** Total transport costs involved in moving a cargo including extra costs such as tariffs and insurance. Transfer costs are highest for people because of the very steep cost of insurance.

**transfer price** The price set by an organization for goods which are sold from one section of the organization to another. These prices can be used to minimize taxes.

**transformation** The changing of data into another form. In this way, absolute distance may be plotted as time-distance in a *cartogram.

**transformation of data** It is possible to make inferences about data when they show a *normal distribution. However, many data are skewed, with an asymmetrical distribution. It is possible to transform the distribution to make a 'normal' shape. This may be done if the distribution has one mode. One of the most powerful transformations is to use logarithmic values for the data since logarithms 'shrink' the spread of data. A milder transformation which may be applied is the use of square roots and square values. The mean and standard deviation may then be calculated. However, the question of what is 'normal' is not always readily defined.

**transform fault** Faults which are at right angles to *sea-floor spreading. They run transverse to the faults across the *oceanic ridge. The ridge is displaced.

**transhumance** A seasonal movement of people and animals between different grazing grounds. Shepherds leave their lowland winter quarters, and move to upland, summer pastures. A farmer practising transhumance is not a nomad, since he has two fixed abodes.

**transitional zone** The area of a city immediately surrounding the *CBD. It developed during the nineteenth century for residential purposes but is now an area of mixed use such as industry, shops and offices, poor housing, and multi-occupation of units.

**translocation** In soil science, the transfer of substances in solution or suspension from one *horizon to another.

**transpiration** See *evapotranspiration.

**transportation problem** The difficulty of finding the least-cost routes of flows between the origins of goods and their ultimate destinations, given details of transport costs and the volumes of supply and demand.

**transport costs** Costs involved in relaying goods to and from a plant, including payments to transport firms for their services and any cost incurred by a plant in using and maintaining its own fleet of vehicles. Generally speaking, transport costs have fallen relatively as a result of improvements in transport technology and transport infrastructure. Early *location theory was based on transport costs.

**transport geography** A branch of human geography concentrating on the movement of people and goods, the patterns of such movements, the volume of people and goods carried, the price of transport, and the role of transport in economic, political, and social development.

**transverse** Across. A **transverse coast** is an *Atlantic-type coast with the lie of the land at right angles to the coast. A **transverse dune** is at right angles to the direction of the prevailing wind. A **transverse ridge** is one at the sea floor, running at right angles to a mid-*oceanic ridge and often flanking a deep trough.

**travelling salesman problem** A problem of the most efficient use of a transport system in order to visit a series of places.

**traverse** In surveying, a base line from which observations are made. An **open traverse** consists of a number of traverses, each at an angle to the preceding line. With a **closed traverse**, the base lines work back to the origin of the first traverse.

**tree line** The line beyond which trees will not grow. This occurs at high latitudes, as when *taiga gives way to *tundra, or at high altitudes.

**trellised drainage** See *drainage patterns.

**trench** In *plate tectonics, a trough, which may be 4000 m below sea level, on the ocean floor.

**trend line** The lie of the structure of a region.

**trend surface map** A three-dimensional diagram showing the uptake of an innovation through time and distance. Trend surface maps may be used to separate regular patterns of regional trends from localized anomalies which have no overall pattern. Trend surface maps are like filters which cut out short-wave irregularities but allow long-wave irregularities to pass through.

**triangulation** A method of surveying using a base line and two sight lines to make a triangle. The angle from the base line of the feature to be surveyed is taken at one end of the line. The process is repeated at the other end. Given that the length of the base line is known, the location of the object relative to it may be determined.

**Triassic** The oldest *period of *Mesozoic time stretching approximately from 225 to 190 million years BP.

**tributary** A river which flows into another, usually larger one.

**tributary area** See *umland.

**trigonometrical survey** A survey using *triangulation.

**trophic level** An individual layer on the *pyramid of numbers which represents types of organisms living at parallel levels on *food chains. All herbivores live at one level, all primary carnivores on the next level, all secondary carnivores on the next level, and so on. The animals on each level are remarkably distinct in size from those on other levels; there is a clear jump in size between an insect and a bird, for example. Since some organisms alternate between a herbivorous and a carniverous diet, the concept is not always applicable.

**tropical** See *tropics.

**tropical air mass** An air mass formed at the sub-tropical *high. The mass may be formed over arid lands—continental tropical (cT)—or over the sea—maritime tropical (mT).

**tropical cyclone** See *hurricane.

**tropical easterly jet** A westward-moving *jet stream blowing in the upper atmosphere over South-East Asia.

**tropical forest** Forested areas which often extend beyond the tropics and consist of *tropical rain forest and *mangrove forest.

**tropical grassland** *Savanna, *campo, and *llano.

**tropical meteorology** In this field, the boundaries of the tropics fluctuate since they are indicated by the descending limbs of the *Hadley cells and with the centres of the *subtropical anticyclones.

The following are characteristic of tropical meteorology:

1. **Tropical wave disturbances**. These have a wavelength of 2000–4000 km,

travel across 6–7° of longitude a day, and last for about two weeks. Ahead of the trough is a ridge of high pressure bringing fine weather. With the approach of the trough, *cumulus cloud develops, wind *veers and heavy showers fall.

2. **Tropical cyclones**. See *hurricane.

3. *Monsoon depressions.

4. **Subtropical cyclones**. These occur when the cold upper air from high latitudes is cut off to form a wave some 300 km in width. They bring cloud and some rain.

5. **Tropical cloud clusters**. See *squall line.

Small-scale variations such as topography, *local winds, and *ocean currents are also of major importance. Cold ocean currents cause offshore fog, ridding the winds of much moisture. *Sea breezes then carry cool, dry air far inland. See also *Inter-Tropical Convergence Zone.

**tropical rain forest** Tropical forest of trees characterized by buttress roots, long, straight lower trunks, and leathery leaves. The vegetation shows distinct layering: the canopy, or upper layer, at around 30 m; the intermediate layer at 20–5 m; and the lower layer at around 10–15 m. Undergrowth is poorly developed but *epiphytes and *lianas are common. Deciduous trees flower, fruit, and shed their leaves at random; there is no seasonality. The range of plant and animal species is immense and many plants yield important medicinal compounds. The felling of the rain forest causes soil erosion, the destruction of potentially useful species, reduction of oxygen from photosynthesis, and the smoke of burning logs increases the quantity of *aerosols and carbon dioxide in the atmosphere. Some writers suggest that the hydrology of the earth may be altered if all the equatorial rain forest is destroyed.

**tropical revolving storm** *Hurricane.

**tropics** The **Tropic of Cancer** lies approximately along latitude 23° and 30 minutes N. Around 21–2 June, the sun's rays are perpendicular to the ground along this line and the sun exerts its maximum strength in the Northern Hemisphere. Conversely, the sun is overhead at the approximate latitude of 23° and 30 minutes S., the **Tropic of Capricorn**, on 22–3 December when the sun's heat is at its maximum in the Southern Hemisphere. Between these two lines of latitude lie the tropics.

The term 'tropical' is used less exactly in climatology, where some areas outside the tropics are said to enjoy a 'tropical climate'.

**tropophyte** A plant, such as a deciduous plant, which can survive both wet and dry seasons.

**troposphere** The lowest layer of the earth's atmosphere. Within this layer temperatures decrease with height at an average rate of 1 °C per 150 m. This layer contains 90% of the water in the atmosphere, 75% of the total gases, and nearly all the dust and liquid particles.

The depth of the troposphere is 7–8 km over the poles, but extends to 16 km over the tropics. Most of the earth's weather develops within the troposphere. The 'ceiling' of the troposphere is the **tropopause**. This is not a sharply defined layer but a series of overlapping layers separating the troposphere from the *stratosphere.

**trough** In meteorology, a narrow area of low pressure between *highs.

**truck farming** In the USA, the production of flowers, fruit, and vegetables.

**true north, true south** Pointing to the geographical North and South Poles—the northern and southern ends of the earth's axis—and not to the *magnetic Poles.

**true origin** The point of origin of a reference system of a map; the meeting place of the two axes of projection.

**tsunami** A huge sea wave. Most are brought about by earthquakes of 5.5 or more on the *Richter Scale. Other causes include submarine volcanoes, very large *landslides off coastal cliffs, or the *calving of very large icebergs from glaciers in *fiords.

**t-test** See *Student's t-test.

**tube well** A well lined with a pipe.

**tufa** A deposit of calcium carbonate found mostly in deserts along a line of once-active springs, but also in areas of limestone geology. The presence of tufa in areas which are now arid points to a time of heavier rainfall; a *pluvial.

**tuff** See *pyroclast.

**tumulus,** pl. **tumuli** A burial mound.

**tundra** The barren plains of northern Canada, the USA, and Eurasia. Temperatures and rainfall are low so that vegetation is restricted to hardy shrubs, mosses, and lichens. The lower soil is permanently frozen, so that drainage is poor. Marshes and swamps are, therefore, common in summer.

**tundra soil** A dark soil with a thick, peat layer of poorly decomposed vegetation, which is usually underlain by a frozen layer of soil. *Translocation is limited and there is, therefore, little development of *horizons. Tundra soils range from *brown earths in the more humid areas to polar desert soils in arid areas.

**tunnel valley** See *meltwater erosion.

**turbidity** A condition of suspended mud and other particles in a fluid picked up by a **turbidity current**—a churning movement in the fluid caused by earth movements or the downslope flow of debris. Turbidity currents may excavate *submarine canyons.

**turbulence** A type of flow where the particles of the fluid move in irregular paths. **Turbulent flow** is characterized by local, short-lived rotation currents known as vortices. Turbulent flow is classified according to the *Froude number of a stream.

**turnpike** A toll road. Toll roads fell into disuse in Britain with the coming of the railways, but the term is still used for certain toll roads in the USA.

**twilight area** A part of the city characterised by substandard buildings and poor facilities.

**twister** Used to describe a *tornado or a *waterspout.

**typhoon** In the China Sea, a *hurricane.

# U

**ubac** That side of a valley which receives less *insolation; the shaded side.

**ubiquitous material** Notably in *Weber's theory of industrial location, a material, like water, available anywhere and not therefore having a locational pull.

**UDA** See *Urban Development Area.

**ultisol** A soil of the *US soil classification. See *ferruginous soil.

**ultrabasic rock** An *igneous rock with less than 45% silica and more than 55% basic oxide.

**ultraviolet radiation** Short-wave radiation between X-rays and violet light. The *ozone layer absorbs much of this radiation coming in from the sun, but some reaches the earth's surface. A little is necessary for the production of vitamin D in some species, but too much ultraviolet radiation is harmful.

**umland** The area served by a city. The umland is also known as a *sphere of influence, *catchment area, *tributary area, or *urban field.

**uncertainty** The state of mind of an individual who is unable to make any estimate of future events. This differs from *risk in that the odds of an event occurring are known in a risk; uncertainty does not give any odds and all outcomes, expected or not, are possible. In the real world, decisions are often made under conditions of uncertainty since it may be difficult to predict the response of an individual to an event. When decision-makers are faced with uncertainty, they will react according to their nature. Some will assume the worst; others will hope for the best. In the former case, the individual is more concerned with possible future loss in a disaster than with gains. Most decision-makers are in the centre ground—partial optimists.

**unconformable** In geology, of a rock stratum of different *dip or *strike from the underlying strata.

**unconformity** In geology, a break in the sequence of rocks, perhaps formed when strata lying over old rocks were eroded away, after which new strata formed above the old.

**underbound(ed) city** A city where the administrative boundary encloses an area smaller than that of the city itself; the city has 'burst' its bounds.

**undercut slope** The steep slope on the outer curve of a *meander.

**undercutting** Erosion at the base of a slope, such as a cliff or river bank.

**underdeveloped country** A term now largely superseded by *developing country.

**underdevelopment** The original meaning of the term indicated that existing resources had not been exploited. The word is now close in meaning to 'poverty' although some underdeveloped countries have high incomes which are enjoyed by the few. Indicators of undevelopment include high birth rates, high infant mortality, undernourishment, a large agricultural and small industrial sector, low per capita *GDP, high levels of illiteracy, and low *life expectancy.

**underfit stream** Also known as a *misfit stream, this is a stream which flows with narrower meander belts and shorter meander wavelengths than are appropriate to the valley. It is suggested that the valley was initially formed by a river of much greater *discharge than now obtains and that an underfit stream is evidence of climatic change.

**underpopulation** Where there are too few people to develop fully the economic potential of an area or nation; a larger population could be supported on the same resource base. Such a situation obtains in the Amazon Basin, but whether it would be wise to colonize such an area is disputable.

**undertow** A strong current flowing away from the shore and near the sea bed, brought about by the *backwash of the waves.

**unemployment** The state of being involuntarily out of work. The unemployment rate is the number of unemployed as a percentage of the total population of working age. An unemployment level of under 3% is thought of as a natural rate as people change in their jobs, their residences, and their state of health. **Structural unemployment** occurs when the labour market no longer requires a particular skill, as in the case of printing newspapers; new technology and new materials replace older working habits. Unemployment is a more general term than structural unemployment and often reflects trade recession where no jobs are to be had. With **fractional unemployment** jobs are available but not taken up because of immobility or the lack of information.

**unequal slopes, law of** That, in an *asymmetrical ridge, the steeper of the two slopes will be more rapidly eroded than the gentler ones. This will cause the crest of the ridge to retreat.

**uneven development** A condition of an economy which has not benefited equally from development in a regional sense and/or within classes in society. It may also occur between consumer goods and capital goods industries and between sectors of the economy. It may be seen as a result of capitalism, based as it is on competition and *accumulation, but it is not unique to capitalism. State socialism has often led to concentration on one sector at the expense of another.

**unified field theory** The theory that concepts within political geography can be linked together. Thus, early ideas are explored until decisions are made which promote the movement of people, goods, and ideas. These movements take place within a field of circulation. Ultimately, an area emerges as an expression of the initial concept.

**uniform delivered pricing** Pricing a commodity at the same value regardless of the location of the customer. Demand will, therefore, not be affected by distance from the manufacturing point. Uniform delivered pricing is sometimes referred to as *c.i.f. pricing.

**uniformitarianism** The view that the interpretations of earth history can be based on the present-day evidence of natural processes. From this comes the maxim 'the present is the key to the past'. Although the processes may be the same, the rate of change may vary over geological time.

**unit response graph** For any *channelled flow, a *hydrograph which is produced by a storm of known rainfall.

**unloading** The removal, by erosion, of rock or, by ablation, of ice. With removal of rock or ice an exhumed landscape is revealed. The pressure release following unloading may cause the exhumed strata to 'burst' upwards.

**upwelling** The rise of sea water from depths to the surface, bringing nutrients for plankton. Many of the world's best fishing grounds are located at such points. The effect called *El niño is the failure of the Peruvian upwelling.

**urban** Of, living, or situated in a city or town. As no standard figures are given for the size of cities and towns, this concept can be rather vague. In Iceland, a settlement of 300 people is classed as urban; the figure is 10 000 in Spain. An area may be classified as urban by its role as a *central place for a tributary area, providing a range of shops, banks, and offices. A high density of population may also be used as an indicator but the city may include large areas of low density housing.

**urban blight** A run-down area of the city. Some parts of the city become outdated as buildings age and as variations occur in the type of demand. Certain activities, such as small-scale industry and warehousing, have an adverse effect on the urban environment and as neighbourhoods decline, they become prone to vandalism. Erstwhile town houses are changed to multi-occupance. Blighted urban areas of the inner city have now become a political concern and urban renewal schemes have become fashionable.

**urban climates** Built-up areas affect local climates in four major fields.

1. The atmosphere. There are 10–20 times as many *aerosols in the urban atmosphere than in rural regions. Gases such as sulphur dioxide and nitrogen dioxide are at higher concentrations. *Pollution domes are common.

2. Heat. Domestic heating, electricity production, and transport systems all give out heat. Thus, an **urban heat island** is created, with temperatures some 6–8 °C higher than those in the surrounding countryside. The amount of heating seems to be dependent on urban population densities rather than on city size.

3. Air flows. Some buildings form wind breaks; some streets form wind tunnels. *Eddying is common as air 'bounces off' tall buildings.

4. Moisture. *Runoff is rapid and plant life is relatively scarce. *Evapotranspiration is therefore lower and towns are less humid. However, rainfall in towns may be some 6–7% heavier than in the countryside.

**urban density gradient** In a city, the pattern of population density as it decreases with distance from the city centre. The formula expressing this change is:

$$d_x = d_0 \, e^{-bx}$$

where $d_x$ represents the population density at distance $x$ from the city centre, $d_0$ is the central density, $e$ is an exponent of distance, and $b$ is the rate of diminution of population with distance from the centre. Population densities are higher near the centre where the poor live on small areas of valuable land and decline with distance from the centre as the rich locate at the periphery using large areas of cheaper land.

**urban development area, UDA** Declining areas of inner cities which are scheduled for redevelopment. Development is in the hands of private entrepreneurs and is encouraged by, for example, a relaxation of planning regulations.

**urban diseconomies** Financial and social burdens arising from an urban location. These include constricted sites, high rates, traffic congestion, and pollution.

**urban ecology** A view of the city as a total environment for its inhabitants within which people organize themselves and to which people adapt.

**urban field** That area surrounding a city which is influenced by it. The inhabitants of the urban field depend on the city for services such as hospitals, higher education, employment, retailing, marketing, and finance and the city is served in its turn by labour.

The delimitation of urban fields poses problems. For example, the area served by a city newspaper may not be the same as the area served by the city's public transport. The boundary of a city is not demarcated by a single line.

There is a hierarchy of urban fields; smaller fields of a number of towns may be 'nested' within the larger urban field of a city. The fields fall into three zones: a core area composed of the built-up area of the town, an outer area which uses the town for high-order goods and services, and a fringe area which uses the urban area rarely and then only for very high-order goods and services.

**urban fringe** The area beyond the city which is affected by the city in terms of pressure on the land, higher prices, and new buildings.

**urban geography** The study of the site, evolution, morphology, spatial pattern, and classification of towns.

**urban hydrology** Urbanization changes the hydrology of a drainage basin. Roads and artificial surfaces cut down *infiltration and storage while storm sewers speed up the flow of water into rivers. It is suggested that urbanization increases the risk of flooding as rivers respond much more violently to a storm event.

**urbanism** A way of life associated with urban dwelling. Wirth suggested that urban dwellers follow a distinctly different way of life from rural dwellers. Physical and social stimuli are high and urban residents may react by becoming aloof and indifferent in their relationships with others. Stress is higher than in the country, and this is said to account for higher levels of mental illness and crime in the city.

**urbanization** This is the migration of rural populations into towns and cities; an increasing proportion of the world's population resides in towns. Urbanization indicates a change of employment structure from agriculture and *cottage industries to mass production and *service industries. This backs up the view that urbanization results from, rather than causes, social change. This is most notable in the development of capitalism and its attendant industrialization. It is said that the phenomenon of the landless labourer and the concentration of wealth into a few hands encourages urbanization.

Others argue that urbanization is the inevitable result of economic growth with the rise of specialized craftsmen, merchants, and administrators. A further view stresses the importance of *agglomeration economies. The city offers market, labour, and capital with a well-developed infrastructure. Urbanization is a relatively recent process in the Third World where it is more rapid than population growth and where the largest agglomerations are growing most rapidly.

**urbanization economies** Advantages gained from an urban location. These include proximity to a market, labour supply, good communications, and financial and commercial services such as auditing, stockbroking, advertising, investment, industrial cleaning, and maintenance.

**urban managers and gatekeepers** Those who allocate scarce urban resources and facilities. Gatekeepers 'open the gate', usually for housing, to those who qualify and close it to those who do not. Gatekeepers include solicitors, estate agents, and financiers. Managers operate mainly in the public sector and include housing officers and local government councillors and planners.

**urban renewal** The improvement of old or run-down parts of the city, either by *rehabilitation or by clearing and rebuilding.

**urban–rural continuum** The zone of barely perceptible transition from the city to the countryside.

**urban sprawl** Housing, shops, and workshops forming an often haphazard spread of buildings at the edge of a city.

**urban village** A residential area of the city containing a cluster of individuals of similar culture and/or interests.

**U-shaped valley** See *glacial trough.

**US soil classification** The US Department of Agriculture recognized ten major soil groups in *The Seventh Approximation*. **Alfisols** are relatively young and acid soils with a clay B *horizon. **Aridisols** are semidesert and *desert soils. **Entisols** are immature, mainly *azonal soils. **Histosols** are primarily organic in content, developing in marshes or peat bogs. **Inceptisols** are young soils with weakly developed horizons. **Mollisols** are characteristic of grassland, high in *bases and with a thick, organically rich A horizon. **Oxisols** occur in tropical and subtropical areas. They are well weathered and often have a layer of *plinthite near the surface. **Spodosols** have been *podzolized. **Ultisols** develop where summers are wet and winters are dry. They are quite deeply weathered and are often reddish-yellow in colour. **Vertisols** are clay soils characterized by deep, wide cracks in the dry season.

**utility** The satisfaction given to an individual by the goods and services used.

**uvala** A depression formed when two or more *dolines coalesce. The size of the hollow is not important in the recognition of a uvala.

# V

**vadose** Referring to the zone immediately below the ground surface and above the *water table in which the water content varies greatly in amount and position.

**valley glacier** A glacier situated in an upland valley or basin.

**valley train** A plain within a valley sloping down and away from the site of a glacier snout, composed of sands and gravels and containing pebbles and boulders.

**valley wind** An air flow generated as a valley floor is heated by the sun. The warm air moves upslope. Valley winds are at their strongest in valleys of a north–south orientation.

**value** In economics, the money equivalent of any commodity which can be owned, which is in short supply, and which has *utility.

**van Allen radiation belts** Two ionizing areas of high-energy particles surrounding the earth, one at 3000 km above the surface, and the other at around 13 000 km.

**vapour** A gas—water vapour is the gaseous form of liquid water.

**vapour pressure** In meteorology, the pressure exerted by the water vapour in the air. This is a partial pressure since pressure is also exerted by the air itself.

**vardarac** A cold winter wind of Greece.

**variability** The extent to which a set of observations spreads about the mean value.

**variable** A changing factor which may affect or be affected by another. **Qualitative variables** are plotted on a *nominal or *ordinal scale. **Quantitative variables** are usually plotted on a *ratio or *interval scale and the measurements may be *continuous or *discrete.

**variable cost analysis** A method of costing an industrial location in terms of the spatial variations in production and costs. In its simplest form:

$$TC_i = \sum_{j=1}^{n} Q_j \cdot U_{ij}$$

where $TC_i$ = total cost of production at location $i$, $Q_j$ = required quantity of input $j$, $U_{ij}$ = unit cost of input at location $i$.

**variance, $\sigma^2$** The average of the squares of the deviations from the arithmetic mean of a data set. It is a statistic which represents the extent to which a set of observations spreads about the mean. Where the observations are closely grouped, the variance is low. See *standard deviation.

**Varignon frame** A string and pulley model for establishing the *least-cost location. Weights are used to represent the amounts of raw materials needed to make one unit of production. A weight is also used for the finished product. The weights are suspended below their point of origin on the strings and all the strings are tied together in the centre. The point of least costs will be the point at which the central knot stops.

**variscan orogeny** A stage of the *Armorican orogeny.

**varve** A series of paired lake deposits laid down each year by streams entering the lake. It is held that a varve couplet represents the total *fluvio-glacial deposition on a lake floor for one year. Summer deposition brings coarse sediments from meltwater streams; such sediments are from silt to sand in size. In winter the lake surface is frozen so that the water is calm. Under these still conditions, the fine deposits settle out in a thinner layer than that of the summer sediments.

**vector** A force having both magnitude and direction, such as a westerly wind blowing at 50 km per hour.

**veering** Of winds in the Northern Hemisphere, changing direction in a clockwise motion, e.g., from westerly to northerly. The converse applies in the Southern Hemisphere.

**vein** A split or crack within a rock now occupied most commonly by quartz, or by metallic minerals.

**veld** The wild grassland of the interior of South Africa. The veld has been greatly modified by fire and experiments suggest that, when protected from farming or fire, much of the veld may develop into scrub or even forest.

**vent** In geomorpholgy, an opening in the *crust through which volcanic material flows. Some volcanoes have a single, central vent, others have a line of vents or **side vents**, also known as **subsidiary vents**.

**Venturi effect** An increase in the velocity of, for example, wind, as it passes through narrow gaps; a common phenomenon between high-rise buildings.

**vertex,** pl. **vertices** Also known as a *node, in *network analysis this is the place joined by two or more routes (*links).

**vertical exaggeration** The factor by which the side scale of a cross-section is greater than the horizontal scale.

**vertisols** Soils of the *US soil classification found in regions of high temperature where bacteria destroy organic residues; hence the *humus content is low. Alternate wet and dry seasons lead to the alternate swelling and shrinking of these soils. By these processes, horizons become mixed or inverted.

**vesuvian eruption** See *vulcanian eruption.

**village** This is difficult to define in Britain as no upper limit of population has been established. There are moves to reclassify 'villages' with populations of over 8000.

**viscous** Adhesive or glutinous. **Viscosity** is the resistance to flow exhibited by a material.

**visible light** That part of the *electromagnetic spectrum which can be seen by a human eye.

**vital rates** Rates of those components, such as birth, marriage, fertility, and death which indicate the nature and possible changes in a population. Even when population numbers are stable, there may be changes in the vital rates. Vital rates determine population structure, for example, by age and sex.

**viticulture** The cultivation of grapes, usually used to make wine.

**V-notched weir** An apparatus for measuring stream discharge. A plywood dam is constructed across the stream. A 90° notch is cut into the middle of the dam wall, such that water flows through the gap but not over the wall. Discharge (Q) is then calculated from the equation $Q = 1.336 \times h^{2.43}$ where h is the height of the water surface above the angle of the V notch.

**volcanic arc** The line of volcanoes formed from magma rising from the *subduction zone.

**volcanic ash** Finely pulverized fragments of rock and lava which have been thrown out during a volcanic eruption. The term 'ash' is a misnomer.

**volcanic bomb** A block of lava ejected into the air from a volcano. As it is thrown out, it cools and spins, causing the block to be rounded or decorated with spiral patterns.

**volcanic dust** Very fine particles emitted during a volcanic eruption. Such dust may act as *condensation nuclei.

**volcanic eruption** Four basic types of eruption may be recognised. **Hawaiian eruptions** are non-explosive; lava spills out from a fissure. **Pelean eruptions** occur when a plug of acid, viscous lava blocks the vent until the build-up of pressure brings about a violent eruption. **Strombolian eruptions** are on a relatively small scale and are more frequent. They are characterised by the emission of *volcanic dust. **Vulcanian (Vesuvian) eruptions** resemble the Pelean type but the lava is less sticky and less acid.

**volcanic nec**k The passage from the *magma chamber to the central vent of a volcano. When it cools, it solidifies to form a plug of resistant rock. If the surrounding rocks are eroded, the neck may be exposed as an isolated spine.

**volcanic rock** An *extrusive rock, a rock made of *lava.

**volcano** An opening of the crust out of which *magma, ash, and gases erupt. The shape of the volcano depends very much on the type of lava. *Cone volcanoes are associated with thick lava and much ash. *Shield volcanoes are formed when less thick lava wells up and spreads over a large area, thus creating a wide, gently sloping landform. Most volcanoes are located at *destructive or *constructive plate margins.

**von Thünen models** Von Thünen had two basic models. Both were located in an *isotropic plain where there was one market—the city—for surplus agricultural production. One form of transport was available and transport costs increased in direct proportion to distance. No external trade took place, and farmers acted as *economic men. All farmers received the same price for a particular crop at any one time.

The first model postulated that the intensity of production of a particular crop declines with distance from the market since transport costs are higher away from the market and the locational rent is therefore lower. Intensive farming—which demands costly inputs—is profitable only where locational rent is high to cover costs, so intensive farming takes place only near the city.

Von Thünen's second model is concerned with land use patterns. Transport costs vary with the bulkiness and perishability of the product. Product A is costly to transport but has a high market price and is therefore farmed near the city. Product B sells for less but has lower transport costs. At a certain stage, B becomes more profitable than A because of its lower transport costs. Eventually, product C, with still lower transport costs, becomes the most profitable product. The changing pattern of the most profitable produce is therefore seen as a series of land use rings around the city. This phenomenon may be illustrated by a graph showing the varying locational rent of three products, the most profitable product at each point, and the land use pattern which results.

**vortex,** pl. **vortices** See *turbulence.

**vorticity** A measure of the rotation in a fluid or gas. Such rotations occur in the air flows of both depressions and anticyclones.

**V-shaped valley** A river valley V-shaped in cross-section, and thus distinct from the U-shaped cross-section of a *glacial trough.

**vulcanian eruption** Also known as a **vesuvian eruption**, this is marked by periodic lulls during which gas pressure builds up behind the lavas that clog the vent. This blockage is removed by an explosion which throws off *pyroclasts in large quantities.

**vulcanism** The action and formation of volcanoes.

# W

**wadi** In arid areas, a valley or stream course which is usually dry but may occasionally be occupied by a stream after a rare burst of heavy rain.

**Wallace's line** A boundary which may be drawn between the distinct flora and fauna of South-East Asia and those of Australia. The original line as determined by Wallace was modified by Huxley.

**waning slope** The low, concave element at the foot of a hillslope.

**warm front** The boundary zone between the warm air at the centre of a *mid-latitude depression and the cold air over which it is advancing. The arrival of a warm front is marked by an increase in air temperature and a clockwise change of wind direction. As the depression approaches, cloud becomes lower and thicker, changing from *cirrus to continuous *nimbo-stratus which brings rain.

**warm glacier** A glacier which has basal temperatures of around 0 °C. Warmth is imparted to the glacier by friction with the bedrock, by shearing within the ice mass, and from *geothermal heat.

**warm occlusion** An *occlusion where the following cold air undercuts the warm sector but rises above the leading cold air.

**warm sector** The section of warm air in a *mid-latitude depression.

**warping** A very slow deformation of a substantial area of the earth's crust.

**Warsaw Pact** An economic and military union of Albania, Bulgaria, Czechoslovakia, East Germany, Hungary, Poland, Romania, and the USSR. It was formed in 1955, but began to break up in 1968, when Albania left.

**wash** *Swash.

**wash board moraine** Synonymous with de Geer *moraine.

**water cycle** *Hydrological cycle.

**waterfall** A site on the *long profile of a river where water falls vertically. Waterfalls may be found at a band of more resistant rock, at a *knick point, or where *deposition has occurred.

**water gap** A pass cut by a river through an upland or ridge.

**watering place** *Spa.

**water-level weathering** The development and enlargement of tidal pools by weathering and by the action of rock grinding animals.

**waterlogged** Of a soil, when all the pores are full of water.

**watershed** The boundary between two river systems. The watershed marks the divide between *drainage basins, and usually runs along the highest points of the *interfluves.

**waterspout** A type of *tornado made up of a spinning column of water.

**water table** The level below which the ground is saturated. Any hole in the ground will fill with water when the water table has been reached. This level often fluctuates with rainfall. The water table is thus the upper surface of the *ground water.

**wave** A ridge of water between two depressions. As waves reach a shore, they curl into an arc and break. The energy of surface waves is responsible for the *erosion of the coast. Waves also initiate currents along the coast which are a moving force of *longshore drift. The height of a wave is generally proportional to the square of wind velocity.

**wave-built terrace** A flat area of sediment seaward of a wave-cut platform (see *shore platform).

**wave-cut platform** See *shore platform.

**wave energy** Energy generated by the force of ocean waves. The use of this energy is still in the experimental stage, but successful models have been built.

**wave refraction** The change in the approach angle of a wave as it moves towards the shore. As water shallows, waves slow down. This change in speed causes the straight line of a wave to 'bend' so that the line of the wave mirrors the submarine contours. Refraction causes waves to converge on *headlands and diverge in *bays. This means that the energy of the waves is concentrated on the headlands rather than on the beaches.

**waxing slope** The convex element at the foot of a hillslope.

**wealth-consuming sector** *Service industry.

**wealth-creating sector** *Manufacturing industry.

**weather** The state of the *atmosphere at any one place or time. This includes humidity, temperature, sunshine hours, cloud cover, visibility, and *precipitation (fog, rain, snow, sleet, and frost).

**weathering** The breakdown, but not the removal, of rocks. Weathering that causes chemical change is **chemical weathering** and includes the processes of *hydration, *hydrolysis, *oxidation, *carbonation, and some forms of *organic weathering. **Mechanical weathering** is the physical disintegration of the rock, as in *pressure release, *crystal growth, *salt weathering, *thermal expansion, and some forms of organic weathering, such as *chelation, and *bacterial reduction, as in *gley soils.

**weathering front** The zone of contact of the *regolith with the underlying rock.

**weathering pit** Depressions on a flat surface, usually on very soluble rocks, and varying in shape and ranging in size from a few centimetres to several metres in width. Most pits are initiated at a weak point in the rock. *Erosion will enlarge the pits; often two or more pits combine.

**Honeycomb weathering** is a grouping of many, closely spaced pits. **Tafoni** are weathering pits which are cut into near-verticle rock faces.

**weathering rind** The chemically altered 'skin' of rock around an unaltered core.

**weather-vane** A metal rod which can rotate horizontally about a pivot, and which will align itself to the direction of the wind.

**Weber's theory of industrial location** A model of industrial location which assumes that industrialists choose a *least-cost location for the development of new industry. The theory is based on a number of assumptions, among them that markets are fixed at certain specific points, that transport costs are proportional to the weight of the goods and the distance covered by a raw material or a finished product, that perfect competition exists, and that decisions are made by *economic man.

Weber postulated that raw materials and markets would exert a 'pull' on the location of an industry through transport costs. Industries with a high *material index would be pulled towards the raw material. Industries with a low material index would be pulled towards the market.

**weir** Generally speaking, a small dam built across a river. In hydrology, weirs are erected to measure river flow. Water is impounded behind the dam and is fed through a notch. **Sharp-crested weirs** have a sharpened metal plate to dam the stream and a steep-sided notch. **Broad-crested weirs** are wider and lower. The rate of discharge of the river is calculated by different methods at each type of weir. See also *V-notched weir.

**welfare** As used in geography, this denotes an activity to provide for those in need.

**welfare geography** An approach in human geography concerned with social inequality. It considers the areal differentiation and spatial organization of human activity from the point of view of the welfare of the people involved. Welfare geography focuses on those factors which contribute to the quality of human life. It takes up welfare issues such as crime, poverty, homelessness, and the lack of educational and social services. It aims to introduce measures which will bring about a fairer distribution of resources and opportunities.

**West** Sometimes a shorthand term for North America and Western Europe.

**westerlies, westerly winds** Winds blowing *from* the west, most often occurring in *mid-latitudes. The westerlies of the Northern Hemisphere blow from the southwest; those of the Southern Hemisphere blow from the north-west. These Southern Hemisphere westerlies are more constant than those of the north because there are fewer land areas or relief barriers in the south.

**wet bulb thermometer** This instrument is a standard mercury thermometer with its bulb wrapped in muslin, constantly kept wet with pure water. As this water evaporates, the bulb will be cooled and will show a temperature lower than that of a dry bulb thermometer at the same location. If the surrounding air is dry, there will be considerable evaporation and constant cooling. If the air is moist, there will be less cooling.

If the dry bulb and wet bulb temperatures are taken for the same sample of air, the relative humidity of the air can be determined from hygrometric tables.

**wetland** Waterlogged land which may be periodically or permanently covered by water.

**wetting front** The lower limit, in a soil, of water infiltration from above.

**wharf** A landing stage used for waterborne traffic.

**whirlwind** *Tornado.

**WHO** See *World Health Organization.

**wildcat** A speculative drilling in search of petrol or natural gas with no clear evidence that either is present.

**wilderness** A region little touched by man. See *wilderness area.

**wilderness area** An area set aside as a sanctuary for wild plants and animals, and which almost no humans may enter.

**willy-willy** Along the north-east coast of Australia, a *hurricane.

**wilting point** The point at which a plant has to supply water from its own tissues for *transpiration when the soil moisture is exhausted.

**windbreak** An obstacle, usually a hedge or belt of trees, across the direction of the wind to shelter houses, crops, or animals.

**wind chill** The power of the wind to remove the warm air close to the surface of the skin. Cold air replaces air warmed by the body and, the stronger the wind, the more heat is carried away.

**wind energy** Power generated by harnessing the wind, usually by windmills. Early windmills were used to power millstones, pumps, and forges. Future uses may include the generation of electricity but there are drawbacks such as the inconstant nature of the wind, the difficulty of construction, and finding a suitable site.

**wind erosion** *Deflation.

**wind gap** A pass through a ridge cut by a stream that is no longer there, perhaps because of river *capture.

**wind rose** A graph with lines radiating from the centre, representing different wind directions. Bar graphs are drawn from the centre to indicate the frequency of a wind direction.

**wind shear** See *thermal wind.

**windward** Facing the wind.

**winter solstice** In the Northern Hemisphere, the *solstice of 21–2 December, in the Southern Hemisphere, the solstice of 21–2 June.

**World Health Organization, WHO** An international organization, founded in 1948 to promote good health and health care, especially in *developing countries but also to research into new therapies.

# X

**xenophobia** A fear or a rejection of foreigners or of a different ethnic group.

**xeroll** A soil of the *US soil classification. See *chestnut soil.

**xerophyte** A plant which is able to grow in very arid conditions because it has adapted to restrict any water loss. Such adaptations include dense hairs or waxy leaves and the shedding of leaves at the start of the arid season. Succulent xerophytes incorporate water into their structure.

**xerophytic coniferous forest** Forest, mostly evergreen, found in the hilly, semi-arid *subtropics.

**X-ray** Short wave rays of the *electromagnetic spectrum.

# Y

**yardang** A long ridge which has been isolated by the removal by wind erosion of rocks on either side. Yardangs can be 100 m or more in height and can stretch for many kilometres.

**yazoo** A tributary stream which does not join the main stream directly but runs parallel to it for some distance, usually because it cannot breach the *levées which flank the main stream.

**year** The time taken by the earth to orbit the sun—365 days, 5 hours, 48 minutes, 46 seconds.

**young fold mountains** *Fold mountains formed during the *Alpine orogeny.

# Z

**zero population growth** The ending of population growth when birth and death rates are equal. This would require an average number of 2.3 children per family in Britain.

**zero-sum game** A *formal game whereby, on choosing a particular strategy, one competitor's gain is his opponent's loss, gain and loss summing to zero.

**zeuge,** pl. **zeugen** An upstanding rock capped with a harder *stratum, undercut by wind at the base.

**zonal** Phenomena occurring in bands roughly parallel with lines of *latitude.

**zonal flow** The path taken by a wind following lines of *latitude rather than lines of *longitude.

**zonal index** This indicates the strength of westerly winds in the upper air. See *Rossby waves.

**zonal soil** A soil where differences in local rock formation and *lithology are largely masked by the overriding effects of climate. The major zonal soils are *tundra soils, *podzols, *Mediterranean soils, *chernozems, *chestnut soils, and *ferallitic soils.

**zonal winds** Winds, such as the *trades or the *westerlies, which are associated with particular *latitudinal zones.

**zone of assimilation** The area which increasingly develops the functions of the *CBD; the CBD of the future, characterized by whole-scale redevelopment of shops, offices, and hotels.

**zone of discard** That area, once a part of the *CBD, but now in decline and characterized by low-status shops and warehouses, and vacant property.

**zone of overlap** An area served by more than one urban centre, i.e., within two or more different *urban fields.

**zone of vacuum** An area with no urban alliance. Such an area is characteristic of developing nations with low levels of urbanization but is rare in the West.

**zooplankton** The animal component of *plankton.

**z-score** A method of standardizing variables measured on interval or ratio scales. If different variables are measured in different units, they may be changed into standard scores—z-scores—by expressing the values in terms of the *standard deviation:

$$\text{z-score} = \frac{\text{deviation score}}{\text{standard deviation}}$$

where the deviation score is the difference between the value and the *arithmetic mean.